500 ESSENTIAL
GARDEN PLANTS

500 ESSENTIAL
GARDEN PLANTS

Edited by
Annette Timmermann

© 2004 Rebo International b.v., Lisse, The Netherlands

Edited: Annette Timmermann
Texts: Angelika Franz (Shrubs), Christian Hesse (Herbs), Brigitte Lotz (Climbers and Bulbs),
Andrea Rausch (Annuals, Bulbs, Pests and Diseases), Kerstin Walter (Perennials),
Werkstatt München/Karen Dengler (Roses)

Translation:
Rosetta International, London, UK;
Anthea Bell in association with First Edition Translation Ltd., Cambridge, UK;
Quality Translations

Photographs:
© Baumschule Rohwer: pages 258, 302 (below), 305, 307, 314 (below), 317, 325,
340, 342 – 345, 347, 348, 350, 354, 355, 357, 360, 362, 365, 382 (below), 385
© Ellen Fischer: pages 12, 154, 176, 335, 382 (above)
© Florastar-Bildarchiv: pages 36 (Kreusch), 38, 256 (Güse),
260 (Güse), 364 (Seibold), 370 (Kreusch)
© laif/P. S. Kristensen: page 44
© Reinhard Lintelmann: pages 90, 298, 362, 365, 384, 387
© Kerstin Walter: pages 127, 130, 143, 160, 185, 194, 206, 213, 219, 222, 224
© Annette Timmermann, Stolpe: all other photographs

Proofreading: Jeffrey Rubinoff, Emily Sands, Eva Munk

ISBN 90 366 1704 9

Contents

Foreword   6

Bulbs   8

Annuals   78

Perennials   118

Herbs   230

Roses   264

Shrubs   298

Climbers   362

Pests and diseases   388

Glossary   393

Index   403

Foreword

As the days get longer and the first buds sprout in the first spring light, it is again time to devote ourselves to tending our plants in our gardens, terraces or balconies. Is there anyone who has never toyed with striking new color notes in unaccustomed places, different combinations of plants or trying out a new variety? In the gardening shop nearest you or one of the innumerable garden centers, you will find an abundant selection of plants which flourish in our climate.

We offer you detailed portraits of 500 garden plants which can be readily obtained through any shop, because they are among the most popular and best-selling of plants. In our selection, resistance to frost is one of the most important criteria – but it cannot be adopted for all plants, because gardening would not be half as pleasant without a few delightfully flowering and fragrant exotic plants. As a result, some of the plants in this book have only limited winter-resistance. Other criteria include resistance to diseases and pests, problem-free combinations with other plants, and especially pleasing fragrance, bloom and color.

Our editor, Annette Timmermann, holds a degree in landscaping and works for a plant wholesaler in Northern Germany. She has chosen these 500 plants for you and provided brilliant color photographs to illustrate many of them. The texts were written by professionals, and are arranged so you can check quickly and specifically whether a specific plant meets your requirements.

We have divided this book into commonly used plant categories, within which the plants are arranged alphabetically by their botanical names.

The title of each plant entry contains the most frequently used English name of the plant. Where different names are used in different geographical regions, we have tried to provide as complete a list of these names as possible in the text.

The text describing each plant tells you about the origin, growth, flowering, propagation, and care of the plant. If a plant is known to have medicinal or healing properties, if it attracts butterflies or bees or is especially sensitive to certain diseases, we have noted it as well. In addition, from page 388 onwards we have described ways of dealing with plant diseases and pests without using chemicals.

Our extensive glossary explains the technical terms used in this book. It will also help you in deciphering the Latin names of plants.

Small yellow boxes next to the text draw attention to the most important information about a particular plant. The symbols used here have the following meanings:

○	prefers sun
◑	prefers partial shade
●	prefers full shade
❆	frost sensitive
❆ ❆	semi-hardy
❆ ❆ ❆	hardy
◌	prefers porous soil
◓	prefers moist soil
◖	prefers wet soil
✖	poisonous plant
❀	fragrant

In addition, the book provides information on flowering seasons, width and height of growth.

Please note:
Some of the plants listed in this book are toxic! This is designated by an x and is generally also stated in the text. Please bear in mind that children are especially attracted by the brilliant colors of flowers and fruit. If you have children, please take this warning and its consequences to heart and avoid the use of these plants as far as possible.

In addition, some of these plants may cause allergic reactions. Persons with a tendency to allergies and allergic reactions should take the appropriate references in the text seriously and stay away from such plants.

Bulbs

Bulbs are indispensable in any garden, as the first spot of color in the garden in spring, and as magnificent blooms in summer and autumn. They brighten up flower beds and borders and many of them make exellent cut flowers. Elegant and hardy, they look wonderful in rockeries. Others will brighten up rooms indoors with their cheerful colors, particularly those which are treated to flower early in winter. Bulbs and tubers absorb the nutrients needed to produce flowers through their leaves. This is why the leaves must not be cut back after the plant has finished flowering. Bulbs are bud-like storage organs consisting of fleshy, scale-like leaves, wrapped around each other, while tubers are thickened fleshy roots which serve the same purpose of storage. Propagation from existing plants is much quicker than raising from seeds. In the case of tubers, plants are propagated by dividing the tubers with at least one eye (a potential shoot) in each section. Many of the summer-flowering species are tender and should only be planted out after the middle of May. The storage organ (bulb or tuber) is lifted in autumn. After brushing away the earth (do not wash), they are stored in a well-ventilated, dry, frost-free place. The hardy species which flower mostly in spring or autumn can be planted between late summer and autumn. As a rule of thumb, the bulb or tuber should be planted to a depth three to four times the size of the bulb. The soil should be loosened to a depth of 8 in and all weeds should be removed. Bulbs will grow very well in ordinary, well-drained garden soil but will need extra watering during the growing and flowering period. Whether they are planted in a sunny or shady position will depend on the species.

Allium giganteum

Allium giganteum

Allium giganticum

ⓘ

Family: Alliaceae
Flowering season: summer
Height and spread: 60 × 6 in
Situation: ○
Moisture requirement: ◊
❊ ❊
❊

This impressive plant grows wild in the Himalayas. Its large, gray-green, strap-shaped leaves grow from the round bulb in spring. They give off an oniony smell when crushed and frequently wither before the flowers appear. The sturdy flower stalk carries the striking spherical flower umbels which appear in midsummer and consist of more than 50 star-shaped individual flowers with projecting stamens. They are violet to pink depending on the variety, and the flower head can reach a diameter of 4–8 in. Bulbs are planted 4–6 in deep in the soil in autumn. Alternatively, seeds can be collected from the seed heads just before they open and sown directly in the autumn or in spring. The soil should be well-drained and alkaline, and the plant flourishes in a sunny or partially shaded position. In winter, it is advisable to provide some frost protection by covering the plants with their own leaves or with bracken. Other species include *A. christophii* (star of Persia) which is purple, and *A. moly* (golden garlic) which is bright yellow.

Crown anemone

Anemone coronaria 'De Caen'

Anemone coronaria

ⓘ

Family: Ranunculaceae
Flowering season: spring
Height and spread: 16 × 6 in
Situation: ◑
Moisture requirement: ◊
❊ – ❊ ❊ *(with protection)*

This sun-loving garden anemone is native to the Mediterranean region and the Middle East. The varieties in the 'De Caen' group have large, cup-shaped single flowers 3 in wide. They appear from April or May until the summer. The colors of the numerous varieties range from pink and mauve to shades of blue and white, with a striking center of dark stamens in most cases. The leaves are reminiscent of parsley. The dark, flat rhizomes are planted in the autumn (frost protection will be necessary) or at the end of winter about 2 in deep in frost-free soil. They should first be soaked in water for 24 hours. Since the plant needs a dry period of dormancy, it is best to lift the tubers and over-winter them in frost-free conditions. In this case, they can also be divided immediately. These plants demand little attention, but they should always be mulched and dry. The soil should be humus-rich and well-drained. Anemones are popular cut flowers.

Arum

Arum

The genus *Arum* contains about 20 species, most of them blooming in spring. They are native to southern and Central Europe, North Africa and western Asia. The large arrow- or heart-shaped leaves, some with striking markings, appear in autumn. The characteristic feature of arums is the prominent spadix inflorescence encircled by the tall leaf-like spathe, designed to attract insects. Depending on species, the spathe is yellowish white, greenish or with brown markings. The flowers mostly give off an unpleasant smell, or in the case of *A. creticum* a sweetish one. After the flowering period in spring, orange red, poisonous berries are formed. The tubers are planted in late summer or autumn 4–6 in deep in the soil. Arums also seed themselves with ease. The soil should be an evenly moist humus which does not dry out. In partial shade the dying leaves turn a beautiful golden color. *A. italicum* and *A. maculatum* are hardy. Caution: parts are poisonous and the juice of the berries causes skin irritations.

Arum

ℹ

Family: Araceae
Flowering season: spring
Height and spread: 12 × 6 in
Situation: ◑
Moisture requirement: ◐
❄ ❄ ❄
✖
❀

Canna

Canna

More than 50 *Canna* species are native to moist, marshy areas in tropical and subtropical regions of the Americas. By crossing different species, many varieties have been created, for instance from *C. indica* (Indian shot). The bright gladioli-like flowers appear in clusters or panicles in many colors, predominantly red but with pink, orange to yellow variations. The decorative leaves resemble banana leaves and can get as long as 24 in. They turn green or scarlet-gold in color. Rhizomes are planted about 4 in deep in the middle of May when the risk of frost is past. Divided rhizomes should each have at least one "eye" or shoot bud. Seeds can be grown in a warm place indoors and the seedlings planted out in early spring. During the growing season they need plenty of water and feeding. Faded blooms should be removed regularly. In frost-free areas the rhizome can be left in the earth protected by a thick mulch; otherwise, they should be lifted before the first frost and stored in peat in a frost-free place.

Canna

ℹ

Family: Cannaceae
Flowering season: summer
Height and spread: to 7 × 2 ft
Situation: ○
Moisture requirement: ◐
❄

Autumn crocus

Autumn crocus, meadow saffron

Colchicum autumnale

Almost 50 species are native to central and western Europe and North Africa. *C. autumnale* is found in the wild in wet meadows. Many varieties are the result of crossing several species, producing large-flowered varieties on tall stems which may reach a height of 12 in. The flowers are white, pink or purple. The cup-shaped flowers develop from the corm in bunches from late summer to autumn, usually before the leaves. The glossy green, lance-shaped leaves are up to 12 in long and die back in summer. When dormant in late summer, corms can be removed and planted about 4 in deep in the soil. A sunny situation is preferable with a moist, well-drained alkaline soil. Many species and varieties of autumn crocus are excellent for naturalising in the garden, for growing in borders with perennials and in rockeries. Caution: all parts are toxic, and the seeds contain the poisonous alkaloid colchicine.

ⓘ

Family: Colchicaceae
Flowering season: autumn
Height and spread: 6 × 3 in
Situation: ○
Moisture requirement: ◊
❅ ❅ ❅
✖

Montbretia

Crocosmia masoniorum

This large-flowered species is native to the province of Natal in South Africa. The flower heads appear freely on arching stems above the leaves in the midsummer and consist of up to 20 funnel-shaped, bright orange-red single flowers. The long sword-shaped, ribbed leaves grow almost as big as the flower heads themselves, up to 3 ft. Corms can be bought or divided from existing clumps. They are planted about 3–4 in deep in spring after the last frost. They thrive best in fertile well-drained soil in full sun. Especially in the first winter months and during periods of frost, they need a thick, protective covering, for instance of leaves or peat with a plastic sheet over it. In very cold regions, it is best to lift the corms and over-winter them in frost-free conditions. During the summer, crocosmias must be watered and fed generously. *C. x crocosmiiflora* is similar but slightly shorter and less hardy with small flowers.

ⓘ

Family: Iridaceae
Flowering season: summer
Height and spread: 40 × 3 in
Situation: ○
Moisture requirement: ◊
❅ – ❅ ❅ *(winter protection)*

Montbretia

Crocosmia masoniorum 'Lucifer'

The popular variety 'Lucifer' is a development of the species of montbretia which is native to South Africa. It has strikingly large, fiery-red, single flowers up to 2 in long which appear in midsummer on arching stems. The mid-green, narrow lanceolate leaves form a pretty contrast. The corms should be planted in spring when the risk of frost is past, about 3–4 in deep in a free-draining, fertile soil in full sun. During the first winter months in particular, and in subsequent periods of frost, they should be protected with a thick layer of leaves or peat covered with plastic sheeting. In cold regions the corms should be lifted and stored in a frost-free place. During the summer, the plants need plenty of water and feeding. They are striking when grown in groups and the cut blooms are also stunning in a vase. Examples of further varieties are 'Emily McKenzie' with large orange flowers and 'Norwich Canary' with small yellow flowers, both about 22 in tall.

ℹ

Family: Iridaceae
Flowering season: summer
Height/spread: 40 × 3 in
Situation: ○
Moisture requirement: ◌
❄ – ❄ ❄ (winter protection)

Crocus

Crocus

Crocuses enrich the spring and autumn with their distinctive blooms. In spring, they are a harbinger of the warmer weather to come, while the autumn-flowering species have the effect of prolonging the summer. More than 80 known species are native to southern Europe, the Middle East and Central Asia. The numerous large-flowered garden varieties are mostly cultivars of *C. chrysanthus* x *C. vernus*. The range of varieties is large and they differ widely from the species, with the colors of the goblet or cup-shaped flowers ranging from violet through many shades of yellow, blue, purple, and white, as well as many two-colored varieties. The exceptional deep orange stamens are a striking feature. The narrow, grass-like leaves appear either together with the flowers, or in the case of some autumn-flowering species only after the flowers. Propagation is from the corms planted in the autumn in the case of the spring-flowering species and in late summer in the case of the autumn-flowering ones. They should be planted about 2–4 in deep and spaced about 4–6 in apart. Seeds can be harvested before the capsules burst open and sown directly in pots. Crocuses are best planted in clumps, for example in borders and rockeries. Shade-tolerant varieties can be naturalized among trees, and many are suitable for growing in pots. The soil should be well-drained and some species should be kept dry in summer when they are dormant, and watered again in the autumn. It is advisable to lift the corms every three to five years and transplant them to another location. Protection from frost should be provided in harsh winters.

ℹ

Family: Iridaceae
Flowering season: spring or autumn
Height and spread: 2–6 × 2 in
Situation: ○
Moisture requirement: ◊
❆ ❆ ❆
✿

ℹ

Family: Iridaceae
Flowering season: spring
Height and spread: 2–4 × 4 in
Situation: ○
Moisture requirement: ○
❄ ❄ ❄
❀

Crocus chrysanthus

Crocus chrysanthus

Native to the Balkans, Romania and Turkey, this is one of the earliest species to flower in spring. The species produces compact flowers on short stalks which are golden yellow, sometimes with bronze-colored markings. The many cultivars are up to 4 in tall and have flowers in various shades of yellow, white and blue and violet. The green leaves are narrow and oblong. The corms are planted in the autumn 2–3 in deep in the soil. The plants tolerate light or partial shade and are happiest in rather sandy well-drained soils which are only slightly moist in the autumn. They are undemanding to grow, but it is recommended that they should be dug up every three to five years after the flowering season, stored in a cool, dry place, and planted in a different location in the autumn. They fit very well with low perennials and in borders as well as in woods and among trees. They should not be planted in lawns which are mowed often.

Species crocus

Crocus speciosus

ℹ

Family: Iridaceae
Flowering season: autumn
Height and spread: 6 × 2 in
Situation: ○
Moisture requirement: ○
❄ ❄ ❄

This autumn-flowering species is native to Asia Minor, the Caucasus, Iran and the Crimea. The flowers appear by themselves before the leaves throughout September and October, with long, bell-shaped blossoms on long, heavy stalks. They range from dark blue to violet depending on variety, with dark or pure white veining. The flowers open wide and reveal the strongly fringed orange stigma and stamens. After flowering, grass-like leaves up to 6 in long appear the following spring. The round corms are planted about 2 in deep in the soil in August. The ideal location is full sun with good well-drained soil. Species crocuses look well among low perennials, and they are outstanding in rockeries as well as among trees and shrubs. They are excellent for wild gardens because they increase rapidly by offsets and seed themselves. Well-known varieties are 'Albus' (pure white) and 'Conqueror' (dark blue, large-flowered).

Crocus tommasinianus

Crocus tommasinianus

Well-known for its slender, soft violet flowers, this species is native to southern Hungary and north-west Bulgaria. It flourishes there with a preference for subsoils containing lime. The flowers appear very early, often even in late winter. Compared with other species, the varieties have richer purple colors, and the outer petals are often silvery. The flowers are 1–2 in long. The tripartite seed vessel forms numerous seeds, so the plant is easily self-sown and therefore good for naturalizing. As with all the spring-flowering species, corms are planted in the autumn. The position may be partially shaded, but the soil must be well-drained. It thrives among low perennials, in rockeries as well as among shrubs and trees. It can also be planted in lightly mown grass. Varieties include 'Ruby Giant' (rich purple, sterile flowers), 'Barr's Purple' (purple and violet), and 'Whitewell Purple' (red and violet).

ⓘ

Family: Iridaceae
Flowering season: spring
Height and spread: 3–4 × 1 in
Situation: ○
Moisture requirement: ◊
✿ ✿ ✿

Crocus vernus

Crocus vernus

This popular crocus species is native to central and southern Europe. The many varieties are mostly large-flowered, with colors ranging from white to blue and violet, with many numerous tones and color combinations. The long, narrow leaves are predominantly white and appear after the flowers. In order to preserve the characteristics of the variety, propagation is by corms that will be planted in the autumn 3–4 in deep. Depending on the variety, many of these crocuses tolerate partially shaded positions, preferring fairly sandy well-drained soils which are only slightly moist in the autumn. They are easy to look after, but it is recommended every three to five years to lift them after they have flowered, and keep them in a cool, dry place before planting them in a different position in the autumn. They are excellent in borders with perennials and beds, among trees and shrubs, or in pots. They should not be planted in lawns because of the competition for nutrients, and because their leaves should not be cut.

Crocus vernus

ⓘ

Family: Iridaceae
Flowering season: spring
Height and spread: 4–6 × 2 in
Situation: ○
Moisture requirement: ◊
✿ ✿ ✿

Cyclamen

Cyclamen

Family: Primulaceae
Flowering season: spring and autumn
Height and spread: 12 × 12 in
Situation: ◑
Moisture requirement: ◌
❄ – ❄ ❄ ❄
❁

Cyclamens are native to Europe and Asia. Depending on the species, they flourish in a variety of situations from moist forests to dry Alpine positions, and they flower either in spring or in autumn. The delicate flowers are fragrant and consist of five petals curving backwards, up to 1 in long. The many varieties of the florist's cyclamen, *C. persicum*, tend to be larger. The main colors are white and shades of pink and red. The leaves are rounded or heart-shaped, the upper side often has silvery markings giving a marbled effect. Leaves of the autumn-flowering species last well into the spring. Cyclamens thrive in partial shade in humus-rich well-drained soils which may contain a little lime. They do not tolerate being waterlogged. The flat tubers are planted in summer about 1–2 in deep so that they are only just evenly covered with earth. Seed can be sown from winter to spring. The seeds germinate easily in the dark, with a little soil lightly sieved over them. Cyclamens look nice in rockeries, among trees and shrubs, or as an indoor plant in pots.

Cyclamen

Cyclamen mirabile

Family: Primulaceae
Flowering season: autumn
Height and spread: 3 × 3 in
Situation: ◑
Moisture requirement: ◌
❄ ❄ ❄

This miniature species is native to south-west Turkey. The pale pink flowers with toothed petals are very slim and up to 4/5 in long. They appear in the autumn at the same time as the heart-shaped leaves which are up to 6/5 in long. When they develop, the upperside of the leaves is often flushed pink, later becoming green, while the underside is reddish. Normally grown in pots in a cool greenhouse, the tubers are planted at a very shallow depth so that their tops almost reach the surface of the soil. The best soil is a humus-rich well-drained soil mixture. They should be kept cool but frost-free. During the growing season, they are watered regularly and given a weak nitrogen fertiliser about every two months. When the leaves begin to die down, watering and the humidity are reduced; during the period of dormancy, they must be kept completely dry. Seeds can be sown from winter to spring. If grown outdoors, a protective covering, for example bracken, should be put in position when frost is likely.

Cyclamen

ⓘ
Family: Primulaceae
Flowering season: autumn/winter
Height and spread: 10 × 10 in
Situation: ◑
Moisture requirement: ◌
❄
✿

*F*lorist's cyclamen

Cyclamen persicum

The wild species is native to the eastern Mediterranean region. Numerous varieties have been derived from it, both large-flowered as well as small-flowered miniature varieties, mainly in white, pink and red colors, either with simple flowers or with frilled, bearded or corrugated ones. The species flowers from the end of winter into spring, while available cultivars flower from late summer to the end of winter. They thrive in light, cool conditions, but do not tolerate full sun. During the growing season, the soil should always be slightly moist and the plant should be fed regularly. It is important to always water from below. While dormant, they should be kept dry. Although bred as house plants, they can also spend the summer and autumn in the open. They are attractive with autumn plants including heathers such as *Calluna* and grasses such as *Carex*. Seeds are sown in late winter at 61°–64°F and germinated in the dark. Tubers in pots can be transplanted after flowering, with the top sticking out a little above the soil.

Dahlia

Dahlia

Dahlias are native to Mexico. By intensive cross-breeding, an enormous range of hybrid varieties have been produced, divided into ten groups. They exist in almost every color (apart from blue), in every form and size, with flowering periods extending far into autumn. The flower heads consist of external petals or ray florets surrounding a small disc of florets in the center. The opposing leaves are mostly tripartite. When the plant above ground has died, the tubers are lifted and stored upside down in an airy place at a temperature of 39°–46°F. In spring, seeds can be sown at 64°–68°F. Propagation is usually by division of the tubers, each piece having at least one "eye" or shoot bud. If the soil is dry they can be planted out in the spring, with the tubers about 5 in below the surface of the soil. The bulbs can be soaked in water for 24 hours before planting. The ideal soil is humus-rich, loose and permeable. In summer it should be watered generously and fed well. Tips for better flowering are to cut back the flower buds to three to five and to remove wilted flower heads regularly.

ⓘ

Family: Asteraceae
Flowering season: summer
Height and spread: 7 × 2 ft
Situation: ○
Moisture requirement: ◌
❋
attracts bees and butterflies

opposite: Dahlia ›Akita‹

Decorative-flowered dahlias
Dahlia 'Akita'

ⓘ

Family: Asteraceae
Flowering season: summer
Height and spread: 40 × 24 in
Situation: ○
Moisture requirement: ◊
❄

The group of decorative-flowered dahlias provide an opulent display of floral splendour far into the autumn. The blossoms are fully double with no clear disk, since most of the disc florets have transformed themselves into petals. The petals are low and open, sometimes turning inwards at the edge, and an expert referring to the 'depth' of a flower means that it has as many layers of petals as possible. The variety 'Akita' is enchanting with an extraordinary form and color. The large, chrysanthemum-shaped flowers are brown and red with bright tips. Among the tall varieties for cutting and flower borders are 'Elegance' (lemon with white tips, 3 ft), 'Eveline' (globular white with a touch of purple, 3 ft) and 'Severin's Triumph' (pink, 5 ft). There are also many compact varieties such as 'Berliner Kleene' (salmon pink, 16 in) and 'Autumn Sunburst' (orange, 16 in). Notes on cultivation are given in the introductory page to the dahlia section.

Pompon dahlias
Dahlia 'Bantling'

Dahlia 'Bantling'

Family: Asteraceae
Flowering season: summer
Height and spread: 44 × 24 in
Situation: ○
Moisture requirement: ◊
❄

Pompon dahlias are simply small ball-flowered dahlias. The term is used to describe varieties with flowers smaller than 2 in in diameter. Ideally the petals should be completely rolled up so that they form little tubes into which one can look. The name 'pompon' comes from the French word for the little woollen balls on the caps of French sailors. The height of most varieties ranges between 20 in and 48 in. They form upright bushy clumps, flower tirelessly and are extremely rugged. The variety 'Bantling' forms clumps up to 48 in high and has bright orange to orange-red flowers from summer until autumn. Further varieties include 'Moor Place' (wine-red, 4 ft), 'Noreen' (pink, 3 ft), 'Small World' (white, 4 ft) and 'Valentine' (yellow, 3 ft). Notes on cultivation are given in the introductory page to the dahlia section.

Dahlia 'Brandaris'

Semi-cactus-flowered dahlias

Dahlia 'Brandaris'

ℹ

Family: Asteraceae
Flowering season: summer
Height and spread: 48 × 24 in
Situation: ○
Moisture requirement: ◊
✻

Semi-cactus-flowered dahlias are a successful form intermediate between cactus-flowered and decorative-flowered dahlias, so division into the correct group is not always easy. The petals are pointed like the cactus-flowered dahlias, but they are only rolled up at the top. Otherwise, they are flat and open like the decorative dahlias. The flower heads are normally larger than those of the cactus dahlias. The variety 'Brandaris' is very distinctive, with yellow-centerd orange flowers and a height of up to 4 ft. Shorter varieties for flower beds include 'Aspen' (white, 16 in), 'Corona' (red and orange, 24 in) or 'Red Pygmy' (strong red, 12–16 in). Medium to tall varieties for cutting and flower borders include 'Germany' (strong red, large flowered, 4 ft), 'Coronation' (yellow, 5 ft), 'Ludwig Helfert' (bright yellow and orange, very striking, 4 ft), 'Nivea' (white, 5 ft) and the well-known 'Firebird' (yellow with red tips, 4 ft). Notes on cultivation are given in the introductory page to the dahlia section.

Ball-flowered dahlias

Dahlia 'Charles Dickens'

Ball-flowered dahlias belong to the oldest forms introduced into Europe. They are what many dahlia enthusiasts describe simply as 'dahlias'. The petals fit closely together; they are rolled up for more than half their length and they look like little bags Only ball and pompon dahlias have these unified, solid-looking flowers. Genuine ball dahlias have one completely round compact flower head, but it may be a slightly flattened spherical form. The size is roughly that of a tennis ball or an orange. The growing height is mostly between 3–4 ft but there are also shorter varieties. 'Charles Dickens' is a tall, very rugged, purple flowering variety. There are many others, such as 'Kenora Fireball' (red, 4 ft), 'L'Ancresse'(pure white, 4 ft, very free-flowering), Little Tiger (red and white, 24 in), 'Noblesse'(bright yellow, 48 in) and 'Wotton Cupid'(pink with cream markings, 4 ft). Notes on cultivation are given in the introductory page to the dahlia section.

ℹ

Family: Asteraceae
Flowering season: summer
Height and spread: 48 × 24 in
Situation: ○
Moisture requirement: ◌
❄

Collerette dahlias

Dahlia 'Don Lorenzo'

These dahlia flowers have just one ring of broad petals surrounding a circle of shorter florets usually of a different color, surrounding the central disk. Botanically this disk consists of stamens which do not form an independent ring but fit tightly against the petals. The name 'Collerette' comes from the appearance of the inner petals. These dahlias are very popular with bees. A particularly attractive proven garden variety is 'Don Lorenzo'. It has red and yellow flowers and reaches an average height of 4 ft, or in good situations as much as 5 ft. It has a very upright habit. 'Herz As' is a shorter variety, up to 20 in, with pink flowers and light pink collars. Other recommended varieties are 'Chimborazo' (maroon flowers with yellow collars, to 4 ft), 'Clair de Lune' (cream and pale yellow, to 4 ft), 'Stefanie Hertel' (black red with brighter collars, 4 ft). Notes on cultivation are given in the introductory page to the dahlia section.

ℹ

Family: Asteraceae
Flowering season: summer
Height and spread: 48 × 24 in
Situation: ○
Moisture requirement: ◌
❄
attracts bees and butterflies

Water lily-flowered dahlias

Dahlia 'Gay-Princess'

ⓘ

Family: Asteraceae
Flowering season: summer
Height/spread: 3–5 × 2 ft
Situation: ○
Moisture requirement: ◊
❄

Water lily-flowered dahlias were formerly included within the group of decorative dahlias, but they now form a class of their own with their shell-shaped flowers which are strongly reminiscent of water lilies. The flower center is double so that the disk cannot be seen; however, the number of the petals is smaller than that of the decorative dahlias. The petals of the water lily dahlias are flat, opened and slightly curved upwards. Their height varies from 24 in to 5 ft depending on variety, most being in the 3–4 ft range. They are suitable for beds, flower borders and cutting. 'Gay Princess' is a small-flowered variety which blooms brightly to raspberry pink and can be 5 ft high. Further examples include the well-tried garden variety 'Gerrie Hoek' (pink, 4 ft), 'Glorie van Heemstede' (rich yellow, small-flowered, 4 ft), 'Pearl of Heemstede' (pale silvery pink, 3 ft), 'Sabine' (pink and white, 4 ft), and 'Souvenir' (pink, 5 ft). Notes on cultivation are given in the introductory page to the dahlia section.

Cactus-flowered dahlia

Dahlia 'Horido'

The extremely popular cactus-flowered dahlias (*D.* x. *hortensis*) do not belong to the older, established species, but were only introduced to Europe at the end of the last century. They owe their elegant appearance to the rolled petals, densely packed with pointed tips. These are rolled from the tip for most or all of their length, unlike semi-cactus dahlias where only half of the petal is rolled. The name does not come from the prickly-looking flowers, but from the fact that they resemble the flowers of particular cactuses. The color combination of 'Horido' is especially popular. Its flowers are yellow with orange tips and grow to a height of about 3 ft. Shorter varieties are 'Autumn Fairy' (orange, 16 in), 'Cheerio' (wine-red with white tips, 20 in) and 'Park Princess' (bright pink, 24 in). Medium to tall varieties are 'Purple Gem' (purple-pink, a popular older variety, 32 in), 'Marianne Strauss' (pink, 3 ft), 'Pfitzer's Joker' (scarlet with white tips, 3 ft), and 'Primaner' (red, 5 ft). Notes on cultivation are given in the introductory page to the dahlia section.

ℹ

Family: Asteraceae
Flowering season: summer
Height and spread: 40 × 24 in
Situation: ○
Moisture requirement: ◊
❄

Orchid-flowered dahlia

Dahlia 'Jescot Julie'

Lovers of the unusual should not deny the Miscellaneous group a place in the garden. Orchid-flowered dahlias do not form a class of their own but are assigned to the Miscellaneous group, which contains all varieties not assigned to any of the other nine groups. As the name suggests, its exotically moulded flowers strongly resemble the flowers of orchids. 'Jescot Julie' is very popular because of its interesting color combination, having orange-yellow petals with purple undersides. It is very free-flowering and grows about 3 ft high. Another recommended variety is the pink and yellow 'Pink Giraffe' which also belongs to the orchid-flowered dahlias because of its flower shape. These giraffe dahlias are older varieties which owe their name to the fact that the petals have markings which recall the skin pattern of a giraffe. Notes on cultivation are given in the introductory page to the dahlia section.

ℹ

Family: Asteraceae
Flowering season: summer
Height and spread: 40 × 18 in
Situation: ○
Moisture requirement: ◊
❄

attracts bees and butterflies

Single-flowered dahlia

Dahlia 'Loki Schmidt'

ⓘ

Family: Asteraceae
Flowering season: summer
Height: to 5 ft
Situation: ○
Moisture requirement: ◊
❄
attracts bees and butterflies

This group still preserves the natural character of its Mexican ancestors. It has single flowers with a yellow center of florets encircled by a row of petals. If there is a second row of petals, the flowers are described as duplex dahlias. The yellow disk forms a beautiful color contrast with the petals and is very attractive to bees. The dwarf varieties also belong here, of smaller growth and flower size and therefore outstandingly suitable for bedding out, flower borders, window boxes, pots and tubs. They are sown in spring at 64°–68°F. The variety 'Loki Schmidt' is orange-red with yellow stripes. Further examples include 'Preston Park' (scarlet, 32 in), 'Irene van der Zwet' (yellow, 24 in), 'Kardinal' (red, 5 ft), 'Nelly Geerlings' (scarlet, 20 in) and 'Roxy' (purple, 16 in, with dark leaves); and duplex dahlias: 'Bishop of Llandaff' (reds, 12 in) and 'Fascination' (purple and pink, 4 ft). Notes on cultivation are given in the introductory page to the dahlia section.

Dahlia 'Tsuki yori no shisha'

Antler dahlia

Dahlia 'Tsuki yori no shisha'

These varieties are popular for their unusual flower form. They do not have a class of their own, most belonging to the cactus or semi-cactus groups of dahlias, and others to the decorative dahlias. Their characteristic feature is petals divided more or less strongly at the ends. The variety 'Tsuki yori no shisha' is particularly unusual with strongly fringed petals and flower heads about 4 in across, making it excellent for cutting. Further examples of the tall varieties are 'Ambition' (purple, 4 ft), 'Dentelle de Venice' (white, 4–5 ft), 'Rhea' (fiery red, 4 ft), 'Trampoline' (purple, 4 ft), and 'Veritable' (purple and white, 4 ft). Notes on cultivation are given in the introductory page to the dahlia section.

ⓘ

Family: Asteraceae
Flowering season: summer
Height: 3–5 ft
Situation: ○
Moisture requirement: ◌
❄

Freesia varieties

Freesia

Family: Iridaceae
Flowering season: summer
Height and spread: 3 ft
Situation: ○
Moisture requirement: ○
❄
❀

The parent species of the numerous hybrid varieties came from South Africa. The strongly fragrant sweet-smelling funnel-shaped flowers up to 3 in long appear on one side at the end of the flowering stems with 8 to 10 flowers on each stem. As well as single flowers, there are also double varieties in all the brightest colors. The narrow, sword-like leaves grow as a fan from the base. In the autumn, the corms are lifted from the soil and overwintered in a frost-free place. In this case, any offsets can be removed, planted in pots or tubs and covered with soil. If left they will flower in the spring. Otherwise they can be planted outdoors about 2 in deep in mid-May. Seeds can be sown at the end of winter at 64°–68°F. Propagation demands a certain amount of effort. The plants thrive best in a warm, light situation with fertile soil. While flowering, they should be watered and fed weekly, watering being stopped after flowering. The pretty cut flowers are available throughout the year through greenhouse cultivation.

Freesia species

Freesia

Family: Iridaceae
Flowering season: summer
Height: to 20 in
Situation: ○
Moisture requirement: ○
❄
❀

Many freesia species have their 'roots' in South Africa, frequently coming from the eastern and western parts of Cape Province. The corms of *F. corymbosa* develop straight pointed leaves up to 8 in long. Depending on variety, the flowers are a more or less intensely fragrant, colored creamy white, bright yellow or pale pink with yellow throat. They are on average a little less than 1 in in length, smaller than those of the large-flowered hybrids. *F. lactea* is charming with its fragrant white flowers tinged with purple. They are propagated in the same way as the hybrids. The corms cannot survive frost and should therefore be overwintered in a cool, frost-free space. Corms planted in the spring will appear early in the summer. At first the young plants should be lightly shaded, but after they have hardened off they will thrive in the sun. They are especially decorative planted in groups.

Fritillary species

Fritillaria

ℹ

Family: Liliaceae
Flowering season: spring
Height/spread: to 60 × 12 in
Situation: ○
Moisture requirement: ◊,
dry to slightly moist well-drained
❀❀ – ❀❀❀
❀

There are nearly 100 species of fritillary which are native to the Mediterranean, south-west Asia and western North America. Their flowering period ranges from spring to early summer and the flowers are usually bell or cup-shaped, hanging singly or in small groups. The narrow, straight leaves are lanceolate. Their habitats are very varied, ranging from forests to open meadow areas and mountainous regions. The original growing conditions must be considered in cultivating them. Some species enjoy dry, sunny locations with well drained soil, such as *F. michailowsky*, which has purple and red flowers with a yellow-tipped interior, and *F. persica* with dense spires of blue and purple flowers. These species are outstandingly suitable for rockeries. Others enjoy rather moist, cool, shady conditions and grow well at the edges of ponds. An example is *F. camtschatcensis* with its almost black bell-shaped blossoms. Seeds can be sown in autumn in a frost-free place. Propagation is much quicker with bulbils which are planted in autumn at a depth of four times their height.

Crown Imperial

Fritillaria imperialis

ℹ

Family: Liliaceae
Flowering season: spring
Height and spread: 40 × 12 in
Situation: ○
Moisture requirement: ◊
❀❀❀
❀

This impressive cottage garden plant is a native of Afghanistan, Iran and the western Himalayas. The thick stem carries a ring of 5 to 8 large, nodding bell-shaped flowers which appear in spring. They are yellow, orange or red depending on variety, with a musky smell which is somewhat unattractive. Above the flowers is a bunch of leaf-like bracts. It has broad lanceolate glossy green leaves. The flat bulbs, as big as a fist, are planted in early autumn about 8 in deep. Any bulbils can be removed in the summer for propagation; sowing seed in autumn is equally possible. The best position is a light to partially shaded situation without direct midday sun, in a fertile well-drained soil. Work well-rotted manure or organic compost into the soil before planting. Keep moist throughout the growing season. Do not remove any leaves which turn yellow; they must be left to die back on their own. It is a fine plant for borders and cutting.

S nake's head fritillary

Fritillaria meleagris

The snake's head fritillary is a native of Europe up to the Caucasus and a protected plant in most countries. Its great attraction is its purple to brown and red bell-shaped flowers with their striking chequerboard marking. There are also white and pink varieties. The grey-green, grass-like leaves are not very numerous. It is normally propagated by bulbils; sowing from seed is also possible but it takes a much longer time. The seed capsules are brown when mature. The little flat round bulbs are planted 2–3 in deep, preferably in groups, in late summer or early autumn. Caution, the bulbs are poisonous. Since the plants are found in moist meadows in nature, they also need a moist, humus-rich, slightly acid soil when cultivated. They like a sunny or partially shaded location, but they must not be waterlogged. It is recommended to work the soil with compost before planting. It is good for the woodland margins or the moist soil near the edge of a garden pond.

ⓘ

Family: Liliaceae
Flowering season: spring
Height and spread: 12 × 3 in
Situation: ◑
Moisture requirement: ◌
❄ ❄ ❄

33

Snowdrop

Galanthus

When snowdrops appear at the end of winter, spring is at the door. They are native throughout Central and southern Europe and western Asia. The domestic species *Galanthus nivalis*, the common snowdrop, thrives on loose, humus-rich soils in partially shaded situations and is a protected plant in most countries. Each bulb forms two blue-green leaves up to 8 in long with hanging cup-shaped flowers about 4/5 in long. These consist of three external petals longer than the three interior, green-tinged ones. The species also includes double varieties. *G. elwesii*, the large flowered snowdrop, has flowers 1 1/2 in long and begins flowering very early, from mid-winter. It also grows in dry, sunny locations. In the autumn, bulbs are planted in the soil 2–4 in deep in small groups. Through self-sowing, thick clumps will quickly form. The plants are undemanding and will flourish for years in the same space. They are pretty in woodland areas, planted in clumps of grass, or in pots.

ⓘ

Family: Amaryllidaceae
Flowering season: spring
Height/spread: 4–8 × 4 in
Situation: ◑
Moisture requirement: ◐
❋ ❋ ❋
❀

Gladiolus

Gladiolus

The *Gladiolus* is a genus of about 180 species which include some of the most popular summer-flowering plants and cut flowers. The species are native to South Africa, the Mediterranean region, the Arabian peninsula, northwest and eastern Africa, Madagascar and western Asia. Since the late 18th century, when gladioli were introduced to Europe from South Africa, new cultivars have been constantly developed. These vary in flower size, form, color and frost tenderness. The tall garden hybrids resulting from crossing several South African species are particularly popular. Their funnel-shaped flowers appear from spring to early autumn depending on variety, each thick stem carrying a flower spike whose flowers open successively from the bottom upwards. When new flowers develop, the older ones die. A flower consists of six petals: a projecting upper central petal, three usually rather smaller lower petals forming a lip, and two backward-curved side petals. The flowers often combine two or more colors in all hues except blue and black. The upright, narrow leaves are light to dark green and almost always sword-like. The plant's height varies from 3 in –5 ft. Gladioli are increased by the freely-forming cormlets which are removed in the autumn and planted in spring. The main pests and diseases from which they can suffer are leatherjackets, thrips, slugs and snails, aphids and gray mould.

Sword lily

Gladiolus 'Rose Supreme'

Gladiolus hybrid

ⓘ

Family: Iridaceae
Flowering season: summer
Height and spread: 60 × 6 in
Situation: ○
Moisture requirement: ◌
✻
❀

Prone to: fusarium tuber rot,
gray mould, thrips, aphids and
infestation by snails

The parent species of many popular garden hybrids mainly come from Africa and southern Europe. The hybrid 'Rose Supreme' has salmon pink flowers with a cream-white heart and is typical of the many cultivars which exist in almost all colors and forms. The range extends from the large-flowered hybrids 5 ft tall with more than 20 flowers on each spike to the dainty flowers of the miniature or Nanus hybrids 16–24 in appearing in smaller spikes in early summer. The funnel-shaped single flowers always come into bloom from the ground upwards. The flat corms are planted 4–6 in deep in spring. Planted continuously until the end of June, they bloom until late summer. Gladioli like a warm, sunny position, ideally protected from the wind with fertile well-drained soil. In dry summers they must be watered, and fed once growth starts to appear. As cut flowers, they are cut as soon as the first flower bud is showing color. In the autumn, the stems are cut down to the to the soil, then the bulbs are lifted and cleaned and stored in a dry, well-ventilated place at 41°–50°F.

Large-flowered gladiolus hybrid

Gladiolus 'Peter Pears'

ⓘ

Family: Iridaceae
Flowering season: late summer
Height: 6 ft
Spread: 14 in
Situation: ○
Moisture requirement: ◐
✻

Prone to: fusarium tuber rot,
gray mould, thrips, aphids and
infestation by snails

This frost-sensitive perennial gladiolus is a large-flowered hybrid which is ideal for cutting and showing. The narrow, sword-like mid-green leaves grow erect from the corm. 28 flower buds up to 5 1/2 in long appear in late summer on dense, uniform spikes, developing into salmon-pink flowers with red throats. Up to 12 may be open simultaneously. Propagation is by young offset corms which in spring are planted 4–6 in deep in well-drained fertile soil in a sunny, sheltered part of the garden. The shoots are very tender when they emerge and should therefore be covered with a paper bag or a flowerpot when there is a risk of early frosts. As soon as the spikes have achieved a third of their ultimate height, a potassium-rich liquid fertilizer should be applied every 10–14 days to help ensure magnificent flowering.

Gladiolus callianthus

Gladiolus callianthus

This individual perennial is native from Mozambique to Eritrea. Long, narrow leaves develop from the corms to a height of 16 in. In summer, fragrant white flowers appear, up to ten on each stem. The crimson throat marking is prominent. They are propagated by flat corms, either purchased or offsets separated from the mother plant during its dormant period, planted 4–6 in deep in spring. Sowing seed in spring is also possible. Gladioli like a warm, sheltered, sunny situation with fertile, well-drained soil. They are well suited to borders or summer flower beds, rockeries and for cutting. Frost-sensitive species such as this one can be over-wintered in a dry, airy room at 41°–50°F. When the leaves turn yellowish-brown in the autumn, the stems are cut down to soil level, the bulbs are lifted, the earth is cleaned off them, and they are stored in a frost-free place.

Family: Iridaceae
Flowering season: summer
Height and spread: 40 × 2 in
Situation: ○
Moisture requirement: ◊
❄
❀

Prone to: fusarium tuber rot, gray mould, thrips, aphids and infestation by snails

Gladiolus cardinalis

Gladiolus cardinalis

This perennial is native to the western Cape Province of South Africa. Its funnel-shaped, wide-opening red flowers with a decorative white stain on the lip are very attractive. Up to 12 single flowers 2 in in diameter appear on slightly curved spikes. The sword-like leaves can achieve a length of 36 in. They can be propagated by flat corms which may be bought, or offsets can be removed from the mother plant while it is dormant. These are planted 4–6 in deep in spring. Sowing seed in spring is also possible. Gladioli like a warm, sheltered, sunny situation with fertile, well-drained soil. They are good in herbaceous borders and flower beds, in rockeries and for cutting. Like all frost-sensitive species, *G. cardinalis* can be overwintered in a dry, well-ventilated room at 41°–50°F. When the leaves turn yellowish-brown in the autumn, the stems are cut down to soil level, the bulbs are lifted, the earth is cleaned off them, and they are stored in a frost-free place.

Family: Iridaceae
Flowering season: summer
Height and spread: 8 × 3 in
Situation: ○
Moisture requirement: ◊
❄

Prone to: fusarium tuber rot, gray mould, thrips, aphids and infestation by snails

Gladiolus papilio

Gladiolus papilio

ℹ️

Family: Iridaceae
Flowering season: Late summer
Height: 36 in
Spread: 26 ft
Situation: ○
Moisture requirement: 💧
❄️ ❄️

Prone to: fusarium tuber rot,
gray mould, thrips, aphids and
infestation by snails

The ornamental perennial is native to South Africa and belongs to the *Gladiolus* genus which has about 180 species and over 10,000 hybrids and cultivars, bred for gardening purposes and for cut flowers. The rhizomes of the plant spread through underground spurs and the species is particularly suitable for planting in mixed beds and for growing for cut flowers. Its erect, sword-like, mid-green leaves make slender fans about 18 in long. From 5 to 10 bell-shaped, flowers appear on each tall, arching flower stem in late summer. They are up to 2 in long and the color varies from light yellow to greenish yellow flushed with purple. When the leaves die down, the bulbs should be lifted, dried and treated with fungicide about every 14 days. Propagation is by separating young rhizome offsets during the dormant period. After being dried and kept in a frost-free place, they can be planted outdoors in the spring.

Marsh Africaner

Gladiolus tristis

ℹ️

Family: Iridaceae
Flowering season: spring
Height and spread: 60 × 2 in
Situation: ○
Moisture requirement: ○
❄️
✿

Prone to: fusarium tuber rot,
gray mould, thrips, aphids and
infestation by snails

This early summer-flowering species also comes from South Africa. The spikes can carry 20 funnel-shaped single flowers. These are green-tinged pale yellow or creamy white, sometimes with reddish brown tones. In the evening it gives off an intense fragrance. The flower stems are narrow and wiry, and the long, very narrow leaves are often pointed at the tip. The flat corms are planted 4–6 in deep in spring. To grow them for earlier flowering, they can also be brought on in a cool greenhouse. Gladioli prefer a warm, sunny, sheltered situation with well-drained soil. They are suitable for flower beds and borders, rockeries and for cutting. Frost-sensitive species like this one are over-wintered in a dry, airy room at 41°–50°F. In autumn when the leaves have turned yellowish-brown, the stems are cut down to the soil level. The bulbs are then dug up, cleaned and stored.

*A*maryllis

Hippeastrum

Hippeastrum is a genus of about 80 bulb species, native to South America where it thrives in the mountains, savannah and forests of the tropical and subtropical regions. Many large-flowered hybrids which are commonly (and inaccurately) known as Amaryllis are grown as house plants. The perennial bulb-forming plant has dark to mid-green strap-shaped leaves, which develop with or immediately after the flower. The umbels with two to six open funnel-shaped flowers appear from January to April and are white to red depending on variety. *H. aulicum* has carmine flowers, *H. vittatum* white ones with red markings and *H. striatum* coral-pink with a green central strip. The plant causes illness if eaten. The hybrid *H. x. acramannii* is one of the few varieties which can survive a short time in the open at 32°F. It should be protected in the garden with a deep winter mulch. Other frost-sensitive varieties should be kept as indoor plants or in the conservatory. Propagation is by offsets.

ⓘ

Family: Amaryllidaceae
Flowering season: winter, spring
Height: 20 in
Spread: 12 in
Situation: ○
Moisture requirement: ◓
❄
✖

*B*luebell

Hyachinthoides hispania

The bluebell is a bulbous perennial closely related to the *Scilla* family and is native to light woodland regions of Spain, Portugal and North Africa. A spreading plant, it easily becomes naturalised in the grass of wild or woodland gardens as well as being a useful ground cover plant in herbaceous borders. Great clumps of upright, strap-shaped, dark green leaves sprout from the bulbs which are about 2 1/2 in wide. Clusters of blue, bell-shaped flowers appear in spring. The cultivars Excelsior, La Grandesse and Rosabella have violet and blue, white, and violet and pink flowers. The plant can cause skin irritation, and illness if eaten. Propagation is by seed sown as soon as the seeds are mature, or by bulbils in summer. If the flowers are not removed when over, the bluebell will self-seed. The rugged species tolerates almost any soil, but it does best in a fertile, moist, well-drained one.

Hyachinthoides hispania

ⓘ

Family: Hyacinthaceae
Flowering season: spring
Height: 16 in
Spread: 4 in
Situation: ◑
Moisture requirement: ◓
❄ ❄ ❄
✖

41

*H*yacinth

Hyacinthus orientalis

ⓘ

Family: Hyacinthaceae
Flowering season: spring
Height: 12 in
Spread: 26 ft
Situation: ○ – ◑
Moisture requirement: ⬤
❄ ❄ ❄
✖
❀

The strongly scented bulbous plant *H. orientalis* is native to Turkey, Syria and Lebanon. From the wild species the many varieties of garden hyacinths with their larger, more prolific flowers have been developed, perfect for spring bedding as annuals, in borders and also as early-flowering pot plants for use in the house and garden. The light green basal leaves, 6–14 in long, cover the lower half of the flowering stem. In the spring, upright clusters of up to 40 bell-shaped tubular florets appear, the color depending on the variety: for instance, 'Amethyst' (lilac), 'Ostara' (deep blue), 'Blue Jacket' (dark blue), 'Queen of the Pinks' (pink). The available range embraces white, yellow, orange, pink, red, blue and violet flowers. In the first year of planting, the inflorescence is very flowery and dense, but in subsequent years the density of the flowers decreases. All parts are poisonous if eaten, and contact with the bulbs can intensify skin allergies. Propagation is by offsets removed in the period of dormancy during the summer.

*S*pider lily

Hymenocallis narcissiflora

ⓘ

Family: Amaryllidaceae
Flowering season: summer
Height: 24 in
Spread: 12 in
Situation: ○ – ◑
Moisture requirement: ⬤
❄
❀

This bulbous perennial with its strangely shaped flowers is native to the Andes of Bolivia and Peru and is the most widely cultivated species of *Hymenocalli*. Semi-erect, basal, strap-shaped, dark green leaves grow from the round bulbs. They are up to 24 in long and enclose the lower half of the flowering stem. In summer, umbels of up to five scented, white flowers appear, sometimes with green striped markings inside and with stamens which are bent over the secondary crown. Propagation is by bulbils which can be planted in pots or in the open in spring. Because it is frost-sensitive, the plant should be lifted in the autumn before the first frost. After wintering in a cool, dry space at 41°–50°F, the bulb can be grown indoors in April and planted in the garden when the risk of frost is past, in a light protected position in full sun. It is ideal for flower borders or mixed beds.

Irises

Irises

Gardeners who grow irises have chosen one of the finest of all bulbous or rhizomatous flowers. The genus comprises some 300 species, most of them native to the northern hemisphere. Depending on the species, the flowering season is from spring to summer. The flowers consist of three outer petals, known as the falls, and three inner petals, called the standards. Bearded irises, sometimes described as 'the poor man's orchids,' owe their name to the striking 'beard' of white or colored hairs on their large, spectacular flowers. They are suitable for borders and natural gardens; borders devoted entirely to irises are particularly effective. The compact botanical species are usually perennial, and are particularly good in rock gardens. The best planting time is late summer or early autumn, but they can also be planted in spring. Irises should be grown in sun or partial shade. Most species will thrive in normal garden soils containing sand and humus, not too moist and rather alkaline. Others, such as *Iris ensata, I. laevigata* and *I. sibirica* prefer damp or even swampy soils, and make good water-garden plants. For optimum development, they should not be placed too close together or in the shade of other plants. If the plants lose vigour or the groups become too dense, they can be divided after three to five years. Dwarf irises such as *I. danfordiae* and *I. x hollandica* need to rest in a dry state in summer. The bulbs should be dug up, dried off, kept in an airy place and planted out again in autumn. Propagation, depending on the species, is by division of the rhizome or by separating offsets from bulbs.

Bearded iris

Iris barbeta

ℹ

Family: Iridaceae
Flowering season: spring, early summer
Height: 2–28 in
Situation: ○
Moisture requirement: ◐
❄ ❄ ❄
✖

The bearded irises are a sub-genus of the iris family with about 300 species, and they are the kind most frequently cultivated in the garden. The bearded irises have large creeping rhizomes on the surface, sword-like, usually wide leaves arranged like a fan, and single or branched stems according to species. From spring to early summer, one or more flowers appear on each stem with well developed erect inner petals ('standards') and drooping outer petals ('falls'). The 'bearded' is derived from the white or chromatic hairs on the falls. The flowers are in many colors depending on species or variety. For instance, *I. iberica* has brown-veined cream-colored or white blossoms, *I. humilis* has yellow flowers, *I. lortetii* has white flowers with pink and chestnut ledges or points and *I. susiana* shows gray ones, deep purple veined blossoms with black markings. All species are poisonous. The plants are propagated by dividing the rhizomes.

Iris barbeta

46

*I*ris chrysographes

Iris chrysographes

The rhizomatous beardless plant of the Sibirica group of irises is native to the Chinese regions of Sezuan and Yunnan. As a hardy species, it is especially suitable in open beds. The grassy leaves are gray-green and up to 20 in long. Unbranched stems, each with two pleasantly deep, purple-red, scented flowers appear in the early summer. The three falls carry yellow markings. The variety 'Black Knight' has very dark purple flowers. All parts cause illness if eaten and the juice causes skin irritations. Each of the rhizomes increasing under the surface forms several offsets each year and can increase infinitely. For propagation, the rhizome should be divided in late summer to early autumn and planted directly in their final location in full sun or bright shade at intervals of about 8 in. The rhizomes should also be divided if after growing for a number of years the clumps have become too large or have lost their vigour.

Family: Iridaceae
Flowering season: early summer
Height: 16–20 in
Situation: ○
Moisture requirement: ◐
✿ ✿ ✿
✖
❀

*D*utch irises

Iris × Hollandia

The unpretentious Dutch hybrids have been cultivated in gardens for a long time and with their graceful forms and bright colors they are well suited to colorful borders and also as cut flowers. The bulb produces wide grass-like, sword-shaped, gray-blue leaves and slim, elegant flowers ranging from white through yellow to blue and deep purple. The three standards and three falls often have contrasting colors and patterns. Examples of popular varieties are 'Golden Harvest' (dark yellow), 'Ideal' (dark blue) and 'White Perfection' (pure white). They normally flower in early summer but when specially prepared they can be forced to flower at other times of year. All parts of the plant can cause illness when eaten and the juice can cause skin irritations. Propagation is in summer by offsets which will usually flower in the second year.

Family: Liliaceae
Flowering season: summer
Height: 16 – 24 in
Situation: ○
Moisture requirement: ◐
✿ ✿ ✿
✖

Iris histrioides

Iris histrioides

Family: Iridaceae
Flowering season: spring
Height: 4–6 in
Spread: 2–3 1/2 in
Situation: ○
Moisture requirement: ◐
❊ ❊ ❊
✖

The bulbous perennial flowers in spring and is one of the Reticulata group of irises. It is native to the north of Asia Minor, Turkey and northwest Iran. This especially hardy plant may flower as early as February if the weather is not too cold. With a height of up to 6 in, this small species is ideal for planting in rockeries, raised beds or tubs. The upright squared leaves are bright to mid-green. Similar in form to those of all iris species, the flowers of *I. histrioides* have petals consisting of three deep blue and violet standards and three large falls with darker coloring and a golden yellow central marking. One or two flowers appear on each stem. The hybrid 'Major' has larger royal blue flowers, while 'Katharina Hodgkin' has creamy-white flowers with bluish and yellow coloring. All parts of the plant are poisonous. Propagation is by removing bulbils in the autumn and planting them again immediately in neutral to alkaline soil. The plant should be kept dry during the summer dormant period.

Iris magnifica

Iris magnifica

Family: Iridaceae
Flowering season: spring
Height: 12–24 in
Situation: ○
Moisture requirement: ◐
❊ ❊ ❊
✖

This bulbous lily species belongs to the Juno group of irises and is native to the central mountains of Asia. A rugged plant, it is hardy in warmer parts of the country and is suitable for sunny, open beds in the garden. Glossy mid-green leaves up to 7 in long grow from the fleshy-rooted bulbs. Up to seven, 3 in long flowers appear on each stem in early to mid spring, with three large falls and three smaller standards. The flowers are pale lilac, with a pale yellow and white marking in the center of the falls. The plant is poisonous like all iris species and causes illness if eaten. It can be propagated by separating offsets, and planting them direct in well-drained, neutral to slightly alkaline soil in full sun. When planting, it is important to ensure that the fleshy roots are not damaged.

*I*ris reticulata

Iris reticulata

This widely popular easily cultivated iris species is native to the Middle East and Asia Minor. The small, delicate flowers appear as early as February and the plant is ideal for rock garden, for early spring beds and for growing in containers and pots. The bulb is surrounded by a net-like ('reticulated') covering and produces 1–2 narrow, sword-like, ribbed, gray-green leaves. After flowering, the leaves grow to about 12 in. The 2 – 2,5 in flowers have a slight scent of violets and are strikingly colored. The violet-blue standards are curved upwards, while the side-ways-set fall is deep purple-blue with an orange central marking. There are many cultivated varieties, such as the pale blue 'Cantab,' the dark blue 'Harmony' and the purple 'Pauline'. All parts of the plant are poisonous. Propagation is by offsets which are taken after the leaves die down in summer. They are kept in a cool dry place until planted in the autumn.

🛈

Family: Liliaceae
Flowering season: spring
Height: 2 – 6 in
Situation: ○
Moisture requirement: ◐
❄ ❄ ❄
✖
❀

49

Summer snowflake

Leucojum aestivum

ℹ

Family: Amaryllidaceae
Flowering season: spring/summer
Height: 18–24 in
Spread: 3 in
Situation: ○ – ◑
Moisture requirement: ◗
❈ ❈ ❈
❀

Like the snowdrop, this bulbous perennial is native to wet meadows, slopes and other moist locations in Europe, Asia Minor and the Balearic Islands. The species has been cultivated as a garden plant for centuries. With its strong growth it is especially suitable for beds, near water and in rough grass in the wild meadow garden. The strap-shaped upright leaves are glossy dark green and up to 12 in long. In early summer, up to eight white blossoms with green tips appear on each stem; they have a slight smell of chocolate. The variety 'Gravetye Giant' grows a little higher and flowers earlier. It also outdoes the type species in the number and size of its flowers. Propagation is by offsets, taken after the leaves have died down. The summer snowflake requires a cool, moist humus-rich soil. The bulbs should be planted only in autumn when they are dormant, about 5–6 in deep, separated into groups.

Spring snowflake

Leucojum Vernum

ℹ

Family: Amaryllidaceae
Flowering season: spring
Height: 8–12 in
Spread: 3 in
Situation: ◑ – ●
Moisture requirement: ◗
❈ ❈ ❈

The spring snowflake is native of the deciduous woods of southern and eastern Europe and it thrives when cultivated in groups in mixed beds, in wild woodland gardens, on moist meadows and near water. Upright glossy dark green leaves grow from bulbs up to 1 in thick. Each flower stem up to 6 in high carries one or two cup-shaped white flowers with green tips in March and April. The leaves die back when the flowering period is over. For easier germination, the peduncles with the seed capsules then bend towards the soil. The very robust variety *L. vagneri* blooms as early as late winter with two flowers on each stem, while *L. carpathicum* has white blossoms with yellow tips. In addition to self-seeding, the plant can be propagated by bulbils in the late summer or by sowing seed directly when it is mature. The spring snowflake requires deep, humus-rich soil in a partially shaded to shaded situation.

Lily

Lilium

The lily genus consists of about 100 species and innumerable hybrids. Lilies are among the longest-cultivated plants of the northern hemisphere. The species are native to North America, Europe, Asia and the Philippines and vary considerably in the shape, size, form and color of the flowers. To classify the varieties, lilies have been grouped into nine divisions, based on the species from which they were developed. These are: Asiatic hybrids, Martagon hybrids, Candidum hybrids, American hybrids, Longiflorum hybrids, Trumpets and Aurelian hybrids, Oriental hybrids, other hybrids, and true botanical species. Lily bulbs consist of overlapping scales, the bulbs being arranged in a rhizome-like manner in some species. These produce upright, mostly unbranched stems up to 10 ft tall, each carrying individual flowers or flowers arranged in bunches, panicles or umbels. The lily flowers consist of six homogeneous petals arranged in a star shape with six stamens in the center. The anthers on the filaments make a characteristic 'T' arrangement. The flower shapes include bowl, funnel, trumpet and Turk's cap (turban). The range of flower colors includes all hues with the exception of blue and black. The flowers may be single colored, striped, speckled or double with papillae. Depending on species, lilies can be increased by separating larger clumps or removing bulb offsets. Seeds do not breed true.

Possible pests include leatherjackets, lily beetles, thrips, aphids, slugs and snails. Mice and squirrels may eat bulbs and young growth, and lilies may also suffer from various fungal and viral diseases.

Golden rayed lily

Lilium auratum

ⓘ

Family: Liliaceae
Flowering season: late summer/early autumn
Height: 2–6 ft
Situation: ◑
Moisture requirement: ◐
✸ ✸ ✸
❀

L. auratum, the golden rayed lily, is one of the most beautiful and elegant representatives of its species. It is native to Japan where it flourishes among bushes and low grass on mostly volcanic soils. Its sturdy stems may be up to 8 ft high depending on position, carrying glossy dark green leaves up to 8 in long along its whole length. From July to September, bunches of 6 to 30 scented bowl-shaped flowers appear, extremely prominent and up to 12 in long. Their color is white with colored spots and golden yellow or crimson red bands which almost reach from the depth of the throat to the tips of the petals. Among the best-known known varieties, *L. a. plathyphyllum* differs from the type species with its wider leaves, larger flowers and larger flower cluster. Propagation is by seed or offsets, which should be planted in well-drained acid soil.

Madonna lily

Lilium candidum

ⓘ

Family: Liliaceae
Flowering season: summer
Height: 3–6 ft
Situation: ○
Moisture requirement: ◐
✸ ✸ ✸
❀

The Madonna lily is one the oldest ornamental plants and was already growing in northern Lebanon and Palestine in biblical times. From there, it has spread to the north and west and today it occurs in the wild in southeastern Europe up to the eastern Mediterranean. Already in the autumn after flowering, a rosette of new, light green, lanceolate basal leaves begins to appear, giving some winter protection to the plant. The stem, up to 6 ft high, is covered with small, flat lanceolate leaves. The outward-facing flowers appear in mid-summer, forming scented clusters of 5 to 20 blooms. The broad trumpet-shaped flowers are pure white wit bright yellow anthers. Stems and leaves die down after flowering. Propagation of the Madonna lily is by offsets which are planted from July to August. The bulb is planted just below the surface in neutral to alkaline soil.

*E*aster lily

Lilium longiflorum

The Easter lily is widely grown for flower arrangements and bridal bouquets. It is a native of southern Japan and Taiwan, where it is found not in the mountains but near the sea. The roots form stems bearing glossy dark green lanceolate leaves up to 7 in long. The scented white flowers appear in small clusters in mid-summer. They are trumpet shaped and achieve a considerable size of 6 to 8 in. The anthers are yellow. Seeds germinate quickly above ground and often after ten months have produced plants ready to flower. The plant is normally grown under glass. Because they are frost-sensitive they are not very suitable for planting in the open. However, they make an attractive container plant, planted in alkaline soil and kept in partial shade.

ⓘ

Family: Liliaceae
Flowering season: summer
Height: 16–40 in
Situation: ◑
Moisture requirement: ◐
❄
✾

Lilium hybride

*R*egal lily

Lilium regale

ℹ

Family: Liliaceae
Flowering season: summer
Height: 24–80 in
Situation: ○
Moisture requirement: ◐
❋ ❋ ❋
❀

L. regale, the regal lily, is often nominated as the most beautiful of its family because of its impressive flowers. It was only discovered at the beginning of the 20th century in the Chinese province of Szechuan. However, from there it rapidly spread throughout the world. The plant is superb in garden borders without strongly alkaline soil. Because of its intense scent, it should be near but not too close to the living room. It is stem-rooting and produces straight or arching stems with glossy dark green leaves 2–5 in long. In July, umbels of up to 25 trumpet sha-ped flowers appear. They are pinkish-purple outside and white inside with a deep yellow throat. The anthers are golden yellow. The ample seeds are formed sponta-neously and germinate above ground within 14 days if they have not dried up too much. In frost-free conditions the seeds will quickly produce many seedlings. These should be protected from late frosts which can often lead to the loss of the whole plant

Oriental hybrids

Lilium 'Black Beauty'

'Black Beauty' is one of the oriental or Japanese hybrids, the aristocrats of the hybrid lilies for their striking especially flowers, handsomely formed and magnificently colored. They probably derive from east Asian species *L. auratum*, *L. japonicum* and *L. speciosum*. 'Black Beauty' can grow up to 7 ft tall and is well suited to planting in borders. Its mid-green lanceolate leaves are alternate. In July and August bunches of medium-sized, scented blossoms appear, whose individual petals are of the Turk's cap type, strongly recurved. They are scarlet with a greenish center and white petal edges. Propagation is by seeds or offset bulbs. When sowing seed, it should be remembered that lilies from the oriental hybrids group are slow and difficult to germinate so that seedlings sometimes only form in the second year. When offset bulbs are ripe, they can be sown either directly in the open, in a situation protected in winter, or in a deep seed tray under glass.

Family: Liliaceae
Flowering season: summer
Height: 5–7 ft
Situation: ◑
Moisture requirement: ◗
❊ ❊ ❊
❀

Trumpet lilies

Lilium 'Bright Star'

This robust plant belongs to the group of trumpet and Aurelian hybrids and is derived from the Asiatic lily species, *L. regale*, *L. henryi* and *L. sargentiae*. It is particularly effective in borders and in large containers, but it is also excellent as a cut flower. It has mid-green, oval to straight leaves. The large, scented flowers appear in the July and August. They are creamy white with an orange-yellow star-shaped mark in the center. The turban-shaped petals are reflexed at the tip. 'Bright Star' can be increased by division at the planting time, from bulb offsets and by sowing. The seeds germinate in the dark and must be covered with soil. The bulbs are sown under glass in spring. The plant prefers a warm, sunny location and tolerates lime soils.

Family: Liliaceae
Flowering season: summer
Height: 3–5 ft
Situation: ○
Moisture requirement: ◗
❊ ❊ ❊
❀

Muscari latifolium

ⓘ

Family: Hyacinthaceae/Liliaceae
Flowering season: spring
Height: to 8 in
Spread: to 16 ft
Situation: ○ – ◑
Moisture requirement: ◐
❄ ❄

Grape hyacinth

Muscari latifolium

This bulbous perennial is a native of south-west Asia where it flourishes in light pine forests. It is a fairly small species which is especially suitable for border planting and for rockeries. The grape hyacinth has individual semi-upright, wide, lance-shaped, mid-green leaves up to 12 in long. The thickly-arranged tiny oval flowers appear on tapered spikes 1/5–2 1/2 in long in spring. The lower blossoms are dark purple while the upper ones are lighter and less strongly colored. Propagation is by division of older colonies in late summer or by sowing in early summer, when at least three years must be allowed before the first flowers appear. Self-sowing also takes place. The bulbs are planted about 4 in apart 2 1/2 to 3 in deep well-aerated soil. The plant requires a warm, protected situation in well-drained, not too moist soil. Grape hyacinths are sometimes vulnerable to viruses.

Daffodil

Narcissus

Daffodils are the widely known, widely varied members of the genus Narcissus, among the most popular garden plants and known in ancient Egypt and Greece. The species is native to Europe and North Africa where it thrives in fields from sea level to sub-alpine altitudes as well as in forests, rock fissures and the edges of streams. Since the 18th century, intensive cross-breeding has taken place both professionally and among amateur daffodil enthusiasts. For instance, today there are more than 14,000 different varieties of the 50 species, and new ones are still being added every year. Daffodils have bulbs tapering to a point with roots which regenerate themselves in stage of growth. The basal leaves are linear to strap-shaped, or sometimes grass- or rush-like. They grow at the same time as the flower stems. Daffodils are grown for their attractive flowers, mostly variations of yellow and white, separately or in combination, which appear in spring, or sometimes in autumn or winter. They consist of a main crown with six individual petals and a secondary crown which is a central cup containing the stamens. For classification purposes, the many varieties are grouped internationally in 12 divisions, according to origin and type of flowers, as follows: Trumpet daffodils, Large-cupped daffodils, Small-cupped daffodils, Double daffodils, Triandrus daffodils, Cyclamineus daffodils, Jonquilla daffodils, Tazetta daffodils, Poeticus daffodils, Species and wild variants, Split-corona daffodils, and Miscellaneous.

*T*rumpet daffodils

Narcissus

ℹ

Family: Amaryllidaceae
Flowering season: spring
Height: 16–24 in
Spread: 3–6 in
Situation: ○ – ◑
Moisture requirement: ◐
❄ ❄ ❄
✖

The extremely resistant representatives of the trumpet daffodil division mainly result from cross-breeding of *N. pseudonarcissus* forms. Depending on variety, they bloom in early spring with white, yellow or two-colored (bicolor) flowers with white, yellow, orange or pink. Each stem produces a single forward-facing flower with a trumpet as long as or longer than the petals of the star-shaped main crown. Varieties include 'Cantatrice', 'Empress of Ireland' and 'Mount Hood' (white flowers), 'Golden Harvest', 'King Alfred' and 'Viking' (yellow flowers), 'Alpine Glow' and 'Rima' (white petals and pink trumpets), and 'Bravoure' and 'Newcastle' (white petals and yellow trumpets). The juice of daffodils can cause skin irritation. Propagation is by offsets which can be removed after the leaves have died down and which are then stored in a cool dry place until they are planted in autumn.

Large-cupped daffodils

Narcissus

Like most of the other species and varieties, daffodils of the large-cupped division flower in mid-spring. They are well adapted to planting among shrubs and in grass. In addition, it is a distinguished cut flower. The flower color is white and yellow as well as bicolor with white, yellow, orange or pink. The plant produces one flower on each stalk, and the size of the cup is at least one-third of the length of the petals, but never longer than them. The large-cupped daffodils have mainly been produced by crossing trumpet and poeticus daffodils, creating a great variety of forms. As well as the color, the shape of the cup also varies from long and rounded to wide and flat. The edge too can be strongly crimped in various ways. 'Cansip' and 'Stainless' are varieties with white petals and cups, 'Binkie' and 'Daydream' have lemon yellow petals with a paler or white cups, and 'Salome' and 'Passionale' have white petals and pink cups. The juice of daffodils is poisonous. Propagation is by offsets.

Tazetta daffodils

Narcissus

The daffodils of the tazetta division of daffodils are hybrids resulting from crossing *N. tazetta* and *N. poeticus*. The small-flowered varieties have up to 20 flowers on a single stem and the large-flowered varieties three to four, so a single plant can perform like a bunch. The tazetta hybrids have strong stems and broad leaves. The fragrant flowers appear from April to May with spreading petals and small cups. The bicolor varieties predominate, such as 'Geranium', 'Laurens Kloster' and 'Orange Wonder.' 'Silver Chimes' has white flowers, and 'Yellow Cheerfulness' yellow ones. Some cultivars are not completely hardy and should therefore be kept in a cool greenhouse. A covering of bracken is recommended as frost protection for all varieties. Contact with the juice of the plant can lead to skin irritations or can aggravate allergies.

❶

Family: Amaryllidaceae
Flowering season: spring
Height: 16–24 in
Spread: to 6 in
Situation: ○
Moisture requirement: ◐
❉ ❉ ❉
✖

Narcissus

❶

Family: Amaryllidaceae
Flowering season: spring
Height: 10–18 in
Spread: to 3 in
Situation: ○
Moisture requirement: ◐
❉ ❉
✖
❀

Lent lily

Narcissus pseudonarcissus

Family: Amaryllidaceae
Flowering season: spring
Height: 6–14 in
Situation: ○
Moisture requirement: ◑
❄ ❄ ❄
✖

This widespread daffodil is a wild species native to much of Europe is. It flourishes in light woodland, in meadows and on stony mountain slopes. The bulbous perennial occurs in varied forms and is equally suitable for planting in flower beds, borders, windows boxes and bowls for indoors as soon as the flowers have died down. Its upright, strap-shaped, would tire, mid-green leaves are 3 in long. Bicolor blossoms appear in early spring with slim cream-colored petals and yellow trumpets. The juice of the daffodil can cause skin irritations. The plant is propagated by dividing when the leaves have died back in early summer or later in the early autumn.

Miscellaneous daffodils

Narcissus 'Tête-a-Tête'

Family: Amaryllidaceae
Flowering season: spring
Height: 6 in
Spread: 2 in
Situation: ○
Moisture requirement: ◑
❄ ❄ ❄

This robust hybrid perennial is an example of the miscellaneous division of daffodils. It distinctive feature is its dwarf habit, making it particularly suitable for rockeries and in bowls for the house. Its mid-green leaves are narrow and strap-shaped. From March to April, one to three flowers about 2 1/2 in across open on each stem. Its has dark golden yellow petals with even darker yellow trumpets. As with all daffodil varieties, the juice of these hybrids can cause irritation if in contact with skin. Propagation is by offsets. It thrives best in any fertile soil which should be kept moist during the growing season.

Guernsey lily

Nerine sarniensis

N. sarniensis is a bulbous perennial native to South Africa its received its popular name because it has been cultivated for many years on the Channel Island of Guernsey. The bulbs supposedly reached the island after a shipwreck on the coast. The plant has upright, strap-shaped, mid-green leaves which appear after flowering. The flowers appear in umbels in September and October and are among the most beautiful of all nerines. They are orange-pink and have striking, protruding stamens and petals corrugated at the edges. The variety *N. s. corusca* 'Major' has scarlet flowers. Propagation is by bulbils or seeds in late summer. Seedlings must be grown for three years in a temperature of at least 59°F in winter before they will flower. All parts of the plant cause illness when eaten. The Guernsey lily requires well-drained, sandy soil and full sun. During the growing season, it should be watered regularly, and kept in a sunny, dry place when dormant in summer.

ⓘ

Family: Amaryllidaceae
Flowering season: early autumn
Height: 18–24 in
Spread: 5–6 in
Situation: ○
Moisture requirement: ◐
❄
✖

65

Chincherinchee

Ornithogalum thyrsoides

ⓘ

Family: Hyacinthaceae
Flowering season: summer
Height: 12–28 in
Spread: 4 in
Situation: ○
Moisture requirement: ◗
❄
✖

This robust bulbous perennial is native to Cape Province in South Africa, where it is widely cultivated for cut flowers. As a garden plant, it is good in groups in mixed borders; otherwise, it is an excellent conservatory or house plant. Chincherinchee is outstanding as a cut flower because it continues flowering in a vase until the last blossom and lasts for up to four weeks. The semi-upright, narrow, lanceolate, bright green leaves appear before the flowering period which is from June to August. The many star-shaped flowers appear in dense, pyramidal clusters. They are white with cream-colored or green-toned background. Each bulb develops three to five inflorescences which appear in sequence, usually at four week intervals. All parts of the plant are poisonous and cause serious illness if eaten, and the juice can cause skin irritations. They are propagated by offset bulblets in autumn or by seeds sown under glass in spring.

Striped squill

Puschkinia scilloides

ⓘ

Family: Hyacinthaceae
Flowering season: spring
Height: to 8 in
Spread: to 2 in
Situation: ○ – ◑
Moisture requirement: ◗
❄ ❄ ❄

The striped squill is a bulbous perennial native to Turkey and the Lebanon. It is closely related to the *Scilla* and the *Chionodoxa* families. It is very suitable for planting in rockeries and under bushes in sunny or partially shaded situations. Its basal, lanceolate leaves die back in the early summer. In March and April dense flower spikes appear on stems about 6 in high; these consist of about six light blue, bell-shaped flowers 4/5 in across which carry a slightly darker marking on each petal. The variety 'Alba' has pure white flowers. The plant is propagated easily by seeds or bulbils. If bulbils are removed in August or September, they should be planted as soon as possible, in order to prevent them drying out, at a depth of 1–1 ¹/₂ in. Over-wintering may require a covering of leaves or bracken. In spring, it is also possible to sow seeds which are lightly covered with earth. After about three years, seedlings will flower for the first time. They are most effective planted in groups.

66

Buttercup, crowfoot

Ranunculus asiaticus

Family: Ranunculaceae
Flowering season: spring/early summer
Height: 8–18 in
Spread: to 8 in
Situation: ○
Moisture requirement: ◐
❀

The buttercup is one of the many species of the Ranunculus genus. It is native to southeast Europe and the Middle East and was introduced to Europe in 1596 where it was long regarded as a precious rarity. In the garden, the buttercup, with its intensely colored, bowl-shaped flowers is best planted in groups in beds and borders. The large number of varieties is divided into four groups derived from the primary species *R. asiaticus*: the Turkish buttercup with mostly double flowers which appear earliest in the year; the Persian buttercup with large single or semi-double flowers; the French buttercup with large, loose double flowers which easily bend the stalk with their weight; and the peony-flowered buttercup with large, double flowers, which look like little peonies and which can be increased by seed as single varieties. Depending on variety, the buttercup's flowers are white, yellow, orange, pink or red. They all have three-lobed pale to mid-green basal leaves.

Ranunculus

S*iberian squill*

Scilla siberica

The Siberian squill is a species of *Scilla*, one of about 90 different bulbous perennial species native to the Ukraine, Georgia and Azerbaijan and northern Iran, although not Siberia as the name would imply. It flowers early and spreads quickly, and in the garden is well suited for planting among shrubs, under trees or to naturalising in grass. The two to four half-bent, strap-shaped basal leaves appear in spring at the same time as the flowers. Each bulb has up to three flower stems 6 in long, each with two to five azure blue bell-shaped blossoms about $1/3$ in wide hanging from them. The variety 'Alba' has pure white flowers, while 'Spring Beauty' has deep blue ones and grows up to 10 in high. Propagation is by division or by bulbils which are removed in the autumn and planted again immediately in humus-rich soil about 4–5 in deep. With the exception of 'Spring Beauty,' all varieties can also be propagated by seed.

Family: Hyacinthaceae
Flowering season: spring
Height: 4–8 in
Spread: 2 in
Situation: ○ – ◑
Moisture requirement: ◊
❄ ❄ ❄

Tulip

Tulip

The tulip belongs to the *Liliaceous* family with its 100 or so different species and its still more numerous varieties. The species are native to the hot, dry regions of Europe, Asia and the Far East. Already about 1,000 years ago, tulips from the broad steppes of western Asia were introduced into the gardens of the sultans and the caliphs. In the mid-16th century, the first tulip bulbs were introduced to Europe where commercial cultivation was quickly established. The Netherlands are today the unchallenged stronghold of tulip growing. In the garden, tulips are grown in beds, borders and containers for their bright colors, both species and hybrid tulips being popular for these purposes. The young shoot developing from the tulip bulb has a hard tip which can pierce a solid layer of soil. The unfolded leaves are stemless and straight to lance-shaped, growing from the base and sometimes also from the stem. Each stem usually carries a single large, elegant flower. The six petals of varying width form flowers which are usually egg-shaped, cup-shaped or lily-shaped, and sometimes also fringed. They are single-colored, patterned or multi-colored. For clearer classification of the many varieties, tulips are subdivided into 15 different classes which go back to the two main groups of the species and garden tulips. They are largely distinguished by the features of the flowers. Examples appear on the following pages.

Tulipa 'Prof. Röntgen'

Parrot tulip

Tulipa 'Prof. Röntgen'

ⓘ

Family: Liliaceae
Flowering season: early spring
Height: 14 – 26 in
Situation: ○ – ◑
Moisture requirement: ◗
✿ ✿ ✿
✖

Parrot tulips are late-flowering garden tulips which have come into being through random mutation from other varieties. With their long-lived flowers – up to four weeks – they are impressive as bedding plants in the garden and also as cut flowers. The single flowers are cup-shaped with unusually feathered edges. The cups are up to 4 in across and flatten in warm sunshine or at the end of the flowering period when the petals separate. The stalks are often bent down to the ground by the weight of the flowers. The colors of parrot tulip flowers range from white and yellow through orange, pink and red to purple, and they are often marked unevenly in several shades. Varieties include 'Estella Rijnveld' (red and white flowers), 'Texas Gold' (golden yellow with a red edge) and 'Prof. Röntgen' (red and yellow). The leaves can be up to 14 in long. All parts of the plant cause illness if eaten. Propagation is by offsets removed in the summer. These are cleaned and stored in a cool, dark, dry place until they are planted in the autumn.

Lily-flowering tulips

Tulipa

ⓘ

Family: Liliaceae
Flowering season: early spring
Height: 18 – 26 in
Situation: ○ – ◑
Moisture requirement: ◗
✿ ✿ ✿
✖

Lily-flowering tulips are late blooming tulips which often extend their flowering period into June. They are highly regarded as a garden plant, particularly for their slim, elegant, lily-like flower shape, and they are excellent in formal beds and also as cut flowers. They grow up to 26 in high and have leaves up to 16 in long. The narrow, single, cup-shaped flowers consist of petals tapering off upwards to a point and reflexed (bending outwards). Depending on variety, the flower colors range from white to yellow, pink to red or magenta, and these are sometimes have flame-shaped markings or are suffused with a contrasting color. The variety 'Aladdin' is scarlet with a narrow, cream-colored boundary, 'Astor' is bronze yellow with apricot-pink shading and 'White Triumphator' has pure white flowers. Like all tulip species, the lily-flowered ones are poisonous plants. Propagation is by offsets in the autumn. Unlike other tulip varieties, lily-flowered tulips are not suitable for raising from seed.

T*riumph tulips*

Tulipa

Triumph tulips with their weather-resistant large flowers carried on sturdy, stable stems result from crosses between single early tulips and Darwin hybrid tulips. They are early to medium flowering species, blooming from at the end of April and the beginning of May. They are suitable for bedding and as clumps in the garden as well as being especially good for raising as cut flowers. The single, cup-shaped flowers 2,5 in across appear in a large number of colors such as dark purple, red, pink, yellow and white. Some varieties have contrasting markings or are suffused with a contrasting color. The fresh green upright leaves are 4 – 14 in tall. All parts of the plant cause illness if eaten, and contact can aggravate skin allergies. Triumph tulips are propagated by removing offsets which should be planted in the autumn. The plant requires a sunny to partially shaded location and a light, fertile, neutral to acid soil.

ⓘ

Family: Liliaceae
Flowering season: spring
Height: 14 – 24 in
Situation: ○ – ◑
Moisture requirement: ◗
❄ ❄ ❄

73

Darwin hybrid tulips

Tulipa 'Apeldoorn'

i

Family: Liliaceae
Flowering season: spring
Height: 24 in
Situation: ○ – ◑
Moisture requirement: ◐
❄ ❄ ❄
✖

Flowering in mid to late spring, Darwin hybrid tulips have large flowers and strong stems, making them especially suitable for planting in clumps, at the front of beds and as cut flowers. The single, red and orange flowers of 'Apeldoorn' have a striking black base inside, bordered with yellow, and black anthers. This robust division also includes yellow-flowered varieties such as 'Golden Apeldoorn.' At the end of the flowering period, the slim calyxes of the flowers open. In spite of their size, the flowers are very weather-resistant and still stand upright after strong rain. The leaves grow to 4–14 in long. The plant is poisonous and can irritate the skin. Propagation is by offsets which should be planted in the autumn about 4 in deep in well-drained, humus-rich soil, 4–6 in apart.

Tulipa 'Golden Apeldoorn' and 'Apeldoorn'

Tulipa 'Apricot Beauty'

Single early tulips

Tulipa 'Apricot Beauty'

Single early tulips are very common in flower beds and mixed borders, because of their early flowering, general robustness and problem-free cultivation. They also make distinguished container plants and cut flowers. They flower in April or earlier when forced. 'Apricot Beauty' has cup-shaped flowers of gentle salmon pink tinged a soft orange-red at the edges, growing singly on strong stems. The mid-green leaves are lanceolate. Like all tulip species, these are poisonous plants which irritate the skin and cause illness when eaten. The perennial bulbous plant can be propagated by offsets in the autumn.

🛈

Family: Liliaceae
Flowering season: spring
Height: 14 in
Situation: ○ – ◑
Moisture requirement: ◐
❄ ❄ ❄
✖

Double early tulips

Tulipa 'Willemsoord'

ⓘ

Family: Liliaceae
Flowering season: spring
Height: 12 – 16 in
Situation: ○ – ◑
Moisture requirement: ◊
❄ ❄ ❄
✖

The double early tulips are among the most popular garden plants because of their heartiness and problem-free cultivation. They too flower in spring, but in comparison with the single varieties, they have larger flowers with two or more circles of petals carried on sturdy stems. They are ideal for planting in groups or for formal beds in the garden because the individual plants produce very uniform flowers all at the same time. Underplanting with small spring flowers, forget-me-nots or garden pansies can enhance the effect of double early tulips. The leaves are 4 – 14 in long. The double, bowl-shaped flowers are up to 3 in wide and, depending on variety, colors range from scarlet to yellow or white, often suffused or patterned by another color. The variety 'Carlton' has scarlet flowers, 'Willemsoord' is pinky-red with white markings and 'Monte Carlo' is dark yellow. All parts of the plants are poisonous. Propagation is by offsets taken after the leaves have died down; they should be stored in a cool, dark place until planting time in autumn.

Single late tulip

Tulipa 'Queen of Night'

ⓘ

Family: Liliaceae
Flowering season: spring
Height: 24 in
Situation: ○
Moisture requirement: ◊
❄ ❄ ❄
✖

Single late tulips are highly valued as garden plants because of their good growing properties, their resistance to rain and their long flowering period. They are effective in mixed borders with gray-leaved plants and indoors as flowers in vases. A good example is 'Queen of Night,' with wide, lanceolate, gray-green leaves and deep purple-red, silky, cup-shaped flowers appearing individually on each stem in late spring. All parts of the plant are poisonous. Propagation is best achieved by taking offsets. 'Queen of Night' and others of this division are fairly undemanding plants. The ideal situation is in full sun, protected from the wind, in well-drained fertile soil.

Species tulips

Tulipa praestans 'Unicum'

Tulipa ›Unicum‹

'Unicum' is a variety of the species *T. praestans*, which is native to Kazakhstan and Tajikistan and was discovered there at the beginning of the 20th century. This undemanding tulip is easy to grow and especially suitable for planting in rock gardens. From the small bulb, a sturdy stem grows with 3–6 upright wide, lanceolate, gray-green leaves with creamy white edges. Both stem and leaves are densely covered with fine hairs. In spring, up to five bowl-shaped, single blossoms appear on the stem. They are bright paprika red with a small, central, yellow spots and blue-black anthers. All parts of the plant are poisonous and contact can cause irritation of the skin. This hardy variety can be increased by removing offsets which are planted in the autumn.

❶

Family: Liliaceae
Flowering season: spring
Height: 12 in
Situation: ○
Moisture requirement: ◗
❄ ❄ ❄
✖

Arum lily

Zantedeschia aethiopica

Zantedeschia aethiopica

This rhizomatous plant is native to moist, marshy areas in Lesotho and South Africa from Cape Province to the Drakensberg mountains, and it is now a successful garden plant. However, it must be grown in a sunny, protected situation and covered in winter with a thick bed of mulch to protect it from frost. While the type species is very tender, the variety 'Crowborough' is less frost-sensitive. The large rhizome produces semi-upright, shiny, light green, arrow-shaped leaves. From spring to the middle of summer, a succession of creamy white spathes 6 – 8 in long, each with a funnel-shaped base and a pointed corner develop at the end of each stem. The cream yellow spadix projects a little from the spathe. The variety 'Apple Court Babe' is much smaller, 'Green Goddess' has spathes with light green markings and yellow in the center, while 'White Sails' has white spathes which open for a long time. The plant causes illness if eaten and the juice can lead to skin irritation. Propagation is by dividing the rhizomes in late summer or autumn, or by sowing ripe seed at a temperature of 70 – 80°F.

❶

Family: Araceae
Flowering season: spring / summer
Height: to 35 in
Spread: to 24 in
Situation: ○
Moisture requirement: ◗
❄ ❄
✖

Annuals

What would a year in the garden be like without colorful annuals? Whether they are grown in flowerbeds or containers – pots, tubs and window boxes – without their magnificent blooms our gardens would lack an important natural element, since they are favorite sources of food for honey bees, bumble bees and butterflies. Annuals complete their entire growth cycle in a single year, while biennials form leaves in their first year and do not flower until the second. Depending on their origins, annuals will grow in various different situations, in light soils or soils rich in humus, but almost without exception they do not tolerate excessive moisture. As a rule, ordinary garden soil contains enough nutrients for annuals in the open ground, but it is advisable to add fertiliser to the potting compost when they are grown in containers, and if necessary to feed again later, for instance with fast-acting liquid fertilisers. Although most annuals love the sun, some prefer a shady situation. Depending on their genus, species and variety, they will flower at various times from spring to autumn. There is no cause for regret when the first frosts cut them down, for their seeds, either dispersed by the plants themselves or harvested by the gardener, provide the material from which to raise the next generation. A wide range of seeds and young plants are also commercially available, so that gardeners who like to experiment can try something new every year. F1 hybrids, obtained by crossing pure-bred male and female plants, are of particularly reliable quality, and will grow vigorously and flower freely. Many annuals can also be easily propagated from cuttings grown indoors in conditions of high humidity.

*A*frican lily

Agapanthus africanus

Agapanthus africanus

ⓘ

Family: Alliaceae
Flowering season: summer
Height and spread: 47 × 24 in
Situation: ○
Moisture requirement: ◐
❄

The African lily is a native of South Africa, and there are about ten species. The best-known garden species is *Agapanthus africanus*. The attractive, usually rounded inflorescences consist of 10 to 30 funnel or bell-shaped flowers, either white or in various shades of blue, depending on the variety. They last well as cut flowers. The large, strap-shaped, fleshy leaves form a rosette close to the ground. African lilies like sunny, warm situations. It is advisable to overwinter them in a frost-free place, although some varieties can survive out of doors covered with a thick layer of mulch. However, as they do not like to be frequently dug up and transplanted, it is best to grow them in pots from the first even if they are to be planted out. They like moist, well-drained, nutritious soils, and during the growing season they need regular watering and feeding once a month with fertiliser. New plants are easily obtained by division of the rhizomes in spring. Simply replant the pieces of rhizome at a shallow level, covering them lightly with soil.

*H*ollyhock

Alcea rosea

Alcea rosea

ⓘ

Family: Malvaceae
Flowering season: summer
Height and spread: 5 × 2 ft
Situation: ○
Moisture requirement: ◌
❄ ❄ ❄
bees and butterflies

Hollyhock is an old cottage plant. Its ancestors were native to southeastern Europe and southwest Asia. Their tall, erect spikes of flowers grow from a basal rosette. The flowers are single or double and come in a wide range of colors, including white, yellow, pink and red, depending on the species. Because the plants flower from bottom to top, they flower for a long time. Although botanically the hollyhock is a herbaceous perennial, most hollyhocks are grown as biennials and sown every year – either in early spring in the house or directly outdoors in May. The pale green, rough, hairy leaves are often attacked by rust in spring. If this happens, the affected leaves should be immediately removed. Hollyhocks need a rich, heavy soil as well a lot of water. They must therefore be watered regularly and mulched with manure or compost. They also need a sheltered position where they are protected from the wind such as against a wall or fence, or supported by stakes.

Love-lies-bleeding

Amaranthus caudatus

This species originates from tropical and subtropical America and has been natura-lised in southern Europe for a very long time. This means that this species does best in a sunny situation. It produces drooping racemes of crimson flowers, reminiscent of fox-tails, which keep for a long time. The large leaves are ovate and light green, and arranged in alternate pairs on strong, erect stems. The 'Viridis' variety grows 30 in high and has yellow-green hanging racemes. Besides these species and varieties with hanging racemes, there are also some with erect panicles such as *A. tricolor* which has red foliage. It is raised from seed in spring and when there is no longer any danger of frost, it can be sown directly outdoors. Amaranthus can be grown in borders and in tubs and is an excellent cut flower. It also looks very good dried and butterflies are much attracted by the plant. It needs loose, light, deep soil, enriched with manure and a sunny situation to promote good growth and flowering.

ℹ

Family: Amaranthaceae
Flowering season: summer
Height and spread: 40 × 28 in
Situation: ○
Moisture requirement: ◊
❈
attracts butterflies

Snapdragon

Antirrhinum majus

Snapdragons are native to the Mediterranean where they grow as herbaceous perennials. In cooler climates they are not hardy, but they flower until late in the autumn. There are very low varieties of 6–8 in for borders and balconies, as well as very tall varieties up to 4 ft which need staking. Recently, trailing varieties have been developed. The single flowers are borne in erect spikes which flower from the bottom to the top. When pressing the base of the flower, it opens like a mouth. The flowers come in a variety of colors, ranging from white, yellow, oran-ge to red, pink and purple. At first, the stems are herbaceous but later they beco-me woody. The leaves are ovate, mid-green and shiny. Snapdragons are easy to raise from seed in pots in early spring. The young plants will survive some slight frost after planting out. Remove faded spikes to prolong the flowering period. Although they grow in moist soil, they do not tolerate being waterlogged.

Antirrhinum majus

ℹ

Family: Scrophulariaceae
Flowering season: summer
Height/spread: to 48 × 18 in
Situation: ○
Moisture requirement: ◊
❈

Marguerite

Argyranthemum frutescens
(syn. Chrysanthemum frutescens)

ⓘ

Family: Asteraceae
Flowering season: summer
Height/spread: 16–40 × 28 in
Situation: ○
Moisture requirement: ○ *but well-drained*
❄

The white-flowering wild form of *A. frutescens* (often known as *Chrysanthemum frutescens*) is native to the Canary Islands. It is a bushy shrub but it can also be grown as a standard. It is ideal for borders, balconies or tubs depending on their height. The flowers come in colors other than white such as yellow and pink and can be single or double. The narrow, deeply cut, pinnate leaves are very decorative, but are often concealed by the mass of flowers. It is easily propagated by cuttings. It needs light, well-drained soil and a sunny position. Fertiliser should be applied regularly during the growing season. It is advisable to remove dead flowers regularly. Although this species is usually grown as an annual, it can survive in a frost-free environment. It will continue flowering in a conservatory.

Argyranthemum frutescens

82

Begonia

Begonia semperflorens

There are now many varieties of this species, which originates in Brazil. It is a compact, many-branched plant which grows between 8 and 14 in high. They come in a wide range of colors, including white, salmon, pink and red. The plants flower uninterruptedly with single or double flowers until late autumn. The leathery leaves are bright to dark green or reddish-brown depending on the variety. It can be raised from seed in late winter, but it is quite a lengthy process. *B. sempervirens* needs a light soil mixture because of its fine, fibrous roots. It should only be planted outdoors when the risk of frost is past. They are very robust plants and therefore ideal for large areas, but like all begonias they are very sensitive to frost. They prefer rich soil with plenty of humus, moist but not waterlogged and partial shade. The more recent varieties only thrive in the sun.

Family: Begoniaceae
Flowering season: summer
Height and spread: 14 × 12 in
Situation: ◑
Moisture requirement: ◊
❄

Tuberous begonia

Begonia-tuberhybrida

The wild form of the tuberous begonia is native to the high mountainous regions of South America. The group includes erect-growing varieties ideal for borders, balconies and pots or large-flowered trailing begonias for hanging baskets. Begonias come in almost every color except blue and green and can be single or double. The Elatior begonias are similar, but the rose-like flowers are more delicate and come in red, pink or orange. The asymmetric, pointed leaves are bright to olive green. The easiest way to propagate tuberous begonias is by division of the tubers. These are planted in humus-rich soil with the hollow side facing upward. The soil must be kept moist at all times and the young plants should only be planted out when there is no longer any danger of frost. Tuberous begonias need rich soil with plenty of humus and protection from wind and rain. During the flowering season, they should be watered generously, but not excessively.

Family: Begoniaceae
Flowering season: summer
Height and spread: 20 × 12 in
Situation: ◑
Moisture requirement: ◊
❄

Common daisy

Bellis perennis

ℹ

Family: Asteraceae
Flowering season: spring
Height and spread: 8 × 8 in
Situation: ○
Moisture requirement: ◐
❈ ❈ *(cover with straw)*

The common daisy is native to Europe and Asia Minor. It is cultivated as a biennial, which means that the rosette of basal, oblong, oval leaves develops during the first year and flowers the following spring. The flower heads are considerably larger than those of the indigenous daisy – they can reach up to 1 $\frac{1}{4}$ in in diameter. There is a wide range of varieties with simple, double and pompon flowers, ranging from white to pink and red. It is raised from seed in summer. If the young seedlings are planted out in autumn, they must be protected with brushwood in winter. Daisies are very easy to grow. They should be planted in fertile soil, in sun or partial shade. As early spring-flowering plants, they will brighten up borders, window-boxes and flower-tubs. They also make attractive cut flowers. They have a tendency to self-seeding. If you want to prevent this, remove the flower heads immediately after flowering.

Calceolaria integrifolia

Calceolaria integrifolia

This colorful calceolaria grows as a semi-shrub in its native Chile and can reach up to 4 ft in height. They are not hardy and are therefore normally grown as annuals. They form bushy or compact sub-shrubs depending on the variety and some of them make excellent cut flowers. The single flowers with their pouch-like under-lip are borne in dense clusters. Besides the original bright yellow species, there are also varieties with reddish flowers which contrast beautifully with the bright green foliage. The plant is raised from seed in late winter or by cuttings which are best taken in late summer. However, they should only be planted out when there is no longer any danger of frost. They need watering regularly but never over the flowers. It is important to feed the plant while flowering and remove the dead flowers and seed heads to encourage flowering.

ⓘ

Family: Scrophulariaceae
Flowering season: summer
Height and spread: 20 × 12 in
Situation: ○
Moisture requirement: ◊
❋

China aster

Callistephus chinensis

This popular cottage garden plant, which originates in China and Japan, has been cultivated in Europe for two centuries. There are a large number of varieties and strains such as low dwarf asters, bushy, compact asters for borders and tall asters grown as cut-flowers. The flowers also vary enormously in color and shape, ranging from reddish and violet-blue to white, yellow and two-tone. The flowers are single or double, spherical, star-shaped, radial or pompon-shaped and can reach up to 6 in in diameter. China asters are raised from seed in early spring and planted out after the risk of frost is past. They grow best in moist, but not waterlogged soil in a sunny position where they are protected from the wind. Flowers which wither without obvious reason must be removed immediately, but not thrown on the compost. It is advisable to plant asters in a different site every year. Removing the first flowers when they are wilted helps to encourage the production of flowers on side shoots.

Callistephus chinensis

ⓘ

Family: Asteraceae
Flowering season: summer
Height and spread: 28 × 18 in
Situation: ○
Moisture requirement: ◊
❋

Safflower

Carthamus tinctorius

Family: Asteraceae
Flowering season: summer
Height and spread: 40 × 12 in
Situation: ○
Moisture requirement: ◌

This annual plant, also known as bastard saffron, can be found in Asia Minor and as far east as India where it grows on dry, sunny plains. It has an upright habit and many-branched stems. The thistle-like heads are carried on the vigorous stems which are entirely covered with leaves. The flowers are yellow, orange or white depending on the variety which contrast beautifully with the glossy, dark green leaves with prickly edges. In their country of origin, they are used to make red and yellow vegetable dyes while oil is extracted from the seeds. Elsewhere they are planted in borders and wild gardens. They make excellent cut flowers and look very beautiful when dried. They can be planted directly outdoors after the risk of frost is past or raised from seed in pots and planted out later. They like fertile, light, well-drained soil because of their long tap roots.

Celosia-plumosa

Celosia-plumosa

Celosia are native to subtropical Africa and America. They are erect, many-branched plants which include low, dwarf varieties and tall types. They owe their Latin name to their flower heads which look like feathery plumes. The intense, bright colors of the yellow, orange, pink or red flowers will brighten up any garden in summer. Its relative, *C. a. cristata* (cockscomb) has very exotic, equally colorful flower heads which are shaped like a cockscomb. The plants are covered with lanceolate, light green leaves. They should be sown in February to flower in May. Celosias are very sensitive to cold and do not like cool, rainy weather, which can lead to foot and root rot. Always plant celosias in rich, very well-drained soil in a warm, sunny position. To use as dried flowers, the flower heads must be cut when in full bloom and hung head down in a cool, airy place.

ℹ

Family: Amaranthaceae
Flowering season: summer
Height and spread: 32 × 16 in
Situation: ○
Moisture requirement: ◊
❄

Centaurea

Centaurea americana

A genus of almost 500 plants which includes *C. americana*, a species native to the southern states of the United States. The annual centaurea is related to the indigenous cornflower (*C. cyanus*) but flowers slightly later with larger, lilac-pink tubular flowers whose outer ray petals – a characteristic feature of cornflowers – project further. *C. americana* is ideal for cottage gardens or in borders in wild gardens. It is also an excellent cut flower which lasts for a long time. It is raised from seed in spring, either in seed trays and pots indoors or a little later directly outdoors. Centaureas grow best in well-drained, fertile soil with plenty of humus. Apart from that, centaureas are easy to grow and need very little care.

ℹ

Family: Asteraceae
Flowering season: summer
Height and spread: 40 × 8 in
Situation: ○
Moisture requirement: ◊
❄

attracts bees

Centaurea

Cornflower

Centaurea cyanus

The cornflower grows wild from the Mediterranean area to North America and Chile. Intensive breeding has raised many varieties, including low-growing pot plants and tall varieties grown for cut flowers. Today, besides the wild blue form, white, pink and red varieties which may be either single or double are available. The flower-heads consist of a number of tiny tubular florets, with the outer florets longer than the others and standing out from them. Bees and butterflies like to visit cornflowers, so they are good plants for a wildflower bed as well as in borders and rock gardens. The lanceolate leaves have woolly hairs on the undersides. The cornflower is easy to cultivate, but will grow best in sunny situations in well-drained, chalky garden soil. In mild areas, seed can be sown directly in the open in late spring or autumn; the advantage of autumn sowing is that flowering will begin early. In colder climates, it is best to raise the seedlings under cover from February to March.

ⓘ

Family: Asteraceae
Flowering season: summer
Height and spread: 36 × 10 in
Situation: ○
Moisture requirement: ◌
❄
Attracts bees and butterflies

ⓘ

Family: Ranunculaceae
Flowering season: summer
Height / spread: to 5 ft × 1 ft
Situation: ○
Moisture requirement: ◑
❄

Larkspur

Consolida ajacis

The annual larkspur is native to the regions around the Mediterranean. It is an upright, sparsely branching plant. The large, solitary, spurred flowers are borne in long racemes. Depending on the variety, the single or double flowers are blue, violet, pink, red or white. The flowers appear in early summer, the vibrantly colored spikes rising elegantly above the fern-like foliage. Larkspur can be sown directly on the site in spring or autumn. The plants sown in autumn flower earlier but some protection during winter. The single-flowered varieties tend to self-seed quite spontaneously. The seeds are usually available in mixed batches. Larkspurs should be planted in a sunny position, protected from the wind. It is best to plant tall varieties against walls and fences. It grows best in fertile, moist calcareous soil. It looks very beautiful in cottage gardens and wild gardens and is a perfect cut flower which keeps for a long time.

Cosmos

Cosmos bipinnatus

This species is native to Mexico and Brazil. It is a vigorous growing plant with stiff, erect, well-branched stems, carrying delicate, very beautiful, anemone-like white, pink or red flowers which can reach 4 in in diameter. The main flowering season is late summer, during which the plant flowers prolifically until the first frost. The finely cut leaves are very decorative and add to the daintiness of the plant. Cosmos can be sown directly outdoors in their permanent position; some early flowering specimens can be sown and grown in a seed tray indoors. Be careful: snails are very partial to young cosmos. Cosmos prefer light, sandy soil but will also tolerate partial shade. Dead flowers must be constantly removed in order to encourage the production of more flowers. Cosmos should be picked just as the petals open if they are intended as cut flowers.

ⓘ

Family: Asteraceae
Flowering season: summer
Height and spread: 48 × 18 in
Situation: ○
Moisture requirement: ◊
❄

89

Carnations and pinks

Dianthus

Carnations (*D. caryophyllus*), including perpetual-flowering and border carnations, and pinks such as Indian pinks (*D. chinensis*), including modern and garden pinks, are all excellent flowers for the summer border. While *D. caryophyllus* is native to southern Europe, *D. chinensis* is native to China. Carnations have many colored flowers which are usually double and fragrant. They are ideal for herbaceous borders, window-boxes and as cut flowers. Indian pinks are usually pink or red. Both types have narrow, gray-green or blue-green leaves. They are raised from seed in a cold greenhouse or frame and planted out in the middle of May; many carnations can also be propagated by cuttings in autumn. Both types grow best in fertile, calcareous soil in a sunny, warm position. They dislike excessive moisture in the soil which could lead to fungus disease. Removing dead flowers will encourage repeat flowering, and Indian pinks can be cut back strongly after the first wave of flowering. Most varieties are sensitive to frost.

ⓘ

Family: Caryophyllaceae
Flowering season: summer
Height and spread: 32 × 8 in
Situation: ○
Moisture requirement: ◌
❊ – ❊ ❊ ❊
❀

Sweet William

Dianthus barbatus

ⓘ

Family: Caryophyllaceae
Flowering season: summer
Height and spread: 24 × 12 in
Situation: ○
Moisture requirement: ◊
❋ ❋ ❋
❦

Sweet William is native to southern Europe but has been cultivated in gardens for a long time. They are typical cottage garden plants which are usually grown as biennials. There are also modern, annual varieties which flower the same year they have been sown. There are many varieties of Sweet William, including dwarf forms which are ideally suited to flower-beds and herbaceous borders while the taller strains make excellent cut flowers. The deliciously fragrant single or double flowers are borne in terminal heads in a wide range of colors including white, pink, red, purple or two-tone, which rise elegantly above the dark green foliage. Annual varieties are sown in early spring so that they are ready to flowers in mid-summer, biennials are sown a little later. The latter should be protected with a layer of brushwood. Sweet Williams grow best in fertile, calcareous soil and watered only moderately. They hate being waterlogged. If intended as cut flowers, they should be cut when a few flowers in the flower head have opened.

Diascia

Diascia

Diascia

ⓘ

Family: Scrophulariaceae
Flowering season: summer
Height/spread: to 12 × 20 in
Situation: ○
Moisture requirement: ◊
❋

This decorative plant, native to South Africa, has only recently been introduced into gardens use. The most common varieties are *D. barberae* and *D. vigilis*. They are cushion plants with slender pendulous stems. They are very good for growing in window-boxes and hanging baskets. The pale pink, salmon-colored or red flowers – the color depending on the variety – seem to float above the glossy dark green leaves. They are borne in dense panicles and are very weather-resistant. They can be raised from seed in spring and propagated by softwood cuttings in late spring or semi-ripe cuttings in summer. They grow best in moist, well-drained, light soil in a sunny position. Diascia hate excessively dry or wet conditions and will even tolerate poor soil. After the first flush of flowers, cut the plant back to encourage repeat flowering. A useful tip: do not plant in conjunction with vigorous plants.

Foxglove
Digitalis purpurea

Digitalis purpurea

This biennial species is native to west and central Europe and North Africa. In the wild, it grows on the edge of woods and in clearings. In the first year, the basal rosette with large, lanceolate, hairy leaves develops from which the imposing spikes will grow during the second year. The large, downward-pointing, tubular, single flowers which are flecked inside are usually directed towards the light so that the spike appears one-sided. In nurseries, seeds are mostly sold in mixed-color batches which include white, pink and red. The best time for sowing is the period of May to June. You can also wait until the ripe seeds fall out. Remove the central spike when it has finished flowering to encourage the flowering of side-shoots later on. Foxgloves look very good in wild gardens and in front of ever-green shrubs such as conifers, rhododendrons or azaleas because they prefer partial shade. Foxgloves grow best in a slightly acid, humus-rich soil. Be careful: all parts are poisonous.

ℹ

Family: Scrophulariaceae
Flowering season: summer
Height/spread: to 56 × 24 in
Situation: ◑
Moisture requirement: ◌
❋ ❋
✖

Yellow foxglove
Digitalis grandiflora

The large-flowered foxglove which is a close relative of the ordinary foxglove is native to east and central Europe, southern Russia and Asia Minor. It can be found on the edge of mountain forests or in clearings. The wild form is a protected species. With its tall raceme, it is one of the most impressive woodland plants. In contrast to the ordinary foxglove, the flowers of *D. grandiflora* are bright yellow, veined with brown inside and grouped on one side of the spike. The oblong, lanceolate leaves are covered with fine hairs. Although a perennial evergreen, it is usually cultivated as a biennial because this is how it produces the most beautiful flowers. It has a tendency to self-seed spontaneously but it is also possible to buy seedlings from the nursery or garden centre (in the herbaceous plants section). In contrast with the ordinary foxglove, the yellow foxglove prefers well-drained calcareous, humus-rich soil but hates being waterlogged. In the garden, it is best planted between and in front of woody plants. It also likes a well-sheltered position and partial shade such as near walls. Be careful: all parts are poisonous.

ℹ

Family: Scrophulariaceae
Flowering season: summer
Height and spread: 48 × 20 in
Situation: ◑
Moisture requirement: ◌
❋ ❋ – ❋ ❋ ❋
✖

Cape marigold, African daisy

Dimorphoteca pluvialis

Dimorphoteca pluvialis

ⓘ

Family: Asteraceae
Flowering season: summer
Height and spread: 20 × 12 in
Situation: ○
Moisture requirement: ◊
❄

The cape marigold is native to South Africa where they grow as perennials. In our country they are grown as annuals because of the cold climate. They have an erect, bushy habit. The large, daisy-like flowers only open when the sun is out. At night and in bad weather conditions, they remain closed. The original species is white with a violet center but it also comes in violet shades or with bizarre spoon-shaped flowers. *D. sinuata* comes in various shades, including white, orange, apricot and yellow. The leaves are oblong and narrow. The plant is raised from seed in spring indoors and planted out when the danger of frost is past. Cape marigolds are easy to look after, but do not like excessive dampness. They will tolerate long periods of drought and should be kept only slightly moist. They also appreciate a light application of fertiliser now and again. Dead heading will encourage repeat flowering.

Wallflower

Erysimum cheiri

ⓘ

Family: Brassicaceae
Flowering season: spring
Height and spread: 28 × 16 in
Situation: ○
Moisture requirement: ◊
❄ ❄
✖
❀

This species of semi-shrub is still often referred to by its old name *Cheiranthus cheiri*. It is native to southern Europe where it grows in the wild. In gardens it is cultivated as a biennial with an erect habit. The upright-growing stems are covered with dark green, lanceolate leaves. The velvety, very fragrant flowers are borne in dense, terminal spikes. They are single or double and come in a wide range of shades including red, orange, brown and yellow. In spring their warm colors add a cheerful note to flower beds. It is raised from seed in the house in spring, or directly outdoors in summer. Young plants or seedlings should only be planted out when there is no longer any danger of frost. Plants which are left outdoors in winter must be covered with brushwood to protect them from frost. Because of its flowering time, it can be combined with bulb plants and other spring flowering biennials. The tall varieties make beautiful cut flowers. The time to cut wallflowers is when they are in full bloom. They need rich, loamy soil but dislike being waterlogged. Be careful: the seeds are poisonous.

Californian poppy

Californian poppy

This annual poppy species is native to California. It forms a bushy, cushion-like shrub. The large, saucer-shaped flowers have a silky texture and only open in the sun. The flowers, which can be single or double, come in a range of brilliant colors, including yellow, orange, various shades of pinks and reds and creamy white. The flowers look very delicate and dainty as do the finely divided, silver-green leaves. Californian poppies are best sown in spring directly outdoors since they would be difficult to plant out because of their long tap roots. The flowering season can be extended by successive sowing. The plant also self-seeds very easily. It thrives in light, sandy soil in a very sunny, warm position. It should be kept only very slightly moist but does not need regular feeding. If planted in the right position and not over-watered, it is very easy to grow.

Californian poppy

ⓘ

Family: Papaveraceae
Flowering season: summer
Height and spread: 20 × 6 in
Situation: ○
Moisture requirement: ◊
❋

Gazania

Gazania

Gazanias originate in South Africa. There are also many compact-growing hybrids. The flower stems emerge from the basal rosette, each stem carrying a large, gerbera-like flower. They come in a wide range of colors and shades, predominantly yellow, orange and red with a dark, central ring. Gazanias are sun-loving plants. They love warm, very sunny positions, the flowers remaining closed in cloudy, rainy weather. The leaves are narrow and lanceolate, green or silvery-white, depending on the variety. Gazanias are propagated from seed in spring and the seedlings planted out when there is no danger of frost. They can also be propagated by cuttings in late summer. They flower best in warm, dry weather conditions. That is why they should only be watered sparingly and never be allowed to become waterlogged. They must be fed regularly. Dead flowers should be removed to encourage repeat flowering.

ⓘ

Family: Asteraceae
Flowering season: summer
Height and spread: 12 × 10 in
Situation: ○
Moisture requirement: ◊
❋

Gypsophila elegans

Gypsophila elegans

Family: Caryophyllaceae
Flowering season: summer
Height/spread: to 40 × 12 in
Situation: ○
Moisture requirement: ◌

This annual species, which is native to Asia Minor and the Caucasus, forms a bushy, densely branched shrub with slender stems. The numerous, white or pink, small star-shaped flowers are very similar to pinks and are borne in dense panicles which almost conceal the lanceolate, gray-green leaves. The best time to sow is spring in a seed tray indoors or a little later directly outdoors where they are to flower. Successive sowing at intervals of 14 days will ensure flowering throughout the summer. Gypsophilas love sun and warmth and grow best in poor, light, calcareous soil. They must be watered and fed only very sparingly because the plants tend to suffer from rot if waterlogged. The plant's delicate, dainty appearance make it an ideal plant for summer-flowering borders. Its pleasant fragrance also make ideal as a cut flower. Gypsophilas combine beautifully with roses.

Sunflower

Helianthus annuus

Family: Asteraceae
Flowering season: summer
Height and spread: up to 10 × 2 ft
Situation: ○
Moisture requirement: ◑

The sunflower is native to the western United States where Indians used it as a food and extracted oil from it. Besides the tall, single-stemmed varieties there are also low, bushy, branched species, ideal for window-boxes and tubs which are stronger and do not need support. The center of the large flower head, which can measure up to 12 in in diameter, consists of small, inconspicuous, tubular florets which produce the seeds after they have been pollinated. Birds are very fond of these seeds. The central florets are surrounded by sterile ray florets which come in a wide range of colors, including yellow, red, brown and white. The flowers are single or double depending on the species. They can be sown directly outdoors in spring or early summer, 1 in deep and 20 in apart. They can also be raised from seed on a window-sill and planted out later. Although the plants need plenty of food and water, they dislike being waterlogged. They keep very well as cut flowers if the ends of the stems – the last inch – are plunged in boiling water for 30 seconds.

Everlasting or straw flower

Helichrysum bracteatum

Straw flowers are native to Australia where they are perennials, but in most gardens they are cultivated as annuals. The tall varieties form erect shrubs with stiff, upright stems which carry terminal flower heads, while the low-growing varieties form a bushier, more branched shrub. There are now new hanging forms which are ideal for window-boxes and hanging baskets. The single or double flowers are available in a wide range of colors, including yellow, orange, pink, red, violet and white. The paper-like petals means they can survive in very hot weather conditions. They can be sown in early spring in a seed tray the house or later directly outdoors. They hate rainy weather. The soil must be very well-drained and dry very quickly after the rain. The plants require only moderate feeding. It is important to dead head regularly. Straw flowers should be cut when in bud, tied in loose bunches and hung upside down in a cool room.

ⓘ

Family: Asteraceae
Flowering season: summer
Height/spread: to 44 × 24 in
Situation: ○
Moisture requirement: ○
❄

Heliotrope

Heliotropium arborescens

ⓘ

Family: Boraginaceae
Flowering season: summer
Height/spread: to 24 × 18 in
Situation: ○
Moisture requirement: ◌

❄

✤

attracts bees

Heliotropes are native to Peru where they grow as a semi-shrub. At first they grow upright, developing only later into a bushier shrub with a low trunk. The deep blue to reddish-violet flowers, grouped in corymbs, bloom uninterruptedly all through the summer, but they do not like rain. The have a delicious fragrance which attracts bees and butterflies. The intense colors of the flowers contrast beautifully with the oblong-lanceolate, olive-green leaves. Heliotrope is propagated by cuttings in spring or summer. It can be raised from seed from January onward. The young plants should be pinched out several times to promote bushy growth and not be planted out until the risk of frost is past. The plants need regularly feeding to ensure abundant flowering. Watering is a delicate matter because the plant must be neither too dry nor too wet. Excessive drought leads to brown spots on the leaves. Regularly dead heading is important. Heliotropes should over-winter in a light position at a temperature of 54–59°F.

Impatiens Neu Guinea

Busy lizzie

Impatiens

ⓘ

Family: Balsaminaceae
Flowering season: summer
Height/spread: to 16 × 12 in
Situation: ◑
Moisture requirement: ◐

❄

The most popular species of this genus are the busy lizzie (*I. walleriana*) and the New Guinea series. The former is native to the mountainous regions of East-Africa while the New Guinea series is the result of the crossing of two species native to New Guinea. The Impatiens in the New Guinea series have noticeably larger flowers than the busy lizzie, narrower leaves and an upright habit. The leaves are very decorative, pale to dark green, with reddish or yellow markings, depending on the species. Busy lizzies have a compact habit and thick fleshy stems and flower prolifically, as the name suggests. The flowers, which are usually red, pink or violet, come also in white and orange or multi-colored. The plant can be raised from seed or propagated by cuttings in spring, but can only be planted out when they is no longer any danger of frost. Both species need plenty of water, especially when they stand in direct sun, and they must never be allowed to dry out. During the flowering period, feed regularly but only in small amounts.

Hare's tail grass

Lagurus ovatus

Hare's tail grass is native to the Mediterranean and the Canary Isles. It forms dense, erect tufts while the dwarf varieties have a more cushion-like habit. Each stem carries an ear, grouping ovoid inflorescences, covered in woolly white hairs and reminiscent of a hare's tail. The leaves are narrow and linear. It can be grown as an annual or biennial. If sown in spring directly outdoors or in small pots, it will flower in mid-summer. If sown in late summer and overwintered frost-free, it will already flower in late spring. Hare's tail grass is easy to grow and thrives in dry, sunny positions. It is particularly suited to rockeries but it also looks very good in colorful summer beds. Hare's tail grass is also very attractive planted in small groups. The flowers are cut fresh or dried and look very good in flower arrangements. If you intend drying the ears, it is best to cut them before they are completely open.

ⓘ

Family: Poaceae
Flowering season: summer
Height and spread: 20 × 12 in
Situation: ○
Moisture requirement: ◌
❄
❄ ❄ *(biennial)*

Mallow

Lavatera cachemiriana

This mallow species is native to Kashmir in northern India where they grow as perennials. In cooler climates, they are mainly cultivated as annuals. They grow very tall and bushy. In summer, these striking shrubs are real eye-catchers with their large, funnel-shaped, silky, rose-coloured flowers, borne in elegant panicles. The large, round to heart-shaped leaves are three to five-lobed. It is best raised from seed, either in early spring in a seed tray in the house or later directly outdoors in the flowering position. In this case, the plants will have to be thinned out. Dead heading will encourage more prolific flowering. Mallows do best in moderately fertile, light, well-drained soil in a sunny position. Excessive moisture can lead to rust and leaf spot (yellow brown spots). This is why they should be planted in a different place every year. They do very well against house walls where they can over-winter in milder climates. It is important to dead head regularly.

ⓘ

Family: Malvaceae
Flowering season: summer
Height and spread: 8–4 ft
Situation: ○
Moisture requirement: ◌
❄ ❄
attracts bees
Prone to: rust and leaf spot

Tree mallow

Lavatera trimestris

ⓘ

Family: Malvaceae
Flowering season: summer
Height/spread: to 48 × 18 in
Situation: ○
Moisture requirement: ○
❄
attracts bees

This species which is native to the Mediterranean forms a tall shrub with an erect, bushy habit. It flowers profusely until the autumn and is a real eye-catcher in any garden. The delicate, funnel-shaped flowers are borne on long stems and are pink, red or whitish, with dark veins, depending on the varieties. They are very popular with bees. The heart-shaped pale green, velvety leaves are very decorative. Mallows are raised from seed, either in seed trays in the house in early spring or directly outdoors in the flowering position in late spring or early summer. In this case the young plants will have to be thinned out. The soil must not be too fertile or damp because mallows hate being waterlogged. Excessive moisture can lead to rust and leaf spot (yellow and brown spots) so they should be planted in a different place every year. However, they will need watering in very dry conditions. It is important to dead head regularly.

Sea lavender

Limonium sinuatum

ⓘ

Family: Plumbaginaceae
Flowering season: summer
Height and spread: 32 × 12 in
Situation: ○
Moisture requirement: ○
❄
attracts butterflies

Sea lavender is native to the coastal regions of the Mediterranean as its common name suggests. It is a herbaceous, bushy semi-shrub which is grown as annual. The clusters are densely branched and carry a mass of tiny single flowers which attract butterflies in large numbers. Sea lavender comes in a wide range of colors, including white, pink, red, yellow, orange, blue and violet. The flowering stems emerge from a basal rosette of lanceolate, lobed leaves, covered with fine hairs. Sea lavender will flower in mid-summer if raised from seed in a warm greenhouse or indoors, hardened off in a cold frame and then planted out when there is no danger of frost any longer. It is also possible to sow directly outdoors but this will delay the beginning of the flowering period. Sea lavender is easy to grow and requires little care. It thrives in dry, light, slightly calcareous soil and tolerates salt. Flowers intended for drying should be picked when in full bloom. The flowers are hung upside down in a dry, shady place.

Lobelia erinus and bacopa

Lobelia erinus

Lobelia erinus

This lobelia species originates from South Africa where it grows a herbaceous perennial. In our latitudes it is only cultivated as an annual because it is only half-hardy. *L. erinus* is a spreading, cushion-forming plant which trails slightly if grown in a pot. It is much used for edging as well as in window boxes and hanging baskets. The flowering period lasts well into autumn. The tiny flowers are blue, red, pink or white depending on the species, and they are so abundant that they almost conceal the foliage. The best time for sowing is early spring which means that the seedlings will be planted out in May when there is no longer any danger of frost. Lobelias intended as bedding plants can be sown directly outdoors in their permanent site. Nurseries also offer modern varieties propagated by cuttings such as 'Richardii.' Lobelias grow well in partial shade and prefer moderately moist soil. They hate being waterlogged or too dry and need very little food. When they have finished flowering, the varieties raised from seed can be cut back to encourage repeat flowering.

ⓘ

Family: Campanulaceae
Flowering season: summer
Height and spread: 12 × 6 in
Situation: ○
Moisture requirement: ◐
❄

101

Lobularia maritima

Lobularia maritima

ℹ️

Family: Brassicaceae
Flowering season: summer
Height and spread: 12 × 12 in
Situation: ○
Moisture requirement: ◊
❄️
🌼
honey producing

This species is native to southern Europe and the Mediterranean. It is a densely branched bushy plant with a spreading habit if grown on the ground but trailing if grown in a pot. It has numerous, tiny, fragrant flowers with four petals, borne in terminal clusters, which appear irresistible to bees. The flowers are white, pink to violet, depending on the variety. The narrow, grayish leaves are almost 'invisible.' Lobularia is raised from seed in early spring and planted out when there is no longer any danger of frost. It can be sown directly outdoors a little later. This plant needs very little food or water. It prefers calcareous soil and a sunny dry position. This is why it ideally suited as a rockery plant. If cut back strongly and fed generously, it will flower a second time. The flowering season extends from early summer to late autumn.

Stock

Matthiola incana

ℹ️

Family: Brassicaceae
Flowering season: summer
Height and spread: 35 × 16 in
Situation: ○
Moisture requirement: ◊
❄️ ❄️
🌼

Stocks have been cultivated as cottage garden plants since the 16th century. They originate from southern Europe where they grow as semi-shrubs but in cooler regions they are cultivated as annuals or biennials. Nurseries offer bushy growing varieties for planting in flower beds, herbaceous borders and tubs as well as cut flower varieties. The intensely fragrant flowers, which can be either single or double, are grouped in terminal panicles. The colors range from white, yellow, pink, red to blue. The oblong gray-green leaves are usually felted. Plants intended for bedding are sown in spring while those intended as cut flowers can already be sown in winter if they are expected to flower in spring. They can be planted out in the middle of May. Stocks require fertile, slightly alkaline soil because a high pH level prevents club-root. If fed excessively, the stems will grow too tall and weak. If intended as cut flowers, the stems are best cut when at least ten flowers have opened and the plant has been well watered.

Bells of Ireland, shell-flower

Molucella laevis

Bells of Ireland, also known as shell-flower, grows wild in west Asia. The curious, funnel-shaped, green, whorl-like calyces, grouped in long spikes on tall stems, are quite an eye-catcher in the garden. The tiny labiate flowers in the calyx, which from a botanical point of view are merely bracts, are quite inconspicuous. Propagation by seed demands a lot of patience because the seeds do not always germinate reliably, even at the required temperature of 64°F. It is helpful to pre-soak the seeds at 39–46°F. Those who wish to start early can sow in early spring in seed trays. Otherwise, sow directly outdoors in the flowering site. *Molucella* requires fertile, loose soil, a lot of sun and warmth. Besides being excellent cut flowers and ideal as dried flowers, they are also excellent in colorful flower beds. They look best planted in groups.

Molucella laevis

ⓘ

Family: Lamiaceae
Flowering season: summer
Height and spread: 40 × 10 in
Situation: ○
Moisture requirement: ◌ , ✳

Forget-me-not

Myosotis sylvatica

This spring-flowering plant grows wild in Europe, Asia, tropical Africa and Australia. Many varieties have been developed from the original species which are bushier, more compact and flower prolifically. The oblong, lanceolate, hairy leaves are covered by a mass of blue, pink or white single flowers. Forget-me-nots can be raised from seed in spring and planted out in late summer or the following spring. However, it is easier to buy young plants in spring. Forget-me-nots flower best in cool weather conditions. They can survive long periods of frost but only if well protected. They grow well in sunny positions and partial shade and thrive in fertile, loamy, loose soil. They combine beautifully with bulb plants and other biennial spring flowers and make pretty flower bouquets.

Myosotis sylvatica

ⓘ

Family: Boraginaceae
Flowering season: spring
Height and spread: 12 × 6 in
Situation: ◑
Moisture requirement: ◌
✳✳ – ✳✳✳

*T*obacco plant

Nicotiana alata

ⓘ

Family: Solanaceae
Flowering season: summer
Height/spread: to 60 × 12 in
Situation: ○
Moisture requirement: loamy, ◌
❄
❀
attracts butterflies

The tobacco plant is native to southern Brazil and northern Argentina where it grows as a perennial. It has a very bushy or rather compact habit depending on the variety. The nodding tubular flowers, up to 4 in long, are borne in loose clusters. In most varieties, they only open towards the evening when they become very fragrant. In the more modern varieties, the flowers open all day and attract many butterflies. The range of colors has been extended from the original greenish-yellow to crimson, pink and white. The leaves are oblong to ovate and up to 10 in long. It can raised from seed in spring and planted out in May when there is no longer any danger of frost. Because of the large leaves and large number of flowers, the plants must be watered and fed generously during the flowering period. When the weather is warm enough, they also grow in partial shade. Taller varieties must be planted in a sheltered position where they are protected from the wind.

Nicotiana

*T*obacco plant

Nicotiana × sanderae

ⓘ

Family: Solanaceae
Flowering season: summer
Height and spread: 24 × 16 in
Situation: ○
Moisture requirement: loamy, ◌
❄
❀

The parents of this ornamental tobacco plant, *N. alata* and *N. forgetiana*, are native to South America. The plants have a robust, erect habit and flower until autumn. The tubular, five-petalled flowers are grouped in terminal panicles. The pink, red, yellowish or white flowers are very fragrant and attract many butterflies. The oblong to ovate leaves can be as long as 10 in and are also very decorative. Raising tobacco plants from seed requires quite a lot of patience because the seeds can take as much as two to three weeks to germinate. It is recommended to prick off the seedlings into boxes and then harden them off in a cold frame before planting out. The best time to sow is early spring but the young seedlings should only be planted out after mid-May when there is no longer any danger of frost. It is easier to buy young plants from the nursery. Nicotianas thrive in a warm, sunny position but in a warm climate they will also grow in partial shade. They need a lot of food and water which is why loamy, humus-rich, well-drained soil is ideal. Tall varieties should be protected from the wind.

Love-in-the-mist

Nigella damascena

This annual, herbaceous plant grows wild from the Mediterranean to Asia Minor. It is an erect, branched, bushy plant with delicate, terminal flowers, reminiscent of cornflowers. The white, pink, blue or purple flowers are surrounded by a crown of thread-like bracts. The delicate, finely cut leaves further emphasise the dainty appearance of the plant. The brown, globular fruit is an inflated pod with 5–10 seeds and also looks very decorative. It can be sown directly outdoors but only when there is no longer any danger of frost. The flowering period can be extended by sowing at four-weekly intervals. Nigella also self-seeds very easily if you allow the fruits to ripen. The seed pods dry very well but they must be harvested while still closed. Provided nigellas are planted in moist soil in a sunny position, they require very little attention.

ⓘ

Family: Ranunculaceae
Flowering season: summer
Height and spread: 20 × 10 in
Situation: ○
Moisture requirement: ◌–◗
❄ ❄

105

Papaver rhoeas

Poppy

Papaver

ℹ

Family: Papaveraceae
Flowering season: summer
Height and spread: 24 × 12 in
Situation: ○
Moisture requirement: ○
❄ ❄

The Iceland poppy (*P. nudicaule*) is native to the Arctic and sub-Arctic regions where it grows as a perennial. However it is normally cultivated as an annual or biennial. It forms a bushy rosette with deeply lobed, blue-green leaves from which the slender, leafless flower stems emerge. The delicate, saucer-shaped flowers can reach up to 4 in in diameter. The pastel-colored flowers may be pink, red, orange, yellow or white, depending on the variety and flowers in summer. The annual field poppy (*P. rhoeas*) which grows in the wild in Europe and Asia, has silky, gossamer-thin flowers and is up to 32 in high. Flowering only lasts a few weeks in mid-summer. The single or double flowers are mainly red. Both species can be sown directly outdoors in late spring and will still flower the same year. They also self-seed very easily. Poppies look very good in rockeries and wild gardens. The dried seed-capsules add a particularly decorative element in dried flower arrangements. Both species need a lot of sun and plenty of water during long periods of drought.

106

Ivy-leaved geranium

Pelargonium peltatum

Ivy-leaved geraniums are native to South Africa. The name pelargonium is correct from a botanical point of view, although the plant is still commonly known as geranium. Trailing or ivy-leaved geraniums are very branched with trailing stems. The single or double flowers come in a wide range of colors, including several shades of reds and pinks, violet and white. The smooth, lobed leaves are ivy-shaped and very glossy, contrasting beautifully with the bright flowers, grouped in terminal umbels. Ivy-leaved geraniums are usually propagated by cuttings in late summer or spring. Some varieties can be raised from seed but it is quite difficult and time-consuming. Although they can survive long periods of drought they must be watered and fed regularly between spring and late summer, but they do not like to be waterlogged. Removing dead flowers and yellow leaves regularly encourages further flowering. Ivy-leaved geraniums should overwinter in a bright, frost-free place.

ℹ

Family: Geraniaceae
Flowering season: summer
Height: trailing to 5 ft
Situation: ○
Moisture requirement: ◊
❋

Zonale pelargonium

Zonal pelargonium

Zonal pelargonium

Zonal pelargoniums are branching shrubs which are also native to South Africa. They are distinguished by the brown 'zone' or marking on their leaves which have given the groups its name. In the wild, they form bushy shrubs but they can also be trained as standards or pyramids. There are a large number of varieties with double and single flowers whose colors range from red, pink and salmon to white. The leaves are marked with one or more dark zones. In foliage varieties, the dark zones are multi-colored. The scented varieties have a delicious fragrance which could be lemon, rose or mint. They are usually propagated by cuttings in late summer or spring. It can also be raised from seed but this can be quite a tedious process. Pelargoniums thrive in a warm, sunny position where they are protected from the rain. Although they can survive long periods of drought they must watered and fed regularly between spring and late summer. But they hate to be waterlogged. To encourage flowering, remove dead flowers and yellow leaves regularly. Zonal pelargoniums should be overwintered in an airy place.

ℹ

Family: Geraniaceae
Flowering season: summer
Height and spread: 20 × 12 in
Situation: ○
Moisture requirement: ◊
❋
❀ *(scented pelargoniums)*

107

*T*railing petunia

Petunia

ⓘ

Family: Solanaceae
Flowering season: summer
Height: to 5 ft
Situation: ○
Moisture requirement: ○
❊

Trailing petunias were originally developed by Japanese breeders. Since then many new varieties have been developed by European breeders. These petunias have very long stems, covered with dense foliage and trumpet-shaped flowers in many colors. They are real eye-catchers in window boxes and hanging baskets. Depending on the variety, the colors are delicate or very bright, ranging from purple to pale blue, from pink to white. These flowers are remarkably weather-resistant. The *calibrachoa* varieties such as 'Million Bells' flower profusely with smaller blooms. They are usually propagated by cuttings. The parent plants should be overwintered at a temperature of about 50°F. Because of the dense foliage and large number of flowers, petunias need plenty of water and food, so it is important to water and feed petunias weekly with liquid fertiliser containing iron. Otherwise the leaves will soon turn yellow.

Petunia

Petunia

The original species from which garden petunias have been developed is native to Argentina and Brazil. The many varieties which exist today are mostly the result of crossing *P. axillaris* and *P. integrifolia*. They grow either erect, 6–16 in high, or trailing, with stems up to 32 in long, and they are usually grown as annuals because they are not hardy. The single or double axillary, trumpet-shaped flowers come in a very wide range of colors, including some variegated strains with dark centres, dark veins and different colored margin. The slightly hairy leaves, which are quite sticky, are often concealed by the numerous blooms. These are the mini-petunias ('Milliflora' petunias) which have become very popular with gardeners. Petunias are sown in early spring under glass at a temperature of 59°F, pricked out, hardened off and planted out in late May or early June when there is no longer any danger of frost. They thrive in a sunny position and partial shade and must be fed and watered generously during the summer. The more recent varieties are very weather resistant. It is important to dead head regularly.

Family: Solanaceae
Flowering season: summer
Height and spread: 16 × 32 in
Situation: ○
Moisture requirement: ◌
❄

Primrose

Primula vulgaris

Primroses grow wild throughout Europe. They prefer cool weather conditions and can survive harsh wintry weather. However, forced plants are only half-hardy. They have a cushion-like, compact habit and the brightly-colored flowers, grouped in whorls, appear as early as late winter. The flowers of the oxlip (*P. elatior*) are carried in clusters on tall, strong stems up to 8 in high, well above the leaves. Primroses come in almost every color and there are also forms with variegated flowers. Both types form basal leaf rosettes with oblong, round-tipped, bright green leaves which are very fragrant in border primroses. They can be propagated by dividing the clump, but they can also be raised from seed under glass, between early spring and early summer. In order to encourage flowering, the plants should be hardened off in autumn. Primroses also thrive in a sunny position but they need moderately moist, loose soil. Annuals do not need feeding.

Primula vulgaris

Family: Primulaceae
Flowering season: spring
Height and spread: 12 × 10 in
Situation: ◐
Moisture requirement: loamy, ◌
❄ ❄ ❄
✽

Castor oil plant

Ricinus communis

ℹ

Family: Euphorbiaceae
Flowering season: summer
Height and spread: 10 × 5 ft
(annual)
Situation: ○
Moisture requirement: ◌
❈
✖

This exotic plant is native to tropical Africa and India where it grows as a shrub or small tree (up to 26 ft high). Because it is not frost-resistant, it is usually cultivated as an annual. It can nevertheless reach a height of 10 ft in one season. Besides its imposing appearance, it also has strikingly large, palmate leaves which can be red or brown veined, supported by red stems. The rather inconspicuous flowers appear in mid-summer, borne in terminal sprays. The male flowers are yellowish and the female flowers reddish. They are followed later by bright red spiny fruits which look like little chestnuts. It is raised from seed in spring under glass at a temperature of 64–68°F, hardened off and planted out in late May or early June. They must be planted in a sunny, warm, well-drained position. In summer, they must watered and fed generously. Be careful: all parts of the plant, even the colourful seeds, are poisonous. It is therefore recommended that you remove the dead flowers.

Black-eyed susan

Rudbeckia hirta

ℹ

Family: Asteraceae
Flowering season: summer
Height/spread: to 40 × 18 in
Situation: ○
Moisture requirement: ◌
❈
honey producing

The wild form and many of the varieties of *Rudbeckia* are native to North America. Although it is a biennial, it is usually cultivated as an annual and is a real eye-catcher in any garden. It has an upright, branched habit. There are tall varieties and lower, compact forms suitable for growing in pots. The single or double flowers have a brown center, surrounded by orange, yellow, red, brown or even two-toned ray petals, depending on the variety. The flowers can reach 6 in in diameter. The stems and oblong-lanceolate leaves are covered with short, fluffy hairs. It can be raised from seed in early spring indoors or sown directly outdoors in late May. Black-eyed susan is easy to grow but needs to be watered and fed generously and regularly. It also tolerates light shade. If dead-headed regularly, it will flower until the first frost. Cut flowers should be picked when in full bloom.

Rudbeckia hirta

Sweet scabious

Scabiosa atropurpurea

Sweet scabious is native to southern Europe and the Mediterranean. It is an annual with a much-branched, compact habit. The double, fragrant flowers are borne on slender, hairy stems and tend to attract large numbers of butterflies and bees. There are numerous varieties which come in a wide range of colors, including many shades of reds and pinks, blue, violet and white. The pinnate leaves are arranged in opposite pairs and slightly hairy. Plants raised from seed in spring under glass at a temperature of about 64°F flower earlier than those sown in late spring directly outdoors in the flowering position. Seeds are usually sold in mixed colors. Sweet scabious grow best in a sunny, warm position and need fertile, calcareous, well-drained soil. When picking flowers, cut the stems at the first joint to encourage uninterrupted flowering. Scabious look particularly attractive planted in groups.

ⓘ

Family: Dipsacaceae
Flowering season: summer
Height and spread: 40 × 10 in
Situation: ○
Moisture requirement: ◇
❄
✿
honey producing + attracts butterflies

Scabiosa stellata

Scabiosa stellata

ⓘ

Family: Dipsacaceae
Flowering season: summer
Height and spread: 24 × 10 in
Situation: ○
Moisture requirement: ⬤
❄
✿
honey producing + attracts butterflies

This species grows wild in southern Europe (Spain, Portugal, Italy and France) and north-west Africa. It has an erect, branched habit with slender, thread-like stems. The pale blue, almost white flowers are borne in globular umbels which can reach up to 1 in in diameter and are extremely decorative. The cup-shaped, brown or green seed heads are even more striking. The lanceolate-oval, pinnate leaves are 7 in long and slightly hairy. Plants raised from seed in spring under glass at a temperature of approx. 64°F flower earlier than those sown directly outdoors in late spring. Scabious grow best in a warm, sunny position and need fertile, calcareous, well-drained soil. The dried seed heads are often used in flower arrangements. The seed heads should be picked when still green.

Senecio cineraria

Senecio cineraria

Senecio cineraria

ⓘ

Family: Asteraceae
Flowering season: summer (biennial)
Height/spread: to 24 × 12 in
Situation: ○
Moisture requirement: ⬤
❄ – ❄ ❄

This species, often sold in nurseries under the name of *S. bicolor* or *Cineraria maritima*, is native to the Mediterranean. A low, bushy, branched shrub, it is usually grown as an annual because it is only half-hardy. With its gray-white, hairy, pinnate, indented or wavy leaves – depending on variety – it is one of the most popular structural plants in late summer and autumn beds. The yellow daisy-like flowers which appear in the second year are quite inconspicuous compared to the foliage. Plants raised from seed in spring can only be planted outdoors in late May when all danger of frost has past. Senecios are very robust plants. The soil must not be too wet because the leaves would turn green. The white hairs which give the plants their silvery appearance are there as a protection against heat and drought. It grows best in a fertile soil which should be low in nitrogen. Although normally hardy, they should protected against harsh frost.

Solenostemon scutalleroides

Solenostemon scutalleroides

The original species, also known as *Coleus blumei*, is native to tropical Africa and Asia where they grow as sub-shrubs in damp shady places under trees. Their exotic, variegated, colorful, nettle-like leaves with serrated, waved or smooth margins come in many shades and shapes. The tubular two-lipped white and blue flowers are rather inconspicuous. The plant is easily propagated by herbaceous tip cuttings in spring or autumn. It can also be raised from seed in late winter under glass at a temperature of 68°F. The plants will grow in full shade but the leaves will be much more colorful if grown in partial shade. Water with soft water or rainwater and feed regularly. Pinch out the flowers regularly to promote a bushy growth.

Solenostemon scutalleroides

ⓘ

Family: Lamiaceae
Flowering season: summer
Height and spread: 24 × 24 in
Situation: ◖
Moisture requirement: ◌ – ◗
❄

African marigold

Tagetes erecta

The ancestors of this vigorous, erect, many-branched plant are native to Mexico in Central America. There are dwarf varieties (approx. 8 in high), medium forms (12–20 in high) and very tall strains (up to 40 in high). The large single or double, daisy-like terminal flowers are borne mostly singly on the stems. They are usually bright yellow or orange but sometimes also creamy-white. The glossy dark green, pinnate leaves are also very decorative. The plants can be raised from seed in spring indoors or in a cold frame and only planted out when there is no longer any danger of frost. If sown directly outdoors in the flowering position, the beginning of the flowering season will be delayed. They exude a strong but not unpleasant scent and are used as a biological weapon to combat eelworms and other pests in the vegetable garden. Marigolds grow best in a sunny position but will also grow in partial shade. They thrive in rich, moderately moist soil. They can be used in flower arrangements if the smell is tolerated. Removing dead blooms will encourage further flowering.

ⓘ

Family: Asteraceae
Flowering season: summer
Height and spread: 40 × 20 in
Situation: ○
Moisture requirement: ◌
❄

French Marigold

Tagetes patula

🛈

Family: Asteraceae
Flowering season: summer
Height and spread: 24 × 16 in
Situation: ○
Moisture requirement: ◌
❄

This species of *Tagetes* is also native to Central America. It is much smaller and bushier than its the African marigold and even the taller varieties will only reach 24 in in height. The flower heads are single or double and come in a wide range of shades and color combinations of yellow, orange, red-brown and dark brown. The dark green leaves are pinnately divided. *T. tenuifolia*, an elegant plant with slender stems and finely divided leaves, reflects the popularity of the small-flowered wild forms. This variety may have smaller blooms – yellow, orange or brownish depending on the variety – but it flowers prolifically, attracting large number of bees and butterflies. The leaves are even more finely divided than those of the other varieties. Cultivation and propagation is the same as for other marigold species. The lower-growing species and varieties are ideally suited to flower beds, borders and window boxes.

Black-eyed susan

Thunbergia alata

🛈

Family: Asteraceae
Flowering season: summer
Height: 5–7 ft (annual)
Situation: ○
Moisture requirement: ◌ – ◖
❄

This sun-loving climber is native to southeast Africa where it is grown as a perennial. In colder climates, it is grown as an annual of moderate growth, the hairy stems reaching about 5 ft in one summer. The orange, yellow or white flowers have a differently colored, usually dark center ('black-eyed') and are borne singly from the leaf axils. The climber flowers uninterruptedly throughout the summer. The ovate leaves are also very decorative. Sow in late February to ensure flowering from the end of May onward. Prick out several seedlings in a pot and pinch out to encourage bushy growth. Water and feed generously, especially in hot weather, but make sure the plant is not waterlogged.

Verbena

Verbena

The ancestors of many verbena varieties are native to South America. The majority of these colorful plants have a bushy, compact habit while a few have a procumbent habit. The single flowers are borne in large terminal clusters, the colors ranging from pink, red, blue, violet and white to salmon pink. Most have a white center. The dark green, oblong-oval leaves, with their serrated edges, are also very beautiful. The annual varieties usually flower well into autumn. Verbena can be raised from seed in early spring and grown indoors until mid-May when the danger of frost has past. Some varieties can be propagated in spring by cuttings from plants which have been allowed to overwinter. Verbenas grow best in a sunny, warm position in fertile, well-drained soil. Hybrids prefer dry soil in contrast to half-hardy varieties such as *Verbena canadensis*, *V. rigida* and *V. tenera* which need regular watering.

ⓘ

Family: Verbenaceae
Flowering season: summer
Height and spread: 20 × 20 in
Situation: ○
Moisture requirement: ◌ – ◐
❄ – ❄ ❄

Trailing Verbena

Verbena

The ancestors of the trailing verbena varieties originate in South America. The range of these trailing varieties has recently greatly expanded as result of intensive research by breeders. New varieties such as 'Tapien' or 'Temari' can develop trailing shoots or stems up to 40 in long. They have a vigorous, much-branched habit which makes them ideally plants for hanging baskets, window boxes and ground cover in the garden. The flower heads are borne on short side-shoots so that the plants are completely covered with a mass of flowers. These come in various shades of pink, blue and red and are extremely weather-resistant. The dark green leaves are finely pinnate or ovate with serrated edge, depending on the variety. Modern varieties are propagated by cuttings. Trailing verbenas must be watered and fed regularly and generously to ensure uninterrupted flowering. They hate dry conditions. It is also important to remove dead blooms regularly.

ⓘ

Family: Verbenaceae
Flowering season: summer
Height and spread: to 40 × 20 in
Situation: ○
Moisture requirement: ◌ – ◐
❄

Viola cornuta

Viola cornuta

ℹ

Family: Violaceae
Flowering season: spring and autumn
Height and spread: 6 × 16 in
Situation: ◑
Moisture requirement: ◊ – ◐
❋ ❋
❀

These popular flowers are the result of cross-breedings between *Viola tricolor* and *V. wittrockiana* whose wild forms are native to Central Europe. These small herbaceous shrubs are usually cultivated as annuals or biennials although some varieties are frost-resistant. They have a compact habit which becomes spreading, even procumbent with time. The flowers which measure 4/5 in in diameter are considerably smaller than those of the garden strain but they flower prolifically from spring to autumn. The range of colors is enormous, the basic colors being white, yellow, pale blue and violet. The flowers can also be multi-colored. The ovate leaves have a serrated edge. Autumn-flowering strains should be sown in June or July in a cold frame or directly outdoors. Spring-flowering strains are sown indoors in January in small pots. Violas grow well both in the sun and partial shade but will do better in cool site than a warm one. The soil must be fertile, moist and well-drained.

Viola cornuta

Garden pansy

Viola wittrockiana

Viola wittrockiana

The garden pansy is native to Europe and the Mediterranean. Much research has been carried out by breeders in recent years so that the number of varieties on offer is quite enormous. The large, single flowers consist of five overlapping petals in an ever-increasing range of shades and color combinations. The dark green leathery leaves are lanceolate-oval. Plants flowering in autumn are sown in June or July, either in pots or in the flowering position. The ideal temperature for germination is about 59°F. Sowing indoors in winter will produce flowering plants two to three months later. If the plants are allowed to overwinter outdoors, it is advisable to protect them from frost with a layer of bracken. They grow well in damp, rich soil, in the sun and in partial shade but they hate being waterlogged.

ⓘ

Family: Violaceae
Flowering season: spring and autumn
Height and spread: 12 × 16 in
Situation: ◑
Moisture requirement: ◌ – ◑
❋ ❋

Zinnia

Zinnia elegans

These colorful, annual zinnias grow wild in Mexico. The numerous, erect-growing varieties come in various sizes, from low strains for growing in pots and borders to tall strains, intended as cut flowers. The daisy-like flowers are found in every color except blue; they may be single or double, dahlia-flowered, cactus-shaped or pompon-shaped, large-flowered or small-flowered. They like warmth and are very susceptible to frost. The leaves are heart-shaped to oval and up to 2 ½ in long. *Z. angustifolia* includes small-flowered, single forms whose blooms are reminiscent of wild flowers. The main colors available are red, orange and violet and sometimes bicolor. Because zinnias thrive in warm conditions, it is advisable to sow indoors in spring at a temperature of about 59°F. They grow best in rich, well-drained soil in a sunny position. Feed at weekly intervals during the flowering season. They flower less profusely in cool, wet summers.

Zinnia elegans

ⓘ

Family: Asteraceae
Flowering season: summer
Height / spread: to 36 × 12 in
Situation: ○
Moisture requirement: ◌
❋

Perennials

Daisies, carnations and delphiniums are popular herbaceous perennials, as are pampas grass, ferns and water-lilies, although they look so different. In this section, perennials include not only all herbaceous plants but also ferns, grasses, marsh-plants and water-plants and a number of climbers, so long as they live three years or more and their shoots do not become woody. However, bulbous and tuberous plants have a section of their own because there are so many of them.

With perennials, the shoots above ground level usually die off in autumn while the root system survives the winter in the soil. In spring, new shoots are produced and the perennial comes back to life. This amazing process is very fascinating: lilies of the valley, peonies and Michaelmas daisies mark the change of seasons. They only flower for two or three weeks but by skilful planning and combination there will be a succession of flowers in the garden throughout nearly the whole year. Perennials live longer than summer flowers and do not need to be planted every year, while they reach maturity much earlier than shrubs. However, they should rejuvenated by division or replacement every three to four years to maintain healthy growth and prolific flowering.

Perennials require very different conditions as far as soil, light and temperature are concerned. They come from all over the world and have often been cultivated, propagated and bred specially for many centuries. Many wild species are protected plants. The better their position in the garden meets their requirements, the better they will perform. So it is sensible not to put a woodland plant in a sunny flower bed where it will need constant watering to keep it alive, when there are numerous sun-loving, Mediterranean plants which love such dry conditions. The right plant exists for every place in the garden – it is a matter of deciding which one goes where.

Bear's breeches

Acanthus spinosus

Family: Acanthaceae
Flowering season: summer
Height: 4 ft
Spread: 24 in
Situation: ○
Moisture requirement: ○
❀ ❀ ❀

Acanthus is native to the Mediterranean: it thrives in well-drained soil in a sunny position and hates being waterlogged. If planted in a sheltered position, it will form an impressive shrub in a very short time. The white flowers with green bracts borne in tall spikes give the acanthus a striking appearance, and it is a very attractive foliage plant even when it is not flowering. Their glossy, dark green, lanceolate leaves are deeply cut, serrated and spiny. In antiquity, acanthus became an ornamental feature in architecture, the Corinthian order of columns having capitals consisting of stylised acanthus leaves. The long spikes can be dried upside down in a dark room and used in dried flower arrangements. It is propagated by division in spring, while larger numbers can be raised from seed. In late autumn, it can also be propagated by root cuttings. The thorny leaves of this handsome, architectural shrub make it unsuitable for a family garden where children play.

Yarrow

Achillea filipendulina

Family: Asteraceae
Flowering season: summer
Height: to 4 ft
Spread: to 24 in
Situation: ○
Moisture requirement: ◐
❀ ❀ ❀

Yarrow has been a very popular shrub for a long time. This is reflected in the wide range of varieties and strains with different height and size of flowers now available – the original wild species is native to Europe and Asia Minor. The variety 'Gold Plate' is particularly tall, reaching a height of up to 4 ft, while 'Altgold' only reaches 24 in. *A. filipendulina* has an erect habit and lanceolate, gray-green, finely cut, hairy leaves. In summer, it produces tiny yellow flowers grouped in large, flat umbels carried on thread-like stems. These fragrant flower heads make excellent cut flowers which last a long time. They look very pretty in flower arrangements, whether fresh or dried. Yarrow thrives in a warm, sunny position and well-drained soil. To ensure vigorous growth and prolific flowering, the shrubs should cut back. They combine beautifully with grasses and blue flowering plants such as salvias (*Salvia*).

Achillea filipendulina

*Y*arrow

Achillea millefolium

Gardens in the open sun need frequent watering if they contain a large number of magnificent, but thirsty, flowering shrubs. But there are many reasons for reducing watering to a minimum: protection of the environment, conservation of water, and the fact that hoses may be banned in times of drought as well as the time consuming nature of watering.

Plants which are used to dry conditions are therefore very useful, and yarrow is an excellent example. Native to the temperate regions the northern hemisphere, it grows wild in meadows, wasteland and on waysides. It is easily identified by its creeping rootstock and erect stems. The leaves are gray-green and fern-like, the individual leaflets being lanceolate and covered with fine hairs. The tiny white flowers are grouped in flat umbels, carried on vigorous, leafy stems. Yarrow flowers profusely and the flowers look good in fresh or dried flower arrangements. As a medicinal plant, it stimulates the metabolism. It thrives in a sunny position in warm, well-drained soil and is propagated by division in spring. There are a large number of varieties available in a wide range of colors.

ⓘ

Familie: Asteraceae
Flowering season: summer
Height: 32 in
Spread: 24 in
Situation: ○
Moisture requirement: ◌
❄ ❄ ❄

Sneezewort

Achillea ptarmica

Family: Asteraceae
Flowering season: summer
Height: to 24 in
Spread: to 24 in
Situation: ○ – ◐
Moisture requirement: ◖
❄ ❄ ❄

This species thrives in rich, moist soil, but it hates being waterlogged. Sneezewort is native to Europe where it has been cultivated as a garden plant for a long time. It grows wild in North America. Sneezewort is a vigorous growing shrub which spreads very easily in sunny and partially shaded places because of its creeping rootstock. The leaves are dark green and the individual leaflets are narrow and lanceolate with a serrated edge. In summer it produces a mass of tiny white flowers, borne in large, loose umbels. The best known variety is 'The Pearl' because its white flowers are double. Sneezewort produces beautiful cut flowers which are often used by florists. It is propagated by division in spring or autumn.

Monkshood

Aconitum carmichaelii 'Arendsii'

Family: Ranunculaceae
Flowering season: autumn
Height: 4 ft
Spread: 20 in
Situation: ○ – ◐
Moisture requirement: ◖
❄ ❄ ❄
✖

Blue is rare as a color in the garden, which is why monkshood is so popular. It produces violet-blue flowers which appear quite late in the summer so that they are even more noticeable and useful. It has an upright, compact habit and its vigorous flower stems do not need staking. The species originates from China but there are many varieties and forms whose flowers come in a wide range of shades of blue, also differing in height. The unusually deep blue flowers of A. c. 'Arendsii' are hooded and borne on high, branched racemes 32 to 50 in tall, the height varying according to the fertility of the soil. They flower for a long time and make excellent cut flowers. The large, dark green leaves are deeply serrated. This variety was developed in 1945 by the German breeder Georg Arends after whom it is named. It is propagated by dividing large plants in spring or autumn. But be careful: this plant is very poisonous and is not suitable for gardens used by children.

Aconitum carmichaelii 'Arendsii'

*F*ive-fingered maidenfair fern

Adiantum pedatum

This elegant maidenhair fern is native to North America and differs considerably from its relatives both in its appearance and in that it is hardy. The popular name refers to the unusual shape of the fronds which are drooping and pedate. The individual, light green fronds are lance-shaped and borne at right angles on black-brown stems. They are very attractive and can be used as green foliage in fresh flower arrangements. It is propagated by the spores contained in the capsules situated on the underneath of the older fronds. This fern spreads easily with its creeping rhizomes, quickly forming dense groups. It thrives in moist soil, rich in humus and slightly acidic. It grows best in partial shade and in a humid atmosphere. It is propagated by dividing older plants in early spring.

ⓘ

Family: Adiantaceae
Height: 20 in
Spread: 20 in
Situation: ◑
Moisture requirement:
❄ ❄ ❄

Alchemilla mollis in the front

*L*ady's mantle

Alchemilla mollis

i

Family: Rosaceae
Flowering season: spring/summer
Height: 12 in
Spread: 12 in
Situation: ○ – ◑
Moisture requirement: ◌ – ◌
❄ ❄ ❄

Lady's mantle is a wild plant native to Europe and western Asia. Its flowers are small, star-shaped and borne in loose corymbs. Their delicate greenish-yellow color contrasts agreeably with the colorful flowers in the garden. The plant's low-growing shoots prevent weeds from growing so that it makes an ideal ground cover for sunny and partially shaded flower beds. Lady's mantle is also very good as a scree plant. The gray-green palmate leaves are very distinctive and have clearly inspired its common name: the shallow, rounded lobes with their serrated edges look like a flowing mantle. After rain, the leaf edges hold tiny water drops which glisten attractively. The plant also has medicinal properties and is said to alleviate gynecological problems.

Lady's mantle is easy to grow and self-seeds very readily if the flowers are left on the plant. It can be raised from seed or divided in spring or autumn.

Water plantain

Alisma plantago-acquatica

The water plantain is native to Europe, Asia and North America where it grows in water. The leaves are pointed, oval to elliptic and bright green. The loose panicles of white or pink flowers are very attractive in summer. The flowers are arranged is whorls as if on several 'levels.' It is best to plant water-plantain on its own in an open sunny position where it can seen when it is flowering.

This erect-growing marginal water plant needs permanently wet soil at the water's edge or in water at a depth of 8 in where it forms tuberous roots. It is an ideal plant for planting on the edge of a pond. It self-seeds very easily which means that it can spread quickly in favourable conditions and may need to be kept in check.

ⓘ

Family: Alismataceae
Flowering season: summer
Height: 28 in
Spread: 20 in
bank and marsh plant
Situation: ○
Moisture requirement: ●
❋ ❋ ❋

Anemone hupehensis

Anemone hupehensis

A. hupehensis is an ideal plant for growing in partial shade. It produces numerous brightly colored, saucer-shaped flowers, borne in loose panicles, well into the autumn. It is a many-branched shrub with a vigorous rootstock and the dark green leaves are deeply divided, coarsely serrated and slightly hairy. The wild form of this species grows mainly in the Himalayas but it can also be found in Japan although it is much rarer there. It has been used as a parent to several hybrids, including 'September Charm,' whose flowers are pale pink on the inside and deep pink on the outside, a beautiful combination of shades.

The plants grow best in deep, loose soil enriched with humus. Anemones spread readily, soon forming large clumps thanks to numerous runners. The plants do best in moderately fertile, slightly acid soil. They are propagated by division in spring or by root cuttings in autumn. The wild species can be raised from seed in autumn.

Anemone hybrida hupehensis

ⓘ

Family: Ranunculaceae
Flowering season: summer / autumn
Height: 28 in
Spread: 20 in
Situation: ○ – ◑
Moisture requirement: ◯ – ◐
❋ ❋ ❋

Anemone

Anemone × hybrida 'Honorine Jobert'

ℹ

Family: Ranunculaceae
Flowering season: summer/autumn
Height: 4 ft
Spread: 24 in
Situation: ○ – ◐
Moisture requirement: ◌ – ◑
❋ ❋ ❋

The form 'Honorine Jobert' was already popular in European gardens in the 19th century. This is not surprising because its white, saucer-shaped flowers with their contrasting golden yellow stamens are produced throughout the summer and are very striking in light partial shade. The leaves are dark green, deeply divided with thin wiry stems. This hybrid is the result of crossing the wild species, which are native to the Himalayas, southern China and Japan. It is very similar to *A. hupehensis* in habit and growing conditions since this species is one of its parents. 'Honorine Jobert' will spread quickly and form large clumps if planted in a sunny position or in partial shade in free-draining humus-rich soil. It can be propagated in spring by division of the rootstock and in autumn by taking root cuttings which are allowed to root in a compost low in nutrients in a frost-free place.

Snowdrop windflower

Anemone sylvestris

ℹ

Family: Ranunculaceae
Flowering season: spring
Height: 12 in
Spread: 12 in
Situation: ○ – ◐
Moisture requirement: ◌ – ◑
❋ ❋ ❋
✖

A. sylvestris is a wild plant which is native to central Europe, the Caucasus and Siberia. While 'Honorine Jobert' adds a touch of light when there is very little color left in the autumn garden, its relative *A. sylvestris* is a beautiful spring flowering plant. The white, cup-shaped flowers have a yellow center, surrounded by a crown of yellow stamens. The slightly nodding flowers grow singly or in pairs on slender stems. The mid-green leaves are divided with a serrated edge and are hairy underneath.

This carpeting perennial spreads very easily because of its vigorous runners, especially if not constricted by other plants. As a woodland plant, it grows best in sun or partial shade under trees or bushes. The soil should be calcareous and rich in humus. By dividing the plants after flowering and directly in position, a carpet of flowers is soon created. In the autumn, it can be raised from seed or propagated by root cuttings. Be careful: this plant is poisonous.

*F*alse anemone

Anemonopsis macrophylla

This plant is much sought-after and hard to find, but avaitable at some specialist nurseries. The false anemone is native to the mountainous regions of Japan and therefore fully hardy. In habit, it is reminiscent of *A. x hybrida* 'Honorine Jobert' but the flowers are waxy and purplish-blue. The nodding flowers are carried on the slender, branched stems of this elegant perennial. The dark green leaves are pinnate and strongly serrated. The false anemone thrives in leaf mould in partial to complete shade. The soil must always be moist; if not, plants may die in hot summers through lack of water. If all the conditions are right, the false anemone will live a long time and flower profusely during the summer, brightening up shaded or even dark parts of the garden. It combines very well with ferns because they thrive in similar conditions. It is propagated by division in spring or raised from seed immediately after harvesting the seeds.

ⓘ

Family: Ranunculaceae
Flowering season: summer
Height: 32 in
Spread: 20 in
Situation: ◯ – ◑
Moisture requirement: ◐
❄ ❄ ❄

*G*olden marguerite

Anthemis tinctoria

Anthemis tinctoria

In the past, the flowers of *A. tinctoria* were used to dye wool (hence its Latin name), but it is now a rare protected plant. It is native to the Mediterranean and loves sunny, dry conditions. This vigorous, upright-growing plant flowers profusely from early summer till autumn. The tiny, yellow flowers, reminiscent of daisies, are carried singly on strong stems and last a long time as cut flowers. The dark green leaves are doubly-pinnate and fern-like.

It thrives in well-drained, sandy to stony soil but even in the best conditions, it is quite short-lived. It should be cut back vigorously after flowering in order to promote new growth. It is propagated in spring by basal cuttings. Older plants can therefore be replaced by young plants which will flower more prolifically.

ⓘ

Family: Asteraceae
Flowering season: summer
Height: 35 in
Spread: 20 in
Situation: ◯
Moisture requirement: ◌
❄ ❄ ❄

127

Columbine

Aquilegia canadensis

🛈

Family: Ranunculaceae
Flowering season: spring
Height: 24 in
Spread: 16 in
Situation: ◑
Moisture requirement: ○
❀ ❀ ❀

A. canadensis is one of the most beautiful aquilegias, a wild species native to North America where it grows in woodland. It has been cultivated and propagated for a very long time. These vigorous plants are extremely decorative with their fine foliage. They have an erect habit, the dark green leaves are fern-like with the individual very narrow. Aquilegia flowers are usually bicolor and this wild species is no exception. Their inner petals are yellow while the outer ones are bright red, spur-shaped and curved backwards. The pendant, bell-shaped flowers are carried on slender stems. They make ideal cut flowers.

A. canadensis grows best in partial shade in well-drained, sandy soil. They are not only ideal for well-established gardens with large shrubs and trees, but also for less sunny parts of rockeries. It is propagated by seed directly after the seeds have ripened or by division in late summer.

Granny's bonnet

Aquilegia vulgaris

🛈

Family: Ranunculaceae
Flowering season: spring
Height: 24 in
Spread: 16 in
Situation: ○ – ◑
Moisture requirement: ○
❀ ❀ ❀
✖

A. vulgaris is native to Europe where it is occasionally seen on the edge of woods. In gardens, it is one of the most popular plants with an an upright, branched habit. The dark green leaves are rounded and divided into leaflets and gray-green on the underside. The pendant flowers are borne in loose panicles and are usually of one color, blue-violet. A white form 'Nivea' is now also available. The curved, hook-shaped spurs are very distinctive.

A. vulgaris thrives in a sunny position or partial shade in light, moist, humus-rich soil. The plant self-seeds readily but the process can be accelerated by gathering the seeds as soon as they are ripe and sowing them in the flowering position. Older plants can be propagated by division of the powerful rootstock. Be careful: this plant is poisonous.

Aquilegia vulgaris

*T*hrift

Armeria maritima

Thrift should always be present in family garden. Children love it because of its colorful, round flower heads which look as if they float above a carpet of grass. In addition, the petals make a pleasant rustling noise when touched – almost like tissue paper. *A. maritima* is native to Northern Europe and as far as west Siberia. It is an evergreen clump-forming sub-shrub with a compact habit and stiff stems with dark green, linear leaves, reminiscent of grass. In spring it produces white, red or pink flowers on wiry, leafless stems. It grows best in well-drained sandy soil in a sunny position. Thrift is easy to grow and flowers profusely. It enjoys dry conditions but hates being waterlogged. It is a good edging plant and is perfect for planting at the front of a border so that children can also see it. It is also ideal for planting in window-boxes and tubs if the drainage is good. It is propagated by dividing older plants in early spring or autumn.

ⓘ

Family: Plumbaginaceae
Flowering season: spring
Height: 6 in
Spread: 12 in
Situation: ○
Moisture requirement: ◊
❄ ❄ ❄

129

Wormwood

Artemisia alba 'Canescens'

ⓘ

Family: Asteraceae
Flowering season: summer
Height: 20 in
Spread: 12 in
Situation: ○
Moisture requirement: ◊
❋ ❋

This is a magnificent ornamental shrub with silver-gray foliage which will provide a beautiful background for brightly colored flowers. Wormwood developed gray foliage as a means of adapting to intense sun, and *A. alba* is native to the Mediterranean region. *A. a.* 'Canescens' has particularly silvery leaves, and the name of the variety means 'growing white.' If artemisia is planted in a very sunny position in well-drained soil and warms up quickly, it will grow well. The addition of sand will further improve the soil. It combines beautifully with other gray-leaved shrubs such as santolina and lavender.

Wormwood is a branched, bushy shrub. The evergreen leaves are finely and curling and a few sprigs look very beautiful added to a bunch of flowers. The gray-yellow flowers are borne in slender spikes but they are rather inconspicuous. It is propagated in spring by division or cuttings. It should be carefully protected from damp conditions in winter.

Artemisia alba 'Canescens' in the front

130

Goat's beard

Aruncus dioicus

This tall-growing plant looks rather like a bush when it is fully grown, but it does not become woody and dies down to ground level in autumn. In spring, young shoots are produced again. It is native to the damp forests of western and central Europe and the eastern part of North America. Ideal for large, shady gardens, it thrives in deep, damp, moderately fertile soil in partial shade but it will also grow in shady positions in very damp soil. The large leaves are dark green and compound, consisting of several lanceolate leaflets with deeply serrated edges, carried on tall stems. In summer, it produces tiny, creamy-white flowers, grouped in long plumes. *A. dioicus* is dioecious which means it has both male and female flowers, the male flowers being the most impressive. This plant looks best at the back of the border, for instance in front of a fence or wall. It thrives in the dappled shade of trees and looks especially attractive near water. It can be raised from seed immediately after harvesting the ripe seeds or by division in autumn. Be careful: this plant is poisonous.

ⓘ

Family: Rosaceae
Flowering season: summer
Height: 6 ft
Spread: 5 ft
Situation: ○ – ◑
Moisture requirement: ◊ – ◉
❄ ❄ ❄
✖

Maidenhair spleenwort

Asplenium trichomanes

While most ferns, being woodland plants, prefer a humus-rich acid soil, the maidenhair spleenwort prefers damp crevices in rocks and needs a more alkaline soil. It is native to the rocky regions of the northern temperate zone where it grows in carbonaceous and silicific rocks. However, it is not as demanding in the garden as might be expected and will often find its place in the cracks of old damp walls. It grows best in rock gardens on an appropriate rocky soil with sufficient moisture. The fern remains low, its pinnate fronds growing low over the earth and spreading through rhizomes, soon forming large groups. The mid-ribs are black and the individual leathery, oblong to rounded pinnae are bright green. The fern is an evergreen which means its fronds do not die back in autumn, unlike many other ferns and shrubs. Propagation is by division or sowing of the spores; the latter method should only be attempted by an expert gardener.

ⓘ

Family: Aspleniaceae
Height: 6 in
Spread: 12 in
Situation: ◑
Moisture requirement: ◉
❄ ❄ ❄

Alpine aster

Aster alpinus

Family: *Asteraceae*
Flowering season: *spring*
Height: *8 in*
Spread: *12 in*
Situation: ○
Moisture requirement: ◐
❀ ❀ ❀

Most people know asters as Michaelmas daisies, meaning that they are autumn-flowering plants, but there are a couple of species which seem to have confused the seasons. One is *A. alpinus*, which is a spring-flowering plant. As the plant's Latin name suggests, it is native to alpine regions where it grows on mountain slopes, meaning that it prefers poor soil. It has a compact habit and forms groups as time goes on. The basal leaves are spatulate while those higher up are linear to lanceolate. The attractive flower heads have yellow centre florets, surrounded by purple ray florets.

The plant look very good in herbaceous borders and in large rock gardens. Its flowers last a long time both in the garden and in flower arrangements. It is advisable to add plenty of sand to the soil before planting to improve the drainage. A regular dose of lime in spring is also helpful. *A. alpinus* is propagated by divis on in autumn and can be raised from seed in spring, although it also self-seeds. Because it is short-lived, it is important to start in good time to produce young plants.

Aster 'Monte Cassino'

Michaelmas daisy
Aster novi-belgii

Aster novi belgii

The tall Michaelmas daisy is one of the most beautiful autumn-flowering aster species with a large number of varieties. Their main disadvantage is they are more prone to mildew than other aster species. It is native to the eastern part of North America and this reflected in the name of the species *A. novi-belgii*, because New Belgium was the old name of the State of Virginia. It is a tall, erect plant which should be staked because of the weight of its flowers. It spreads though runners and forms large groups. The brightly colored flower heads are borne in loose, branched panicles. The leaves are lanceolate with a smooth edge and cover the entire stem. Asters thrive in rich, fertile soil in a sunny position. They look very effective at the back of herbaceous borders. Propagation is by division in autumn. 'Dauerblau' which has blue-purple flowers produces some of the most beautiful cut flowers of the autumn, as does 'Royal Velvet' with semi-double, red-purple flowers and 'Crimson Brocade' with pink-red, semi-double blooms.

ℹ

Family: Asteraceae
Flowering season: autumn
Height: to 3 ft
Spread: to 24 in
Situation: ○
Moisture requirement: ◐
❊ ❊ ❊

Michaelmas daisy
Aster pringlei 'Monte Cassino'

Those who love to have flowers in the house will adore this variety: 'Monte Cassino' produces numerous small, white flower heads which look beautiful combined with other brightly colored flowers in a vase. In the garden it looks very good combined with rudbeckias, monkshood and brightly colored dahlias and will provide a real visual delight throughout the autumn. The ancestors of this variety are native to North America. *Aster pringlei* (sometimes sold under the name *A. ericoides*) has a powerful rootstock, an erect habit and slender, branched stems. The white flower heads have yellow center florets which are borne singly on slender stems. The bright green basal are lanceolate with a smooth or slightly serrated edge, while the leaves on the stems are narrow and linear. 'Monte Cassino' is not completely hardy so it needs to be protected from the frost during winter, with bracken. It is propagated by division in autumn.

ℹ

Family: Asteraceae
Flowering season: autumn
Height: 24 in
Spread: 16 in
Situation: ○
Moisture requirement: ○
❊ ❊

Astilbe

Astilbe × arendsii

Family: Saxifragaceae
Flowering season: summer/autumn
Height: variable
Spread: variable
Situation: ○ – ◑
Moisture requirement: ◐
❄ ❄ ❄

Astilbes include hardy herbaceous perennials which thrive in partial shade in moist soil, enriched with humus. They are very effective in a well-established gardens under old trees and near pools and ponds. If planted in a sunny position, the soil must be moist at all times while excessive sun could lead to leaf damage. In perfect conditions, astilbes form vigorous thickets. The foliage is fern-like and the individual leaflets are ovate to lanceolate with serrated edges. In summer they produce tiny flowers, borne on strong stems in loose, feathery panicles. They flower for a long time and look very effective in dried flower arrangements. The plants are only cut down in spring so as to enjoy the beautiful flowers during the winter. They can be divided for propagation at the same time.

There are many species and varieties. *A. x arendsii* 'White Gloria' grows up to 3 ft high with large panicles of white flowers. One of the most beautiful dark red varieties is *A. x arendsii.* 'Fanal' which only grows up 24 in high.

Astilbe x arendsii und Geranium

Masterwort

Astrantia major

Astrantia is a striking flowering plant which is very popular among gardeners because of its elegant appearance. It has a bushy habit and deep green, slightly glossy, tripartite leaves with coarsely serrated margins and magnificent blooms. The rounded, pale pink flower umbels are surrounded by a crown of white, pink or greenish bracts. The individual flowers are so tiny that they are usually only perceived as umbels, which in fact look very good in a vase.

They grow best in partial or full shade because this species is native to the mountain forests of Central and Eastern Europe. They associate very well near bushes, under light trees, in front of fences and walls. They need fertile, damp but well-drained soil. If the conditions are right, *A. major* will self-seed but for quicker results the ripe seeds can be sown immediately after harvesting. Older plants can be divided in spring.

Astrantia major

ⓘ

Family: Apiaceae
Flowering season: summer
Height: 24 in
Spread: 16 in
Situation: ◑ – ●
Moisture requirement: ◊
❅ ❅ ❅

Aubrietia

Aubrieta × cultorum

Aubrietias have been cultivated for a very long time. For instance, *A. x cultorum* was developed as early as the 19th century and today there are many more varieties available. Its ancestors originated from the mountainous regions near the Mediterranean and Asia Minor. *Aubrieta* is a mat-forming, spreading species. The blue-green leaves are evergreen, hairy, ovate to oblong and arranged in rosettes. The flowers which are grouped in loose clusters are usually purple. There are also varieties with blue, white and very occasionally reddish flowers. 'Bressingham Pink' has double, pink flowers.

Aubrietias are perfect for planting at the front of herbaceous borders and in rock gardens. They grow best in moderately fertile, well-drained alkaline soil and associate well with candytuft (*Iberis*) and *Arabis*. Aubrietias must be pruned with great care because older plants can easily look bare if pruned too vigorously. Cut back after flowering and feed generously to encourage vigorous, compact growth. It is propagated by cuttings in late summer and by division in early autumn.

ⓘ

Family: Brassicaceae
Flowering season: spring
Height: 2 in
Spread: 20 in
Situation: ○
Moisture requirement: ◊
❅ ❅ ❅

Yellow alyssum

Aurinia saxatilis

ⓘ

Family: Brassicaceae
Flowering season: spring
Height: 12 in
Spread: 16 in
Situation: ○
Moisture requirement: ◌
❄ ❄ ❄

This species thrives on stony soil and will feel at home in traditional rock gardens, screes, tops of walls, steps and small cracks between paving stones and in walls. It is easy to grow and long-lived, provided it is in a sunny position. It is native to the mountainous regions of Central and southeastern Europe as well as Turkey. It is a low, evergreen, bushy plant which becomes woody at the base so that, from a botanical point of view, it is a sub-shrub. The leaves are gray-green and hairy, obovate to linear with serrated margins and often also pinnatifid and arranged in rosettes. The bright yellow flowers are grouped in dense corymbs.

Aurinias are ideal for growing in tubs. It they grow too large, they can be cut back hard; this will stimulate new growth and a more compact habit. The soil should be given a lime treatment in the spring because it needs to be slightly alkaline. The plants are propagated by cuttings in summer.

Bergenia

Bergenia cordifolia

ⓘ

Family: Saxifragaceae
Flowering season: spring
Height: 16 in
Spread: 16 in
Situation: ○ – ◐
Moisture requirement: ◌ – ◓
❄ ❄ ❄

Bergenias have evergreen, leathery leaves. They look particularly effective when planted in dense groups or strips. *B. cordifolia* has a flat, creeping rootstock and forms dense groups. The dark green leaves, which are round to oval and puckered, turn red in winter as a result of frost. The flowers are pink, bell-shaped and grouped in dense clusters borne on vigorous red stems.

Bergenia is native to the Altai mountains in Central Asia, Mongolia and Siberia. It is a vigorous plant which thrives in well-drained soil, in full sun or partial shade but it also tolerates occasional dry conditions. It is propagated by division or rhizome cuttings after flowering in spring or in autumn. Old plants have a tendency to become bare but this can be prevented by regular division. The most popular varieties include 'Silverlight' with white flowers which turn pink with time and 'Morning Red' which has deep red-purple flowers borne on red-brown stems.

Knotweed

Bistorta officinalis 'Superba'
(syn. Persicaria bistorta)

Bergenia cordifolia

Knotweed should be high on the list of anyone wanting to create a wild garden: it is a robust, vigorous-growing plant which produces very decorative flower heads which look most effective planted in groups and last a long time both in the garden and in flower arrangements in the house. Knotweed thrives in moist, fertile soil in a sunny or partially shaded position. If the conditions are right, it will form dense groups as it spreads by means of creeping runners. Because of its vigorous growth, it may crowd neighbouring plants. This can be resolved by cutting the runners back regularly. It is ideal for damp areas of a wild garden and near ponds. The leaves of B. officinalis 'Superba' are deep green, the basal leaves are ovate and the stem leaves are triangular. In spring, they produce tiny, pale pink flowers grouped in cylindrical spikes carried on slender, wiry stems. Older plants are propagated by division in spring or autumn.

There are two particularly pretty knotweed varieties, namely *B. affinis* 'Superba' which only grows 8 in high and B. amplexicaulis (syn. *P. amplexicaule*) 'Firetail' with spikes of bright red flowers that are produced well into the autumn.

ⓘ

Family: Polygonaceae
Flowering season: spring/summer
Height: 28 in
Spread: 20 in
Situation: ○ – ◑
Moisture requirement: ◊
❀ ❀ ❀

Marsh marigold

Caltha palustris

Family: Ranunculaceae
Flowering season: spring
Height: 12 in
Spread: 12 in
bank and marsh plant
Situation: ○
Moisture requirement: 💧
❄❄❄
✖

Although becoming rarer, the marsh marigold can still be seen growing in slow-flowing, unpolluted waters in large parts of the northern hemisphere. It is readily available from water garden centers and in the garden it will thrive in permanently moist soil near pools or in shallow water, at a depth of 8 in in a sunny position. In the right conditions it will grow bushy and form clumps. The dark green leaves are glossy, kidney-shaped and lightly toothed. The bright yellow, cup-shaped flowers, reminiscent of buttercups, are grouped in loose clusters.
It can be propagated by division after flowering in late spring, but it also self-seeds quite readily in the right conditions. To prevent unwanted spreading, it should be planted in pots, sunk in the marshy soil. Be careful: this plant is poisonous.

Campanula carpatica

Campanula carpatica

Campanula carpatica

Family: Campanulaceae
Flowering season: spring/summer
Height: 10 in
Spread: 6 in
Situation: ○
Moisture requirement: ○ – ◐
❄❄❄

There is a wide range of campanulas which all look very different and enjoy different growing conditions – it is therefore very important to choose the right plant for the right place. C. carpatica is a low-growing species which is ideal for sunny rock gardens and also for window-boxes and tubs. It is native to Eastern Europe and western Siberia, has a compact habit and does not form runners as other campanulas do (such as *C. poscharskyana*). Their pale blue, bell-shaped flowers are borne singly on tall, wiry, leafless stems. Campanulas flower prolifically for a very long time. The leaves are rounded to heart-shaped.
C. carpatica grows best in alkaline, loamy soil, rich in humus, in a sunny position. It will also grow in screes and cracks in paving stones if moist enough. They combine beautifully with carnations (*Dianthus*) and thrift (*Armeria*). The best-known varieties include 'Blue Clips' with pale purple flowers and 'White Clips'. It is propagated by division of older plants in spring or autumn.

Peach-leaved campanula

Campanula persicifolia

Every garden should include campanulas, and *C. persicifolia* would be an excellent choice because it is particularly beautiful. The characteristic bell-shaped flowers are grouped in tall, erect clusters close to the slender stem and look very good in herbaceous borders and in colorful flower arrangements. In order to support the stems weighed down by the weight of flowers, it is advisable to plant taller herbaceous perennials nearby or support by staking.

The peach-leaved campanula is native to Europe. The dark green, narrow, lanceolate leaves are arranged in rosettes. It tends to spread easily through runners. The white or pale blue bell-shaped flowers ornament the garden over a long period. It thrives best in fertile, humus-rich, alkaline soil in sunny and partially shaded positions. Snails are fond of the young leaves and its important to take measures to control this in good time. It is propagated by division in spring or autumn.

Campaula persicifolia

ⓘ

Family: Campanulaceae
Flowering season: summer
Height: 32 in
Spread: 12 in
Situation: ○ – ◑
Moisture requirement: ◔ – ◕
✿ ✿ ✿
Prone to: infestation by snails

Sedge

Carex hachijoensis 'Evergold'

It is not easy to find plants for shady parts of the garden, but sedge thrives in shade and its variegated foliage with luminous, creamy-white stripes will brighten 'problem' areas. The wild form is native to the forests of Japan and has dark green leaves, while the evergreen variegated variety with the evocative name 'Evergold' was specifically developed as a garden plant. It forms rather low but dense clumps and their long, linear leaves arch elegantly towards the ground. The rather inconspicuous flowers which are grouped in dark brown spikes appear in spring. Sedge is easy to grow and not fussy about its position. It grows well in moderately moist, loose soil, rich in humus. The very fact that it keeps its leaves in winter also makes it more vulnerable. Being exposed to hot sun in frosty conditions can be very dangerous for the plant, because water is evaporated through the leaves, but the plant is unable to absorb moisture through the leaves because the soil is frozen. It should be protected with bracken in winter to prevent drying.

ⓘ

Family: Cyperaceae
Flowering season: spring
Height: 10 in
Spread: 16 in
Situation: ◑ – ●
Moisture requirement: ◕
✿ ✿

Centaurea

Centaurea montana

ⓘ

Family: Asteraceae
Flowering season: summer
Height: 20 in
Spread: 24 in
Situation: ○ – ◑
Moisture requirement: ◑
❊ ❊ ❊

This shrub has many features which make it a very popular plant. The flower heads are a rare blue color. The thistle-like central florets are surrounded by slender, star-shaped ray florets and are reminiscent of a cornflower – which is in fact a close relative. But unlike the cornflower, *C. montana* is a perennial and flowers twice a year. Regularly dead-heading will ensure repeat flowering and also unwanted self-seeding.

C. montana is native to the mountainous regions of Europe where it grows in meadows and clearings. They have a spreading habit and a creeping rootstock. Its gray-green leaves are lanceolate and smooth-edged. The young leaves are slightly woolly underneath. It thrives in well-drained, fertile, calcareous soil. It is ideal for flower beds whether in the sun or partial shade. Besides the blue wild form, there are also white and pink flowering varieties; they all make excellent cut flowers. They are propagated by division in autumn and self-seed very easily.

Centaurea montana

Red valerian

Centranthus ruber

Very few perennials flower longer than red valerian, which is why it looks so beautiful in summer flower arrangements. Its is true that the star-shaped flowers are very small, but they are a beautiful deep pink and grouped in impressive panicles or umbels. The 'Albiflorus' variety has white flowers, borne above the gray-green, slightly fleshy leaves. The individual leaflets are ovate to lanceolate, with a smooth or serrated edge. The stems tend to become woody at the base and grow upright, forming compact plants. They combine beautifully with globe thistles (*Echinops*).

It is native to the rocky regions and gravel beaches of the European Mediterranean. This explains why it needs a lot of warmth, but apart from this it is easy to grow, thriving on poor, chalky, well-drained soil. It grows in stony soil and cracks, but hates being waterlogged. It the conditions are right, it will propagate itself by self-seeding for an informal effect. It can be raised from seed in spring or autumn.

ⓘ

Family: Valerianaceae
Flowering season: spring/summer
Height: 24 in
Spread: 18 in
Situation: ○
Moisture requirement: ◌
❄ ❄ ❄

Bugbane

Cimicifuga simplex

This plant's late flowering makes it a valuable addition to any garden. Its slightly fragrant, creamy-white, star-shaped flowers, borne in candle-like spikes, will brighten up damp, shady areas under trees and near walls and fences at the end of the flowering season. *C. simplex* is native to Asia where it is found mainly in the mountain meadows of Japan, Mongolia and Kamchatka. Once the plant has become established, which can take several years, it forms impressive thickets, pushing up young shoots from the base. It is long-lived and is easy to grow. Its deep green leaves are deeply divided, the individual leaflets ovate, lobed with a serrated edge. The flowers are borne in slender, arching spikes on dark brown stems which sometimes need staking. Bugbane grows best in humus-rich, moisture-retaining soil which never dries out completely. It does not like positions in full sun. It is propagated by division in spring or by sowing the ripe seeds in autumn.

ⓘ

Family: Ranunculaceae
Flowering season: autumn
Height: 4 ft
Spread: 24 in
Situation: ◑ – ●
Moisture requirement: ◐
❄ ❄ ❄

Convallaria majalis

ⓘ

Family: Convallariaceae
Flowering season: spring
Height: 6 in
Spread: 10 in
Situation: ◐ – ●
Moisture requirement: ◊

❄ ❄ ❄

✖

❀

*L*ily of the valley

Convallaria majalis

Most of the year, lilies of the valley lead a shadowy existence but in spring, when they flower, they really steal the show. There are many reasons for having lilies of the valley in the garden: they have a wonderful fragrance and thrive in the shade under trees where other plants would not grow, while the creeping rhizomes which develop from the crowns soon form a carpet of flowers.

Lilies of the valley are a protected species in the wild. It is native to the woods and meadows in the mountains of the northern temperate zone. The pendant, bell-shaped, pure white flowers are grouped on arching stems, followed later by red fruits. The leaves are mid to dark green, slightly shiny and elliptic to lanceolate. The basal leaves are always in pairs, sometimes in threes. Lilies of the valley grows best in moist soil with plenty of leaf mould but they also tolerate dry conditions. They combine beautifully with lungwort (*Pulmonaria*) and violets. They are propagated by division in autumn or spring. Be careful: lilies of the valley are poisonous and particularly dangerous for small children because the flowers are so attractive.

Coreopsis lanceolata

ⓘ

Family: Asteraceae
Flowering season: summer
Height: 12 in
Spread: 14 in
Situation: ○
Moisture requirement: ◊

❄ ❄ ❄

*C*oreopsis

Coreopsis lanceolata

The bright yellow flowers have a dark gold-yellow center which looks like an eye. At a distance the colorful flowers are quite similar to marguerites but the ray florets have a serrated edge. They look very beautiful in fresh flower arrangements. The plant has a bushy habit and flowers profusely on branched stems. The deep green leaves are narrow to lanceolate and pinnatipartite. Regular dead heading will encourage growth and further flowering. The plant should be cut back after flowering.

It is native to North and Central America. It thrives in warm, well-drained, fertile soil in sunny position. It can be raised from seed in spring or division in spring and autumn.

Pampas grass

Cortaderia selloana

If there is one ornamental grass which has successfully become a garden staple, it is the pampas grass. A solitary plant par excellence, its long silvery plumes can be seen from a distance and are particularly attractive against a background of autumn colors. Its common name reveals its place of origin – it is native to the pampas, the extensive grassy plains in Argentina and Uruguay. In the garden it forms magnificent thickets with gray-green, arching, strap-shaped leaves. The leaves have rather sharp edges which makes handling quite difficult. The tiny, silvery flowers are grouped in dense, plume-like spikes. The plants are dioecious, which means that the male and female flowers are on different plants, the spikes of the female flowers being denser and more erect. They grow best in loose, well-drained, fertile soil in a sunny position. During the growing season, it should be watered and fed regularly from the side. It does not like being waterlogged or watered from above. The shrub can be protected from winter damp by tying the foliage together to face upwards. It should only be cut back in spring. Pampas grass is propagated by division. There are several varieties such as 'Sunningdale Silver' which grows up to 10 ft high and 'Pumila,' which only reaches 5 ft in height.

ℹ

Family: Poaceae
Flowering season: summer/autumn
Height: 8 1/2 ft
Spread: 5 ft
Situation: ○
Moisture requirement: ◊
❅ ❅ ❅

Cortaderia selloana

Larkspur

Delphinium-hybrids

Delphiniums have been popular in cottage gardens for a long time. There are many interesting varieties of this stately plant, collected and planted by enthusiasts. The varieties were developed in ancient times from wild species and native to Europe and Asia where they grow in mountainous regions in meadows and on the edge of woods. There, they grow in cool, moist soil which is never waterlogged. These conditions should be met when selecting a place in the garden. Varieties are divided into groups, based on their ancestry. These groups differ greatly in habit and in the shape of the flowers:

The Large-flowered or Elatum group includes the largest number of varieties and is never is frequently found in gardens. The plants have an erect habit and the flowers are all borne in spikes. The plant grows up to 5–7 ft in height and 3 ft in spread. They are splendid solitary plants.

The Belladonna group includes smaller plants, more branched varieties with looser spikes. They reach a height of 4 ft and a spread of 20 in. These delphiniums look very good in a herbaceous border.

The Pacific group includes varieties similar to those in the Elatum hybrids. They are short-lived and are therefore usually cultivated as annuals and biennials. Their dense, candle-like spikes can grow up to 6 ft high and 32 in wide, depending on the species.

Be careful: if swallowed, delphiniums can cause nausea, and the leaves can cause skin irritation.

❶

Family: Ranunculaceae
Flowering season: summer
Height and spread: variable
(according to species and variety)
Situation: ○
Moisture requirement: ◗
❄ ❄ ❄

*L*arkspur

Delphinium 'Black Knight'

ⓘ

Family: Ranunculaceae
Flowering season: summer
Height: 6 ft
Spread: 32 in
Situation: ○
Moisture requirement: ◐
❀ ❀ ❀

This 'Black Knight' is one of the most popular variety in the Pacific group. The intense dark-purple color of the flowers is unrivalled by any other variety. All individual flowers are cup-shaped with a black eye in the center. The flowers are borne in extraordinarily tall, dense spikes. The basal leaves are deeply lobed with serrated edges. It is a vigorous-growing plant with a stately appearance which will look splendid in any garden. But its height also makes it more vulnerable to high winds than the lower varieties. The plants should be staked with bamboo sticks very early on when the young shoots are only 12 in high. The supports should 'grow' with the plant. Varieties in the Pacific group are short-lived and 'Black Knight' is no exception. The plants should be replaced after two years because they lose their flowering ability. They can be raised from seeds because the seedlings will have the same flower color as the parent.

*L*arkspur

Delphinium 'Berghimmel'

ⓘ

Family: Ranunculaceae
Flowering season: summer
Height: 6 ft
Spread: 32 in
Situation: ○
Moisture requirement: ◐
❀ ❀ ❀

This variety, which has double, cup-shaped, sky blue flowers, with white eyes, is particularly popular with gardeners. The flowers are borne in very tall, extremely dense spikes which are quite vulnerable to high winds. The rootstock is fleshy and the dark green leaves are deeply divided with serrated edges. This variety is part of the Elatum group. It often flowers a second time in autumn, but not as profusely. To ensure a second flowering, it is advisable to cut the plant back to 4 in above ground level and water and feed it regularly. The soil must never be allowed to dry out completely. In addition, the plant must given weekly doses of a compound fertiliser following the manufacturer's instructions on the packet. Indeed, too much of a good thing is as bad as not enough. Moreover, the plant needs an airy, open space where it is not constricted by other plants. Otherwise, it will flower less profusely and become prone to mildew. It is propagated by cuttings in summer and by division in autumn.

Larkspur

Delphinium 'Fanfare'

The traditional color of delphiniums is dark blue but breeders have greatly increased the range available: 'Fanfare' has striking, pale pink-purple flowers which have a silvery sheen in the sun and a white eye which contrasts with the rest of the petals. The double, cup-shaped flowers are grouped very tall, densely set spikes. Because of their height and weight, they are very vulnerable to high winds and should be supported very carefully well before the flowers are produced. The plant is cut down to 4 in above ground after flowering.
This variety is part of the Elatum group. It is vigorous pant with a fleshy rootstock. The deep green, basal leaves are deeply divided and serrated. It thrives in fertile soil in a sunny position, sheltered from the wind. By watering and feeding regularly, the plant may flower a second time in autumn. It is propagated by cuttings in summer or by division in autumn.

Family: Ranunculaceae
Flowering season: summer
Height: 7 ft
Spread: 3 ft
Situation: ○
Moisture requirement: 💧
❄❄❄

Deliphinium 'Völkerfrieden'

Larkspur

Delphinium 'Völkerfrieden'

The deep blue flowers with white eyes are the distinctive feature of this variety. It is a vigorous plant with bright green, deeply divided basal leaves with serrated edges. It is part of the Belladonna group and has slender, loosely branched spikes. It does not grow as tall as the other two groups. What many gardeners saw as a disadvantage became a plus when it came to combining it with other herbaceous perennials and achieving a harmonious effect. Shorter varieties are easier to fit in borders and flower beds. Delphiniums look very beautiful planted among shrub roses and brightly colored flowers such as fleabane (*Erigeron*) and lilies (*Lilium*), or ornamental shrubs such *calamagrostis x acutiflora*. The varieties in the Belladonna group need well-drained, fertile soil in a sunny position and often produce a second flowering. They combine beautifully with dahlias in autumn. They are propagated by cuttings in summer or division of older plants in autumn.

Family: Ranunculaceae
Flowering season: summer
Height: 4 ft
Spread: 20 in
Situation: ○
Moisture requirement: 💧
❄❄❄

Garden chrysanthemums

Dendranthema-hybrids

Chrysanthemums are excellent, reliable flowering shrubs which brighten up borders in autumn and are an excellent source of colorful, cut flowers. Botanists have recently reclassified many plants previously classed under *Chrysanthemum* in the *Dendranthema* genus. Besides the approximately 20 wild species, there are some 5,000 known varieties. The genus includes not only herbaceous perennials, but also annuals sold as cut flowers at florist's shops in autumn, which are tender herbaceous plants used by nurseries to produce cut flowers by forcing the plants under glass. But as far as gardens are concerned, herbaceous perennials are the most interesting varieties because you do not need to buy and plant them every year. Most varieties available on the market have been developed from species native to Russia, China and Japan. They are bushy plants with lanceolate to ovate, more or less deeply lobed, alternate leaves on sturdy stems. The leaves and flowers are both aromatic – although not every one likes the smell. Garden varieties can be grouped according to the flowering period: there are early, medium-early and late-flowering varieties. Early-flowering varieties with branched stems bearing clusters of flowers will bring color to the garden while late varieties will bring warmth to autumn flower beds and borders. Another important aspect is the shape of the flower which varies enormously, ranging from single, anemone-centered, incurved, intermediate or reflexed to double, pompon-shaped. Individual varieties and their growing requirements will be described in the following entries.

ℹ

Family: Asteraceae
Flowering season: summer / autumn
Height: c. 12 in – 5 ft
(according to species and variety)
Spread: 12 in – 4 ft
(according to species and variety)
Situation: ○
Moisture requirement: ◊ – ◖
❄ ❄

Garden chrysanthemum

Dendranthema × grandiflorum
(syn. Chrysanthemum-Indicum-hybrids)

Dendranthema x grandiflorum

What an inexperienced eye would see as a single flower is in fact a flower head. It consists of numerous, tiny, individual blooms, grouped in a globular flower head with long ray florets on the outside and shorter tubular florets in the center. The proportion of ray florets to tubular central florets differs according to the variety. Single flower heads have up to five rows of flat ray florets while the large center is filled with short, yellow tubular flowers. Recommended varieties include 'Clara Curtis' which flowers in early autumn with pink flowers and a greenish center which turns yellow later, height 28 in; and 'Dawn Mist' which flowers early with pale pink flower heads and yellow center, height 4 ft. Anemone-shaped flower heads are also single but the tubular center florets are longer so that they form a taller hemisphere. Recommended varieties include 'Sally Ball' which flowers with yellow-orange flower heads in early autumn, height up to 4 ft, and 'Yellow Pennine Oriel' which flowers early with yellow flower heads, height up to 4 ft.

ⓘ

Family: Asteraceae
Flowering season: summer/autumn
Height: 12 in – 5 ft
(according to species and variety)
Spread: 12 in – 4 ft
(according to species and variety)
Situation: ○
Moisture requirement: ◌ – ◖
❋ ❋

Dendranthema

Garden chrysanthemum

Dendranthema × grandiflorum 'Ritter Tom Pears' (syn. Chrysanthemum-Indicum-hybrids)

It is possible for gardeners to influence the size and number of flower heads. By pinching out some of the buds, the remaining buds develop into larger flower heads. On the other hand, if as many blooms as possible are wanted, the tips of the shoots are pinched out in spring when the plant is 8 in tall. This will promote the development of lateral shoots and the number of flowers which naturally will be a little smaller. They are borne in many-branched clusters which should be supported so that they are not damaged by wind and driving rain.

The variety illustrated here has reflexed flower heads and flowers in early autumn. It grows up to 32 in high and is called 'Ritter Tom Pears.' The double spherical flower heads have numerous flat ray florets which curve downward and inward. Other recommended varieties with reflexed flower heads include 'Madeleine' which flowers in early autumn with pink flower heads, height up to 4 ft; and 'Red Wendy' which flowers early with red flower heads, height up to 4 ft.

Garden chrysanthemums thrive in fertile, humus-rich soil with neutral to low pH in a sunny, sheltered position. They should be watered generously in the growing season and fed regularly with liquid compound fertiliser. These chrysanthemums are also sensitive to frost. In colder parts of the country they should winter indoors in a cool bright place. In places where frost does not occur very often, a thick layer of mulch will be sufficient to protect from the cold. The plants are only cut back in early spring because the old shoots serve as a protection against the cold. Chrysanthemums are planted and divided in autumn when there is no longer any danger of frost and so that they can become well-established in their new site. Chrysanthemums are propagated by cuttings of basal shoots.

Chrysanthemums with pompon-shaped flower heads produce numerous curved ray florets with rounded ends. Recommended varieties include 'Poppet' which flowers profusely in early autumn with small, yellow flower heads, height up to 24 in; and 'Salmon Fairie' which flowers late with salmon-colored flower heads, height up to 20 in.

Family: Asteraceae
Flowering season: summer/autumn
Height: c. 12 in – 5 ft
(according to species and variety)
Spread: c. 12 in – 4 ft
(according to species and variety)
Situation: ○
Moisture requirement: ○ – ◐
❄ ❄

Pinks and carnations

Dianthus caryophyllus

Carnations immediately evoke the image of an old cottage garden. Today their intense fragrance is usually only found in florist's shops since scented carnations have become less common in the garden. Tastes differ but those who dislike highly-bred florist's carnations should not reject the whole genus because there is a very wide choice of beautiful plants, such as the biennial Sweet Williams (*Dianthus barbatus*), annual and perennial carnations and pinks, and several wild herbaceous forms, which would all look very good in gardens. Florists mainly sell carnations which have been forced as annuals in greenhouses and should not be confused with garden carnations.

Dianthus caryophyllus, a wild species native to the Mediterranean, has been used by many breeders as a basis for many garden varieties. It forms low clumps of usually gray-green or deep green, linear leaves, similar to grass. The flowers are usually borne singly or in clusters of two or three. Depending on the species, the flower are plain-colored or edged or flecked with a different color. The varieties flower prolifically and are excellent as border plants, in window-boxes and tubs. They prefer sandy, chalky well-drained soil. It is important to dead head regularly in order ensure abundant flowering the following year. After the second year, the plant begins to flower less. It can be raised from seed in late winter in the greenhouse or on the window-sill, the seedlings being planted outdoors when all danger of frost has passed.

ⓘ

Family: Caryophyllaceae
Flowering season: summer
Height: 20 in
Spread: 16 in
Situation: ○
Moisture requirement: ◊
❄ ❄ ❄
❀

Maiden pink

Dianthus deltoides

ℹ️

Family: Caryophyllaceae
Flowering season: summer
Height: 6 in
Spread: 12 in
Situation: ○
Moisture requirement: ◌
❀ ❀ ❀

Low-growing, clump-forming herbaceous perennials are very useful as edging plants in borders or the fill gaps in flower beds. The maiden pink is one of those perennials. It is native to Europe, North America and west Siberia where it grows in well-drained, poor soil and is a protected species. The clump-forming habit of this variety is reminiscent of that of a tuft of grass. The individual leaves are linear and pointed, deep to olive green and glossy. The numerous, red-violet flowers produced from June to autumn are borne on branched stems.

This variety is very easy to grow. All it needs is warm, sandy, well-drained soil in a sunny position. They are ideal plants for rock gardens, wild gardens and window-boxes because they survive long periods of drought without suffering too much. They can be propagated by division in spring and autumn but they also self-seed very easily. As well as the species, recommended varieties include red flowering varieties such as 'Brilliancy' and 'Splendens' and white-flowering varieties such as 'Albus.'

Dianthus plumarius

Pink

Dianthus plumarius

ℹ️

Family: Caryophyllaceae
Flowering season: spring
Height: 10 in
Spread: 14 in
Situation: ○
Moisture requirement: ◌
❀ ❀ ❀
❀

This variety is very much what people imagine a pink should look like: the fragrant flowers with deeply fringed petals are borne in clusters on branched, upright stems, while the foliage is blue-green and grass-like. This variety forms large clumps with woody basal shoots. It is particularly decorative in sunny rock gardens where it readily spreads over stones, along paths, steps or on top of garden walls. The soil should be chalky, but not too dry. It is a good cut flower but is also suitable for growing in tubs.

The European wild form has been cultivated for a long time and there are many varieties available on the market whose flowers come in a wide range of colors, especially pinks and reds as well as whites. They are all easily propagated by division in autumn.

Bleeding heart

Dicentra spectabilis

Bleeding heart is a well-known herbaceous perennial and has been grown in cottage gardens for a very long time. Its exotic origin is not immediately apparent. In fact, *Dicentra spectabilis* is native to Asia where it grows in the shady forests of China and Korea. It was only introduced into Europe in the 19th century. It has a bushy habit and fleshy, brittle roots which must be treated carefully when working the soil around the plant. In spring, the plant produces arching clusters or racemes of pendulous, pink, heart-shaped flowers with long, shiny white, protruding inner petals. The leaves are pale green and fern-like which die down very soon after flowering. The empty space can then be filled with other plants such as ferns or primulas.

Bleeding heart grows well in any well-drained soil, enriched with humus, in partial shade. It can be raised from seed in spring or propagated by root cuttings also in spring.

The 'Alba' variety has white flowers and is more sensitive to late frosts than the pink wild form. The dwarf variety (*Dicentra eximia*) only grows 12 in high.

ⓘ

Family: Fumariaceae
Flowering season: spring
Height: 24 in
Spread: 24 in
Situation: ◑
Moisture requirement: ◐
❄ ❄ ❄

Dicentra spectabilis

155

Great leopard's bane

Dorinicum pardalianches

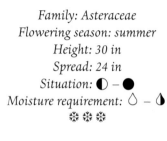

Family: Asteraceae
Flowering season: summer
Height: 30 in
Spread: 24 in
Situation: ◑ – ●
Moisture requirement: ○ – ◐
❊ ❊ ❊

In spite of the daisy-like flowers of the great leopard's bane, it is only distantly related to the ox-eye daisy or marguerite. The yellow flower heads are produced in summer on slender, branched stems and look very good both in the garden and in fresh flower arrangements. The plant has a bushy habit and fleshy roots with underground runners which spread rapidly. The leaves are brilliant green, slightly hairy and heart-shaped. It is native to the light woodland of Western Europe. This is why in the garden it prefers cool, loose soil in partial or full shade. It can be raised from seed or propagated by division in spring or autumn. There is another variety available in nurseries, *D. orientale*, (syn. *D. caucasicum*) which only grows 18 in high and flowers in spring.

Dryopteris filix-mas

Male fern

Dryopteris filix-mas

Family: Dryopteridaceae
Height: 3 ft
Spread: 32 in
Situation: ◐
Moisture requirement: ◐
❊ ❊ ❊
✖

Ferns are among the easiest plants to grow. As a wild plant, they are used to looking after themselves. If planted in the right place where the conditions replicate those of their natural habitat, they will grow without any problem. In the wild, most ferns can be found in forests where they thrive in damp, humus-rich, lightly acid soil in partial shade.

The male fern is familiar to many people from their walks through woods and forests. It grows wild in Europe and North America and spreads far and wide by means of rhizomes. Its arching fronds develop from a short shoot and form a funnel-shaped crown. The young shoots are bright green, turning deep green with time. The lanceolate fronds are almost pinnate and the stems are covered with scales. Male ferns thrive in moist conditions and are ideal for planting along ponds in shady positions. Ferns are propagated by spores. In male ferns, the spores are stored in brown spore capsules situated underneath the fronds. Male ferns can be propagated by sowing these spores. Nevertheless, propagation is easier by the division of rooted runners. Be careful: although the male fern is a medicinal plant its active agents can be poisonous if taken in too large a quantity.

Globe thistle

Echinops ritro

The globe thistle is an extremely versatile plant which looks beautiful in fresh and dry flower arrangements as well as in the garden. It has a bushy, erect habit and very long branched flower stems, carrying globular flower heads with tiny blue flowers. The leaves are narrow, sharply divided and hairy. They are gray-green on top and downy gray underneath with fine thorns along the edges. Planted on its own, it is a real eye-catcher in the garden, but its thorny leaves may be a disadvantage in gardens where children play.

The globe thistle is ideal for a sunny flower bed because it prefers moderately fertile, warm, dry soil. It is native to southeastern Europe where it grows in dry meadows and light groves. It combines beautifully with tall ornamental grasses which require similar growing conditions. Globe thistles hate being waterlogged, especially in winter when it could be quite damaging. In parts of the country where rainfall is high, they should be protected in winter. They are raised from seed or propagated by division in spring or by root cuttings in autumn.

ⓘ

Family: Asteraceae
Flowering season: summer
Height: 5 ft
Spread: 3 ft
Situation: ○
Moisture requirement: ◊
❀ ❀ ❀

Echinops ritro

157

Foxtail lily

Eremurus robustus

ℹ

Family: Asphodelaceae
Flowering season: spring/summer
Height: 8 ft
Spread: 3 ft
Situation: ○
Moisture requirement: ◊
❄ ❄

Foxtail lilies are very striking plants when in full bloom. The fleshy root system produces majestic plants with tall flowering stems crowned by impressive spikes of star-shaped flowers. The single, shallowly cup-shaped flowers are bright pink, gradually fading until they are almost white. The basal, strap-shaped, blue-green leaves die off soon after the plant has finished flowering. By combining it with ornamental grasses, the unsightly gap will pass unnoticed.

In order to grow well and flower abundantly, it must be planted in well-drained warm soil, with plenty of sand, in a sunny, sheltered position. The foxtail lily is native to Central Asia where it grows in dry, stony, even poor soil, but does not tolerate long periods of rain. The tall spikes should be supported if necessary. In winter, it should be protected from the cold (and the rain) before the first frost arrives. It can be propagated by sowing or division after the plant has finished flowering.

Fleabane

Erigeron 'Dunkelste Aller'

ℹ

Family: Asteraceae
Flowering season: summer
Height: 24 in
Spread: 18 in
Situation: ○ – ◑
Moisture requirement: ◊ – ◐
❄ ❄ ❄

Fleabane is one of the most popular herbaceous perennials and cut flowers. Its daisy-like flowers are very similar to those of asters. There are many varieties available on the market whose flowers come in a wide range of colors such as white, pink, purple and blue. The variety 'Darkest of all' has been developed from the North American wild form *Erigeron speciosus*. The semi-double, purple flower heads consist of long, narrow ray florets and a yellow center. This variety produces many flowers and looks very beautiful in the garden or in fresh flower arrangements, combined with yellow-flowering achilleas, white-flowering gypsophilas or blue flowering salvias. The basal leaves are gray-green and lanceolate. The flowering stems tend to lean to one side and should be supported with bamboo canes. It thrives in fertile, well-drained soil in a sunny position, but it will also grow in partial shade. If the flowering stems are cut down just above ground level after flowering and the plant is fed generously, it may flower again later in the season. It is propagated by cuttings in spring.

Eryngium

Eryngium × oliverianum

Interesting gardens depend on unusual plants such as eryngium to attract attention. It combines beautifully with yarrow and ornamental grasses. It would be a pity if its foliage became concealed by its companions, so it is best to plant with a little space around it. The leaves are extremely prickly. The ovate, dark green leaves have prominent veins, the basal leaves are lighter in color and the stem leaves are deeply lobed. All the leaves have a spiny margin. The tiny, steel blue flowers are grouped in large, cylindrical flower heads, borne on sturdy, branched stems. The flower heads which are surrounded by linear, spiny bracts can be used in fresh and dry flower arrangements. Eryngium has an upright bushy habit. *Eryngium x oliverianum* is the result of a cross between *Eryngium giganteum* and *E. planum*. They grow best in a sunny, dry position in deep, well-drained, very poor soil where their tap roots can develop freely. They can be propagated by division in spring or root cuttings in winter.

ⓘ

Family: Apiaceae
Flowering season: summer
Height: 32 in
Spread: 20 in
Situation: ○
Moisture requirement: ◊
❉ ❉ ❉

Eryngium x oliverianum

159

Family: Asteraceae
Flowering season: summer
Height: 7 ft
Spread: 3 ft
Situation: ○ – ◑
Moisture requirement: ◊
✽ ✽ ✽

Hemp agrimony

Eupatorium purpureum

Herbaceous perennials include small, clump-forming plants as well as large specimens which look more like shrubs such as hemp agrimony. It does not become woody and dies down to ground level in autumn, producing new shoots again in spring. It is an imposing shrub in summer when it reaches a height of 6 ft. The dark green, lanceolate, slightly serrated leaves are arranged in whorls along the purplish stems. The tiny, bright pink to red-purple, tubular flowers are grouped in terminal rounded umbels. Hemp agrimony is native to the damp forests of North America and therefore needs damp, fertile soil, rich in humus. Although it prefers partial shade, it will also grow in a sunny position as long as the soil never dries out completely. It forms a vigorous, robust shrubby plant if the conditions are right. It is ideal for wild gardens, around ponds and in the rear of borders. It combines beautifully with *Rodgersia* and *Lythrum*. It is propagated by division in early spring or autumn.

Euphorbia

Family: Euphorbiaceae
Flowering season: spring
Height: 4 ft
Spread: 3 ft
Situation: ○
Moisture requirement: ◊
✽ ✽

Euphorbia

Euphorbia characias

The sun-loving plant is native to the Mediterranean. Even in less favored latitudes, it will develop into a magnificent bush if planted in a warm, sheltered position, for instance in front of a sunny wall, in loose, well-drained, moderately fertile soil. It is an evergreen with an upright habit, keeping its gray-green, lanceolate leaves throughout the winter. The individual shoots are biennial: the plant flowers on the previous years wood which should be cut back after flowering if seeds are not required. *E. characias ssp. Wulfenii* has greenish-yellow individual flowers with equally greenish-yellow nectar glands. It does not have the dark eyes typical of many euphorbias. This species has red-brown nectar glands. It is susceptible to cold winds and excessively fertile soil can lead to frost damage. It is advisable to protect the plant against frost in winter with a layer of bracken or other foliage. Be careful: wear sloves when handling this plant because the milky juice contained in all the parts of the plant is poisonous and causes skin irritation, so gloves should be worn when handling this plant. It is not suitable for a garden with children.

Euphorbia

Euphorbia cyparissias

This Euphorbia is native to Europe where it grows in dry, stony meadows and in dunes. It is a vigorously growing plant which spreads by means of runners wherever the conditions are right. It prefers poor, loose, well-drained soil and a sunny position. It is ideal for the larger wild garden where it can develop to its full potential. In smaller gardens its size must be controlled by the regular removal of suckers and division of the parent plant. The small, yellow-green – often also red – individual flowers are borne in dense umbels. The blue-green, linear leaves can sometimes become tinged with orange. In autumn the foliage turns yellow.
E. cyparissias is propagated by division and cuttings of basal shoots. It can also be raised from seed. Be careful and wear gloves when handling this plant because the milk-like juice contained in all the parts of the plant is poisonous and causes skin irritation, so gloves should be worn when handling this plant. It is not suitable for a garden frequented by children.

Family: Euphorbiaceae
Flowering season: spring
Height: 16 in
Spread: 16 in
Situation: ○
Moisture requirement: ◌
❄ ❄ ❄
✖

Euphorbia

Euphorbia polychroma

All show and no substance is the motto of this euphorbia: its small, yellow-green flowers are grouped in dense, terminal umbels. The flower heads are surrounded by striking, bright yellow bracts, arranged in such a way that they look like petals. This gives the otherwise inconspicuous flower heads a particular prominence. The flowers which appear in spring are produced over a period of several weeks. It has a rounded, bushy habit with slightly hairy, ovate to lanceolate, bright green leaves, tinged with red. The foliage turns a beautiful autumn color. This species is native to Central and southeastern Europe where it grows in forests and groves. It grows best in cool, fertile, chalky soil in a sunny position or partial shade. It can be propagated in many ways: by division in spring or autumn, from seed from winter to spring or by cuttings in spring. Be careful: the milk-like juice contained in all the parts of the plant is poisonous and causes skin irritation, so gloves should be worn when handling this plant. It is not suitable for a garden with children.

Family: Euphorbiaceae
Flowering season: spring
Height: 20 in
Spread: 20 in
Situation: ○ – ◑
Moisture requirement: ◍
❄ ❄ ❄

Meadowsweet
Filipendula palmata

Family: Rosaceae
Flowering season: spring/summer
Height: 32 in
Spread: 24 in
Situation: ○
Moisture requirement: ◐ – ●
❄ ❄ ❄

Filipendula is a popular plant in water gardens. It thrives in moist conditions and its pink, feathery panicles borne on tall, branched stems above the foliage are quite striking. It is ideal for planting along ponds and if the conditions are right it will soon develop into a majestic plant which also spreads quite easily by means of creeping runners.

F. palmata is native to Asia where it grows in damp meadows and wetlands in eastern Siberia, China and Japan. The dark green leaves are five-lobed and the individual leaflets deeply serrated. As might be expected, it needs loamy, moisture-retaining soil, enriched with humus and preferably a sunny position. It is propagated by division in spring or autumn, by cuttings in spring or from seed in autumn.

Blanket flower
Gaillardia × grandiflora 'Kobold'

Family: Asteraceae
Flowering season: summer/autumn
Height: 12 in
Spread: 12 in
Situation: ○
Moisture requirement: ○
❄ ❄ ❄

This gaillardia is particularly colorful and will thrive in sunny flower beds. The flower heads consist of bright red, yellow-tipped ray florets and dark red, tubular florets in the center. Its abundant flowering puts it on a par with other summer-flowering plants. However, it is important that the plant does not exhaust itself because this would shorten its lifespan. If you want to ensure prolific flowering the following year, you must feed the plant regularly during the growing season and cut it back hard in early autumn. During this 'prescribed' rest period, it will regenerate itself and develop into a bushy plant again. It should be replaced after three years. The hybrid was developed by breeders from wild species native to North America where it grows wild in the prairie. The foliage is deep green, the basal leaves are deeply cut and the stem leaves are lanceolate with smooth edges. It thrives in fertile, well-drained soil in a sunny position. It can be propagated from seed under glass at the end of the winter, by division in spring or by root cuttings in autumn.

Gaillardia x grandiflora 'Kobold'

Gentian

Gentiana sino-ornata

Those who associate gentians with Alpine landscapes will be surprised: gentians are in fact native to China and need to be protected against frost during winter, but that is the only disadvantage to this plant. If planted in the right place in the garden, it will grow happily and flower profusely. *G. sino-ornata* has a mat-forming, spreading habit. The foliage is mid-green, linear with pointed ends. The deep-blue, bell-shaped flowers are borne singly at the end of stems. This variety differs from other gentian varieties in that the trumpet-shaped flowers have interior green stripes. It thrives in moist, lime-free soil, rich in humus, in a sunny position or partial shade. It is suitable for rock gardens and at the front of herbaceous borders where it will provide welcome color at a time when other plants have stopped flowering.

Gentiana sino-ornata

i

Family: Gentianaceae
Flowering season: autumn
Height: 6 in
Spread: 12 in
Situation: ○ – ◐
Moisture requirement: 💧
❄❄

Geranium

Geranium

The geranium genus comprises a wealth of different forms: there are 300 species and countless varieties. These plants are easily cultivated, long-lived perennials, and in moderate climates will grow almost anywhere with the exception of very damp situations. Most species will do well in normal garden soils, in sun or partial shade, but they never like waterlogged soil. The leaves are usually bright green, with five lobes, and often fragrant. Sometimes the rosettes of leaves will even live through the winter. The flowers are borne in umbelliferous inflorescences, and in most species are cup-shaped, but some are star-shaped. The color spectrum ranges from white, pink and purple to blue, and certain species have decorative veining. The flowering season, depending on the species, is from spring to late summer. Geraniums are very versatile plants: low-growing species such as the bloody cranesbill (*G. x sanguineum*), which is about 8 in in height, make good ground cover, and are extremely suitable for rock gardens, troughs, or dry-stone walls; *G. himalayense* and the free-flowering *G. x magnificum* can also be combined effectively with other ornamental perennials, grasses and roses. *G. silvaticum*, which can reach a height of 30 in, does best on moist soil in partial shade, and is an excellent companion plant for shrubs and trees. Geraniums should be planted in groups for the best effect. With all species, it is a good idea to remove faded flowers and leaves to encourage new growth. The quickest and easiest way to propagate these plants is by division.

Crane's-bill

Geranium himalayense (syn. G. grandiflorum)

ⓘ

Family: Geraniaceae
Flowering season: spring/summer
Height: 12 in
Spread: 20 in
Situation: ○
Moisture requirement: ◊
❀ ❀

When in search of undemanding ground cover, most gardeners turn to flat-growing shrubs such as *Cotoneaster dammeri* or *Potentilla fruticosa* rather than a herbaceous perennial. But for sunny parts of the garden, the crane's-bill is one of the most beautiful alternatives. It is native to the Himalayas where it grows in woodland clearings and mountain meadows. It grows best in cool, fertile soil but will also tolerate dry conditions. The rootstock, with its vigorous runners, forms thick mats which suppress weeds. The purple-blue, trumpet-shaped flowers with white eyes are borne on branched stems in late spring. The bright green leaves are deeply lobed and the individual leaflets are serrated. To cover large areas as quickly as possible, lift, divide and plant again, either in early spring or late summer.

The most common variety available in nurseries is the very popular variety 'Gravetye' (syn, *G. grandiflorum* var. *alpinum*) with small leaves and large reddish-purple flowers.

Crane's-bill

Geranium × magnificum

ⓘ

Family: Geraniaceae
Flowering season: spring/summer
Height: 20 in
Spread: 24 in
Situation: ○
Moisture requirement: ◊
❀ ❀ ❀

This variety has been cultivated for a long time and was developed by breeders from species growing wild from the Caucasus to Persia. Its vigorous, bushy growth is a useful plant for controlling weeds. For best results, plant close together and allow to spread. *Geranium x magnificum* combines well with other flowering herbaceous perennials. It is particularly suitable for informal gardens with a country look. It is also very good for cut flowers.

It grows best in fertile, well-drained soil in a sunny position or partial shade. If the conditions are right, the crane's-bill will grow happily and flower profusely. The purple-blue flowers marked with dark veins are saucer-shaped and grouped in small clusters. The gray-green, hairy leaves are round and deeply lobed. The leaves are pleasantly aromatic and turn orange-red in autumn. It is propagated in early spring or late summer by dividing older plants before or after flowering.

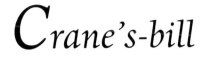

Crane's-bill

Geranium renardii

The white flowers of this crane's-bill are clearly veined with purple-brown but because these flowers are produced for only a few weeks, this variety is usually planted as an ornamental foliage plant. The gray-green, kidney-shaped leaves are lobed with serrated edges and covered all over with short, fine hairs which feel very velvety to the touch. There is no doubt that this plant is an eye-catcher even when not in bloom. It is best planted at the front of herbaceous borders or as an edging plant around borders. It looks particularly good in combination with gray-leaved plants (for instance artemisia or santolina).

G. renardii is native to the Caucasus where it grows wild in mountain meadows. It is vigorous, compact, clump-forming plant. It grows best in well-drained soil in a sunny position, but hates being waterlogged. It is propagated by division in spring or autumn or raised from seed in spring.

Family: Geraniaceae
Flowering season: spring
Height: 12 in
Spread: 12 in
Situation: ○
Moisture requirement: ◊
✽ ✽ ✽

Geranium

167

Bloody crane's-bill

Geranium sanguineum

Geranium sanguineum

ⓘ

Family: Geraniaceae
Flowering season: spring/summer
Height: 12 in
Spread: 20 in
Situation: ○ – ◖
Moisture requirement: ◌
❋ ❋ ❋

This variety is native to Europe and the Caucasus where it grows in mountain meadows. It grows best in a sunny position or partial shade and is ideal for planting in rock gardens or along paving-stones which it will soon partially cover with its trailing shoots. The soil should be chalky, warm and well-drained. If necessary, the soil can be improved by the addition of sand and lime. *G. sanguineum* has very aromatic, deeply divided, slightly hairy leaves which turn yellow in autumn. The red-purple flowers are borne singly on branched stems. There are many varieties available in nurseries which come in a wide range of pink and purple shades as well as white ('Album') – reflecting the lasting popularity of the bloody crane's-bill. It is propagated by division in autumn and by cuttings in spring. It can also be raised from seed in spring.

Crane's-bill

Geranium sylvaticum

ⓘ

Family: Geraniaceae
Flowering season: spring/summer
Height: 24 in
Spread: 16 in
Situation: ◖
Moisture requirement: ◖
❋ ❋ ❋

While the previous *Geranium* varieties all loved sunny positions, this variety prefers partial shade and moist soil. It grows throughout Europe, Turkey and the Caucasus and as far as Siberia and Central Asia where it grows in woodland, as the Latin name suggests. In the right conditions, it develops deep roots and forms a compact plant. The mid-green leaves are mostly basal and deeply lobed with serrated edges. The red-purple, saucer-shaped flowers are borne on branched stems. The species flowers prolifically over a long period. It grows best in fertile, moist soil in partial shade. It is ideally suited to shady flower beds, in front of a hedge or wall as well as under trees. It is propagated by division in spring or autumn. The 'Mayflower' with pale blue flowers and white centers. The white-flowering 'Album' are very attractive.

*A*vens

Geum coccineum

Although thornless, *Geum* is a member of the rose family. The wild species is native to Turkey, the Balkans and the Caucasus. It has a bushy, spreading habit. The dark green leaves are slightly hairy and remain on the plant throughout the winter. The basal leaves are irregularly pinnate, the terminal leaflets are kidney-shaped and larger than the lateral ones. The stem leaves are unlobed with serrated edges. The bowl-shaped flowers are produced in spring and borne singly on branched stems. The petals are orange-red with prominent yellow stamens. Avens is a floriferous plant which is easy to look after. It grows best in cool soil, rich in humus, in a sunny position. It will also grow in partial shade but will flower less profusely. It should be dead headed regularly and cut back immediately after flowering to encourage a second flowering in the autumn. Older plants are divided in autumn or spring to rejuvenate the plants or for propagation.

Geum coccineum

ℹ

Family: Rosaceae
Flowering season: spring/summer
Height: 20 in
Spread: 12 in
Situation: ◯ – ◐
Moisture requirement: ◌ – ◍
❀ ❀ ❀

*G*round ivy

Glechoma hederacea

Ground ivy is a very interesting plant because it is so versatile: it makes excellent ground cover, but can be invasive. It has a trailing or creeping habit depending on where it has been planted. This means that it is ideal for planting in window-boxes, hanging-baskets as well as ground cover in the garden. The wild species, now a protected species, is native to Europe where it grows in woods and forests. It can also be found in the Caucasus, Siberia, Central Asia and Japan. The aromatic foliage is kidney-shaped, but heart-shaped near the base, with notched margins. The wild species has plain dark green leaves but in the 'Variegata' variety they are edged with white and silver. The inconspicuous blue-purple flowers are borne in erect spikes. Ground ivy prefers fertile soil, rich in humus and partial shade. It also grows in the shade but should never be planted in full sun. If the conditions are right it will spread rapidly. If it is too invasive, it can be checked by cutting back or removing the underground runners. It is easily propagated by planting rooted runners. Be careful: this plant is poisonous.

ℹ

Family: Lamiaceae
Flowering season: spring
Height: 6 in
Spread: variable
Situation: ◐
Moisture requirement: ◌ – ◍
❀ ❀ ❀
✖

169

Glyceria

Glyceria maxima

Family: Poaceae
Flowering season: summer
Height: 32 in
Spread: variable
bank and marsh plant
Situation: ○
Moisture requirement: ●
❀ ❀ ❀

This ornamental grass is a beautiful foliage herbaceous perennial, suitable for moist areas in large gardens. It forms large, spreading clumps with erect flower spikes. The wild species, now a protected plant, is native to Europe and Asia and has strap-shaped, mid-green leaves. But the most common variety available in nurseries is 'Variegata' with cream-striped leaves, tinged with pink at the base. The tiny, inconspicuous, greenish flowers are borne in loose panicles.

Glyceria needs wet, fertile soil and a sunny position. It is ideal for planting along ponds and in shallow water up to 8 in deep. It can be propagated by division in spring.

Gypsophila

Gypsophila paniculata

Family: Caryophyllaceae
Flowering season: summer
Height: 32 in
Spread: 3 ft
Situation: ○
Moisture requirement: ◌
❀ ❀ ❀

Beautiful flower arrangements can be further enhanced by the addition of other decorative flowering plants – this is true of flower beds as well as fresh flower arrangements. Gypsophila is particularly beautiful planted in combination with brightly colored flowering plants and roses. The numerous, tiny, white flowers are borne in graceful, delicate panicles and provide a magnificent background to the neighbouring plants. The flower stems are strongly branched, slender and wiry. They make excellent cut flowers, both in fresh or dry flower arrangements.

The wild species is native to southern Europe, the Caucasus and western Siberia. They have a vigorous rootstock which grows deep into the ground and spreads well in light, sandy and deep soil. Gypsophila takes a long time to become established but once established, it is very long-lived. The leaves are blue-green, fleshy, lanceolate and pointed. It is propagated from seed or cuttings in spring. 'Bristol Fairy' is a popular variety with double white flowers which grow aller than the species.

Sneezeweed

Helenium 'Moerheim Beauty'

ⓘ

Family: Asteraceae
Flowering season: summer
Height: 32 in
Spread: 20 in
Situation: ○
Moisture requirement: ◌
✤ ✤ ✤

Many plants have been named after the sun, the most famous being the sunflower. Its botanical name *Helianthus* is derived from the Greek word for sun – *helios*. This is also true of the botanical name for sneezeweed – *Helenium* – which is indeed very sun-like: the wild form is native to North America and has bright yellow, daisy-like flowers with prominent centers. Its great popularity as a garden plant and cut flower has prompted breeders to develop varieties in yellow, orange and red shades: 'Moerheim Beauty' has copper-red flowers. These varieties look very good planted together in a sunny herbaceous border: 'Butterpat' has bright yellow flowers and 'Goldrausch' golden-yellow flowers with brown markings. They also combine beautifully with goldenrod (*Solidago*), yarrow (*Achillea*) and ornamental grasses such as *Miscanthus*.

Sneezeweed has a very erect habit, the shoots becoming slightly woody at the base. The dark green leaves are lanceolate and slightly serrated. It will grow in any garden soil but hates being waterlogged. It is propagated and rejuvenated by division in spring or autumn.

Helenium 'Moerheim Beauty'

Sunflower

Helianthus × multiflorus

Most plant-lovers first became acquainted with sunflowers in childhood, sowing the seed in a pot on the windowsill, planting them out in the garden and watching in amazement as they developed into dramatically tall flowers. This will have been the annual sunflower species which dies down after the seeds have ripened. There is no doubt that annual sunflowers are fascinating to watch as they grow taller and taller, but perennial herbaceous sunflowers such as *H. x multiflorus* are much less work. It is a floriferous perennial which lasts a long time as a cut flower. The flower heads consist of bright yellow ray florets and golden-brown tubular central florets and remain smaller than most of the annual species. The coarse leaves are dark green, lanceolate to ovate. This hybrid was developed from varieties are native to North and Central America. It grows best in well-drained, moderately fertile soil in a sunny position. In the right conditions, it can soon spread and cover large areas. The spread can be checked by cutting back the runners. *H. x multiflorus* is propagated and rejuvenated by division.

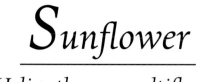

ⓘ

Family: Asteraceae
Flowering season: summer/autumn
Height: 5 ft
Spread: 24 in
Situation: ○
Moisture requirement: ◊
❃ ❃ ❃

Heliopsis

Heliopsis helianthoides

The yellow flower heads, which are very reminiscent of ox-eye daisies, flower for a very long time and look very beautiful in a vase. The flowers which are produced until well into the autumn are borne on sturdy, branched stems. The wild form which is native to North America has an upright, robust habit. The leaves are dark green, lanceolate to ovate with serrated edges. They feel quite rough because they are covered with bristly hairs. It grows best in fertile, well-drained soil in a sunny position in the garden. Regular dead heading will extend the flowering period. Heliopsis will also benefit from regular feeding. It is propagated in spring by cuttings – older plants are divided in spring or in autumn after flowering. It is advisable to rejuvenate the plant after three years by division in order to encourage flowering. Heliopsis combines beautifully with other yellow-flowering herbaceous perennials such as *Helianthus, Helenium, Rudbeckia* and *Monarda*.

ⓘ

Family: Asteraceae
Flowering season: summer
Height: 3 ft
Spread: 24 in
Situation: ○
Moisture requirement: ◊
❃ ❃ ❃

Christmas rose

Helleborus niger

ⓘ

Family: Ranunculaceae
Flowering season: winter
Height: 12 in
Spread: 12 in
Situation: ◑
Moisture requirement: ◐
❄ ❄ ❄
✖

The Christmas rose is one of the best known herbaceous perennials. It owes its name to its extraordinary flowering time. Its nodding, white flowers do not always flower exactly at Christmas, but they appear during the winter or early spring, depending on the weather. Anyone seeing only the white flowers might wonder about the plant's Latin name *nige*r – which means black – but looking at the roots the reason will soon become obvious.

The wild species is native to the Alps and Carpathian mountains. It is an evergreen, clump-forming perennial which spreads through rhizomes. The dark green, glossy leaves are deeply lobed with serrated edges and relatively hardy but must be protected against frost in severe weather. The terminal flowers which are borne singly or in clusters of two and three are also excellent cut flowers. Christmas roses grow best in deep, moist, fertile, chalky soil, enriched with humus in a sheltered position, for instance in front of a wall or a fence. It is propagated by division in late summer or raised from seed immediately after the seeds have ripened. Be careful: this plant is poisonous.

174

Lenten rose

Helleborus orientalis

The early flowering season of Lenten roses is one of the reasons why they are so popular in gardens. There are many varieties available on the market. *H. orientalis* self-seeds very easily, producing white, pink, red and green flowers. It is not surprising that this wide range of colors should arouse the interest of collectors. The wild species is native to southeastern Europe and the Caucasus. It is a vigorously, spreading plant with dense evergreen foliage on sturdy stems. The glossy, basal leaves are dark green, deeply divided and slightly serrated. The nodding, saucer-shaped flowers are borne singly. They are white, tinged with green and have prominent, bright stamens. Lenten roses grow best in moist, fertile, chalky, loamy soil, rich in humus and in partial shade. If the soil is moist enough, it will also grow in a sunny position. It can be raised from seed immediately after the seeds have ripened, but it also self-seeds very easily.

🛈

Family: Ranunculaceae
Flowering season: winter/spring
Height: 20 in
Spread: 20 in
Situation: ◑
Moisture requirement: ◐
❄ ❄ ❄
✖

175

Tawny day lily

Hemerocallis fulva

It is not easy to choose the right kind of day lily for the garden because the choice of varieties and hybrids is so vast. *H. fulva* is undoubtedly one of the most beautiful wild species. Native to China and Japan, it was later introduced into Europe. It is a clump-forming plant with fleshy roots and strap-shaped, mid-green, ridged, arching leaves – the habit is very reminiscent of that of ornamental grasses. The trumpet-shaped flowers are similar to lilies, but each one only flowers for one or two days. However, since the buds do not open all at the same time, the flowering period lasts for several weeks. The orange-brown flowers are borne in clusters on tall, branched stems from June to August. By also planting early-flowering varieties, the flowering season can be extended. The position must be chosen with great care because day lilies must be able to grow without being disturbed. They grow best in fertile soil in a sunny position or partial shade. Propagation is by division in spring or autumn.

ⓘ

Family: Hemerocallidaceae
Flowering season: summer
Height: 3 ft
Spread: 30 in
Situation: ○ – ◐
Moisture requirement: ◌ – ◗
❀ ❀ ❀

Hemerocallis lilioasphodelus

ⓘ

Family: Hemerocallidaceae
Flowering season: spring
Height: 24 in
Spread: 24 in
Situation: ○ – ◐
Moisture requirement: ◌ – ◗
❀ ❀ ❀
❀

Day lily

Hemerocallis lilioasphodelus (syn. H. flava)

This variety has been cultivated for a very long time. In China, its country of origin, it has been grown for generations as an ornamental and medicinal plant which later became naturalised in southeastern Europe. It is a large, vigorous, clump-forming, spreading plant with fleshy roots and ridged, strap-shaped, arching leaves. The yellow, bell to funnel-shaped flowers have short stalks and are borne in large clusters on long stems. They are not only very beautiful but they are also very fragrant. *H. lilioasphodelus* thrives in cool, fertile soil in a sunny position or in partial shade. It looks very impressive in large groups and is ideal for planting near ponds. It is very important to plant them where they will be able to spread without being moved. The are also ideally suited to wild gardens because they naturalise very easily. They are propagated by division in autumn. A useful tip when growing day lilies: buds which do not open should be removed because it is a sign of pest infestation.

Day lily

Hemerocallis 'Marion Vaughn'

Day lilies are very popular plants both among gardeners and breeders. This is reflected in the very large number of varieties available. Most varieties have creamy-white, yellow, orange or reddish flowers, but there are a few with blue-purple flowers. Some flowers have stripes and many of them are double – the passion for collecting knows no limit. The particularly floriferous and robust variety 'Marion Vaughn' is deliciously fragrant with pale yellow, funnel-shaped flowers and petals with a creamy, raised midrib which only last a day or two. Although they are not suitable as cut flowers, they look very striking in the garden. They grow best in cool, fertile soil in a sunny position or partial shade. This variety is less invasive than the wild species and therefore very popular in small gardens. It is propagated by division in spring or late autumn.

Family: Hemerocallidaceae
Flowering season: summer
Height: 32 in
Spread: 24 in
Situation: ○ – ◑
Moisture requirement: ◊ – ◖
❋ ❋ ❋
✿

Coral flower

Heuchera micrantha diversifolia 'Palace Purple'

Coral flowers are a good choice when colorful foliage is wanted. The leaves are basal, lobed and toothed, and they are dark red-purple with a metallic sheen. The plant forms low but spreading clumps of leaves and shoots which become a little woody at the base. In the right conditions it soon covers a large area so that it is ideal as ground cover or to fill gaps between other plants. Coral flowers look very good with ferns or hostas.
This variety has been developed from the North American wild species. It grows best in damp, well-drained soil in partial shade. The tiny, white, bell-shaped flowers which are borne in loose panicles on red-brown, wiry stems appear in spring. The elegant panicles also look very decorative in fresh flower arrangements. Only part of the leaves die off in winter because the plant is in fact semi-evergreen. That is why it must not be completely cut back in autumn. Only the dead flowers and leaves should be removed. It is propagated by division or cuttings in summer after the plant has finished flowering.

Family: Saxifragaceae
Flowering season: spring/summer
Height: 20 in
Spread: 16 in
Situation: ◑
Moisture requirement: ◖
❋ ❋ ❋

Plantain lily

Hosta species and hybrids

This is a genus of approximately 70 species which are native to China, Japan and Korea. Many of these species are cultivated because of their beautiful basal, glossy, lanceolate to heart-shaped foliage. Hostas form large clumps with fleshy leaves and make excellent ground cover but they also look very good on their own or in tubs. There are numerous varieties with a wide range of variegated foliage, the green leaves marked with white, cream or bright green. Variegated hostas are ideal for brightening up partially shaded areas in the garden. The leaves are often used in flower arrangements. Hostas prefer moist, fertile, loamy soil and a sunny position or partial shade. They look very good with astilbes. They come out rather late in spring which is why it is advisable to mark the place where they are so that the rootstocks does not get damaged by accident when gardening around them. The trumpet-shaped, white, bluish or purple flowers are borne in clusters. The plant is propagated by division in autumn; the fleshy roots of older plants are quite tough so a knife is sometimes needed. Each piece must have at least one eye. It is vitally important to protect hostas from slugs and snails, especially during wet summers.

There are numerous variegated varieties of *H. fortunei* such as 'Aureomarginata' which has mid-green leaves with creamy-white edges and violet flowers.

ⓘ

Family: Hostaceae
Flowering season: summer/autumn
Height: variable
Spread: variable
Situation: ○ – ◑
Moisture requirement: ◐
❀ ❀ ❀

179

Hosta

Hosta 'Hadspen Blue'

Family: Hostaceae
Flowering season: summer
Height: 12 in
Spread: 20 in
Situation: ◐
Moisture requirement:
❄❄❄

Low-growing hostas are ideal as ground cover but they also look good in tubs or pots and will do well even in a north-facing window box. 'Hadspen Blue' is a slow growing variety with blue-green, heart-shaped leaves with marked veins and gray blooms. The leaves can grow up to 6 inches wide. The violet, trumpet-shaped flowers are borne in dense racemes on tall stems, well above the foliage. The name Hadspen is a tribute to a country estate near Castle Cary in Somerset in southern England. The gardens and attached nursery are open to the public and of particular interest to hosta lovers, containing a wide collection of the plants.

'Hadspen Blue' grows best in damp, well-drained, fertile soil. A layer of mulch will ensure that the soil remains evenly moist. Hostas are propagated by division in late summer or early spring. Snails and slugs can cause a lot of damage to the leaves in a wet summer.

Hosta 'Hadspen Blue'

Hosta

Hosta sieboldiana

This variety is one of the most impressive of all the hostas. It is a slow-growing variety native to Japan, and it forms a large clump with a fleshy rootstock and beautiful large, bluish-gray leaves, ovate to heart-shaped with prominent veins which can grow up to 18 in long. In summer, it produces bluish-white, bell-shaped flowers, borne in racemes which rise just above the foliage. This variety looks best planted on its own so as to make the most of the beautiful foliage. Older plants can be real eye-catchers but when choosing a place to plant them, it is worth remembering that hostas only come out in late spring, so the site will look bare for quite a long time.

H. sieboldiana grows best in cool, fertile soil in partial shade. If planted in full sun, the leaves will become gray and unsightly. It can be propagated by division in spring or autumn. The dead leaves should be removed in autumn to prevent them from rotting in wet weather.

Family: Hostaceae
Flowering season: summer
Height: 24 in
Spread: 3 ft
Situation: ◐
Moisture requirement: ◊
❋ ❋ ❋

Hosta sieboldiana

181

Candytuft

Iberis sempervirens

i

Family: Brassicaceae
Flowering season: spring
Height: 12 in
Spread: 16 in
Situation: ○
Moisture requirement: ◊ – ◆
❄❄❄

Candytuft is an amazing sight when it flowers in spring, the foliage being almost completely concealed by a mass of snow-white flowers. In addition, it is a very undemanding plant which is easy to grow – what more could one want? *I. sempervirens* is native to southern Europe and Turkey. Strictly speaking, this is not a true herbaceous perennial but a sub-shrub because the shoots become woody. It is an evergreen with dark green, linear leaves with smooth edges. It is densely branched with a bushy, spreading habit and arching stems.

The cross-shaped flowers do best on lime soil which is not too rich. It looks especially beautiful in paving which it partially covers, flourishing in the gaps between the stones. Propagation is by the sowing in spring and by division in the autumn. The variety 'Schneeflocke' (syn. 'Snowflake') is also to be recommended because it remains lower than the type at up to 10 inches and grows more compactly.

Inula

Inula hookeri

i

Family: Asteraceae
Flowering season: summer
Height: 30 in
Spread: 18 in
Situation: ○ – ◐
Moisture requirement: ◊ – ◆
❄❄❄

As well as appealing to people, this vigorous perennial with its mass of scented, brilliant yellow flowers is also attractive to bees and other insects. This ecological benefit is another good reason for planting *I. hooker* which will thrive on well-drained soil in a sunny or partially shaded herbaceous border a permeable soil. It will rapidly form a heavy clump and it will survive periods of drought without problems. It also looks handsome planted naturally in groups in large gardens which will attract bees in profusion.

The plant is native to mountainous regions of the Himalayas. The free-growing foliage consists of leathery, elliptical to lanceolate, serrated, hairy leaves. The daisy-like flowers have a central disk surrounded by long, very narrow, yellow petals. The orange-yellow center is formed of short, tubular disc florets. The flower heads appear individually or in bunches on slim, stiff stems growing above the leaves. Propagation is by sowing or division in spring.

Inula hookeri

Red-hot poker

Kniphofia caulescens

The red-hot poker adds grandeur to the perennial garden. The tall flower spikes are an impressive attraction in sunny herbaceous borders as well as indoors in vases. The individual small tubular flowers are densely packed together into large terminal spikes. The flowers are initially coral-red, turning to creamy white as they open. Since they open sequentially from the bottom of the spike, the flower heads have a multicolored appearance during the flowering season.

Kniphofia caulescens is from heavy growth and develops a fleshy rootstock. Its basal, leathery, strap-shaped, arching, gray-blue leaves are reminiscent of ornamental grasses. Native to the mountain regions of South Africa, the plant requires a warm, sheltered location. The soil should be fertile, humus-rich and well-drained, since the fleshy rootstock is very sensitive to being waterlogged. In the growing season, the soil should be watered to keep it moist. Some winter protection against frost and continuous rain is necessary. The stems of the clump can be tied together so that the rain does not fall inside it. The perennial is pruned only in spring. It can be increased by division after the flowering season is over.

ⓘ

Family: Asphodelaceae
Flowering season: summer/autumn
Height: 4 ft
Spread: 24 in
Situation: ○
Moisture requirement: 💧
❄ ❄

183

Dead nettle

Lamium maculatum

ⓘ

Family: Lamiaceae
Flowering season: spring/summer
Height: 8 in
Spread: various
Situation: ◯ – ◐
Moisture requirement: ◗
❄ ❄ ❄

Uncovered soil quickly dries out and inevitably attracts weeds. If on the other hand it is given a close covering of vegetation, the moisture will be preserved and unwanted seedlings have hardly a chance. Ground cover plants are therefore invaluable in a low-maintenance garden. This decorative dead nettle species, *L. maculatum*, is an excellent choice for shady, moist areas of the garden. It forms dense carpets of full, green leaves with a silvery pattern. The perennial is semi-evergreen, so it should not be pruned in the autumn; only the dried up shoots should be removed. The individual leaves are oval to heart-shaped and grow freely. In spring, little pink to red to purple tubular flowers appear continuously in clusters at the end of the stems.

The original distribution of *Lamium maculatum* extends all the way from Europe to North Africa and Asia Minor. It favors moist, humus-rich soils in partial shade or shade and it does well among trees and shrubs. It is increased by division in spring or autumn or by cuttings until late spring.

Marguerite, ox-eye daisy

Leucanthemum vulgare
(syn. Chrysanthemum leucanthemum)

ⓘ

Family: Asteraceae
Flowering season: spring
Height: 36 in
Spread: 24 in
Situation: ◯
Moisture requirement: ◊ – ◗
❄ ❄ ❄

The marguerite is an essential plant in a low-maintenance informal country garden. The brilliant white blossoms are excellent planted in the herbaceous border or in groups in contrast with colorful perennials such as phlox and delphiniums, which they set off to perfection. The natural distribution of the species extends from Europe through the Caucasus to Siberia, and it is also found in North America. It has been cultivated throughout the world for so long that it no longer seems to give the impression of a wild plant.

The marguerite is easy to grow and thrives in all normal garden soils in sunny situations. It quickly forms large, bush-like clumps with runners. The foliage is dark green, the basal leaves being spoon-shaped and deeply serrated, while the stem leaves have less pronounced serration or none at all. The terminal flower heads consist of long, white petals surrounding a center of yellow disc florets. The marguerite is short-lived, but it can be increased by division in spring or autumn. It self-seeds freely. Among the most beautiful varieties of marguerite is *L. x Superbum* 'Wirral Supreme' which has double flowers.

Lamium maculatum

*K*ansas gay feather

Liatris spicata

In planning the garden, it is good idea to have some vigorous perennials which look handsome in themselves but also provide bunches of cut flowers for flower arrangements indoors. The perennial *L. spicata* is excellent for the purpose, with its handsome red to mauve flowers of strikingly unusual form. It is ideal for sunny beds and can also provide decoration on verandas and terraces in containers. It combines well with grasses such as fountain grass, Pennisetum, and the cone flower, *Rudbeckia*.

Native to the meadows of North America, it is long-lived with a fleshy rootstock and an upright habit. The leaves are straight and reminiscent of ornamental grasses. The long, basal leaves form a bush, while the leaves on the flowering shoots are shorter. The red to mauve blossoms are formed in dense, cylindrical spikes 8 in long on stiff stems. In contrast to most other perennials, the flowers open from the top of the spike downwards. So when the final flowers open at the lower end of the spike, the top ones have already bloomed, but they are sometimes taken for flower buds by inexperienced observers. The plant enjoys a fertile soil. Older plants can be increased by division in the spring.

🛈

Family: Asteraceae
Flowering season: summer
Height: 24 in
Spread: 12 in
Situation: ○
Moisture requirement: ○ – ◐
❄ ❄ ❄

185

Sea lavender

Limonium latifolium (syn. L. platyphyllum)

Family: Plumbaginaceae
Flowering season: spring/summer
Height: 32 in
Spread: 18 in
Situation: ○
Moisture requirement: ◐
❀ ❀ ❀

Good accompanying plants play an important role and they should not be ignored in designing the garden. During its flowering season, the sea lavender is covered with a cloud of little, lavender-colored flowers. The branching flower heads are supported by wiry stems growing from basal rosettes. The flower clusters can be cut for immediate use in a vase indoors or they can be dried and used in dried flower arrangements. The leathery leaves are dark green, spoon-shaped to elliptical and the growing clump becomes woody with time.

The natural distribution of the species extends from Central and southeast Europe as far as southern Russia, flourishing in dry meadows. In the garden, it also requires a well-drained soil, ideally an alkaline sandy soil. It should be planted in a warm situation in full sun; it happily survives occasional periods of drought. It combines very well with gray-leaved perennials. It can be increased by sowing in spring, dividing older plants in autumn, or by root cuttings in winter.

Lobelia

Lobelia × speciosa

Family: Campanulaceae
Flowering season: summer
Height: 3 ft
Spread: 12 in
Situation: ○ – ◐
Moisture requirement: ◐ – ◑
❀ ❀

Lobelien are a guarantee of glowing color in the garden. The blue flowering annual bedding plant and balcony plant known as trailing lobelia (L. erinus) is widespread but the perennial lobelias (Lobelia x speciosa) are less well known. Numerous varieties are offered by specialist nurseries, and those with fiery red, red-violet and pink flowers are particularly popular. However, the short-lived perennials require a little effort if they are not simply to be replaced with new ones each spring. They are sensitive to longer periods of frost and they must be very well protected with a mulch or over-wintered in a light, cool, frost-free room. After two years the amount of flowering reduces.

The leaves of these lobelias are mostly full green, but the upper surface of the leaves of some varieties are red or reddish-brown. The leaves are predominantly downward-pointing, oval-shaped and slightly hairy. Up to 1 ft tall, they produce numerous spikes of flowers in various colors. These lobelias are best planted in fertile, humus-rich garden soil. Propagation is by division in spring.

Lupinus

Garden lupin

Lupinus hybrids

Garden lupins are old cottage garden plants. They are derived from the many-leaved lupin *L. polyphyllus*, an economically useful plant home native to North America. They are used in the vegetable-growing industry as an intermediate crop to improve soil quality, since it has the ability to increase the nitrogen content of the soil with the aid of the bacteria in its roots. The perennial varieties for the garden offer a wide choice of attractively colored, or frequently bicolored, flowers arranged in dense spikes which flower continuously. They form bushes of dark green, sometimes bluish colored foliage consisting of palmate leaves; the individual leaflets being oval to lanceolate.

Lupins prefer a deep, fertile, well-drained, humus-rich neutral to slightly acid soil in full sun. Regular applications of compost are rewarding. Since the fine foliage appears early in the year, they are excellent plants for herbaceous borders. Faded blooms should be cut off immediately so that the plant's strength is not wasted forming seeds. Propagate with basal cuttings taken from non-flowering side shoots in spring.

ⓘ

Family: Fabaceae
Flowering season: spring/summer
Height: 32 in
Spread: 20 in
Situation: ○
Moisture requirement: ◌
❄ ❄ ❄

187

Rose campion

Lychnis coronaria

ⓘ

Family: Caryophyllaceae
Flowering season: spring/summer
Height: 24 in
Spread: 16 in
Situation: ○
Moisture requirement: ○
❊ ❊ ❊

With a new garden there is always a great demand for quick results. The problem is that trees and shrubs are mostly bought as young plants and will take several years to achieve their desired potential. An interim solution can be provided by summer-flowering perennials such as this rose campion gives a bright and colorful effect when planted in groups. The perennial is short-lived, however, quickly achieving its best performance. Even in its first year it will produce numerous magenta flowers in the first year and it self-seeds very easily. The individual saucer-shaped flowers are admittedly small but they open in loosely branched clusters raised on gray stalks. The rosettes of predominantly basal leaves are silvery-gray ovate to lanceolate, making dense foliage.

The perennial is native to stony areas in southeast Europe, Central Asia and the Himalayas. It likes a sunny space with well-drained soil. Particularly in winter, waterlogged soil can lead to rotting of the roots. Dead plants should be removed in spring; self-sown seedlings can be planted in the corresponding holes. Conscious propagation can be by seed sown in the spring or by division of the plants in late summer.

Gooseneck loosestrife

Lysimachia clethroides

ⓘ

Family: Primulaceae
Flowering season: spring/summer
Height: 3 ft
Spread: 24 in
Situation: ○ – ◑
Moisture requirement: ◐
❊ ❊ ❊

Lysimachia virtually looks after itself in the garden with minimum attention so long as it is planted in the right situation. After a phase of acclimatisation, the perennial will thrive in sunny or partially shaded parts of the garden in moist and fertile soil. In the best location, it tends to spread rampantly with creeping stems, but this can be controlled by division.

The wild perennial is native to China and Japan. Its freely-appearing leaves are light green, lanceolate to ovate, turning to an orange-red color in the autumn. In bloom it has a striking appearance with its numerous, tiny, white, star-shaped flowers opening continuously in late summer on dense arching flower spikes which resemble a gooses' necks. As the flowering period continues the spikes straighten up. Lysimachia looks very beautiful next to water and associates well with day lilies (*Hemerocallis*), *Rodgersia* and knotgrass (*Bistorta*). Propagation is by root cuttings taken in spring.

Dotted loosestrife

Lysimachia punctata

Many perennials come into their heyday with their summer flowers and this is very true of the dotted loosestrife. Its clusters of golden yellow flowers on upright spikes provide a display for more than two months, after creating an energy reserve for the next season. The flower spikes have a very natural appearance, combining well with bergamot (*Monarda*) or knotgrass (*Bistorta*), and they can also be used for cut flowers. The full, green, elliptical pointed leaves appear freely in pairs or whorls on the flowering stems.

L. punctata is native to Central and southeast Europe where it spreads naturally in river banks and marshy areas. Over the years, it will form bushy groups, but it is not rampant. If required, it can be one reduced or increased by division of the clumps in spring or autumn. The ideal situation is a moist, fertile soil in the partial shade; a sunny location is also possible if the soil is moist enough. The plant is ideal for planting at the edges of ponds.

🛈

Family: Primulaceae
Flowering season: spring/summer
Height: 3 ft
Spread: 24 in
Situation: ○ – ◑
Moisture requirement: ◗
❄ ❄ ❄

Loosestrife

Lythrum virgatum

Lythrum virgatum

Permanently moist garden soil is hopeless for growing geraniums, petunias or African marigolds. But instead of trying to dry and firm the soil by drainage, it is also possible to choose plants which particularly enjoy these conditions. *L. virgatum* is a beautiful choice for moist to wet, fertile soils in sunny or partially shaded situations. It thrives in moist borders and boggy meadows, perhaps in combination with certain irises (*Iris sibirica*), gooseneck loosestrife (*Lysimachia clethroides*) or *Filipendula*. It can be planted even in the wet soil at the edge of a garden pond. The plant is native to Central and Eastern Europe. It develops into a clump with woody shoots growing from the base. Its flowers are bright purple-red carried in slender spikes on tall stems. They look very natural in spite of their striking color. The lanceolate, dark green leaves cover the flowering stems. Propagation is by cuttings in spring from non-flowering side shoots or by division of clumps in autumn or spring.

ⓘ

Family: Lythraceae
Flowering season: summer
Height: 3 ft
Spread: 20 in
bank or marsh plant
Situation: ◯ – ◑
Moisture requirement: ◐ – ●
❀ ❀ ❀

Plume poppy

Macleaya cordata

For particularly striking garden design, a good rule is to use dramatic or unique plants like the plume poppy which has an unusual appearance and forms an imposing bush. It is hard to believe that it is actually a member of the poppy family. When fully grown, it has a rounded structure with large, decorative, rounded or heart-shaped leaves with serrated lobes, and above them, elegant, feathery flower plumes. Its form and its subdued coloring work best against a neutral background, such as a wall, a fence or a hedge. The individual small flowers are bright pink and are carried on ochre stems. The upper sides of the leaves are blue-green while the undersides look gray-green because of their hairs. The whole plant contains an orange-brown latex-like juice. *Macleaya cordata* is a wild perennial native to China and Japan. It prefers a moist soil and sunny locations. Under favorable conditions it can become rampant; if so, prompt intervention is desirable, cutting the underground runners. Propagate by, dividing the clumps in the spring or autumn.

ⓘ

Family: Papaveraceae
Flowering season: summer
Height: 7 ft
Spread: 4 ft
Situation: ◯
Moisture requirement: ◐
❀ ❀ ❀

190

Musk mallow

Malva moschata

Many classics simply never go out of fashion. This is true of many garden plants and of mallows in particular. For generations, they have been found in cottage gardens together with their close relative, the hollyhock (*Alcea rosea*). The natural distribution of the musk mallow extends from Europe to northwest Africa and Asia Minor. It forms a bush with woody shoots branching out richly from the base. It is popular for its bright pink, flat, saucer-shaped flowers, which appear in clusters which are also very good for cutting. The flower buds open themselves sequentially over many weeks. Also available is a white-flowering variety, 'Alba'. The finely divided, kidney-shaped leaves of *M. moschata* smell slightly of musk.

Mallows may make no special demands for their situation and fertile garden soil in sun or partial shade suit them well. In spring, they can be propagated by seeds sown in spring or by cuttings from non-flowering shoots taken in the early summer.

ℹ

Family: Malvaceae
Flowering season: spring / summer
Height: 24 in
Spread: 16 in
Situation: ○ – ◑
Moisture requirement: ◌ – ◖
❄ ❄ ❄

Malva moschata with Lavandula angustifolia

191

Shuttlecock fern, ostrich fern

Matteuccia struthiopteris

Family: Woodsiaceae
Flowering season: summer
Height: 3 ft
Spread: 20 in
Situation: ○ – ◑
Moisture requirement: ◊
❀ ❀ ❀

Many perennials had already conquered large parts of the world on their own before they were discovered as garden plants. The shuttlecock or ostrich fern is distributed throughout almost the whole of the northern temperate zone. In riverside forests in the wild as well as in the garden, it thrives in moist, partially shaded regions. In suitable situations, it can form large thickets through its invasive underground rhizomes. It is very suitable for the water garden, but it must not be waterlogged. The soil should be humus-rich and neutral or slightly acid. In small gardens, it should be thinned regularly. The fern is a marvellous sight when the young, pale green, snail-shaped crosiers unfurl themselves in spring. Once fully unfurled, the pinnate fronds bend outwards, forming a slightly funnel-shaped clump which looks like a shuttlecock – hence one of its common names. The individual fronds are lanceolate; they do not develop any spores because they are sterile. For reproduction, the fern forms fertile fronds in the centre of the funnel. These are green at first, turning brown when mature, and look a little like ostrich feathers. Propagation by sowing spores is time-consuming and difficult; it is better and easier to divide the crown in the autumn.

Blue poppy

Meconopsis grandis

Family: Papaveraceae
Flowering season: spring
Height: 4 ft
Spread: 20 in
Situation: ◑ – ●
Moisture requirement: ◊
❀ ❀ ❀

True blue is an unusual color in plants and the sight of it must have made the plant-collector's heart beat faster. With its blue flowers, *M. grandis* is an even more exciting find, since blue poppies are a particular rarity and no doubt all the more sought-after. The perennial large meconopsis is available from specialist nurseries. It belongs to the same family as the familiar domestic poppy (*Papaver rhoeas*) and its nodding, flat, cup-shaped flowers with their silky petals are similar in form, but bright azure blue. Its orange-yellow stamens make a beautiful contrast, while the sturdy stalks are reddish-brown when grown.
The perennial is native to the Himalayas and needs acidic soil with plenty of leaf mould, and a cool, sheltered situation in partial shade. It grows erect and has green, mainly basal leaves growing in rosettes. The individual leaves are ellipti-

Meconopsis grandis

cal, serrated and hairy. This poppy is short-lived and should be propagated by division after flowering. If it does not have enough moisture, it dies without forming seeds. Another blue-flowering poppy species is *M. betonicifolia*, but its flowers are smaller.

Mertensia

Mertensia simplicissima

These ground cover plants love the sun and tolerate extreme dryness. *M. simplicissimus* is a native of the sandy coastal regions of Japan and develop low, creeping carpets of dense shoots which suppress weeds. So to avoid the problems of regular garden watering during the warm summer months, this plant is an excellent choice. The soil should be poor and very well-drained, which can be achieved by adding sand and grit to ordinary garden soil. The plant has fleshy, blue-gray, round to spatula-shaped leaves which grow in rosettes. It even thrives in gaps between stones. In summer, the rather inconspicuous, blue, tubular flowers open all together at the end of upright, flowering shoots. Propagation is by dividing the plants in spring.

Family: *Boraginaceae*
Flowering season: *summer / autumn*
Height: *12 in*
Spread: *12 in*
Situation: ○
Moisture requirement: ○
❄ ❄ ❄

Miscanthus sinensis, in the front

Miscanthus

Miscanthus sinensis 'Silberfeder'

ⓘ

Family: Poaceae
Flowering season: summer/autumn
Height: 7 ft
Spread: 5 ft
Situation: ○
Moisture requirement: ○ – ◕
❋ ❋ ❋

Tall, decorative grasses such as miscanthus make attractive individual feature plants. Feathery flowers appear at the end of the garden season, making a filigree attraction which will survive wind and weather for a long time. Alternatively, they can be cut off in the autumn, dried and used in flower arrangements. The actual pruning should not be done until the early spring because the leaves serve as winter protection. The plant is very effective as a background to a border. The original species is native to China and has been used in Europe to create over 100 hybrids. Today, there are varieties with different growth heights and flower colors, and one (*M. s.* 'Zebrinus') with a striking leaf pattern of golden horizontal markings. A breeder who has specialised in this plant is Ernst Pagels of Eastern Friesland in the Netherlands who has created a long list of successful varieties. The leaves of the variety 'Silberfeder' are strap-shaped, arching and ornamented with a white central marking. The tiny flowers are first pink and later become silvery. They are carried in loose, feathery panicles at the end of the stems. Miscanthus prefers fertile, dry to fresh soil in a sunny position. It is increased by division in spring.

Water forget-me-not

Myosotis palustris (syn. M. scorpiodes)

The biennial forget-me-not *M. sylvatica* will be familiar to all plant lovers since childhood, but there are also perennial relatives. The flowers of the water forget-me-not are azure blue with yellow eyes, form in loose clusters appearing as beautiful bunches in spring. The plants make spreading clumps with free-growing alternate lanceolate leaves. As both the common and the botanical name suggest, *M. palustris* (Latin for 'marshy'), the water forget-me-not requires a moist situation. The plant is native to Europe, Turkey and Siberia. It is suitable as a ground cover plant in a water garden and for planting at pond edges. In suitable situations, it freely self-seeds itself and it can be increased intentionally by sowing seed or taking cuttings immediately after flowering. It combines beautifully with primulas (*Primula pulverulenta*), the ostrich fern (*Matteuccia*), the sensitive fern (*Onoclea*) and the globe flower (*Trollius*).

ⓘ

Family: Boraginaceae
Flowering season: spring/summer
Height: 12 in
Spread: 8 in
Situation: ○
Moisture requirement: ◐ – ●
✤ ✤ ✤

Yellow water lily

Nuphar lutea

The domestic yellow water lily is an aquatic plant with floating leaves reminiscent of true water lilies (*Nymphaea*) and a vigorously creeping rootstock. It is native to still or gently flowing waters in Europe, Asia Minor, Central Asia and Siberia, but pollution has caused its decline in the wild. The species is only suitable for larger garden ponds, ideally with a depth of 7 ft. In smaller ponds, it is better to plant a dwarf variety of the true water lily (*Nymphaea* hybrids, for instance, 'Chromatella' with bright yellow flowers).

The flowers of the yellow water lily are bright yellow, cup-shaped and similar to those of the globe flower (*Trollius*). They are scented and project on stems above the water. The dark green leaves are heart-shaped, tending to circular. When the water level is low, they too will project above the water surface on long stalks. It should be planted in a fertile aquatic compost and can be increased by division in spring or autumn.

ⓘ

Family: Nymphaeaceae
Flowering season: summer
Water depth: to 10 ft
Spread: 7 ft
water plant
Situation: ○
Moisture requirement: ●
✤ ✤ ✤

Nymphaea alba (Monet's Garden, Giverny)

*C*ommon white water lily

Nymphaea alba

ℹ

Family: Nymphaeaceae
Flowering season: summer
Water depth: 2–7 ft
Spread: 7 ft
water plant
Situation: ○
Moisture requirement: ◗
✿ ✿ ✿

Who woudn't recognize the common white water lily? Numerous varieties with yellow, pink or red flowers all trace their ancestry back to the white water lily. This species is native to Europe, Asia Minor and the Caucasus and thrives in still, deep water. The scented flower is completely white with yellow stamens; initially, it is cup-shaped, but later opens further, giving it a star-shaped appearance. The rounded, shiny, floating leaves on long leaf stalks and reddish in the young stage and later take on their mid green color. The deep split which divides the leaf into two lobes is typical.

Water lilies form a branching rootstock. They need sun in order to form many flower buds. The preferred depth depends on the size of the rootstock; young plants are first inserted only into aquatic soil a maximum of 10 in below the water level. Provided that the water does not freeze completely in winter, water lilies can survive frost. They can be increased by division in the spring. A dwarf water lily that thrives even in large ponds is the deep red flowering *Nymphaea* 'Froebelii.'

Blue-eyed Mary

Omphalodes verna

O. verna, or blue-eyed Mary, is a ground cover plant suitable for partially shaded parts of the garden. It can very good under trees, planted in humus-rich soil in front of walls or hedges which throw a shadow on it. The species is a woodland plant native to southeast Europe. It spreads by developing numerous runners so that with time it will cover the ground with a covering of green leaves, reliably suppressing weeds. Its leaves are light green, lanceolate to heart-shaped, carried on long stalks. In spring, tiny, azure blue flowers with white eyes open in loose clusters all over it; they are slightly reminiscent of its distant relative, the forget-me-not.

O. verna combines happily with ferns and it is especially beautiful as an under-planting for azaleas and rhododendrons. It is increased by division in autumn.

ℹ

Family: Boraginaceae
Flowering season: spring
Height: 8 in
Spread: 8 in
Situation: ◗
Moisture requirement: ◌ – ◗
❄ ❄ ❄

Royal fern

Osmunda regalis

The royal fern is one of the largest ferns in the world and at the same time one of the most beautiful. The fronds of old specimens can be up to 7 ft long. It is found in both northern and southern temperate zones. It develops a thick rhizome which rises upright above the soil when the fern is older. The freely produced, light green, sterile fronds are pinnate or bipinnate, the leaflets are oval or oblong, and bend outwards. The fertile fronds appear in the center, enclosed by the infertile fronds. The upper half carries spore capsules which can be recognized by their light brown color.

The royal fern needs a moist, humus-rich neutral to acid soil in a partially or completely shaded situation. It is ideal for planting at the edges of ponds so long as it is not waterlogged. It is increased mainly by sowing the spores as soon as they are mature in late spring, since the heavy rhizomes cannot be successfully divided.

ℹ

Family: Osmundaceae
Flowering season: summer
Height: 5 ft
Spread: 32 in
Situation: ◗
Moisture requirement: ◗
❄ ❄ ❄

Peony

Paeonia species and hybrids

The genus *Paeonia* consist of about 30 species, which in turn have produced a large and increasing number of varieties. Most of them are herbaceous perennials, but there are also upright deciduous shrubs known as tree peonies. The area of natural distribution of the genus ranges throughout the temperate regions of Europe, Asia Minor and Asia. Particularly in China, the Asiatic species such as *P. lutea* and *P. suffruticosa* have been grown in gardens for more than 1,000 years. From this ancient tradition, some of the most beautiful varieties have been raised. At first only the true peony known as *P. officinalis* was grown in gardens in Europe.

The peony varieties are divided into groups according to the respective wild species from which they originate. The largest is still the Paeonia Officinalis group. However, the most important today is the Paeonia Lactiflora group to which most of the perennial peonies grown in Europe belong. In addition, tree peonies are increasingly available: these mostly belong to the Paeonia Suffruticosa group, and more rarely to the Paeonia Lutea group.

The flower colors of peonies are bright, extending from white and yellow to pink, red and deep red shades. According to the number of petals, the anemone flowers are described as single, semi-double and double. Peonies require a neutral to acid, deep, well-dug, fertile soil. They are long-lived plants which, left to themselves will increase happily over decades in the same position. They should be planted in early autumn and propagated by sowing, division or cuttings. Caution! All parts of the peony can cause illness if eaten.

ⓘ

Family: Paeoniaceae
Flowering season: spring/summer
Height: 2–3 ft
(according to species and variety)
Spread: 2–3 ft
(according to species and variety)
Situation: ○ – ◑
Moisture requirement: ◊ – ◖
❄ ❄ ❄
✖

199

Garden peony

Paeonia 'Globe of Light'

ⓘ

Family: Paeoniaceae
Flowering season: summer
Height: 36 in
Spread: 36 in
Situation: ○
Moisture requirement: ◌ – ◖
❄ ❄ ❄
✖
❀

This variety belongs to the Paeonia-Lactiflora group, derived from a species which is native to Southeast Asia and eastern Siberia, also known as the Chinese peony, Japanese peony or noble peony. 'Globe of Light' forms a perennial erect bush and is highly regarded for its large, anemone-shaped, fragrant flowers. The petals are pink-red, while the stamens in the center are golden yellow; they look like reduced petals and are known as petaloids by botanists. To achieve the largest flowers, a general fertilizer low in nitrogen should be applied in early spring and a number of individual flower buds should be removed so that the others will then develop better. The varieties have dark green, pinnate leaves, the individual leaflets being oblong to oval shaped. Propagate by dividing older plants in the early autumn, but the plants will need several years in order to flower. The buds which will form shoots should only be covered by 1 in of earth.

Among the most popular varieties of this group is 'Sarah Bernhardt' which has very large, double, fragrant, shimmering, bright pink flowers with ruffled petals.

Paeonia 'Globe of Light'

Tree peony

Paeonia 'Kamada-nishiki'

Paeonia suffruticosa

Many tree peony varieties with names such as this were bred in Japan. They derive from a tree peony native to Southeast Asia and belong to the Paeonia-Suffruticosa group. Tree peonies grow slowly, but very handsomely. They have woody shoots and only form a few flowers. This type species has single, bright pink flowers, but this variety has double flowers; the outer petals are dark pink and the inner ones bright pink. The leaves are dark green with a gray-green underside, alternate and feathered. The individual leaflets are elliptical and pointed.
Tree peonies are valuable plants which should receive a favoured space in the garden. They require a fertile, well-drained neutral to acid soil. They are planted in early autumn. In the first winter, they are vulnerable to frost and should be protected; the early growth is always endangered by late frosts. Pruning is not necessary; only the seed cases and any dead wood should be removed. Propagation is by cuttings taken from semi-ripe cuttings in the summer. Growing from seed is also possible but takes several years.

ⓘ

Family: Paeoniaceae
Flowering season: spring/summer
Height: 5 ft
Spread: 32 in
Situation: ○ – ◐
Moisture requirement: 💧 – 💧
❄❄❄
✖

Tree peony

Paeonia lutea

P. lutea are native to China and Tibet and is the origin of the many peonies in the Paeonia-Lutea group today. It forms a slow-growing shrub whose shoots, being woody, do not die down in winter each year, unlike the ordinary peony. However, long periods of continuous frost are detrimental, so precautions should taken where necessary. The nodding flowers of *P. Lutea* are a bright yellow color. They are cup-shaped and single and mostly appear separately at the ends of the shoots. The stalked shiny leaves are divided into three, the leaflets are divided into pointed lobes. The upper side of the leaf is dark green, while the underside is blue-green. Peonies of the Paeonia-Lutea group lose their leaves in the autumn. They should not be pruned, but faded flowers and dead wood should be removed. They thrive on fertile, neutral to acid soils in sun or partial shade. Propagation is by semi-ripe cuttings in summer.

ⓘ

Family: Paeoniaceae
Flowering season: spring/summer
Height: 3 ft
Spread: 24 in
Situation: ○ – ◐
Moisture requirement: 💧 – 💧
❄❄
✖

Peony

Paeonia officinalis

P. officinalis will be in flower by early summer at the latest: this species has been a popular plant grown in cottage gardens for centuries. The double, purple-red, fragrant flowers are highly regarded today in sunny herbaceous borders and summer flower arrangements, although the flowers only last for a short time. *P. officinalis* is naturally distributed mainly throughout the region of the Alps, Turkey and the Caucasus. It grows into an upright bush. The flowers have numerous, crimped petals and appear at the end of flexible stalks individually or in small groups. The mid-green leaves are feathered and bipinnate, the individual leaflets oblong. 'Alba Plena' has white flowers, sometimes lightly tinged with pink. Propagate by dividing of old plants.

ⓘ

Family: Paeoniaceae
Flowering season: spring/summer
Height: 32 in
Spread: 32 in
Situation: ○
Moisture requirement: ◌ – ◑
✿ ✿ ✿
✖
✿

Iceland poppy

Papaver nudicaule

The Iceland poppy is an endearing perennial for sunny beds, sloping banks, scree gardens and roof terraces. It tolerates dry conditions well and also flourishes in situations which are not well-protected from wind and weather. The soil should be alkaline and well-drained. The species is native to arctic regions – and to Iceland. It forms bushy clumps from predominantly basal leaves which are oval, feathered and deeply split. The hairy leaves are gray-blue in color and contain a latex-like juice. The nodding flower buds are carried on leafless stalks and open into shell-shaped flowers in a range of white, yellow and orange colors. It has a particularly long flowering season with new flower buds continuing to open over several months. It self-seeds with great ease and will spread itself throughout the garden. This can be prevented by cutting the plants down before seed formation, which also encourages the growth of the plants. Propagate by sowing seeds in summer. The Iceland poppy is often grown as a biennial plant because it weakens rapidly as a result of its free flowering.

ⓘ

Family: Papaveracaea
Flowering season: spring/summer
Height: 12 in
Spread: 6 in
Situation: ○
Moisture requirement: ◌
✿ ✿ ✿

Oriental poppy

Papaver orientale

The oriental poppy has been a classic of the perennial garden for generations. As the name suggests, it did indeed come to Europe from the Orient, being native to Turkey, the Caucasus and Iran. It is spectacular with its extremely large flowers appearing in early summer to mid summer. It likes a sunny situation with loose, well-drained soil for its deep-penetrating, fleshy roots. Wet and cold soil in winter can be detrimental.

The oriental poppy is grown for its large, shell-shaped, bright scarlet flowers with silky petals, each of which has a purple-black marking at the base. It combines well with delphiniums or salvias. The flowers appear on strong, bent, stalks which contain a latex-like juice. The deep green hairy leaves are deeply feathered. The individual lobes are lanceolate and serrated. The perennial dies back very soon after flowering, leaving an open space. Cutting back immediately the first flowering can encourage a second flowering in the autumn; in this case, the plant will quickly grow leaves again. Oriental poppies are increased by division or by root cuttings in the early autumn.

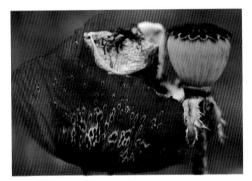

Papaver orientale

ℹ️

Family: Papaveraceae
Flowering season: spring / summer
Height: 24 in
Spread: 20 in
Situation: ○
Moisture requirement: ◌ – ◑
❄ ❄ ❄

Fountain grass

Pennisetum alopecuroides
(syn. P. compressum)

ℹ

Family: Poaceae
Flowering season: summer/autumn
Height: 3 ft
Spread: 32 in
Situation: ○
Moisture requirement: ◌ – ◑
❀ ❀ ❀

When its unusual, bottlebrush-like flowers appear in summer, fountain grass is very striking in the herbaceous border. The tiny single flowers are yellow-green to dark purple-red and appear in small spikes. These are closely packed together in cylindrical flower heads carried on arching stems. It is apparent that nature has spared no efforts to ensure that this ornamental grass attracts attention when it is in flower. The flowers are lovely in fresh or dried flower arrangements. However, outside the flowering season the fountain grass is rather inconspicuous and therefore not very suitable for displaying as an individual feature.

P. alopecuroides is a native of Japan, Korea and Australia. It forms large, bushy clumps over a period of time. Its leaves are strap-shaped and elegantly curved. It does best in a sunny situation with well-drained garden soil, but it is damaged if it becomes waterlogged, particularly in the winter. The leaves are cut back in the spring, when it can be propagated by dividing.

Beard tongue

Penstemon barbatus
(syn. Chelone barbata)

ℹ

Family: Scrophulariaceae
Flowering season: summer
Height: 32 in
Spread: 12 in
Situation: ○
Moisture requirement: ◌
❀ ❀

When growing flowers in the garden for cutting, it is rewarding to choose perennials rarely seen in flower shops. This penstemon is a good example, forming numerous slender spikes of pendulous, tubular and two-lipped pink to red flowers. Regular cutting of some of the stems will encourage flower formation and the flowering period can be extended by removing faded blooms immediately. The perennial is native to the warm southwest of the United States and Mexico. It has a creeping rootstock and loose, upright growth. The shoots of older plants tend to become woody at the base. The predominantly basal leaves are soft green and oblong to oval shaped, arranged in a rosette; the stem leaves are lanceolate. The plants are semi-evergreen, losing only half their leaves in winter. They need a warm, sunny situation with fertile, well-drained humus-rich soil. This tender perennial does not survive the winter in colder regions without protection and it should be wintered in a cool, light space, like fuchsias. Because of its prolific flowering, the plant is short-lived, weakening in the third year. It is propagated using cuttings in summer.

Phlomis

Phlomis russeliana (syn. P. samia)

The flowers of perennials have such diversity of form that you can never be bored with your garden. Phlomis, for example, has very unusual flowers and is unfortunately only rarely seen. It forms tiers of flower clusters which remain decorative even when dried up after flowering. The plant, is in fact, only cut back in spring. The individual flowers are bright golden-yellow, tubular, two-lipped and arranged in clusters. They are carried on erect, wiry stems, making them very good cut flowers.

P. russeliana is native to Turkey. The wild species has unbranched shoots becoming woody with age, growing to a semi-shrub and forming spherical bushes. The mid-green leaves are wrinkled, the basal leaves being heart-shaped and the stem leaves oval. Phlomis requires a sheltered, sunny location, and winter protection is necessary in some areas. The soil should be rather poor, alkaline and well-drained. If the flower heads are not removed after flowering, the plant will self-seed freely. Intentional propagation is by sowing or division in spring.

ⓘ

Family: Lamiaceae
Flowering season: spring/summer
Height: 3 ft
Spread: 3 ft
Situation: ○
Moisture requirement: ◌
❄ ❄

Phlox

Phlox species and hybrids

There are nearly 70 species of *Phlox* and their appearances differ so widely that a family relationship would often not be suspected. There are the tall perennials such as *P. paniculata* which also provides excellent cut flowers for summer flower arrangements; and there are also good ground cover species such as *P. subulata* which make a spectacular show with bright carpets of flowers in spring. Nearly all the phlox species are native to North America, and first reached Europe in the 18th century. Its great popularity is owed to its free flowering habit and range of intense flower colors. Today there is an enormous number of varieties. The process of expanding the color spectrum of the flowers began in the 19th century, when the range available included white, pink, red and mauve. Phlox flowers are normally saucer-shaped. The flower center, known as the eye, is often of a different color. The illustration shows 'Eventide,' a variety of *P. paniculata* with pale, lilac-blue flowers.

ℹ

Family: Polemoniaceae
Flowering season: spring/summer
Height: various
Spread: various
Situation: ○
Moisture requirement: ◌ – ◐
❄ ❄ ❄

207

Meadow phlox

Phlox maculata

ℹ

Family: Polemoniaceae
Flowering season: spring/summer
Height: 36 in
Spread: 20 in
Situation: ○
Moisture requirement: ◊ – ◖
❄ ❄ ❄

This tall phlox is a woodland perennial species which is outstandingly suitable for the wild garden. In form and color the flowers are reminiscent of *P. Paniculata* hybrids, but they are a little smaller, look more natural and fit more comfortably into a landscape setting. *P. maculata* is bushy with sturdy stems which are often reddish in color. The leaves are straight to narrowly oval in shape and slightly hairy, appearing opposite each other on the stem. The individual flowers are saucer-shaped and form cylindrical clusters.

The species is native to North America and prefers a sunny situation with well-drained, fertile soil. It is particularly impressive in large groups. In addition to the type species, the variety 'Alpha' has dark pink flowers with dark centers while 'Omega' has white flowers with violet eyes. Both grow to a height of about 3 ft and combine together well in the herbaceous border. *P. maculata* is propagated by division in spring or autumn and by root cuttings in winter.

Phlox

Phlox paniculata

ℹ

Family: Polemoniaceae
Flowering season: summer
Height: 3 ft
Spread: 20 in
Situation: ○
Moisture requirement: ◊ – ◖
❄ ❄ ❄

It is impossible to imagine cottage gardens without this tall phlox. In the garden it thrives best in a sunny situation, with good fertile soil. *P. paniculata* is slim and, upright and forms large clumps with age. The lanceolate leaves are arranged opposite each other on the stems. The terminal cylindrical flower spikes carry saucer-shaped flowers with five petals. It is a very popular cut flower, although giving off a characteristic smell that not everyone likes. The flowering period can be increased by cutting off half the shoots in spring. The same applies to the flower buds, although this takes rather more time. Propagate by dividing folder plants in the autumn or spring or by taking in root cuttings in winter.

Among the most beautiful varieties are 'Starfire' with deep red flowers and 'Graf Zeppelin,' which has white flowers with deep pink eyes. *P. paniculata* combines well with salvias and heleniums.

Phlox paniculata

Moss Phlox

Phlox subulata

The moss phlox has a very different habit from its tall relatives described earlier. It is very low-growing and forms large carpets with numerous short stemmed flowers, making it an excellent ground cover plant. If, however, it is planted in containers or on staging, it also produces attractive trailing growth. Like most of the phloxes, the species is native to North America. Many varieties have been bred with a large range of flower colors, including many shades of pink, red and purple. Among the most popular varieties are 'G. F. Wilson' with light lavender flowers and 'Temiskaming' with deep crimson flowers.

That moss phlox is evergreen with linear curved leaves. The flowers are star-shaped and arranged in clusters. In spring, the leaves disappear almost completely beneath the mass of the small flowers. They are excellent planted in combination with candytuft flowers (*Iberis*). The moss phlox prefers a well-drained, sandy alkaline soil in a sunny situation. It is very undemanding and can also be used for planting scree gardens and roof terraces. It is propagated by cuttings in spring or by division in autumn.

ⓘ

Family: Polemoniaceae
Flowering season: spring
Height: 4 in
Spread: various
Situation: ○
Moisture requirement: ◊
❊ ❊ ❊

209

Obedient plant
Physostegia virginiana

ℹ

Family: Lamiaceae
Flowering season: summer
Height: 32 in
Spread: 20 in
Situation: ◯ – ◐
Moisture requirement: ◊
❋ ❋ ❋

When garden flowers are intended to be 'harvested' for flower arrangements, it is better to choose more interesting species than routine perennials. The individual flowers of the obedient plant are fascinating in the garden as well as in summer flower arrangements because they seem attached to the plant with friction hinges. Their position can be changed without moving them back to the initial position. They are funnel-shaped, two-lipped and arranged in tall flower spikes. The species is native to North America and the flowers are red-purple. The variety 'Summer Snow' is white and the recommended variety 'Vivid' is shorter and flowers later with pinky-red flowers. The obedient plant has an erect habit and a creeping rootstock which forms dense groups over time. The bright green leaves are elliptical to lanceolate and serrated, arranged opposite each other on the stem. It prefers a moist to sunny location with fertile humus-rich soil. If planted in partial shade, it will survive occasional dry periods. It can be increased easily by division in spring. Larger stocks can be created from cuttings taken in the summer.

Polygonatum x hybridum

Salomon's seal
Polygonatum × hybridum

ℹ

Family: Convallariaceae
Flowering season: spring
Height: 4 ft
Spread: 3 ft
Situation: ◐ – ●
Moisture requirement: ◊ – ◊
❋ ❋ ❋
✖

Plant lovers appreciate gardens in which there is a wide variety of species to discover. Even collectors who have amassed a great variety of species should be sure not to omit Solomon's seal from a shady garden where its reserved beauty will not fail to please. The perennial has elegantly bent shoots with angular stalks. Its relatively large, light green and oval-shaped leaves growing regularly from the shoots and the pendulous bell-shaped white flowers are tinged with green. The long-cultivated plant is derived from species which are native to Europe and Asia. It is related to the lily of the valley. The vigorous rhizome of Solomon's seal needs a well-drained, fertile, moist soil. The situation should be sheltered in partial to full shade. As planting companions, ferns are a good choice, for instance, the five-fingered maidenhair fern (*Adiantum*) or the male fern (*Dryopteris*). Specimens can be increased by division at the end of winter. Caution: all parts of the plant are poisonous.

Shield fern

Polystichum tsus-simense (syn. P. luctuosum)

The shield fern will appeal to the perennial lover who has not forgotten the fever of collecting: there are nearly 200 species in the genus *Polystichum*, although some come from tropical regions and in cooler climates will only thrive in the greenhouse. *P. tsus-simense* is native to Southeast Asia. Outdoors in mild regions, the species will survive the winter in a sheltered situation, but elsewhere it must be over-wintered in a cool, light room with a temperature of about 54°F. It forms a crown with delicate filigree fronds rising from a central rosette. The triangular, bipinnate fronds are dark green with some parts bluish; the oval-shaped leaflets are serrated and pointed. It requires well-drained, humus-rich soil in partial or full shade. Individual breeding fronds develop which carry out propagation. They rest on the moist substrate and develop little plantlets. The young plants should be removed from the frond of the parent plant only when they have rooted. Propagation by sowing spores is considerably more time consuming.

Also recommended is the even more intricate *P. setiferum* 'Proliferum Plumosum Densum' which is frost hardy and can be over-wintered in the open.

Polystichum tsus simense

ⓘ

Family: Dryopteridaceae
Height: 16 in
Spread: 16 in
Situation: ◑ – ●
Moisture requirement: ◌ – ◐
❄

Cinquefoil

Potentilla aurea

The genus of these little, rose-like plants includes a wide variety of shrubs and perennials which are among the most popular herbaceous plants. The species *P. Aurea* is native to Europe and Asia Minor. It forms a compact mat of mid-green leaves which are divided into five, serrated, radiating leaflets with hairy undersides. Its popular name 'cinquefoil' means 'five leaves.'

P. aurea grows with low, spreading shoots and develops golden yellow flowers in loose clusters in spring. It is an excellent ground cover plant in a sunny situation. The species tolerates dry conditions and is therefore a good choice for roof terraces or tubs. It thrives in a neutral to acidic, loamy, humus-rich well-drained soil. Propagation is by division in spring or autumn.

ⓘ

Family: Rosaceae
Flowering season: spring/summer
Height: 6 in
Spread: various
Situation: ○ – ◑
Moisture requirement: ◌
❄ ❄ ❄

Auricula cultivars

Primula auricula

ℹ

Family: Primulaceae
Flowering season: spring
Height: 4–8 in
(according to species and variety)
Spread: 4–10 in
(according to species and variety)
Situation: ◯ – ◐
Moisture requirement: ◌ – ◖
❆ ❆ ❆

The genus *Primula* contains more than 500 species, most of them perennials. For greater ease of identification they are divided into groups with similar features. Auricula cultivars are one of these groups. The auriculas have a long history of cultivation and were created by crossings the Alpine auricula *P. auricula* with the cowslip *P. hirsuta*. The relatively large, saucer-shaped flowers are often pink or violet; they appear in bunches above the leaves. The flower center is usually a different color, a white or yellow ring. The basal leaves are light green, oval to round and arranged in rosettes. The flowers or leaves of some auriculas are covered with a white coating secreted by the plant, known as 'farina.' They should not be allowed to get wet while being watered or otherwise, one reason why show auriculas are invariably grown in pots in the greenhouse. Less ambitious gardeners plant their border auriculas in alkaline, humus-rich and well-drained soil. They should always be protected from excessively wet conditions in winter.
Propagate with seeds sown in late autumn. The seeds are covered with only a thin layer of soil covering the seeds. They require a low temperatures in order to germinate.

Primula-Polyantha group

Primula-Polyantha group

ℹ

Family: Primulaceae
Flowering season: winter/spring
Height: to 8 in
(according to species and variety)
Spread: to 6 in
(according to species and variety)
Situation: ◯ – ◐
Moisture requirement: ◌ – ◖
❆ ❆ ❆

Primulas have been grown in gardens for a long time. Polyanthus primulas are the result of complex breeding experiments involving the true cowslip *P. veris*, the oxlip *P. elatior*, the European primrose *P. vulgaris* and the Caucasian primrose, *P. juliae*. They form dense, evergreen rosettes. The basal leaves are dark green, oval-shaped and usually visibly veined. The heavy, slightly hairy flower shoots carry umbels of up to 15 saucer-shaped flowers in various colors, from white to yellow and red and deep purple-blue as well. The flowers have yellow centers.

Polyantha primroses are mostly grown as biennials. Professional gardeners grow them in pots in the greenhouse and bring them to flower in late winter. They can then be kept on the window sill or planted out in the open as harbingers of spring. They will be happy in ordinary garden soil. It is important to plant them in a situation with full sun and evenly moist soil. The perennials can easily be increased by division in spring or autumn. Seed mixtures are sown in summer and flower in the following spring.

Primula

Primula pulverulenta

P. pulverulenta should be present in every water-garden. In spring, the tall spikes of deep red flowers, each with a purple eye, stand out beautifully against the fresh green foliage of young ferns and hostas. They grow best in moderately fertile, damp soil and make excellent border plants which thrive near ponds. The descriptive name of the group, Candelabra – which includes several wild species and their varieties – refers to those species and varieties whose tubular, flat-faced flowers are arranged in tiered whorls up the farinose stem. The following species are among the most popular: *Primula beesiana, P. x bullesiana, P. bulleyana, P. chungensis* and *P prolifera*. Candelabra primulas form basal rosettes of mid-green, lanceolate to ovate leaves with prominent veins and striking midrib. They are mostly semi-evergreen which means that they only lose part of their leaves and survive the winter with a smaller rosette. They are propagated by division in spring or autumn.

Primula pulverulenta

ℹ

Family: Primulaceae
Flowering season: spring
Height: to 3 ft
(according to species and variety)
Spread: to 24 in
(according to species and variety)
Situation: ○ – ◑
Moisture requirement: ◐ – ●
❄ ❄ ❄

Cowslip

Primula veris
(syn. P. officinalis)

ⓘ

Family: Primulaceae
Flowering season: spring
Height: 8 in
Spread: 6 in
Situation: ◑
Moisture requirement: ◌ – ◕
❀ ❀ ❀
✖

The native cowslips are undoubtedly among the best-known of the primula species. Their very distinctive yellow, tubular, nodding, slightly fragrant flowers are borne in dense clusters on sturdy stems. The individual flowers each have five orange-colored flecks in their throat. This is what distinguishes this wild species from the oxlip (*P. elatior*). The basal leaves, arranged in a rosette, are moderately green, wrinkled, lanceolate to ovate with serrated edges and a woolly underside. *P. veris* has been used as medicinal plant since antiquity, but it vital to take the correct dose because the active ingredients can cause poisoning. Like other wild flowers, cowslips have become much rarer in the wild. They look best in wild gardens where they can enjoy the dappled shade provided by the shrubs around them. The soil should be chalky, rather moist in spring and dry in summer. The plant is propagated by division in spring or autumn.

Primula veris

214

Pseudofumaria

Pseudofumaria lutea (syn. Corydalis lutea)

Few plants thrive in dry soil in partial shade. Pseudofumaria is one of those rare plants which brighten up shady parts of the garden. It flowers for a long time and self-seeds easily, thus quickly spreading over a large area. Bushy, extremely ornate, with fleshy, branched shoots and fern-like, bluish-green leaves it produces clusters of yellow flowers. *P. lutea* is native to Europe where it grows in the mountains and deciduous forests. In the garden, it grows best in partial shade in stony, well-drained, humus-rich soil. If planted under large trees, it will need extra watering during prolonged periods of dry weather. It combines beautifully with crane's-bills (*Geranium*) and primroses as well as ferns. This species is rather short-lived so self-seeded seedlings can be used to replace the parent plant. It is propagated by division in early spring.

ⓘ

Family: Fumariaceae
Flowering season: spring/summer
Height: 10 in
Spread: 10 in
Situation: ◑
Moisture requirement: ◌ – ◗
❀ ❀ ❀

Pseudolysimachion

Pseudodolysimachion longifolium (syn. Veronica longifolia)

This plant is known to many gardeners by the less accurate name of Veronica or speedwell. Its racemes of violet-blue flowers look very decorative in sunny herbaceous borders and in fresh flower arrangement and are popular among gardeners. It flowers for a long time in the garden because the side-shoots produce racemes which appear in succession. By cutting back the plant after flowering, it is possible that the plant will flower a second time in autumn. It combines beautifully with roses and herbaceous perennials such as *Helenium* and *Rudbeckia*. The individual flowers are small and funnel-shaped. It is sometimes necessary to support the slender spikes. The moderately green, lanceolate leaves with serrated edges are arranged in whorls along the whole stem. The sturdy shoots grow very erect. Older plants can be divided in autumn. This species grows wild in Central Europe, Asia Minor and as far east as Siberia. It grows best in fertile, loamy soil in a sunny position near water.

ⓘ

Family: Scrophulariaceae
Flowering season: summer/autumn
Height: 32 in
Spread: 20 in
Situation: ○
Moisture requirement: ◗
❀ ❀ ❀

215

Pseudolysimachion (spiked speedwell)

Pseudodolysimachion spicatum
(Syn. Veronica spicata)

Family: Scrophulariaceae
Flowering season: summer
Height: 16 in
Spread: 12 in
Situation: ○
Moisture requirement: ◌ – ◖
✺ ✺ ✺

This species does not grow as tall as its relative *P. longifolia*, and is often just known as veronica. It has a clump-forming habit, the shoots first spreading in a prostrate manner, then growing upright to form a medium-height carpet. It thrives in a warm place in moderately fertile, well-drained soil and can survive periods of drought, which makes it highly suitable for planting in screes and roof gardens. It is native to Europe, Asia Minor and Siberia. The small, blue or blue-violet flowers with long, violet stamens are borne in slender terminal spikes. The leaves are mid-green, linear to lanceolate with serrated edges. It is propagated by division in spring or autumn or by cuttings of non-flowering shoots in summer.

Eagle-like brake

Pteridium aquilinum

Family: Dennstaedtiaceae
Height: to 7 ft
Spread: variable
Situation: ◑ – ●
Moisture requirement: ◌ – ◖
✺ ✺ ✺
✖

Ferns are by no means mere background or gap-filling plants. The eagle-like brake is an imposing, majestic fern which, planted on its own, is a real eye-catcher. It is important to take this fern's spreading habit into consideration because it can cover large areas quickly. This may be desirable in large gardens, but in a small garden, its roots should be contained. For instance, it could be placed in a large plastic container with drainage holes which is then sunk into the ground.
The eagle-like brake can be found in most parts of the world, from the forests of the temperate zone to the tropics. The bright-green, trebly pinnate fronds have very sturdy stems. When a stem is cut through diagonally, the inner vessels are seen to be shaped like the wings of an eagle. In the right conditions, spore capsules will develop on the under-edges of the pinnae. The fronds turn yellow in autumn. The eagle-like brake thrives in cool, humus-rich neutral to acid soil but it will also

Pteridium aquilinum

grow in poor, sandy soil, although in that case it will not grow so tall. It is propagated by division in autumn. Be careful: this fern is poisonous.

*L*ungwort

Pulmonaria saccharata

Lungwort has very decorative foliage and is a beautiful ground cover, ideal for planting along shady borders. It is vigorous, bushy and clump-forming. Its spreading leaves are ideal for suppressing weeds. The elliptic, moderately green leaves are flecked with white. Their flowers add a wonderful touch of color to the garden. These tubular flowers, borne in terminal clusters, are pink when they first come out, becoming tinged with blue and violet as time goes on. As a result, the same plant seems to produce flowers of different colors. The foliage becomes rather unsightly after flowering so that it is best to cut it back. This will also encourage new growth. The wild species is native to Central Europe where it grows in damp forests. It thrives in moist, fertile, humus-rich soil in partial or full shade. If the soil is very moist, it will also grow in the sun. It combines very beautifully with Solomon's seal (*Polygonatum*) or ferns. It is propagated by dividing the clumps in early spring or autumn. Lungwort self-seeds very easily and the young plants can either replanted elsewhere or potted.

Family: Boraginaceae
Flowering season: spring
Height: 12 in
Spread: 24 in
Situation: ◐ – ●
Moisture requirement: ◌ – ◐
✵ ✵ ✵
✖

Pulsatilla vulgaris

*P*ulsatilla
Pulsatilla vulgaris

ⓘ

Family: Ranunculaceae
Flowering season: spring
Height: 8 in
Spread: 8 in
Situation: ○
Moisture requirement: ◌ – ◖
❊ ❊ ❊
✖

The relatively large, bell-shaped flowers are borne singly and appear before the leaves. The flowers are red-violet with striking orange-yellow stamens, which contrast beautifully with the petals. There are also varieties with white or red flowers. They all combine very beautifully with irises.

The wild species is native to Europe. It has a bushy, clump-forming habit. The stems are covered with silver hairs and the leaves are fern-like. *P. vulgaris* grows best in chalky, humus-rich, well-drained soil in a sunny position. It is best raised from seed as soon as the seeds have ripened because they quickly lose the capacity to germinate. This plant has medicinal properties, but can be toxic if incorrectly dosed.

Common buttercup

Ranunculus acris

The common buttercup is a native wild plant, which has been cultivated in gardens for a long time. The common name refers to the bright yellow color of the flowers, which have a very silky sheen. The flowers are cup-shaped with greenish centers and are borne in clusters on slender, branched stems. The wild species is native to the northern temperate zone. It has a bushy habit and short underground runners, but it is not as invasive as its other relatives such as *R. repens*. The leaves are dark green, deeply split and lobed, the individual leaflets are deeply serrated. Be careful: all parts of the plant can cause illness if eaten.

The buttercup is ideal for sunny flower beds, bordering ponds and in marshy soil. It is propagated by division in spring or autumn. The double meadow buttercup 'Flore Pleno' is a very old variety with beautiful double flowers.

Family: Ranunculaceae
Flowering season: spring/summer
Height: 24 in
Spread: 20 in
Situation: ○
Moisture requirement: ◐ – ●
❀ ❀ ❀
✖

Rodgersia

Rodgersia aesculifolia

Many herbaceous perennials are grown less for their flowers than for their attractive foliage. *R. aesculifolia* is one such plant which looks particularly attractive planted on its own and is also excellent in combination with woody plants. When planted in mixed herbaceous borders it should not be planted too close to neighboring plants so that it can be seen in without confusion. The leaves and flower plumes are reminiscent of those of a horse chestnut. The individual leaflets are serrated and have prominent veins.

The wild species is native to central China where it grows in damp forests. It is a vigorous-growing plant which develops powerful underground runners. It grows best in moist, fertile, humus-rich soil in partial shade. If the soil remains constantly moist, it will also grow in a sunny position. However, it hates being waterlogged. The slightly fragrant, tiny, pinkish-white flowers are grouped in branched umbels on sturdy stems covered with brownish hairs. It is propagated by division in spring or from seed in autumn.

Rodgersia aesulifolia

Family: Saxifragaceae
Flowering season: summer
Height: 5 ft
Spread: 3 ft
Situation: ◑
Moisture requirement: ◐
❀ ❀ ❀

Black-eyed susan

Rudbeckia fulgida

ⓘ

Family: Asteraceae
Flowering season: summer/autumn
Height: 28 in
Spread: 20 in
Situation: ○
Moisture requirement: ◊
❄ ❄ ❄

It looks good, it is a perennial and does not mind being neglected – this summarises the black-eyed Susan. This easy-to-grow perennial, native to North America, has large, daisy-like flowers, reminiscent of the marguerite. The outer ray florets are golden yellow while the short tubular central florets are dark brown to black. The flower heads are borne singly on branched stems and last for a long time both in the garden and as cut flowers. If the dead flowers are not removed, the dark centers will still look very decorative in winter, long after the yellow ray florets have fallen off.

Black-eyed Susan has a very upright habit and dark green, lanceolate to ovate, coarsely hairy leaves. It grows well in any well-drained, fertile garden soil and will thrive in sun or shade. It does not mind dry conditions. Because it flowers for such a long time, it is often used for planting in large containers. *R. fulgida sullivantii* 'Goldsturm' is lower than the type species, only growing to 2 ft. The plant combines beautifully with autumn asters and ornamental grasses. It is propagated by division in spring or autumn.

Common arrowhead

Sagittaria sagittifolia

Arrowhead is an ideal plant for growing near ponds and in pools. It is native to Europe, Russia and Siberia where it grows in still or flowing water. The tuberous-shaped roots which develop on the runners become anchored in the loamy soil and rise up to the surface of the water. The arrow-shaped leaves are very distinctive, each leaf endowed with two long 'tail ends' and a long stem. It has striking white flowers with prominent yellow stamens, grouped in whorls along the stems.

Common arrowhead thrives in full and partial shade. It is ideal for ponds and marshy areas. In nature, common arrowhead self-seeds very easily, forming large colonies. It is propagated in spring by carefully separating the tubers or by raising from seed.

ⓘ

Family: Alismataceae
Flowering season: summer
Height: to 20 in
above the water surface
Water depth: to 16 in
bank and marsh plant
water plant
Situation: ○ – ◑
Moisture requirement: ●
❄ ❄ ❄

Sage

Salvia × sylvestris

The intensely blue flowers and very aromatic leaves are perfect reasons for choosing *S. x sylvestris* as a herbaceous perennial for a sunny border. Bees and butterflies are also very attracted by the blue flowers. It is ideal for herbaceous borders where it combines beautifully with old-fashioned, brightly colored perennials such as peonies (*Paeonia officinalis*) and poppies (*Papaver orientale*). It also looks very good with roses. It is bushy and has vigorous, lush-green leaves. The basal leaves are heart-shaped, while the stem leaves are lanceolate with wavy, indented edges. The flowers are two-lipped and surrounded by red-violet bracts. If cut back after the first flowering and fed generously, it may flower again in late summer. The plant thrives in well-drained, warm soil and does not mind dry conditions. It is propagated by cuttings in summer or division in autumn.

ⓘ

Family: Lamiaceae
Flowering season: spring/summer
Height: 32 in
Spread: 12 in
Situation: ○
Moisture requirement: ◌ – ◑
❄ ❄ ❄

*C*otton lavender

Santolina chamaecyparissus

Santolina chamaecyparissus

ⓘ

Family: Asteraceae
Flowering season: summer
Height: 16 in
Spread: 16 in
Situation: ○
Moisture requirement: ◊
❋ ❋

Gray-leaved plants usually originate from warm regions with plenty of sun. The leaves are protected from the sun and heat by a layer of very fine gray hairs which reduce the loss of water through evaporation. There are known as 'professional starvers' in the garden and their foliage allows the most extraordinary color combinations. Cotton lavender is not grown for its tiny, inconspicuous yellow flower heads, but for its very elegant, finely divided, woolly, silver, aromatic foliage. The shoots become slightly woody, which is why it is classed as a sub-shrub. The foliage is evergreen. With regular pruning, its shape can be maintained, preventing it from becoming straggly. It adds a Mediterranean touch to the garden, and being native to the Mediterranean, it needs a lot of warmth and should be planted in sheltered place in poor, well-drained, chalky soil. It is propagated in summer by cuttings of half-ripe side-shoots.

*S*cabious

Scabiosa caucasica

ⓘ

Family: Dipsacaceae
Flowering season: summer
Height: 20 in
Spread: 16 in
Situation: ○
Moisture requirement: ◊
❋ ❋ ❋

This herbaceous perennial flowers all through the summer, if dead headed regularly and fed generously with a liquid compound fertiliser. The species is native to the Caucasus as its Latin name suggests. It grows wild in mountainous regions and thrives in a chalky, well-drained, humus-rich soil in full sun. It is also ideal for planting in tubs. Its blue-violet flowers look very attractive in herbaceous borders and flower arrangements. What many see as a large, single flower is in fact a flower head consisting of blue-violet ray florets and paler tubular central florets. These flower heads are borne on tall, branched, wiry stems and attract bees and butterflies.

Scabious is bushy. Its gray-green foliage consists of lanceolate, smooth-edged, basal leaves and deeply divided stem leaves. It combines beautifully with red-hot pokers (*Kniphofia*). It is propagated by division in spring. 'Clive Greaves' is a beautiful variety with light blue flowers.

Scabiosa caucasia

S*edum*

Sedum species

This is a vast genus of over 500 species, most of which are native to the northern hemisphere. They include not only herbaceous perennials, but also annuals, sub-shrubs and shrubs. All share the ability to store water in their fleshy (succulent) leaves because the genus belongs to the *Crassulaceae* family.

Most of the species and varieties used in the garden are low-spreading, ground-covering plants. They are extremely easy to look after, tolerating dry conditions, and intense sun and growing well in poor, well-drained soil. They are ideal for roof terraces, in front of sunny flower beds, screes, and in pots and tubs. The lea-ves are arranged in opposite pairs or in whorls. The small, star-shaped flowers are usually borne in terminal panicles or flat umbels. The plants are propagated by cuttings in summer. Be careful: certain species can cause illness if eaten.

Family: Crassulaceae
Flowering season: summer
Height: variable
Spread: variable
Situation: ○
Moisture requirement: ◌ – ◑
❄ ❄ ❄

223

Stone orpine

Sedum reflexum (syn. S. rupestre)

ℹ️

Family: Crassulaceae
Flowering season: summer
Height: 4 in
Spread: variable
Situation: ○
Moisture requirement: ○
❊ ❊ ❊

This sedum is a 'professional starver,' native to the rocky regions of Central and Western Europe. It grows in crevices in rocks and along waysides, the main requirement being that the soil should be well-drained. It prefers poor, chalky soil in a sunny position where it will grow very happily. It is ideal for planting at the front of sunny flower beds or on roof terraces. It is very effective in rock gardens and among paving stones because the runners spread to form loose mats which grow over paving stones or steps. The individual evergreen gray-green leaves are cylindrical and pointed and arranged in alternate pairs. In summer, it produces yellow flowers grouped in flat umbels, borne on leafy, reddish-green, upright stems well above the low foliage. The buds are pendulous but the yellow flowers look upward and attract bees and other insects. It is propagated by cuttings in summer.

sedum spectabile

ℹ️

Family: Crassulaceae
Flowering season: summer/autumn
Height: 20 in
Spread: 20 in
Situation: ○
Moisture requirement: ○ – ◐
❊ ❊ ❊

Ice plant

Sedum spectabile

It is well-known that taste is subjective, but there is no doubt that this ice plant is very beautiful. It is best planted along the edge of sunny herbaceous borders so that the erect stems can be easily seen. In summer, it produces small, bright pink flowers, grouped in terminal, flat umbels which attract insects. The fleshy, gray-green leaves are arranged in opposite pairs on the equally fleshy stems. The leaves are elliptic to ovate with serrated or indented edges.

S. spectabilis is native to Southeast Asia. Unlike other sedum species, it prefers permanently moist soil. Particularly in periods of hot, dry weather, it should be given rich compost in spring and needs to be fed regularly to encourage large flower heads. The flower heads should only be removed at the end of the winter because they look very nice dry. One of the most popular varieties is 'Brilliant' which has bright pink flowers.

Houseleek

Sempervivum species and hybrids

The houseleek has been used as a medicinal plant for a very long time and is closely linked to ancient country traditions. It used to be planted on the roofs of houses because it was thought give protection from lightning. The best-known species is *S. tectorum*, the common houseleek. Like most other species in this genus, it has fleshy (succulent) leaves which can store water. The blue-green, red-tipped leaves (the color is very variable) are oval, pointed and arranged in rosettes. *S. tectorum* has a mat-forming habit, its runners producing further rosettes. The red-violet flowers are borne in terminal umbels, reminiscent of those produced by *Sedum* species. Rosettes which have produced a flower head die after flowering. The flower heads can grow up to 6 in high but those of *S. montanum* only reach 4 in; this species has dark green leaves and wine red flowers.

The sempervivum thrives in poor, well-drained neutral to acid soil in a sunny position and it does not mind dry conditions. It looks very good at the front of flower beds, in shallow containers or in window boxes. It is propagated by dividing older plants or rooted rosettes.

ⓘ

Family: Crassulaceae
Flowering season: summer
Height: to 6 in (according to species)
Spread: variable
Situation: ○
Moisture requirement: ◌
❄ ❄ ❄

Sempervivum

225

Goldenrod

Solidago virgaurea

ⓘ

Family: Asteraceae
Flowering season: summer/autumn
Height: 32 in
Spread: 32 in
Situation: ○
Moisture requirement: ◊
❀ ❀ ❀

Goldenrod grows everywhere. Anyone travelling regularly by train who looks out of the window will be familiar with the distinctive silhouette of goldenrod which stands out from other plants in late summer. It grows wild along railway embankments and in wastelands because it likes poor, well-drained soil in a sunny position. In the garden, it looks very good at the back of herbaceous borders or in other parts of the garden. The tiny, individual flowers are borne in branched, arching panicles and are long-lived. Solidagos make colorful cut flowers. They combine beautifully with autumn asters. The slightly hairy leaves are lanceolate with serrated edges, while the stems are covered with leaves right up to the top.
S. virgaurea grows wild throughout Europe, Turkey, the Caucasus and as far as

226

Siberia and Southeast Asia. The other species are native to North America. The 'Goldenmosa' variety is more compact than the wild species and produces larger umbels.

Lamb's tongue

Stachys byzantina (syn. S. lantana)

There are herbaceous perennials which are grown exclusively for their foliage. *S. byzantina* not only looks good, but feels very pleasant to the touch, almost as soft as fur. The elliptic leaves are gray-green, covered with white woolly hairs. The basal leaves are arranged in rosettes while the stem leaves are arranged in opposite pairs. In summer, it produces terminal, gray-felted spikes of small, pink, tubular, two-lipped flowers. These may not impress people much but they attract numerous insects. 'Silver carpet' is a variety which hardly flowers.

This species is native to Asia Minor. It is a mat-forming plant which spreads very easily and is therefore ideal as a ground cover at the front of sunny flower-beds. It prefers poor, well-drained soil and hates being waterlogged which would cause it to rot and die. It is propagated by dividing older plants after flowering. It combines very successfully with autumn crocuses (*Colchicum*) which should be planted amongst the foliage of the lamb's tongue. The large-flowered *S. macrantha* is a close relative which looks very good with roses. The crinkled, soft green leaves are heart-shaped and the large, rose-purple, hooded flowers are arranged in whorls. This species grows up to 2 ft high.

ⓘ

Family: Lamiaceae
Flowering season: summer
Height: 16 in
Spread: variable
Situation: ○
Moisture requirement: ◊
✽ ✽ ✽

Globe flower

Trollius chinensis

Family: Ranunculaceae
Flowering season: spring/summer
Height: 3 ft
Spread: 20 in
Situation: ○ – ◐
Moisture requirement: ◑ – ●
❀ ❀ ❀
✖

T. chinensis is native to the mountains of China where it is found in moist meadows and along river banks. In gardens, it prefers moist, loamy soil near ponds where it looks very attractive. It forms a bushy, branched plant with soft green, long-stemmed, mostly basal leaves which are deeply lobed. The individual leaflets are coarsely serrated. In spring, it produces striking orange-yellow, cup-shaped flowers with long nectaries. By cutting the flower stems back back to the base after flowering and feeding, it is possible to have a second flowering. It is propagated by dividing older plants after flowering. It combines very beautifully with *Iris sibirica* and *Filipendula*. It relative *T. europaeus*, native to Europe, has globular-shaped flowers which appear slightly earlier. Be careful: all parts of the plant are poisonous.

Trollius chinensis

228

Mullein

Verbascum olympicum

The gray foliage of mullein will suggest the atmosphere of a Mediterranean garden. The most important requirement is that it should have plenty of sun; apart from that, it is a very easy plant to grow. *V. olympicum* grows wild on wasteland and railway embankments. The gray, felt-like, broadly lanceolate, fleshy leaves are arranged in large rosettes. The species is fairly short-lived. In the first year, it only produces a basal rosette while the tall, candle-like, branched spike with its bright yellow flowers appears one or two years afterwards. The rosette dies after the seeds have ripened.

V. olympicum is native to Greece and Turkey where it grows in rocky areas. It thrives in warm, well-drained, chalky soil and hates being waterlogged. It self-seeds itself, but can also be raised from seed in spring. There are also longer-lived hybrids available, such as *V. x hybrids*.

ⓘ

Family: Scrophulariaceae
Flowering season: spring/summer
Height: 7 ft
Spread: 24 in
Situation: ○
Moisture requirement: ◊
❄ ❄ ❄

Herbs

Whether grown for their attractive ornamental qualities, for culinary or medicinal use, or for their fragrance, herbs tempt us to give them a place in our gardens or on our patios or balconies. In addition, they attract other natural creatures, for their delicious aromas lure bees and butterflies even to high balconies. Herbs will flourish and fully develop their fragrance in full sun, but in other respects they are easy to grow. Do not over-water, since they will tolerate drought much better than excessive moisture. Nitrogenous liquid manure made from stinging nettles, tansy or milfoil will promote growth, but be careful not to wet the leaves of herbs when applying these fertilisers. There are no limits to the ways you can grow herbs. They can be planted out in a spiral design, or in colorful herb beds, and will even look pretty in pots. The advantage of growing them in containers is that they can be brought indoors in winter. Mediterranean herbs such as basil, oregano and sage will lend a southern atmosphere to any situation. Try growing herbs along paths, so that you can enjoy their delightful fragrance in passing. A small selection of culinary herbs should always be placed near the house, since they taste best freshly gathered, preferably before they flower. Herbs can easily be raised from seed or bought as young plants. Seed-lings of warmth-loving species should be started indoors. As winter approaches, remember that many perennial herbs are not as hardy when container-grown as in the open ground, so cover them with twigs or similar materials, or overwinter them under cover in a light, frost-free place.

Bugle

Ajuga reptans

ⓘ

Family: Lamiaceae
Flowering season: spring
Height: 6 in
Spread: 24–36 in
Situation: ◑
Moisture requirement: ◗
❈ ❈ ❈

Bugle is a member of the *Ajuga* genus which includes approximately 50 species of hardy annuals and herbaceous perennials, semi-evergreen or evergreen creeping rhizomes which make excellent ground cover. *A. reptans* grows in Europe, northwest Africa, Turkey, Iran and the Caucasus. It has attractive, dark green, undivided, at times toothed, leaves arranged in opposite pairs and two-lipped, tubular-shaped, mostly dark blue flowers which appear in spring and early summer. Cultivated varieties make excellent garden plants which thrive particularly well in moist conditions in a sunny or shady position. It can be sown in spring or autumn and propagated by division or by cuttings of rooted runners after flowering. *A. reptans* is a mildly analgesic, astringent herb with laxative properties. It is also used to treat bruises, wounds and burns caused by scalding. In addition, it contains compounds used in the treatment of cancer and in pest control. All the parts of the plant can be used.

Garlic

Allium sativum

ⓘ

Family: Alliaceae
Flowering season: summer
Height: 12–36 in
Spread: 12 in
Situation: ○
Moisture requirement: ○
❈ ❈ ❈
✿

Garlic, one of the oldest herbs known to man, belongs to the onion family. This group comprises approximately 800 species with bulbs, rhizomes or fibrous rootstock which flower in spring, summer or autumn. Most species are native to the dry, mountainous regions of the northern hemisphere. A single bulb produces further numerous secondary bulbs which then form clumps. The flowers are tubular at the base and bell, star or cup-shaped. They are borne in larger or smaller pendant terminal umbels. These mostly spherical flower-heads measure 3/8 to 4 in. *A. sativum* is a sharp herb with a powerful aroma. It is used to fight bacterial infections, lower blood-pressure and cholesterol and lower blood sugar levels and fever by increasing perspiration. In autumn, the bulbs are planted whole or as separate cloves, 2 to 4 in deep in the soil. The bulbs of the white or pink flowering plants, which now contain 5 to 18 cloves, can be harvested the following late summer or autumn. They must be dried in the air and stored in a frost-free place.

Chives
Allium schoenoprasum

Chives shares the same properties as the other members of the onion family but they are milder and rarely used for medicinal purposes. The plants are cultivated for their hollow, cylindrical, dark-green leaves, but the bulbs are also used. Chives are propagated by seed in spring or by division in autumn or spring. They can be planted in any well-drained, fertile soil in a sunny position, but they will also grow in semi-shade. The pale-purple or pure white, bell-shaped flowers are grouped in globular heads 1 in wide. Chives add a delicious flavour to potatoes and eggs. Both the leaves and bulbs are used to garnish and season soups, salads, fromage frais, omelettes and sauces such as remoulade. The flowers have an exquisitely delicate onion flavor.

Family: Alliaceae
Flowering season: summer
Height: 12–24 in
Spread: 4 in
Situation: ○
Moisture requirement: ◖
❋ ❋ ❋
❀

Allium schoenoprasum

Dill

Anethum graveolens

ⓘ

Family: Apiaceae
Flowering season: summer
Height: 4 ft
Spread: 18 in
Situation: ○
Moisture requirement: ○
❀ ❀ ❀
❀

Dill is an aromatic annual with hollow, finely-ridged, erect stems. It probably originates from southwest Asia, perhaps India, but today it is found all around the Mediterranean and western Asia. In the Far East, dill has been known as an important medicinal plant since Biblical times, while in India, dill has been used for centuries both as medicinal herb and as a condiment. The three- to four-fold pinnate oblong or obvate leaves, up to 14 in long, are divided into numerous thin, thread-like, blue-green feathery leaves. Propagation is by successional sowings directly outdoors from March to July, thus ensuring a constant supply. The very small yellow flowers, borne in umbels, bloom in July and August, later producing oval, flat seeds. The freshly chopped leaves add a sharp, refreshing, delicious aromatic taste to fish, eggs and potatoes. In addition, dill promotes digestion and is an excellent diuretic. Sprigs of dill are added to pickles, while the seeds are used in curry powder.

Chervil

Anthriscus cerefolium

ⓘ

Family: Apiaceae
Flowering season: spring
Height: up to 20 in
Spread: 10 in
Situation: ◐
Moisture requirement: ○ – ◑
❀ ❀ ❀
❀

Chervil which grows in Europe and western Asia is an aromatic biennial, usually cultivated as an annual. The hollow stems bear bright green, multi-pinnate, fern-like leaves which smell like aniseed. It grows in any type of soil – also in pots – in sun or partial shade and combines well with other shade-loving kitchen herbs. To ensure a constant supply, chervil is sown outdoors at regular intervals between March and August. In appearance, chervil is similar to parsley. The small white flowers, grouped in umbels, grow from the leaf axils in early summer and are followed by tiny fruits. The leaves must be picked before the plant flowers and are usually consumed fresh. In fact, it is best not to dry chervil because much of the aroma disappears in the process. On the other hand, it freezes very well. Today, it is mainly used in French cuisine where it is served mostly with fish and poultry. Because the fragrance of aniseed is quite delicate and therefore disappears very quickly, chervil is usually added just before serving.

Arnica

Arnica montana

True arnica grows in the wild in the mountain ranges of Central Europe, in peaty areas with acidic soil or in sunny meadows where the soil contains little chalk. It is a protected plant. Its habit of growth is upright, with few branches and the flower stems rise from a strong rosette of leaves. The long leaves themselves are covered with soft hairs and, like the flowers, are aromatic. The bright yellow flower-heads, which have a diameter of up to 3 in, are an eye-catching feature and attract bees and butterflies. The seed-heads, which develop in late summer, resemble dandelion clocks. As a garden plant, arnica prefers dry, acid soils poor in nutrients, and will grow in either sun or partial shade. It is a good perennial for rock gardens or herbaceous borders. The ripened seeds can easily be harvested and sown in autumn directly in the ground where they are to grow. Arnica is a traditional medicinal plant, well known for helping wounds to heal quickly. But a word of warning: if eaten, all parts of the plant will cause severe nausea, and the sap can cause allergies in certain sensitive people.

Family: Asteraceae
Flowering season: summer
Height and spread: 12 × 20 in
Situation: ○
Moisture requirement: ◖
❄ ❄ ❄
Medicinal and aromatic plant
❀
Attracts bees and butterflies

Artemisia

Artemisia ludoviciana

The *Artemisia* genus consists of approximately 300 species of evergreen or semi-evergreen shrubs and herbaceous perennials. Artemisia is found mainly in the northern hemisphere where it thrives in dry soil in the countryside, in copses and among shrubby undergrowth – some species are found in southern Africa and southern America. Artemisia is cultivated mainly for its gray or silvery, aromatic, often divided or multi-pinnate, feathery leaves. It is propagated by seed in spring or autumn in the cool greenhouse, some species can be divided in spring or autumn. Artemisia dracunculus (tarragon) is mainly cultivated as a kitchen herb. There are other species which are bitter herbs used to treat fever and as a vermifuge. *A. ludoviciana* is a herbaceous perennial with rhizomes which throw up lanceolate, downy, silvery-white to gray-green leaves. The brownish-yellow, cylindrical flower-heads appear in mid-summer and continue blooming until autumn. The leaves and stems are used in mixed fragrances and in white or silver borders and flower arrangements.

Family: Asteraceae
Flowering season: summer
Height: up to 4 ft
Spread: variable
Situation: ○
Moisture requirement: ◌
❄ ❄ ❄
❁

235

Borage

Borago officinalis

ℹ

Family: Boraginaceae
Flowering season: spring/summer
Height: 24 in
Spread: 18 in
Situation: ○
Moisture requirement: ○
❀ ❀ ❀

B. officinalis or borage is an annual herb with erect, hollow stems and ovate leaves covered with silvery hairs. It belongs to a genus consisting of hardy annual and perennial species, native to Mediterranean and western Asia. Borage has hairy stems and ovate, alternate leaves, also covered with rough silvery hairs. The blue flowers which appear in summer are star-shaped and grouped in umbel-like panicles. The fruits later develop into small brown to black seeds. Some species have colorful foliage. The name is derived from the Latin word *borra* (stiff hair) and refers to the rough hairs on the leaves. Borage is propagated outdoors by seed in spring. Borage is a herb with a high salt content and diuretic properties. It also has a soothing effect on damaged or irritated tissue. In addition, it has sudorific properties and acts as a mild sedative and anti-depressive. The leaves give a cucumber-like taste to drinks. Finely chopped, it is often added to salads and herb cheeses. In Italy, it also prepared as a vegetable. The fresh flowers are often added to salads or used to garnish dishes.

Borago officinalis

Black mustard

Brassica nigra

The *Brassica* genus consists of 30 hardy species, mostly annual or biennial herbs which are found everywhere on farmland and along river-banks throughout Europe and Asia. *B. nigra* is an annual with a strongly branched stem and lobed, oblong to lanceolate, gray to blue-green leaves. The cross-shaped, gold-yellow flowers appear in summer grouped in bunches. The flowers later develop into small, erect, angular pods which contain black-brown seeds. Black mustard is propagated by seed outdoors in spring. Many parts of the plant are used, namely the leaves, flowers, seeds and oil produced from the seeds. It is a herb with a hot, sharp taste which stimulates the blood circulation and digestive system but irritates the skin and mucous membrane. Externally, it can be used a poultice, mustard plaster and in the bath to treat rheumatic and muscular pain. It is also used to treat infections of the respiratory tract. The young leaves and flowers add a pleasant piquancy to salads. The seeds are ground to make mustard and are often used whole in curry dishes and vegetables preserves. The flowers are used as decorations in punch bowls or as a garnish in salads.

ⓘ

Family: Brassicaceae
Flowering season: spring
Height: 3–10 ft
Spread: 4 ft
Situation: ○
Moisture requirement: ◌
❀ ❀ ❀
❀

Calendula officinalis

Pot marigold

Calendula officinalis

The *Calendula* genus includes 20 to 30 species of hardy, bush-like, fast-growing annuals, perennials and evergreen sub-shrubs native to the Mediterranean. Only *C. officinalis* and its varieties are cultivated as ornamental plants, culinary herbs or medicinal plants. The pot marigold is a bushy, aromatic, long-lived annual with branched stems and pointed, alternate, aromatic leaves. The daisy-like flower heads with orange or yellow ray flowers and yellow, orange, violet, purple or brown tubular central florets appear in summer and continue until the autumn. Propagation is by seed in spring or autumn, after which it often self-seeds. On the Indian sub-continent and in the Arab world, pot marigold is used as a medicinal herb, a fabric dye, in the manufacture of cosmetics and as food. The petals are used in rice and soups as a substitute for saffron and also fresh in salads. Pot marigold is also used internally as a homeopathic remedy and externally to treat skin problems.

ⓘ

Family: Asteraceae
Flowering season: summer/autumn
Height: 20–28 in
Spread: 20–28 in
Situation: ◑
Moisture requirement: ◌
❀ ❀ ❀
❀

237

Coriander

Coriandrum sativum

ℹ

Family: Apiaceae
Flowering season: summer
Height: 20–28 in
Spread: 8 in
Situation: ○
Moisture requirement: ◌
✿ ✿ ✿
❀

The coriander genus consists of two species of annuals which are both native to Southeast Asia and North Africa. *C. sativum* is one of the oldest known herbs which was already cultivated some 3,000 years ago. Coriander was already mentioned in manuscripts of classical antiquity as well as in many medieval herb books. It is an erect annual with very fragrant, serrated, oval pinnatipartite leaves, divided into oblong or linear leaflets. The small, cup-shaped flowers, are borne in terminal umbels, surrounded by large fertile white or purple flower heads which later develop into spherical, light brown fruits. Propagation is by seeds sown in spring. Both the seeds and leaves are used in cooking. Because the leaves and seeds have a different flavor, they are used in different types of dishes. The freshly chopped leaves are much used in south-east Asian cuisine. In medicine, the seeds are used ground, as a liquid extract or as a distilled oil, which is also used in the perfume industry.

Artichoke

Cynara scolymus

ℹ

Family: Asteraceae
Flowering season: autumn
Height: 6 ft 6 in
Spread: 4 ft
Situation: ○
Moisture requirement: ◌
✿ ✿ ✿

The *Cynara* genus consists of ten hardy, perennial, thistle-like, herbaceaus species which grow on well-drained, sunny hillsides around the Mediterranean, in North Africa and Canary Isles. *C. scolymus* is a large, erect, very beautiful shrub with deeply-lobed or pinnate, silver or gray-green leaves with pointed lobes, covered with gray hairs on top and a dense, white, woolly down underneath. It has large spherical flower heads which appear singly or in umbel-like panicles. The flower heads consist of small purple flowers and appear in summer. Artichokes are propagated in spring by sowing in a cool greenhouse and by planting suckers in spring or autumn as well as by cuttings in winter. The overlapping floral bracts and the bottom or heart of the flower heads of some species are edible when still in the bud stage, as are the young leaf shoots. Artichoke is a bitter, slightly salty herb whose active agent cynarin stimulates the liver and gall bladder while reducing the cholesterol level in the blood.

Echinacea purpurea

Echinacea, purple cone flower

Echinacea purpurea (syn. Rudbeckia purpurea)

E. purpurea or purple cone flower is one of the nine hardy perennial herbaceous species which makes up this genus. Echinacea purpurea thrives in the dry prairies, stony mountain slopes and wooded copses of eastern North America. It was already used by native American Indians to treat wounds. The purple cone flower has short, thin, black rhizomes. The erect hairy stems have lanceolate, smooth-edged or slightly toothed or deeply pinnatifid, dark green leaves, covered with rough hairs. The single, daisy-like purple, red or pink flower heads have pointed bracts underneath and striking brown-yellow or orange, oval or cone-shaped centers. It is propagated by sowing seeds in spring, taking cuttings in autumn and early winter, and dividing in autumn and spring. Echinacea was mentioned in the ancient Vedic manuscripts on healing and in Western medicine today it is considered an effective detoxification treatment for the lymphatic system and respiratory tract.

ℹ

Family: Asteraceae
Flowering season: summer
Height: 3–10 ft
Spread: 18 in
Situation: ○
Moisture requirement: ◊
❄ ❄ ❄

239

Arugula salad or garden arugula

Eruca sativa

ⓘ

Family: Brassicaceae
Flowering season: spring
Height: 24–36 in
Spread: 6–8 in
Situation: ○
Moisture requirement: ◌
❊ ❊

The *Eruca* genus consists of five annual and perennial species native to the Mediterranean and eastern Asia, although it is now cultivated in many other places. It was much loved by the ancient Romans who used it in salads. *E. sativa* is a robust, erect, mustard-like annual with asymmetric, toothed leaves. The cream-colored flowers have four petals with purple-colored veins which bloom from late winter to autumn when the slender, erect shoots begin to grow. A constant supply is ensured by sowing outdoors at regular intervals from March to June or in late summer for an autumn harvest. Arugula also has a tendency to self-seed. In the past, arugula was also used to stimulate digestion. Today, it is used mainly in salads because the leaves add a particularly pleasant, peppery taste. Plants which are cultivated in dry, hot regions have a sharper taste and aroma than those grown in moist, fertile soil. Arugula can also be grown in borders among flowers.

Foeniculum vulgare

Fennel

Foeniculum vulgare

ⓘ

Family: Apiaceae
Flowering season: summer
Height: up to 7 ft
Spread: 18 in
Situation: ○
Moisture requirement: ◌
❊ ❊ ❊
✿

Fennel is a hardy herbaceous biennial or perennial, native to the European part of the Mediterranean and Asia. It thrives in the sun in dry soil, especially near the coast. In classical times, fennel was used as an herb and a vegetable. Today, fennel is cultivated almost everywhere in the world, even in Australia. All the parts of the plant are aromatic and taste like aniseed. It develops deep roots and grows slender stems and delicate, thread-like leaves which smell and taste like aniseed. The tiny yellow flowers are borne in flat umbels and later develop into aromatic, gray-brown fruit. It is propagated in spring by sowing from seed or by planting self-seeded seedlings. The biennial type forms a thickened, bulbous stem base and is cultivated as a vegetable. Both leaves and seeds are used in cooking and medicine, especially as a treatment for digestive problems, flatulence and colic. Crushed seeds are used to make herb tea and the oil is used in the perfume industry.

Woodruff

Galium odoratum

Galium is a large widespread genus grouping some 400 annual and perennial species which grow in woodland, thickets, meadows and wasteland. One of the species, *G. odoratum* or woodruff, is a well-known deciduous garden plant which grows in places as varied as Siberia and North Africa. It is an excellent ground cover for shady places. A herbaceous plant with a spreading rhizome root system, it develops erect, angular shoots and basal whorls consisting of six to nine lanceolate to elliptic, bright green leaves with shallow, toothed edges. It forms fragrant, white, star-shaped flowers borne in terminal or axillary umbels from late spring to mid-summer. When ripe, the seeds are sown in a shady, cool greenhouse and the rhizome is divided in autumn or early spring. Woodruff is an astringent, slightly bitter herb which develops a strong aroma when dried. Woodruff has strong, diuretic and relaxing properties. It also stimulates the liver, relaxes cramp and reduces the risk of blood clotting.

ⓘ

Family: Rubiaceae
Flowering season: spring
Height: up to 18 in
Spread: variable
Situation: ◐
Moisture requirement: 💧
❄❄❄
❀

Gaultheria procumbens

Partridge berry

Gaultheria procumbens

The *Gaultheria* genus is made up of 200 species of small, evergreen, flowering shrubs, sometimes rhizomatous. It is native to the Andes, North America, Australia and eastern Asia where it grows in woodland. It also grows in in moist places the Himalayas. Many species are cultivated for their waxy flowers and colorful berries. *G. procumbens*, also known as wintergreen and checkerberry, grows in dry woodland in the eastern regions of North America. It is a creeper with a spreading rhizome root system and therefore makes an excellent groundcover. The shiny, dark green leaves, which are obovate or ovate and toothed, appear at the end of the shoots. When crushed, they emanate a strong, wintergreen smell. In summer, the plant produces pale pink flowers which are single or borne in terminal racemes. The flowers later develop into bright red berries which remain on the plant until spring. The seeds are sown in autumn in a cool greenhouse. Gaultheria is an astringent, aromatic, warming herb with anti-inflammatory properties.

ⓘ

Family: Ericaceae
Flowering season: summer
Height: 6 in
Spread: 3 ft and more
Situation: ◐
Moisture requirement: 💧
❄❄❄
❀

Licorice

Glycyrrhiza glabra

Family: Fabaceae
Flowering season: summer
Height: 4 ft
Spread: 3 ft
Situation: ○
Moisture requirement: ◐ but ○
❊ ❊ ❊

Glycyrrhiza is a genus of 20 summer-flowering perennial species which grow in the Mediterranean, tropical Asia, Australia and America. *G. glabra*, also known as licorice, Spanish juice or black sugar is found in southwest Asia and the Mediterranean. Licorice was already highly valued in ancient Egypt, Assyria and China because the glycyrrhizin it contains is 50 times sweeter than raw sugar, but it only reached Europe in the 15th century. *G. glabra* is a variable perennial with a spreading rootstock, downy stems and leaves divided into oval leaflets and covered with sticky, glandular hairs. The pea-like, pale blue to violet flowers are borne in loose spikes and later develop into oblong pods. Licorice is propagated by seed in pots outdoors in autumn or spring or by root division in early spring. The roots and suckers of this sweet, calming herb are medicinally useful because of their anti-inflammatory and expectorant properties. The plant is also used to make sweets and confectionery by boiling its roots to extract the licorice.

St. John's Wort

Hypericum

Family: Clusiaceae
Flowering season: summer
Height: 2 ft–3 ft 6in
Spread: 2 ft
Situation: ○
Moisture requirement: ○
❊ ❊ ❊
❀

Hypericum, or St. John's Wort, belongs to a genus of 400 species of deciduous, semi-evergreen or evergreen shrubs or semi-shrubs and herbaceous annuals and perennials which are found in many parts of the world. It grows mostly in temperate regions, in woodland and thickets, on mountain slopes and rocks. The leaves are opposite, occasionally whorled and often have beautiful autumn colors. The yellow flowers with their striking stamens are borne singly or in the terminal leaf axils. Some species have berry-like fruits which may contain between three to five capsules. Propagation is by seed, sown in autumn or spring in a cool greenhouse. *H. guttiferae*, the true St John's Wort, grows in Europe in thickets and woods and in the temperate regions of Asia. It is a bitter-sweet, cooling, astringent herb which calms the nerves, reduces inflammation, has antiseptic and analgesic properties and promotes healing. The foliage is poisonous and is not edible.

Hyssop

Hyssopis officinalis

Hyssop belongs to a genus of herbaceous perennials and semi-evergreen or evergreen and deciduous shrubs which thrive in dry soil and can be found from the Mediterranean to Central Asia. The leaves are narrow and lanceolate, ovate or oblong and green to blue-green. The dense spikes of tubular, two-lipped, purple-blue flowers – very occasionally white or pink – appear in late summer. Hyssop is propagated in autumn or spring by seed in a cool greenhouse and in summer by basal cuttings. Hyssop is a perfect plant for the herb garden or rockery, as a low thicket or hedge, near sunny, warm walls or in pots. Hyssop was mentioned in the Old Testament as a medicinal plant with cleansing effect. It is a bitter aromatic herb with expectorant and anti-inflammatory properties. It lowers fever and contains camphor-like essential oils and other compounds which are used in the treatment of bronchial problems. The leaves taste a little like sage and mint and are used to add flavor to pulses and meat dishes.

ⓘ

Family: Lamiaceae
Flowering season: summer
Height: 18–24 in
Spread: 24–36 in
Situation: ○
Moisture requirement: ◊
✽ ✽ ✽
❀

Bay, bay laurel

Laurus nobilis

L. nobilis, bay or bay laurel, belongs to a genus of two species of evergreen trees or shrubs which are native to the Azores, Canary Islands and the Mediterranean where they are found mainly in low copses and rocky soils. Often cultivated as an ornamental plant, L. nobilis, sweet bay or bay laurel is grown for its aromatic leaves which are often used in cooking. The lanceolate, alternate leaves are shiny and dark green. Clusters of tiny, pale yellow flowers on female plants develop into oval, purple-black berries. It is propagated by semi-ripe cuttings in summer and by seeds sown in a cool greenhouse in autumn. Bay laurel is often grown in tubs but, being sensitive to frost, it should overwinter in a cool greenhouse. Whole branches are cut off and dried upside down in a warm, well-aired place. Dried bay leaves are an important ingredient in European cuisine.

Laurus nobilis

ⓘ

Family: Lauraceae
Flowering season: spring
Height: up to 40 ft
Spread: up to 33 ft
Situation: ○
Moisture requirement: ◊
✽ ✽
❀

243

Lavandula angustifolia and Malva moschata

ⓘ

Family: Lamiaceae
Flowering season: summer/autumn
Height: 10 in–4 ft
Spread: 12 in–5 ft
Situation: ◯
Moisture requirement: ◌
❈– ❈ ❈ ❈
✿

*L*avender

Lavandula angustifolia

The *Lavandula* genus consists of approximately 25 species of aromatic evergreen shrubs and semi-shrubs which grow on dry, sunny, rocky hill slopes around the Mediterranean, Canaries, North Africa and can be found as far afield as southwest Asia and India. The gray-green leaves, arranged in opposite pairs, are fernlike and toothed, the edge often turning inward. Lavender is cultivated mainly for the long-stemmed spikes of fragrant, two-lipped, blue, purple or white flowers. Lavender also attracts bees which love the large amounts of nectar contained in the flowers. It is propagated in spring or early autumn by seed in a cold frame or cool greenhouse and in summer by semi-ripe cuttings. Species sensitive to frost should be protected in winter and those in tubs should be allowed to overwinter in a cool greenhouse or conservatory. When intended for drying, the flowers should be cut before they are in full bloom. The essential oil obtained from the flowers of *L. angustifolia* has curative properties and is also used in the perfume industry.

ⓘ

Family: Apiaceae
Flowering season: summer
Height: 7 ft
Spread: 36 in
Situation: ◯
Moisture requirement: ◌
❈ ❈ ❈
✿

*L*ovage

Levisticum officinale

Lovage, also known as love parsley, is a genus with a single perennial species, native to the eastern Mediterranean and more especially to Liguria in Italy. It has strong fleshy roots, hollow stems and slightly pinnate, triangular or diamond-shaped, dark green leaves which can grow up to 3 in long. The leaves have an interesting taste, reminiscent of celery and yeast. The tiny, star-shaped, greenish-yellow flowers are borne in flat umbels which later develop into oval, slightly winged, green fruit. It can be raised from seed in a seedbed or propagated by division in spring. Lovage is a bitter-sweet, calming, very aromatic herb which promotes digestion, relaxes cramps and activates perspiration. It also has diuretic and expectorant properties. Young shoots can be prepared like vegetables while the leaves are used to flavor soups and stews as well as salads. The leaves may irritate the skin.

Wild camomile

Matricaria recutita

Wild camomile, which grows wild almost everywhere in Europe, Asia Minor, Iran, India and even China, is very similar in its chemical composition to *Anthemis nobilis* or common or Roman camomile, but with a less strong aroma. It is a sweetly scented annual plant with erect, strongly branched stems. The single flowers are borne at the end of the long stems. The bright green, deeply lobed leaves have narrow, pointed leaflets. The daisy-like flowers start life with a flat center consisting of hollow, golden-yellow, five-petalled, central florets, surrounded by a crown of white ray-flowers. Gradually, the flat center becomes cone-shaped so that the ray flowers look as if they are sloping downward. Wild camomile is raised from seed in spring and autumn, but it also a strong tendency to propagate by self-seeding. It is a bitter, aromatic, calming herb with anti-inflammatory, antispasmodic, analgesic and healing properties. Camomile has been known as a medicinal herb since antiquity. Camomile oil, on the other hand, was first mentioned only in 1588.

Lemon balm

Melissa officinalis

The *Melissa* genus consists of three herbaceous perennial species which grow in Europe, North Africa and can be found as far as Central Asia. *M. officinalis*, also known as lemon balm, sweet balm and balm mint, has been cultivated for over 2000 years. It is a bushy herbaceous plant with an erect habit. The angular branched stems are covered with hairs and the pale to medium green, oval leaves with slightly serrated edges are arranged in opposite pairs. When crushed, they emanate a strong lemony scent. The two-lipped, pale-yellow flowers, which later develop a white or lilac hue, are grouped in clusters in the leaf axils. Lemon balm is raised from seed in a cool greenhouse and it is recommended that you thin the seedlings as they grow bigger in autumn. Lemon balm is an aromatic, calming, cooling herb which lowers fever, promotes digestion and has antispasmodic properties while relaxing the peripheral blood vessels. It contains lemon-scented essential oils which have anti-viral properties. The freshly chopped leaves are used in salads, soups, sauces, herb vinegar, game and fish dishes to add a delicate lemony flavor.

ⓘ

Family: Asteraceae
Flowering season: spring/summer
Height: 6–24 in
Spread: 4–16 in
Situation: ○
Moisture requirement: ○
❄ ❄ ❄
❀

Melissa officinalis

ⓘ

Family: Lamiaceae
Flowering season: summer
Height: 2–4 ft
Spread: 18 in
Situation: ○
Moisture requirement: ◖ *but* ○
❄ ❄ ❄
❀

Mints

Mints

The genus *Mentha* contains 25 species, all of them highly aromatic. Common mint or spearmint (*Mentha spicata*) smells like chewing-gum, apple mint or round-leaved mint – (*M. x rotundifolia*) lends its fragrance to the mint tea so popular in North Africa, and we are all acquainted with the true peppermint (*M. x piperita*). In the wild, the plants, most of which form rhizomes, grow in moist soils in Europe, Africa and Asia. Mints are cultivated chiefly as culinary and medicinal herbs, but their leaves, pale to dark green or even tinged with red, are very decorative too. In summer, they bear white, pink or purple flowers, depending on the species, usually in dense spikes and very popular with bees and butterflies. If you grow mint in your garden, you can keep gathering fresh leaves to flavor food or make refreshing mint tea. Mints need a situation in sun to partial shade, and rather moist, loamy soil rich in humus is ideal. Since the underground rootstocks of most species spread very vigorously, it is a good idea to restrain their invasive tendency by knocking the base out of a container, sinking it in the soil, and planting the mint in it. The shoots will die down in winter, but come up again in spring. Covering with twigs as protection from frost is advisable, especially in regions where the winters are severe. Mints can be propagated from seed in spring, by division of the rhizomes in autumn or spring, or by cuttings from the tips of the plant taken in spring or summer. There is also a wide range of young plants on sale.

Peppermint

Mentha × piperita

ⓘ

Family: Lamiaceae
Flowering season: summer
Height: 12–36 in
Spread: variable
Situation: ◯
Moisture requirement: ◗
❄ ❄ ❄
✿

The *Mentha* genus consists of 25 species of aromatic, fragrant, herbaceous perennials with rootstocks which grow wild in Europe, Africa and Africa in moist or wet soil and even in shallow water. The erect, branched stems have oval to round leaves whose color ranges from bright or dark green to blue, purple or gray-green. *M.x piperata* has erect, square, often reddish-green stems and a thick woody rootstock. The smooth, oval leaves with clearly marked veins have a sharply toothed edge. The pink to lilac flowers are grouped in loose terminal spikes. It is propagated by division in autumn or spring or by cuttings in spring and summer. These cuttings develop during the growth period. The plant has a spicy fragrance. Mint leaves are among the most popular medicinal herbs because of the antispasmodic and disinfectant properties of its essential oils. Peppermint is used to treat nausea, digestive problems, stomach ulcers, gastro-enteritis, irritable bowel, colic, influenza (especially during the feverish stage) and colds. The leaves contain tannic agents and are used to treat diarrhoea. It is also used externally to treat infections of the respiratory tract, paranasal sinusitis, catarrh, asthma, itching, burns, eczema, neuralgia, rheumatism and insect bites.

Red mint

Mentha × smithiana

ⓘ

Family: Lamiaceae
Flowering season: summer
Height: 3 ft
Spread: variable
Situation: ◯
Moisture requirement: ◗
❄ ❄ ❄
✿

M. x smithiana or red mint is a creeping, spreading perennial with sweetly scented oval to ovate, toothed, downy, dark-green leaves with a reddish hue. The pinkish-red to lilac tubular, sterile flowers are borne in terminal whorls, usually at a distance from each other, but sometimes also close together. It is an aromatic plant whose taste is very similar to that of spearmint. It has stimulant, antispasmodic properties and promotes digestion. Its oil is less strong than that of peppermint and not as pleasant. Internally, it used to treat digestive disorders, colic, flatulence, hiccups, feverish colds in children. It is also used as a taste enhancer in food such as chewing gum and mouthwashes. The leaves are used in the preparation of the well-known English mint sauce and jelly which are a traditional accompaniment to lamb and in the Greek yogurt sauce *tzatziki*.

Apple mint

Mentha suaveolens

M. suaveolens, also known as apple mint or round-leaved mint, is one of the most attractive kinds of mint found in Western and southern Europe, especially in the Mediterranean. It is a vigorous, creeping perennial with irregular stems, oval to round gray-green, toothed, downy, slightly wrinkled leaves with wavy edges. The tubular pink to white flowers which appear in summer are grouped in dense terminal whorls or branched spikes. *M. suaveolens* can become scorched in the strong sun. The aromatic herb has a sweet, appley scent combined with a spearmint fragrance. Because its flavor is superior to that of other mint varieties, it is considered the best flavored and most popular culinary mint. It is also often used to decorate dishes, especially puddings. In addition, the leaves crystallize extremely well because of the fine hairs covering them.

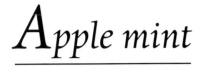

Family: Lamiaceae
Flowering season: summer
Height: up to 3 ft
Spread: variable
Situation: ○ – ◑
Moisture requirement: ◗
❀ ❀ ❀
❀

Horsemint

Monarda

The *Monarda* genus consists of 15 species of hardy annuals and bushy, herbaceous perennials with rootstock and aromatic leaves. They grow on the dry prairies and bushland of North America, but also in damp woodland. Horsemint was used by many North American Indian tribes. The aromatic, mid- to dark green or purple leaves, which may be alternate or opposite, are on single or slightly branched stems. The leaves are lanceolate to oval with a toothed or smooth edge. The leaf veins are raised. The tubular, sage-like white, red or violet flowers often have colored bracts and form capitate, terminal whorl heads. The upper lip of the flower is hooded (galeiform) and erect, the lower lip is three-lobed and broad. Horsemint is raised from seed in spring or autumn in a cool greenhouse, by division in spring or basal cuttings in early summer. Some species exude a scent which resembles that of bergamot. Many are used to flavor meat dishes while other are used to make herbal teas.

Family: Lamiaceae
Flowering season: summer
Height: 3–4 ft
Spread: 18 in
Situation: ○
Moisture requirement: ◗ *but* ○
❀ ❀ ❀
❀

Nepeta cataria mit Geum

ℹ️

Family: Lamiaceae
Flowering season: summer
Height: 12–24 in
Spread: up to 24 in
Situation: ○
Moisture requirement: ◌
❀ ❀ ❀
❀

Catnip

Nepeta cataria

Nepeta is a genus of approximately 250 species of herbaceous perennials and a few annuals which grow in Europe and Asia, North Africa and in the mountains of tropical Africa. They thrive in cold, damp places, in hot, dry areas, on stony slopes or on high mountainsides. Catnip or N. cataria has ovate to lanceolate, aromatic leaves with a smooth, indented or toothed edge, arranged in opposite pairs. In some species, the leaves are covered with downy hairs which gives them a silvery, gray-green appearance. The irregularly two-lipped, white, occasionally yellow, blue or white tubular flowers which grow in whorls. The flowers are grouped in spikes, panicles or clusters and bloom for a long time. It is propagated in autumn by seed in a cool greenhouse, by division in spring or autumn and by cuttings from spring to early summer. Catnip is a bitter, astringent herb with a camphor-like aroma which lowers fever, increases perspiration and has antispasmodic and calming properties. It has a stimulant effect on cats; they eat the plant and love rolling in it.

Basil

Ocimum basilicum

Ocimum is a genus of approximately 65 species of aromatic annual and perennial plants, evergreen herbs and shrubs which grow in the hot tropical regions of Africa and Asia. Aromatic basil later travelled from ancient Egypt to Greece and Rome, where it became a very popular culinary herb. The species most frequently cultivated is *O. basilicum* and its varieties. It is an erect, bushy, aromatic herbaceous annual with linear, ovate, often downy, bright green leaves, sometimes tinged with purple, with smooth or serrated edges. The small, white, tubular, two-lipped flowers, often tinged with pink-purple, grow in loose, downy whorls from the leaf axils. Basil is raised from seed in pots under glass at a temperature of 55°F. In warm regions it is also sown outdoors in late spring or early summer. In spring, it can also be propagated by cuttings. Because basil is very sensitive to cold, it should not be sown or planted out too early or when the weather is still cold. It is an invigorating, warming, aromatic herb with antispasmodic properties. It also lowers fever, promotes digestion and is used in the treatment of bacterial infections and intestinal parasites. In cooking, basil is used above all with tomatoes and in the preparation of pesto, the Italian sauce. The essential oil extracted from basil is used in the perfume industry and aromatherapy, mouthwashes and insecticides.

O. basilicum citriodorum, a type of basil native to northwest India, is a bushy annual or herbaceous perennial with narrow, oval leaves which smell of lemon. The seeds of the white, tubular, two-lipped flowers also have a lemony smell. This kind of basil is particularly good for flavoring herb vinegar and fish dishes.

O. basilicum purpurascens is an erect, bushy, strongly branched annual or herbaceous perennial with small, tubular, two-lipped, pink flowers, grouped in spikes. The ovate leaves tinged with purple-red exude a spicy fragrance.

Family: Lamiaceae
Flowering season: summer
Height: 8–24 in
Spread: 6–18 in
Situation: ○
Moisture requirement: ◌
❄
❀

Evening Primrose

Oenothera biennis

The 125 species of the *Oenothera* genus are mostly native to North America with a few exceptions which originate from South America. The genus includes annuals, biennials and herbaceous perennials with tap roots, some with rhizomes or runners. *O. biennis* or evening primrose is a hardy biennial whose erect or ground-hugging stems have alternate, lanceolate to a greater or lesser extent, whole or lobed leaves with smooth or serrated edges and occasionally with basal rosettes of larger leaves. It flowers between June and August with a profusion of pale yellow flowers which appear towards the evening and which later develop into downy pods filled with tiny seeds. It can be raised from seed in June in a cool greenhouse or directly outdoors between June and August. The seeds produce evening primrose oil which contains gamma-linoleic acid, an unsaturated fatty acid which is used in the manufacturing of hormone-like substances. It also has blood-cleansing properties. The oil is also used in skincare products and cosmetics.

Family: Onagraceae
Flowering season: summer
Height: up to 5 ft
Spread: up to 2 ft
Situation: ○
Moisture requirement: ◌
❄ ❄ ❄

Marjoram

Origanum majorana

i

Family: Lamiaceae
Flowering season: summer
Height: up to 20 in
Spread: 18 in
Situation: ○
Moisture requirement: ◌
❊ ❊
❀

Origanum is a genus of 20 species of aromatic herbaceous, summer-flowering plants and evergreen or semi-evergreen sub-shrubs and shrubs, native to the mountains regions of the Mediterranean and southwest Asia. Most species are valued for their strong aromatic fragrance and are used to enhance the flavor of food. *O. majorana* (marjoram) is a perennial, evergreen sub-shrub with slender, erect, red-brown stems and downy, gray-green ovate or elliptical leaves. The inconspicuous white to pink, tubular flowers appear in late summer. All origanum species are propagated by seed in a cool greenhouse or by divison. They can also be propagated in early summer by basal cuttings of cuttings from non-flowering shoots. *O. majorana* has a more delicate aroma than *O. vulgare* and is best used fresh. The leaves and flowering sprigs are particularly popular in Italian and Greek cuisine where they are used to season meat dishes, soups, tomato sauces and pasta as well as oil and vinegar.

Common or wild marjoram, oregano

Origanum vulgare

i

Family: Lamiaceae
Flowering season: summer
Height: 16–24 in
Spread: 18 in
Situation: ○
Moisture requirement: ◌
❊ ❊ ❊
❀

O. vulgare, also known as wild or common marjoram or oregano, grows wild from Europe to Central Asia. It is a variable, bushy perennial with a woody base and rootstock. The upright or slightly outward-growing purple-brown stems have very aromatic, round to ovate dark-green leaves, often tinged with red. The pale to dark pink or white tubular flowers, surrounded by green bracts tinged with purple, are borne in dense clusters like panicles or umbel-like whorls from mid-summer to early autumn. It is a very aromatic, antiseptic herb with antispasmodic, sudorific and expectorant properties. It also promotes digestion and stimulates the womb. The leaves and flowering sprigs are used to make tea which is used to treat colds, flu, digestive problems and painful menstruation. It is much used in Italian, Greek and Mexican cuisine and in hot spicy dishes with chillies, garlic, tomatoes and onions.

Geranium

Pelargonium

Pelargonium is a genus of approximately 250 species of evergreen herbaceous plants, sub-shrubs, shrubs and succulents which grow mainly in South Africa. The leaves are usually alternate, palmate or pinnate, frequently with a stem and often fragrant. The erect shoots carry terminal, umbel-like clusters of five-petalled flowers. The flowers are bowl, trumpet or funnel-shaped. Pelargoniums, commonly known as geraniums, are propagated by cuttings between spring and autumn but cannot be grown outdoors all year round. That is why they should grown in pots or tubs that can be brought indoors, to a conservatory or greenhouse, during the winter months, and taken out again in the summer. Scented-leaf pelargoniums, shrubby, evergreen herbaceous perennials and shrubs, are cultivated mainly for their leaves which range from mid-green, often variegated, to golden or silvery; they are mostly very varied in shape and color. When crushed, the leaves exude an aromatic fragrance, similar to nutmeg or lemon, and are delicious added to salads. The mauve, pink, purple or white flowers are small and decorative.

ℹ

Family: Geraniaceae
Flowering season: summer
Height: variable
Spread: variable
Situation: ○
Moisture requirement: ◊
✳
❀

Pelagonium

Petroselinum crispum

*P*arsley

Petroselinum crispum

Petroselinum is a genus with three species of biennial plants with thick tap roots which grow on waste land and rocky slopes in the Mediterranean regions of Europe. Parsley is one of the most cultivated culinary herbs in Europe. The vigorous, hollow stems have triangular, densely curled, pinnate, mid-green leaves with serrated edges. Tiny, star-shaped, white or green-yellow, often red-tinged flowers grouped in umbels appear in the second summer and later develop into ovate fruits. Parsley can be raised outdoors from seed between spring and late summer. *P. crispum* is a biennial with white, tap roots and triangular, pinnate, curly leaves with frizzy edges. It is often and for decoration used to flavor and food. *P. crispum neapolitanum*, known as flat-leaved, has flat, dark-green, smooth leaves with a stronger taste. This type is hardier, larger and less sensitive to weather than the curly variety. All varieties of parsley are particularly rich in vitamins A and C.

ℹ

Family: Umbelliferae
Flowering season: summer
Height: up to 30 in
Spread: 24 in
Situation: ○
Moisture requirement: ○
❉ ❉ ❉

*L*esser celandine

Ranunculus ficaria

Ranunculus is a genus of 400 species of annual and biennial plants, herbaceous and tuberous-rooted perennials, some deciduous, some evergreen, native to the northern, temperate latitudes. Many species are water-plants or thrive in damp, wet places. R. ficaria, the lesser celandine, grows in Europe, Western Asia and North Africa. It is a low, spreading, carpet-forming herbaceous plant with fleshy roots and dark green, glossy leaves, serrated or indented along the edges. The yellow, singly borne, shallow, cup-shaped flowers appear in spring. Propagation is by seed in summer or by division in spring and autumn. Most species of the *Ranunculus* or buttercup family contain strong irritants which means they should not be ingested. This includes R. ficaria which is an astringent herb, used in the treatment of haemorrhoids.

ℹ

Family: Ranunculaceae
Flowering season: spring
Height: 6 in
Spread: 12 in
Situation: ○
Moisture requirement: ◐
❉ ❉ ❉
✖

Castor oil plant

Ricinus communis

Ricinus is a genus comprising one tender, shrubby, evergreen species which grows wild in from northeast Africa to western Asia and in many tropical regions. In the tropics, the castor oil plants grows as tall as a tree but in temperate regions, it is cultivated as half-hardy annual. *R. communis* is an erect, well-branched shrub, usually cultivated like an annual. It has alternate, very broad, ovate, toothed leaves which range from shiny mid-green to reddish-purple and bronze-red. The greenish yellow flowers, borne in ovate spikes, appear in summer. The small, red female flowers have striking red stigmas. The gray-brown seeds are contained in spherical, reddish-brown capsules with brown spikes. It can be raised from previously soaked seeds, sown singly in pots, at a temperature of 70°F. All the parts of the plant are extremely poisonous, especially the seeds. Merely touching the leaves can cause skin allergies. The oil extracted from the seed has strong laxative properties and is also used in the manufacturing of soap and cosmetics.

ℹ

Family: Euphorbiaceae
Flowering season: summer/autumn
Height: 3–7 ft
Spread: 3 ft
Situation: ○
Moisture requirement: ◑ *but* ○
❄
✖

Rosmarinus officinalis

Rosemary

Rosmarinus officinalis

Rosmarinus is a genus of three species of evergreen shrubs which grow in dry rocky slopes and woodland in southern Europe and Asia Minor. *R. officinalis* is a dense, bushy, erect, evergreen shrub. Its leathery, linear, dark green leaves which are arranged in opposite pairs are very aromatic. The edges are often rolled in towards the underside. The purple-blue or white, two-lipped, tubular flowers which are grouped in short whorls appear in spring and continue blooming until early summer. Frequently, it flowers again in autumn. It is raised from seed in spring in a cool greenhouse and in summer by semi-ripe cuttings. Rosemary thrives in a sunny position and must be protected from cold winter winds. It is an aromatic, invigorating herb which contains many essential oils. It has anti-inflammatory, antiseptic, antispasmodic, analgesic and sudorific properties. Fresh or dried sprigs of rosemary add a delicious flavor to all lamb dishes as well as many other recipes. Rosemary is an indispensable herb in the kitchen.

ℹ

Family: Lamiaceae
Flowering season: spring
Height: up to 7 ft
Spread: 5–7 ft
Situation: ○
Moisture requirement: ○
❄ ❄
❀

Rue

Ruta graveolens

Ruta is a genus with eight hardy, evergreen and semi-evergreen sub-shrubs or herbaceous perennials which turn woody at the base and grow in northeast Africa and from Eastern Europe to southwest Asia. *R. graveolens* is a small evergreen or semi-evergreen sub-shrub with alternate, sometimes opposite, broad ovate to round, pinnatipartite to deeply lobed leaves. The mustard-yellow, cup-shaped flowers with four fringed petals appear in summer and develop into four-lobed capsules. Rue is raised from seed in spring in cool greenhouse or semi-ripe cuttings in summer. It is a bitter, strong, warming herb with medicinal properties. It is used to alleviate menstrual pains, colic, epilepsy, rheumatic pain and treat eye infections. If ingested, rue can cause an unwell feeling and if it comes into contact with skin in bright sun, it can cause serious skin irritation. When used in cooking to season meat dishes, it should only be added in small amounts.

Ruta graveolens

256

Sage

Salvia officinalis

Salvia is a genus of 900 species found worldwide, especially in the warmer, temperate regions. They are mostly aromatic, annual, biennial or perennial, generally evergreen shrubs and semi-shrubs, a few of them with rhizomes or tuberous roots. Besides *S. officinalis*, all the species are sensitive to frost or half-hardy. The ovate to pinnate leaves with serrated or indented leaves grow in opposite pairs on the square stems. Many of the species are covered with fine hairs. The two-lipped flowers have a straight or hooded upper lip and a lobed, wider underlip. The calyx is tubular, bell or funnel-shaped. Sage or *S. officinalis,* which is a very popular culinary herb, has many well-branched stems, pale gray-green leaves and pink to violet flowers – very rarely white – which appear in summer. Sage is propagated by cuttings in late summer. Depending on the species, sage contains many different essential oils with many different aromas and applications. It is also used to make a tea because of its medicinal properties and it is an important ingredient in herb oils and vinegar.

ⓘ

Family: Labiatae / Lamiaceae
Flowering season: spring / autumn
Height: 1–10 ft
Spread: variable
Situation: ○
Moisture requirement: ◊
❈ – ❈ ❈ ❈
❀

Salvia

Common elder

Sambucus nigra

Sambucus nigra

ℹ️

Family: Caprifoliaceae
Flowering season: summer
Height: up to 20 ft
Spread: up to 20 ft
Situation: ○
Moisture requirement: ◑ *but* ○
❋ ❋ ❋
✖
❀

Sambucus is a genus of 20 species of hardy deciduous shrubs, small trees and perennials which grow in copses and thickets in temperate and sub-tropical regions. *S. nigra*, known as the common elder, is an erect, bushy shrub with powerful stems found in Europe, west Asia and North Africa. It has a cork-like, gray-brown bark and pinnate leaves with five ovate, serrated, medium-green leaflets. The small white to cream flowers have a delicate musk scent and appear in early summer. They are borne in flat panicles or umbels and later develop into spherical black berries. Elder is propagated by seed in autumn in a cool greenhouse or by hardwood cuttings in winter. Both the leaves and raw berries contain poisonous substances which are neutralised by cooking. The flowers are used to make delicious elderflower cordial and fritters. They are also used to flavor liqueurs and punch. The flowers have medicinal properties and are used in the treatment of common ailments, so that elder used to be known as the 'poor man's medicine chest.' The autumn berries are crushed to make juice which is drunk hot in winter to ease colds and to make elderberry wine.

Costmary

Tanacetum

ℹ️

Family: Asteraceae
Flowering season: summer
Height: 6–36 in
Spread: 12–36 in
Situation: ○
Moisture requirement: ○
❋ ❋ ❋
✖
❀

Tanacetum is a genus of 70 species of hardy perennial herbaceous plants, some of them evergreen, which grow in northern temperate regions on rocky hillsides and in meadows. Some of the *Tanacetum* species used to be classed in the *Balsamita*, *Chrysanthemum*, *Matricaria* and *Pyrethrum* genuses. The aromatic leaves are lanceolate or lobed with smooth, serrated or indented edges. The basal leaves are covered with hairs and have a silvery appearance. The terminal, capitate or daisy-like inflorescences, borne singly or in umbels, appear in summer. The yellow, tubular central florets are surrounded by rather inconspicuous white, red or yellow ray florets. *Tanacetum* can be raised from seed in spring at a temperature of 50 to 64°F. In the past, these aromatic, pungent herbs were used in the treatment of stomach and intestinal disorders as well as a vermifuge. However, because it is very toxic, it is no longer used for this purpose. No one with children should grow this plant in their garden. *Tanacetum* contains insect repelling substances and *T. parthenium* helps to alleviate migraine and rheumatism.

Garden thyme

Thymus vulgaris

Thymus is a genus of about 350 small, aromatic, evergreen shrubs and semi-shrubs and woody-based herbaceous perennials which grow wild in dry calcareous soil in Europe and Asia. They have, tubular flowers with five petals. Because there are so many synonyms for the various species and varieties, the classification of this genus is quite complex. Their attractive, creeping habit and the pleasant fragrance of their foliage and flowers, which are attractive to bees, make them popular plants for sunny borders and rockeries. Thyme is propagated by seed in spring in a cool greenhouse and by cuttings of lateral shoots in summer and by semi-ripe cuttings in mid to late-summer. In spring or summer, the rooted cuttings are lifted and potted until they are fully mature. Many species of thyme are used in the kitchen to enhance the taste of a wide range of dishes.

T. vulgaris or garden thyme is a bushy, cushion-forming, hardy, perennial semi-shrub with linear, elliptic, hairy, aromatic gray-green leaves. In late spring and early summer, white to purple flowers borne in whorl-like clusters appear in the leaf axils. Garden thyme is a warming, astringent herb which promotes digestion. It has expectorant, antispasmodic, cough-relieving, antiseptic and fungicidal properties and is used, for instance, in the manufacturing of mouth rinses. Thyme is an indispensable ingredient in Mediterranean cuisine because it keeps its aroma even when food is cooked for a long time. It is an important ingredient in the bouquet garni and is often added to herb oil and vinegar.

ⓘ

Family: Lamiaceae
Flowering season: summer
Height: 12–18 in
Spread: 24 in
Situation: ○
Moisture requirement: ◌
❄ ❄ ❄
✿

Lemon thyme

Thymus × citriodorus

T. x citirodorus is a variable hybrid of *T. pulegioides* and *T. vulgaris*. It is a round, bushy shrub with branched stems and narrow, oval-rhombic to lanceolate, more or less hairy, mid-green, lemon-scented leaves. The flowers are pale pink to lavender with leaf-like bracts around the slightly larger, two-lipped flowers. Lemon thyme is an aromatic, relaxing herb and often used in potpourri. It is also used in aromatherapy to treat asthma and respiratory disorders, especially in children, because the essential oil is not an irritant. In the kitchen, it is used to season spicy dishes.

ⓘ

Family: Lamiaceae
Flowering season: summer
Height: 10–12 in
Spread: 24 in
Situation: ○
Moisture requirement: ◊
❀ ❀ ❀
❁

Continental wild thyme

Thymus serpyllum

Continental wild thyme is a variable, low, spreading semi-shrub with slightly hairy, elliptic, gray-green leaves. The compact terminal whorls of tubular, two-lipped pink to purple flowers appear in summer. Continental wild thyme stimulates digestion and has calming, diuretic, expectorant and antispasmodic properties. It is also used in the treatment of respiratory disorders, laryngitis, gingevitis and alcoholism. In cooking, it is used in the same way as garden thyme.

ⓘ

Family: Lamiaceae
Flowering season: spring/summer
Height: up to 4 in
Spread: 36 in
Situation: ○
Moisture requirement: ◊
❀ ❀ ❀
❁

Nasturtium

Tropaeolum majus

ⓘ

Family: Tropaeolaceae
Flowering season: summer/autumn
Height: 3–10 ft
Spread: 5–7 ft
Situation: ○
Moisture requirement: ◊
❄
❦

Tropaeolum is a genus of 90 species of vigorous-growing, hardy climbing, creeping or prostrate or bushy annuals and herbaceous, often with bulbous roots, native to the cool mountain regions of Central and South America. The alternate, hairy leaves have smooth edges and can be palmate with five to seven lobes or leaflets. Climbing species have funnel-shaped flowers which grow from the leaf axils. The flowers have five unguiculated petals, striking spurs and five inconspicuous, pointed sepals which develop into spherical fruit. Nasturtiums can be sown in pots from April onward and directly in the earth from May onward. Seedlings should only be planted out when there is no longer any danger of frost. Nasturtium is a bitter, antiseptic, invigorating herb with diuretic, expectorant, bactericidal and fungicidal properties. The leaves and flowers are added to salads, the freshly chopped leaves adding a pleasant peppery taste while the flower buds are an excellent substitute for capers.

Valerian

Valeriana officinalis

Valeriana is a genus with more than 200 species of annuals and hardy herbaceous perennials which grow throughout the world – except for Australia – in damp woodland, meadows, river banks and mountains. They are semi-evergreen or ever-green sub-shrubs or shrubs with rhizomes or tap roots. *V. officinalis* is a variable perennial with a short rhizome and irregular, aromatic, pinnate, bright green basal and stem leaves which may have between seven and ten lanceolate, serrated leaflets. The tubular white or pink flowers which appear in summer are grouped in small, round panicles. These later develop into seeds covered with white hairs. It is raised from seed in spring in an open frame or by division in spring and autumn. Valerian has a scent of musk and is a bitter, calming herb with antispasmodic, anal-gesic qualities. It also promotes digestion and reduces blood pressure. It was alrea-dy in use in the 4th century BC when Hippocrates recommended it for treating sleep disorders. The oil is also used in the manufacturing of musk perfume.

ⓘ

Family: Valerianaceae
Flowering season: spring/summer
Height: 3–5 ft
Spread: 16–32 in
Situation: ○
Moisture requirement: ◐
❄ ❄ ❄
❄

263

Roses

opposite: Climbing roses in the garden 'Ton ter Linden'

Growing garden roses dates back almost 5000 years and is presumed to have begun in China. One would no doubt have to go still further back, far into prehistoric times, to discover the very first rose. Today, the genus Rosa embraces a unique variety of wonderful plants, ranging from the wild roses of nature through the wonderfully scented old roses (e.g. Alba rose, Bourbon rose, China rose, Damask rose, Gallica rose, Moss rose) to the colorful modern roses. In turn, within these categories, a great number of hybrids have been produced, including both random mutations and intentionally bred varieties (e.g. Climbing rose, Dwarf rose, Floribunda rose, Hubrid teas, Rambler rose).

Growing roses in the garden is open to all, not restricted to experts. Besides taking into account such criteria as fragrance and color when making your choice, you should bear in mind the situation and the purpose for which the rose is intended: are you planning to lay out a rose-bed, or will you have room only for a dwarf rose in a container? Is the variety you select remontant – meaning that it will have a second flowering during the season – or will it, like many Old Roses, flower only once although over quite a long period? The modern varieties developed from the Old Roses, known as English Roses, sometimes flower from May until the first frosts, and most of them are double and have a beautiful fragrance. Bedding roses are ideal for planting in large areas. This group contains modern, long-stemmed, grafted roses bearing flowers singly (as in the case of the Hybrid teas) or with several blooms on one stem, and the buds are usually elongated. Polyantha and Floribunda roses, which bear their blooms in dense clusters, are also suitable for bedding. Large, vigorous roses, which may be grown as single specimens, in hedges or in groups, depending on the variety, are known as shrub roses, and are very robust and easy to care for. Groundcover roses, as the name suggests, grow outwards rather than upwards. Finally, climbing roses look beautiful on the walls of houses or grown over arbors, but always need to be tied to some kind of support. Ramblers are very vigorous varieties which can grow 6 to 10 feet in a single year. Botanical or species roses such as Rosa arvensis, R. gallica and the R. rugosa hybrids, which offer food and shelter for birds, are very suitable for the wild or natural garden.

That methods of propagation and cultivation of all species and varieties is basically similar and easy to achieve. Roses need a sunny, airy location and protection from strong, cold winds. They prefer fertile, moist but well-drained soil that is regularly mulched and fed. Pests and diseases must be tackled immediately with suitable remedies; roses are frequently affected by aphids, powdery mildew, black spot and rose rust. During the dormant period in winter or early spring, old or damaged wood should be removed and pruning appropriate to the particular variety should be carried out. As a rule, wild roses and their hybrids are less demanding and more resistant than modern roses, but there are many exceptions among the newer roses, such as the hybrid tea R. 'Gloria Dei' or the Floribunda rose. 'Queen Elizabeth' which are both robust plants. As well as the traditional formal rose garden, roses present limitless possibilities in informal landscape gardening. In addition to the effect created by their own variety and the many way in which they can be used together, roses in combination with other plants can often provide stimulating contrasts and harmonious effects. A beautiful combination of color and form is provided, for example, by old roses and plants such as Lilium regale or red foxgloves. A distinguished partner is lavender on account of its fragrance and its contrasting color, and a shrub such as summer jasmine is another good companion, adding its own fragrance to that of the summer roses.

Rambler rose

Rosa 'Albertine'

ℹ️

Family: Rosaceae
Flowering season: summer
Height and Spread: 16 ft × 13 ft
Situation: ○
Moisture requirement: ◌
❁ ❁ ❁
Prone to: mildew

The popular rambler 'Albertine' was bred by Barbier in France and introduced in 1921. It is a very vigorous climber with arching shoots covered with hooked thorns. The young shoots are reddish-green. R. 'Albertine' is a cross between R. wichuraiana and the hybrid tea R. 'Mrs Arthur Robert Waddell,' and is one of the most popular climbing varieties of this group. It is thickly covered with small, glossy, dark green leaves. In mid-summer, small bunches of salmon-pink flower buds open into double, copper-pink, shell-shaped, 3 in flowers which give off a very intense scent. The flowers appear in profusion and the flowering period extends over several weeks. Like most of the *Wichuraiana* ramblers, R. 'Albertine' is robust and resistant to disease, but in periods of great dryness, it is vulnerable to mildew. This rose is especially beautiful grown up fences or walls or scrambling over a pergola, but it can also form a dense bush 5 ft high. It rarely requires pruning, but old wood should be removed from time to time.

Hybrid teas

Rosa 'Alexander'

ℹ️

Family: Rosaceae
Flowering season: summer to autumn
Height/spread: to 7 ft × 3 ft
Situation: ○
Moisture requirement: ◌
❁ ❁ ❁

This exceptional variety with its strong, upright growth was introduced by Harkness in England in 1972. It is derived from of R. 'Super Star' x (R. 'Ann Elizabeth' x R. 'Allgold'). Its large, elegantly shaped flowers are typical of the group of long-stemmed hybrid teas. The 5 in double flowers with their compact tips are bright cinnabar red and scented. The rose is generously covered with shiny, dark green leaves and flowers repeatedly in summer and autumn. R. 'Alexander' is a sturdy hybrid tea resistant to diseases and pests and it also thrives in poorer soil. It is excellent planted as a hedge and beautiful in front of a fence or in beds. However, the dominant red of its flowers demands care in choosing a color arrangement with other plants. When dormant, old or damaged wood and crossing or over-long shoots should be cut out, while the main shoots are shortened to 24 in above the base.

Floribunda rose (patio rose)

Rosa 'Anna Ford'

The floribundas known as patio roses are not necessarily shorter, but they are daintier than their bushy relatives. They are taller and bushier than miniature roses. Harkness in England bred this extremely dependable variety from *R.* 'Southampton' x. *R.* 'Minuetto'. It is a reliable, wide growing, dense bush sort with small, very shiny, dark green leaves and a fine display of flowers throughout summer into autumn. Bunches of cup-shaped flower buds open into semi-double, flat flowers of 1 ½ in with a deep orange-red color turning to pale yellow in the center. They are weakly scented. It was introduced in 1981 and has proved a distinguished rose for growing in tubs, in beds or as a low hedge. Maintenance is fairly undemanding: faded blooms should be removed and old or weak shoots cut out in winter.

❶

Family: Rosaceae
Flowering season: summer to autumn
Height/spread: 18 × 16 in
Situation: ○
Moisture requirement: ◊
❀ ❀ ❀

English Rose

Rosa 'Charles Austin'

Rosa 'Charles Austin'

The variety 'Charles Austin' is one of the oldest of the English Roses, and is still sometimes known under its synonym of 'Ausfather.' It was raised in 1973 by the famous rose breeder David Austin. With its natural, upright habit of growth it makes an excellent plant for mixed borders, combining well with other shrubs and perennials. The rosette-shaped, very full flowers are apricot when they first open and turn paler as they fade. They have an intense, fruity fragrance. English Roses were created in the 1970s by crossing Old Roses with modern Hybrid Teas and Floribundas. Old Roses are those varieties which were available on the market before 1867, the date of introduction of the first Hybrid Teas. The new varieties unite the romantic charm and fragrance of historic roses with the wide color palette and long flowering season of modern roses. A romantic appearance and fragrance are more important features of English Roses than dazzling color or a profuse crop of flowers, and no other plant group can equal them in their range of scents.

❶

Family: Rosaceae
Flowering season: summer
Height and spread: 5 × 4 ft
Situation: ○
Moisture requirement: ◊
❀ ❀ ❀
❀

English Rose

Rosa 'Charles de Mills'

Rosa 'Charles de Mills'

ⓘ

Family: Rosaceae
Flowering season: summer
Height and spread: 5 × 4 ft
Situation: ○
Moisture requirement: ◊
❄ ❄ *(but protect in winter)*
✿

The variety 'Charles de Mills' (synonym: 'Bizarre Triomphant') is a genuine Old Rose of early European origin. Roses in this group are once-flowering, revealing a wealth of wonderfully fragrant blooms in early summer. 'Charles de Mills' is a vigorous Gallica rose, notable for its extremely large and very full, crimson flowers. Gallica roses were cultivated by the ancient Greeks and Romans; rose-breeding from this group began in the Netherlands in the 17th century, and was continued later on a large scale by French rose-growers. Unlike the typically rounded flowers of other historic varieties, the blooms of 'Charles de Mills' are very flat. The upright, slightly pendulous shrubs are very robust and need little attention. Pruning is confined to the removal of old and weak shoots. If larger flowers are required, the breeder recommends cutting back the rest of the plant by a third. This rose is very good in smaller gardens because of its compact size.

China rose

Rosa chinensis 'Cécile Brunner'

ⓘ

Family: Rosaceae
Flowering season: summer to autumn
Height/spread: 30 × 24 in
Situation: ○
Moisture requirement: ◊
❄ ❄ ❄

Upright, slim, low bush rose, with small, elegant, dark green, straight leaves. The numerous perfectly formed cup-shaped double flowers 1 1/2 in in size appear in generous bunches. Each pale pink flower appears from a pointed, tea rose-shaped bud on a long flower stem, making it an ideal buttonhole rose. It has a weak but characteristic scent during its flowering period from summer to autumn. It is also known as R. 'Mignon' or 'The Sweetheart Rose,' and it is often confused with R. 'Bloomfield Abundance,' which, however, is much larger-growing and has less beautiful flowers. R. 'Cécile Brunner' is the cross of a polyantha rose and R. 'Mme de Tartas,' bred by Pernet-Ducher in France and introduced in 1881. It is especially suitable for every kind of planting container and for mixed beds.

China rose

Rosa chinensis 'Old Blush'

This forms an upright, compact, almost thornless bush with shiny, medium-green, pointed leaves. The clusters of dainty, shell-shaped, double flowers of about 2 ½ in are a pale silvery pink, darkening over time and giving off a slight scent reminiscent of sweet peas. As with most China roses, the flowering season of 'Old Blush' is from summer to autumn, with many persistent blooms. Also known as 'Parson's Pink China,' this old rose is undemanding and very resistant. It also tolerates poorer soils as well as north-facing positions and is regarded as one of the best China roses for the garden. On a protected wall, it can be trained as a small climbing when it will grow to a greater height than as a shrub. The species was discovered in China and introduced into Europe in 1781.

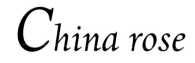

Family: Rosaceae
Flowering season: summer to autumn
Height/spread: 40 ×32 in
Situation: ◑
Moisture requirement: ◊
❀ ❀ ❀

Gallica rose

Rosa 'Complicata'

This vigorous rose forms an open bush of arching branches covered with matt gray-green leaves. The single, flat, wide-opened blossoms of about 4 in are bright pink with paler centers and golden yellow stamens. The flowers give off a light, pleasantly fresh scent. The origin of this old rose is uncertain, but is generally believed that its ancestry includes *R. canina* or *R. macrantha*. It is a beautiful climber scrambling up into an old tree, adorning it with a large number of pendant blooms flowering along the whole length of the shoots in summer. It also makes a natural hedge and is excellent for informal, natural or low-maintenance parts of the garden. *R.* 'Complicata' is undemanding and resistant against disease. It also tolerates poor soils and shade. Its origin and date of introduction into Europe are unknown.

Family: Rosaceae
Flowering season: summer
Height/spread: 7 × 10 ft
Situation: ○
Moisture requirement: ◊
❀ ❀ ❀

English rose

Rosa 'Constance Spry'

ⓘ

Family: Rosaceae
Flowering season: summer
Height and spread: 6 × 5 ft
Situation: ○
Moisture requirement: ◊
❄ ❄ *(but protect in winter)*
❀

This variety is one of those raised by the famous rose-breeder David Austin, and has been on the market since 1961. It is a shrub rose with slightly pendulous shoots and a wide spread. 'Constance Spry' is one of the few English Roses also suitable for growing as a climber and its dense foliage will quickly cover walls or pergolas. The leaves are reddish brown when they first emerge, and then turn to deep green. The peony-shaped, pure pink flowers are very full, with an intense myrrh-like fragrance. They are paler towards the edges, and can reach a diameter of 4 in, but in spite of their size, they are very delicate-looking. This shrub rose, a once-flowering variety, can be grown in many ways: not only as a climber but also on its own or in group plantings. If it is to be trained on a wall, it is advisable to plant it 12 in from the foot of the masonry, so that the rose can always get sufficient moisture. Mulching and regular watering and feeding with fertiliser are essential. Another very beautiful English Rose is 'Shropshire Lass,' which has flat pink flowers.

Alba rose

Rosa 'Cuisse de Nymphe'

This rose is an upright bush with the arching shoots and the gray-green leaves typical of Alba roses. In mid-summer, numerous rosettes of pink and white, double flowers of about 3 in appear with a pleasant, intense scent. The petals bend back on themselves during flowering and become paler at the edges of the flower. This very popular old rose almost certainly originated in the 15th century, or possibly even earlier. However, nothing is known of its origin. *R.* 'Cuisse de Nymphe' ('Nymph's thigh') is also known as *R.* 'Great Maiden's Blush' and as *R.* 'La Séduisante.' It is especially beautiful as a hedging rose and is also excellent for mixed beds. Immediately after flowering, old wood should be removed and over-long shoots pruned to shorten them.

ⓘ

Family: Rosaceae
Flowering season: summer
Height/spread: 7 × 4 ft
Situation: ○
Moisture requirement: ◌
❄ ❄ ❄

Damask rose

Rosa 'Duc de Cambridge'

The very beautiful example of an old rose was bred in France and introduced before 1848. The parents varieties of *R.* 'Duc de Cambridge' are unknown. In older English literature, it is often known as *R.* 'Duke of Cambridge.' It is an upright, very thorny plant with initially reddish, rounded leaves turning dull green. The large, strongly-scented, double flowers appear in bunches and are a deep purple-pink with lighter edges. It is one of the darkest varieties of damask rose. The roses of this group normally bloom on two-year-old wood during the summer, often producing a second flowering on young shoots in late summer. After flowering the main and side shoots should be shortened heavily and over-long shoots should be removed in the autumn. It should be sheltered from strong winds. *R.* 'Duc de Cambridge' is very suitable for growing in beds.

Rosa 'Duc de Cambridge'

ⓘ

Family: Rosaceae
Flowering season: summer
Height/spread: 4 ft × 3 ft
Situation: ○
Moisture requirement: ◌
❄ ❄ ❄

273

Gallica rose

Rosa 'Duchesse de Montebello'

'Duchesse de Montebello'

🛈

Family: Rosaceae
Flowering season: summer
Height/spread: 4 × 3 ft
Situation: ○
Moisture requirement: ◊
✾ ✾ ✾

This rose grows as an upright, loose-growing bush with arching shoots and green leaves which harmonise beautifully with its clusters of double, pale pink flowers, an unusual shade for a Gallica rose. Its globular buds open into medium-sized, flat, cup-shaped flowers. The color of this old rose has often led to the conclusion that it may not be a pure *Gallica* rose, an opinion reinforced by experiments in England where it has produced some repeat-flowering seedlings. It was bred by Laffay in France and introduced before 1829. *R.* 'Duchesse de Montebello' flowers in summer, giving off a sweet scent. It bears partial shade, tolerates poor soils and is good for hedges or planting containers.

Hybrid tea

Rosa 'Duftzauber 84' syn. 'Royal William'

🛈

Family: Rosaceae
Flowering season: summer to autumn
Height/spread: to 3 × 2 ft
Situation: ○
Moisture requirement: ◊
✾ ✾ ✾

The group of large-flowered hybrid teas includes this variety bred by Kordes in Germany and introduced in 1984. It grows as a substantial, upright, thick-stemmed bush with large, matte, dark green leaves. Long-stemmed, elegantly-shaped double flowers 5 in in size and velvety blood red appear in generous abundance in summer and autumn. They have a lovely, strong scent. This robust rose is suitable for growing in beds and borders or it can be trained as a climber. Its impressive, long-lasting, brightly colored flowers are excellent for cutting and displaying in a vase indoors. This hybrid tea is also known as *R.* 'Royal William.' It is resistant against pests diseases and needs little maintenance. In autumn or spring, it should be severely pruned, so that the stems will branch out again with an open, airy center. It was bred from *R.* 'Feuerzauber' and an unnamed seedling.

Rosa 'Duftzauber 84'

Climbing rose

Rosa 'Félicité et Perpétué'

The vigorous, arching, almost spineless climbing rose has very flexible, slim shoots and is therefore described in some catalogues as a rambler rose. It was bred and introduced by Jacques in France in 1827, but its exact parentage is unknown. It seems to be a hybrid of the evergreen rose *R. sempervirens*, and it too is evergreen, with numerous, small, shiny, dark green, pointed leaves remaining until late into winter. In summer, this single-flowering rose produces an abundance of cascading, creamy-white flowers from its pinky-red flower buds. The flowers are double rosettes 1 ¹/₂ in in size and deliciously scented. This versatile rose is excellent scrambling over arbors and pergolas or entwined in trees. It is also attractive planted near still water in which it is reflected. It tolerates poorer soils and lighting conditions, and with will flower even more magnificently only a minimum pruning.

🛈

Family: Rosaceae
Flowering season: summer
Height/spread: 16 × 13 ft
Situation: ○
Moisture requirement: ◌
❄ ❄ ❄

275

Gallica-Rose

Rosa gallica versicolor 'Rosa Mundi'

Rosa gallica 'Versicolor'

ℹ

Family: Rosaceae
Flowering season: summer
Height/spread: 32 × 40 in
Situation: ○ – ◐
Moisture requirement: ◌
❉ ❉ ❉

This is an erect, bushy rose with uneven, matte, medium-green leaves. Known as 'Rosa Mundi', this old rose is a sport of *R. gallica officinalis*, known as 'The Apothecary's Rose' or 'Rose de Provins'. Both roses are similar to each other in every respect except flower color. The semi-double, flat flowers of 'Rosa Mundi' are 2 in in size, striped with bright crimson markings on a pale pink background and a distinct delicate scent. It is the oldest and best known striped rose, flowering prolifically. Native to southwest Asia, it was probably introduced into Europe in the 16th century. Few other roses are better suited to creating low, elegant hedges, and it also shows itself off to advantage in mixed beds. 'Rosa Mundi' prefers well-mulched soil, but it can also tolerate poorer soils and shade. The shoots should be pruned by one-third of their length after flowering.

Floribunda rose (patio rose)

Rosa 'Gentle Touch'

ℹ

Family: Rosaceae
Flowering season: summer to autumn
Height/spread: 20 × 16 in
Situation: ○
Moisture requirement: ◌
❉ ❉ ❉

This group of smaller floribunda roses are described as patio roses, which are excellent trained on terraces or even indoors as pot plants. *R.* 'Gentle Touch' is a cross between *R.* 'Liverpool Echo' x ('Woman's Own' x 'Memento'), produced by Dickson in Northern Ireland and introduced in 1986. With an erect, densely growing, bushy habit, it is covered in shiny, little, dark green leaves which contrast with the large clusters of pale pink flowers. The double, cup-shaped flowers, 2 in in size, have a weak but pleasantly fresh fragrance, and appear dependably in summer until autumn. The variety can be trained as low hedge, as a ground cover or as a standard, and as already mentioned is good for growing in pots. Robust and resistant to pests and diseases, it needs little attention. Winter pruning to thin it out is recommended.

English rose

Rosa 'Gertrude Jekyll'

Rosa 'Gertrude Jekyll'

'Gertrude Jekyll' is also known under its synonym 'Ausbord.' This variety is a vigorous English Rose with an upright habit of growth. Its small, firm buds suddenly and surprisingly unfold into large, rosette-shaped flowers of a rich pink shade with 4 in diameter. The recurved petals at the heart of the flower are a striking feature. The blooms are very full, and have an intense fragrance of the finest Old Rose quality, which has led to the use of this variety to make rose essence. It will delight the eye and the nose in the garden from summer to autumn, and is an ideal rose to plant in borders, especially in the rear because of its height. 'Gertrude Jekyll' is related to the well-known deep pink variety 'The Countryman,' which itself is the result of back-crossing an English Rose with an old Portland Rose. Portland Roses are notable for their remontancy – that is to say, they flower more than once during the season, most profusely in the first, summer flowering, with a smaller crop of flowers in autumn.

ⓘ

Family: Rosaceae
Flowering season: summer
Height and spread: 5 × 3 ft
Situation: ○
Moisture requirement: ◊
❄ ❄ *(but protect in winter)*
❀

Rosa glauca

Rosa glauca (syn. R. rubrifolia)

This wild rose forms an upright bush with arching shoots and especially beautiful leaves. The delicate leaves are initially tinged with violet and later become a light blue-gray tone. In autumn, they take on a deep plum color. Small, loose clusters of single, flat mauve pink flowers with white centers and golden yellow stamens 1.5 in in size open in June and July. Also known as *R. rubrifolia,* it is native to the mountain regions of Central Europe and in autumn it is decorated with numerous bunches of small, round, red rose hips. It is therefore a very rewarding ornamental garden shrub throughout summer and autumn. It is a very robust plant tolerating almost any soil conditions and situation even a north-facing position. The incomparable leaf coloring provides beautiful accents when planted mixed borders or used in flower arrangements.

ⓘ

Family: Rosaceae
Flowering season: summer
Height / spread: 7 × 5 ft
Situation: ○ – ◑
Moisture requirement: ◊
❄ ❄ ❄

Climber rose

Rosa 'Gloire de Dijon'

opposite: Rosa 'Gloire de Dijon'

This famous old climbing rose was bred by Jacotot in France and introduced to the market in 1853. It is probably a cross between an unknown tea rose and *R.* 'Souvenir de la Malmaison', an old bourbon rose. Once classified as a Noisette rose, today it is thought to be a Tea rose mainly because it is hardier than the typically tender Noisettes. The shiny, dark green leaves are tinged red when they are new. It has large, pale apricot to creamy white, double flowers, 4 in in size, in early summer, and often again in autumn. These flowers open flat and quartered and are sometimes tinged with pink in the autumn. The rose has a strong, sweet scent and is very free-flowering. *R.* 'Gloire de Dijon' thrives best on a warm, sunny wall.

Family: Rosaceae
Flowering season: summer to autumn
Height / spread: 15 × 13 ft
Situation: ○
Moisture requirement: ◌
❄ ❄ ❄

Hybrid tea

Rosa 'Gloria Dei' (syn. 'Peace,' Mme A. Meilland)

The introduction of *R.* 'Gloria Dei' by Meilland in France in 1942 was a milestone in the history of the modern rose. Known to English speakers as *R.* 'Peace,' it is one of the most popular roses throughout the world and has also had a great influence on later generations of roses as a parent variety. With a detective's intuition, the breeder crossed [('George Dickson' x 'Souvenir de Claudius Pernet') x ('Joana Hill' x 'Charles P. Kilham')] with 'Margaret McGredy,' and the remarkable result was the creation of this large, vigorous, branching hybrid tea, free-flowering and covered with full, glossy green leaves. In summer and autumn, an abundance of elegantly formed double flowers appear, creamy-yellow tinged with pink towards the edges. At 6 in, the peony-like flowers are large with a light, but delightful scent. The variety is outstandingly suitable for beds, borders, hedges or as a tall rose. It is also an excellent rose for cutting.

Family: Rosaceae
Flowering season: summer to autumn
Height / spread: to 40× 30 in
Situation: ○
Moisture requirement: ◌
❄ ❄ ❄

Large flowered bush rose

Rosa 'Graham Thomas'

Rosa 'Graham Thomas'

ⓘ

Family: Rosaceae
Flowering season: summer to autumn
Height/spread: 4 × 5 ft
Situation: ○
Moisture requirement: ◌
❀ ❀ ❀

With his creations the English rose breeder David Austin has added a new chapter to the group of large flowered bush roses, also known as modern shrub roses. He has succeeded in marrying the charming flower, scent and growth form of old roses with the best properties of the modern roses, including the ability to flower more often or more persistently throughout the year and to cover a rich spectrum of colors. One of these is *R.* 'Graham Thomas', a cross between *R.* 'Charles Austin' x (*R.* 'Iceberg x seedling), a bush rose with bushy, arching growth and straight, shiny, medium-green leaves. The flowers give off a lovely, intense, tea rose scent and open into incomparable, double, clear yellow, shell-shaped flowers, 4 in in size. For best repeat flowering, the regular removing of wilted blossoms is recommended. During the dormant period, dead wood should be cut out and the shoots should be gently pruned from time to time. *R.* 'Graham Thomas' is very beautiful in mixed borders and is also very popular as a cut flower. It was introduced in 1983.

Ground cover rose

Rosa 'Heidetraum'

ⓘ

Family: Rosaceae
Flowering season: summer to autumn
Height/spread: 30 × 48 in
Situation: ○
Moisture requirement: ◌
❀ ❀ ❀

This cross between *R.* 'Immensee' x. *R.* 'Amanda' was created by the German breeder Noack and came on the market in 1988. It is robust and resistant against pests and diseases and needs no special attention. With its vigorous, dense habit and freely-branching shoots thickly covered with shiny, green leaves, it makes a good ground cover for sunny slopes, beds or narrow terraces. The barely-scented deep pink-red flowers appear from summer to late autumn. They are double, shell-shaped, 2 in long and they make decorative clusters along the stem. Other varieties of ground cover rose include *R.* 'Flower Carpet' (bright pink) and *R.* 'Swany (white), and *R.* 'Suma' (red). They are also attractive planted in large tubs. With their varied uses, *R.* 'Heidetraum' and the many other attractive varieties of this group are not only useful for smothering weeds while they have their leaves; they are also invaluable for protecting the soil from erosion. They can be planted individually as accents in the landscape garden.

Moss rose
(R. × centifolia muscosa)

Rosa 'Henri Martin' (syn. 'Red Moss')

This moss rose forms a vigorous, upright bush with flexible twigs which are bent down by the weight of the numerous flowers. It is densely covered with uneven, fresh green leaves. The clusters of globular double flowers are bright carmine red and 3 in in size, carried on wiry stalks. They are strongly scented and in full flower, golden yellow stamens appear. The stems are light green and slightly mossy. Also known as *R.* 'Red Moss,' the variety is very free-flowering in mid-summer and is shown off at its best on pyramidal support; the flowers then cascade all the way down to the ground. This moss rose survives hot, dry summers well, and is also extremely hardy and shade tolerant; it can even thrive in a north-facing situation. Light pruning is recommended after flowering. Its parent varieties are unknown. It was bred by Laffay in France and introduced in 1863.

ℹ

Family: Rosaceae
Flowering season: summer
Height/spread: 6 × 4 ft
Situation: ○ – ◑
Moisture requirement: ◊
❋ ❋ ❋

Large flowered bush rose

Rosa 'Heritage'

A particularly beautiful English rose with lovely, shell-shaped flowers. It was bred by David Austin in England and came on the market in 1984. It forms a solid upright bush, with straight, almost thornless shoots covered with pointed, shiny dark green leaves. Larger or smaller clusters of double pale pink flowers 4 in across appear along the entire length of the shoots; depending on lighting conditions, they sometimes tend towards pale apricot. The strong scent is reminiscent of lemons. It is the result of crossing an unnamed seedling with (*R.* 'Wife of Bath' x *R.* 'Iceberg'). The repeat flowering extends through summer and autumn. It needs fertile, well-mulched soil and is excellent for beds. This rose is typical of those bred by Austin, combining the appearance of an old fashioned shrub rose with an almost never-ending flowering period.

ℹ

Family: Rosaceae
Flowering season: summer to autumn
Height/spread: 4 ft × 4 ft
Situation: ○
Moisture requirement: ◊
❋ ❋ ❋

Damask rose

Rosa 'Ispahan'

ⓘ

Family: Rosaceae
Flowering season: summer
Height/spread: 5 ft × 4 ft
Situation: ○
Moisture requirement: ◌
❊ ❊ ❊

This forms a graceful, upright bush thickly covered with attractive gray-green foliage. The double, shell-shaped flowers, 3 in across, are a warm pink and give off a delightful strong scent, a particular characteristic of most damask roses. Alternatively known as *R.* 'Rose d'Isfahan,' it flowers early in the year and then has quite a long season compared to other varieties of this group. It tolerates fairly poor soil and it is equally suitable for hedges and mixed beds, as well as for planting in containers. It is also recommended for cutting for vases because the flowers survive for a long time in water. This old rose possibly originated in Persia and was already being cultivated before 1832.

Rosa 'Jayne Austin'

English Rose

ⓘ

Family: Rosaceae
Flowering season: summer
Height and spread: 3 × 2 ft
Situation: ○
Moisture requirement: ◌
❊ ❊ *(but protect in winter)*
❊

As its name suggests, 'Jayne Austin' is one of the roses bred by David Austin, and is also known as 'Ausbreak.' Its growth is very dense and branching. The flower is rosette-shaped, a soft yellow with a slight tinge of apricot, and frequently has an eye at the center. The fragrance is reminiscent of lilac. The thin, translucent petals give this rose a very delicate and indeed exquisite appearance, qualities which it owes to its relationship with the remontant Noisette Roses. Noisette Roses have small, delicate flowers, and make good climbing roses because of their slender shoots. 'Charity' is similar to 'Jayne Austin' in this respect, but has larger, slightly cup-shaped flowers in a soft shade of apricot yellow. It is remontant, with a delicious myrrh fragrance. 'Graham Thomas' is one of the best-known yellow English Roses, with medium-sized flowers of an unusually pure color, and a classic Tea Rose fragrance. It is named after the well-known horticulturalist and writer of books on roses.

Alba rose

Rosa
'Queen of Denmark'

This loose-growing, extremely thorny bush has matte, gray-green leaves. It has double, quartered, warm, deep pink flowers 3 in in size; open flowers reveal a green button eye in the center. During the single flowering on the previous year's wood, this old rose gives off an exceptionally lovely, intense scent. Like most albas, it is easily cultivated; it tolerates poor soils or woodland conditions and also thrives in partial shade. It is especially good for growing as a hedge or in mixed beds. This beautiful old rose was probably bred by John Booth in Hamburg became in 1816, perhaps by crossing an unknown seedling with *R.* 'Cuisse de Nymphe.' It came on the market in 1826.

Rosa 'Königin von Dänemark'

ⓘ

Family: Rosaceae
Flowering season: summer
Height / spread: 5 × 4 ft
Situation: ○
Moisture requirement: ◊
❄ ❄ ❄

283

Rosa 'Magenta'

English Rose

ⓘ

Family: Rosaceae
Flowering season: summer
Height and spread: 3 × 4 ft
Situation: ○
Moisture requirement: ◌
❈ ❈ *(but protect in winter)*
❈

This Floribunda rose, introduced by the Kordes rose nursery of Germany in 1954, is grown as a shrub rose. Its leathery, dark green leaves form an attractive contrast with the full, lilac-pink flowers that are borne in dense clusters more than once a year. The flowers may be up to 3 in in diameter, and are borne in such profusion that they can bend the stems. The fragrance is very intense. Shrub roses of the English Rose type are the result of years of rose-breeding, and the range is correspondingly wide. As a rule, they are plants of vigorous growth, robust, free-flowering and can reach heights of up to 6 ft. Most varieties are remontant, flowering more than once a year, and introducing color into the garden when the flowers of other shrubs have faded. Colors range from pink through red to yellow and white, and the blooms may be single or double. Low-growing dwarf varieties, suitable for growing in containers, include the yellow 'Baby Love', 30 x 30 in, and 'Little White Pet', 24 x 30 in, which has small, white, pompon flowers.

Climbing rose

Rosa 'Maigold,' Rosa pimpinellifolia hybrids

ⓘ

Family: Rosaceae
Flowering season: summer to autumn
Height/spread: 8 × 8 ft
Situation: ○
Moisture requirement: ◌
❈ ❈ ❈

Few modern climbing roses can compare with R. 'Maigold' where robustness and disease resistance are concerned. It tolerates the most varied, even adverse, soils and conditions and is extremely hardy. It inherited these properties from its parent varieties R. 'Poulsens Pink' x R. 'Fruhlingstag'. Bred by Kordes in Germany, R. 'Maigold' came on the market in 1953. It is one of the first roses to flower in the year and then delights gardeners with a rich flowering period with some repeat flowering later. It grows vigorously with strong, arching stems covered with numerous reddish thorns and shiny green, sparkling leaves. The deliciously-scented semi-double shell-shaped flowers, 4 in in size, appear in clusters and are a full golden yellow, tinged with orange. It is one of the best roses for unsheltered situations and also excellent for growing up the wall of a house or over a pergola. It can also be trained as a bush rose, but its growth is somewhat uncontrolled.

Rosa 'Magenta'

Damask rose

Rosa 'Mme Hardy'

This rose forms an erect bush thickly covered with leathery, dark green leaves. Elegant pure white flowers 4 in across appear during the flowering period in the summer. They are double quartered rosettes with a green button eye in the center. They give off a pleasant, strong, fresh scent. This splendid old rose also thrives on poor soils and is shade tolerant. It is excellent planted in mixed beds. It was bred by Hardy in France and introduced in 1832. Nothing is known of its origins. A dependable, robust and resistant variety, it demands little maintenance. After flowering, the flowering shoots should be shortened and the bush generally tidied up.

Family: Rosaceae
Flowering season: summer
Height/spread: 5 × 4 ft
Situation: ○
Moisture requirement: ○
❅ ❅ ❅

Rosa 'New Dawn'

Climbing rose (Wichuraiana-Rambler)

Rosa 'New Dawn'

ⓘ

Family: Rosaceae
Flowering season: summer to autumn
Height/spread: 11 × 10 ft
Situation: ◯ – ◑
Moisture requirement: ◊
❄ ❄ ❄

A sport of the single-flowering rambler rose *R.* 'Dr. Van Fleet,' this rose was bred in 1930 by the Somerset Rose Company nursery in the United States. With its introduction, methodical experiments began in the same year to breed modern climbing roses. Accordingly, *R.* 'New Dawn' is of great importance as a parent variety of many modern climbing roses. Its growth is strong, with beautiful, widely branching stems covered with shiny, dark green leaves. From the pointed flower buds, double, shell-shaped 3 in blossoms open in large clusters. They are pale pearl pink and have a lovely scent. The prolific flowering continues into the autumn. Also known as *R.* 'The New Dawn,' it is a simple climbing rose which is very resistant to disease, and is ideal for growing up house walls, on trellises and square pillars or over pergolas. It can also be trained as a hedge or bush rose. *R.* 'New Dawn' tolerates both poor soils and a north-facing situation.

Moss rose (R. × centifolia 'Muscosa')

Rosa 'Nuits de Young'

Moss roses are the result of a mutation from centifolias which had developed moss-like growth on their sepals. However, precise information about when the first mutation to a moss rose occurred is not available. It is only known that *R. x centifolia* 'Muscosa' existed in France in 1700. *R.* 'Nuits des Young' was grown by Laffay in France and was introduced in 1845. It is the darkest of all the moss roses and compared to others, only slightly mossy. Its growth is upright and slim with stiff shoots carrying small, elegant, deep green leaves. The double, flat flowers appear in the summer; they are velvety deep purple and maroon, with golden yellow stamens and may give off a fine fruit scent. The dark reddish brown sepals are mossy. It is especially beautiful with brighter colors in mixed beds and it can also be used for hedges or for planting in containers. Also known as *R.* 'Old Black,' many rose connoisseurs consider it one of the best of the moss roses.

ⓘ

Family: Rosaceae
Flowering season: summer
Height/spread: 48 × 35 in
Situation: ○
Moisture requirement: ◌
❅ ❅ ❅

Large flowered bush rose

Rosa 'Penelope'

Family: Rosaceae
Flowering season: summer to autumn
Height/spread: 3.5 × 3.5 ft
Situation: ○
Moisture requirement: ○
❀ ❀ ❀

The English clergyman and breeder Joseph Pemberton was responsible for the existence of all but a very few of the graceful, strong scented roses known as the hybrid musks found in gardens today. This group of modern bush roses has a short, somewhat chequered history which actually began with the breeding successes of Joseph Pemberton. *R.* 'Penelope' is a cross between the hybrid tea 'Ophelia' and an unnamed seedling which was introduced in 1924. It is an extremely dependable rose, robust and resistant to disease. With its densely branching, bushy growth and its large, dark green foliage, it is very good for hedges and mixed beds. Many clusters of musk-scented, semi-double, shell-shaped flowers, 3 in across, appear in the summer. They are a soft creamy-pink fading to white. With dead heading, *R.* 'Penelope' will give recurrent flowering until the autumn; if left, the flowers will produce small, bright pink rose hips.

Rosa 'Penelope'

288

Large flowered bush rose

Rosa 'Pink Grootendorst'

The vigorous, erect-growing bush rose is a sport of *R*. 'F. J. Grootendorst', a hybrid of the wild rose *R. rugosa* from Japan and western Asia. It was bred by Grootendorst in the Netherlands and introduced in 1923. *R.* 'Pink Grootendorst' is a variety which flowers freely and continuously in summer and autumn, its charming dense flowers appearing in attractive clusters. They are pale pink, double rosettes, 2 in in size with frilly petals and a weak scent. The rose is generously covered with small, leathery, dark green leaves. Compared with the formal elegance of many other varieties, the whole appearance of *R.* 'Pink Grootendorst' radiates an almost cheerful casualness and it is therefore very suitable for growing in mixed beds or as a hedge. It is known for the long life of its cut flowers in water. It is slightly shade tolerant and also thrives on poor soil. It responds well to severe pruning.

ⓘ

Family: Rosaceae
Flowering season: summer to autumn
Height / spread: 4 × 3.5 ft
Situation: ○
Moisture requirement: ◊
❁ ❁ ❁

Incense rose

Rosa primula

This rose forms a vigorous, upright bush with shiny, fern-like foliage. The medium-green leaves give off an aromatic, incense-like fragrance. The single, shell-shaped, primrose yellow flowers 2–1/2 in in size have striking stamens and appear in the late spring on individual, curved, arching side shoots. The blossoms mature to small, spherical, reddish brown rose hips. This wild rose is suitable for sheltered, wind-free situations where its scent can develop well. It thrives in woodland areas on poor soils as well as in gardens. The robust, resistant rose is one of the most beautiful of its kind and requires no particular attention. However it may be heavily pruned in winter when necessary. It comes from Central Asia and/or northern China and was introduced from Samarkand in 1910.

ⓘ

Family: Rosaceae
Flowering season: spring
Height / spread: 7 × 7 ft
Situation: ○
Moisture requirement: ◊
❁ ❁ ❁

*F*loribunda rose

Rosa 'Queen Elizabeth'

ⓘ

Family: Rosaceae
Flowering season: summer to autumn
Height/spread: 7 × 3 ft
Situation: ○
Moisture requirement: ◊
❁ ❁ ❁

With its introduction in 1954, this rose bred by Dr W. E. Lammerts in the United States became a world-wide success, and it would still be hard to find a less demanding, more consistently flowering, modern garden rose. Of vigorous, upright, high growth, it has large, leathery, shiny, dark green leaves. Its long flower buds open into large, double, pale pink, round and then shell-shaped flowers, 4 in across, at the beginning of the season. They appear in big clusters and are slightly fragrant. Also known as 'The Queen Elizabeth Rose,' it is beautiful in mixed borders where it makes an attractive background with its tall, slim growth; it is also an outstanding hedge rose and thrives equally well grown in containers. Finally, it is a popular rose for cutting. Its parent varieties are *R.* 'Charlotte Armstrong' and *R.* 'Floradora', giving it great disease resistance, undemanding soil requirements and shade tolerance. It should be heavily pruned in the dormant season.

*G*round cover rose

Rosa 'Rosy Cushion'

ⓘ

Family: Rosaceae
Flowering season: summer to autumn
Height/spread: 3 × 4 ft
Situation: ○
Moisture requirement: ◊
❁ ❁ ❁

This variety was introduced by Ilsink in the Netherlands in 1979. It makes a dense, low-growing mound with projecting, arching, flowering shoots, carrying beautiful, shiny, dark green leaves. The single to semi-double, shell-shaped, flowers, 2 in in size, are produced in large bunches. They are a pale pinky red with an ivory-cream center and golden yellow stamens. The rose is dependable, flowering through summer and autumn. A cross between *R.* 'Yesterday' and an unnamed seedling, it is pleasantly scented and suitable for planting in beds or as a hedge. Also known as *R.* 'Interall,' it is a robust plant resistant to disease and pests with a fairly low demand for maintenance. Faded blooms should removed and old wood cut to the ground.

Rosa rubiginosa

*D*og rose

Rosa rubiginosa (syn. R. eglanteria)

ℹ

Family: Rosaceae
Flowering season: summer
Height/spread: to 8 × 8 ft
Situation: ○
Moisture requirement: ◊
❋ ❋ ❋

This rose makes a vigorous, upright, bush branching out with very thorny, curved, arching shoots and dark green leaves, which have finely serrated edges and are perfumed, giving off a pleasant apple scent. The single, shell-shaped flowers 1 in in size are dark pinky red with pale centers and golden yellow stamens. They appear abundantly in summer separately or in small bunches. In autumn they produce an abundance of bright red, egg-shaped rose hips which last through the winter. This domesticated wild rose species is robust and resistant to disease and is ideal for planting on its own in a gardening landscape; it is also very beautiful as a hedge rose. It tolerates poor garden soils as well as woodland areas and partial shade. It should be clipped each year to promote new growing shoots, since it is the tips of these which give off their incomparable scent. It may be pruned heavily every winter. Also known as *R. eglanteria*, this wild rose is native to Europe and Asia Minor.

Floribunda rose

Rosa 'Schneewittchen' (syn. R. 'Iceberg')

This famous variety was introduced by Kordes in Germany in 1958. It is one of the many kinds of floribunda roses, which are, strictly speaking, crosses between a polyantha rose and a hybrid tea rose R. 'Schneewittchen' is also known as R. 'Iceberg' and is an upright bush of vigorous rose branched growth with arching flowering shoots generously covered with slim, shiny, light green leaves. The elegantly formed flower buds open into dazzlingly snow-white, double flowers 3 in across; these are initially spherical and later shell-shaped. Numerous large clusters of these flowers appear persistently from summer to late into the autumn, giving off a lovely full, volatile scent. The cross between R. 'Robin Hood' and R. 'Virgo' has something of the grace of moss rose hybrids. It is excellent for cut flowers and is suitable for growing in beds or as a hedge. With pruning, it forms a very beautiful bush about 4 ft in height. As its alternative name, R. 'Iceberg' suggests, it is robust and resistant to disease.

ⓘ

Family: Rosaceae
Flowering season: summer to autumn
Height/spread: 32 × 26 in
Situation: ○
Moisture requirement: ◊
❄ ❄ ❄

Rambler rose

Rosa 'Seagull'

One of the loveliest and most dependable ramblers of the multiflora hybrids is undoubtedly this variety introduced by Pritchard in 1907. It is still controversial whether R. 'Général Jacqueminot' was used for the cross with R. multiflora. Its growth is strong, wide and arching, making it a distinguished climbing rose for small trees, pergolas and strong supports. The plentiful, tapered, oval, gray-green, leaves are enhanced in summer by an abundance of large, compact clusters of small white blossoms with bright yellow stamens. The simple or semi-double flowers are about 1 in in size and they open flat or shell-shaped; they have a lovely, very distinct smell. As usual with rambler roses, pruning is rarely necessary; however, multiflora hybrids shoot strongly from the base and if old wood is not removed, they will in time form an impenetrable tangle, making the plant vulnerable to fungal disease.

ⓘ

Family: Rosaceae
Flowering season: summer
Height/spread: 20 × 13 ft
Situation: ○
Moisture requirement: ◊
❄ ❄ ❄

*P*atio rose

Rosa 'Sheri Anne'

ℹ

Family: Rosaceae
Flowering season: summer to autumn
Height/spread: 12 × 10 in
Situation: ○
Moisture requirement: ◊
❀ ❀ ❀

The ancestors of the patio or dwarf roses of today were undoubtedly miniature forms of a China rose. One of the earliest varieties reached England and later France at the beginning of the 19th century. Its recent history is owed to the work of the American Ralph Moore in growing these roses. *R.* 'Sheri Anne' is a cross between *R.* 'Little Darling' and *R.* 'New Penny' that was introduced in 1973. It forms an upright, compact bush with leathery, glossy, medium-green leaves. The loose clusters of small, pointed flower buds open into very decorative double, goblet-shaped and later, rosette-shaped flowers, 1 in in size. They are bright orange-red with golden yellow stamens in the center. Also known as *R.* 'Morsheri,' it is a robust variety, flowering freely and reliably over a long period. It prefers a sunny situation and needs fertile soil conditions. It is a rewarding rose for cutting and so long as it is properly fed, it will also thrive extremely well planted in containers and window boxes.

Rosa 'Sommerwind'

Dwarf rose

Rosa 'Snow Carpet'

The name of this small rose is descriptive of its habit. The low, horizontally spreading shoots thickly covered with shiny, bright green foliage give the appearance of a carpet, and in summer, it is sprinkled with an abundance of pure white, star-shaped flowers. These appear in clusters and open into slightly scented double, pompon-shaped blooms 1 in in size. The cross of R. 'New Penny' and R. 'Temple Bells' was made by McGredy in New Zealand and came on the market in 1980. It makes an especially pretty ground cover on sunny slopes or in the rock garden and it acquits itself equally well as a foreground planting in flower beds. Like nearly all dwarf roses, it needs a sunny location and care should be taken not to shade it with neighbouring plants. R. 'Snow Carpet' is sometimes listed under the name R. 'Maccarpe.' Given favourable environmental conditions it may flower again in the autumn.

ⓘ

Family: Rosaceae
Flowering season: summer
Height / spread: 6 × 20 in
Situation: ○
Moisture requirement: ◊
❄ ❄ ❄

Ground cover rose

Rosa 'Sommerwind'

R. 'Sommerwind' forms a low-growing, almost dome-shaped, horizontally-branching bush. It was introduced in 1985 and was bred by Kordes in Germany, its known parent being the variety R. 'The Fairy' which was crossed with an unnamed seedling. It has thick, shiny, dark green foliage. Loose flower clusters appear along the whole length of the shoots, opening into double, shell-shaped, pure pink flowers, 2 in across, with frilled petals. They smell lovely and fresh. This robust rose has a strikingly rich flowering period from summer until the first frost. It is excellent on sunny slopes and for growing in borders; it can also be trained as a low hedge or a small standard rose. Like other ground cover roses, R. 'Sommerwind' increases by low, creeping growth so it should not be pruned in the same way as a shrub rose. In the early years, it is sufficient to remove old wood. Careful pruning may take place later. It is also known as R. 'Korlanum', R. 'Surrey' and R. 'Vent d'Eté.'

ⓘ

Family: Rosaceae
Flowering season: summer to autumn
Height / spread: 32 × 48 in
Situation: ○
Moisture requirement: ◊
❄ ❄ ❄

Ground cover rose

Rosa 'Sonnenschirm'

Family: Rosaceae
Flowering season: summer to autumn
Height/spread: 30 × 52 in
Situation: ○
Moisture requirement: ○
❋ ❋ ❋

The many varieties of this group are united by the slightly misleading name of ground cover roses, but they have other qualities and should not be thought of simply for that purpose. All the varieties are vigorous with arching sideways shoots, so they extend in width far more than they do in height. This make them adaptable to many different uses in the garden, and ground cover roses are the obvious choice where horizontal coverage is wanted rather than vertical. *R.* 'Sonnenschirm', created by Tantau in Germany and introduced in 1993, produces dense sideways growth thickly covered with medium-green foliage. The flowers are double, shell-shaped, pale creamy-yellow blooms with golden yellow stamens, 4 in across. They flower in profusion, continuously from summer until autumn. The scent is not strong but it is pleasant and fresh. The variety is particularly beautiful on sunny slopes and is equally suitable for beds or for planting in large containers. It is also known as *R.* 'Broadlands.'

Bourbon rose

Rosa × borboniana 'Mme Isaac Pereire'

Family: Rosaceae
Flowering season: summer to autumn
Height/spread: 7 × 7 ft
Situation: ○
Moisture requirement: ○
❋ ❋ ❋
prone to: Mehltau

This forms a large upright, bush with dark green foliage. The double flowers 5–6 in across are shell-shaped, quartered and dark pink in color. They give off a strong, intense scent similar to raspberries. A characteristic of this long-flowering old rose is that it produces misshapen flowers when it starts flowering in summer but these often become more perfect, the closer it is to autumn. This exceptional bourbon rose of unknown origin was bred by Garçon in France and introduced in 1881. It also makes an excellent climbing rose, tolerant of poor soils and happy in partial shade. However, it is relatively vulnerable to blight.

Bourbon rose

Rosa × borboniana 'Variegata di Bologna'

This forms an upright, slim, arching bush with straight stems and thick, light green foliage. The double flowers 3–4 in across are initially spherical and then become shell-shaped. They are quartered and very striking with irregular purple to carmine markings and spots on a creamy-white background. They give off an intense, sweet scent. The flowering season is normally in summer, but a second flowering in autumn is quite common. This remarkable bourbon rose prefers a sunny, protected situation and a fertile, well mulched soil. It appreciates support and should be lightly pruned in the late winter. It is relatively vulnerable to powdery mildew. It was bred by Bonfiglioli in Italy and introduced in 1909, but its parent varieties are unknown.

Family: Rosaceae
Flowering season: summer
Height/spread: 7 × 5 ft
Situation: ○
Moisture requirement: ◌
❄ ❄ ❄

Shrubs

Ornamental shrubs, whether flowering specimens or conifers, ground-cover plants or grown as hedges or on espaliers, offer long-term pleasure in the garden. Some shrubs, for instance box, can even be used by the ingenious topiarist to create sculptures. Most ornamental shrubs will adapt easily to their situations, but they are best grown in crumbly, well-drained soil and ideal light conditions, and consequently it is essential to prepare heavy soils well before planting. Peat-loving plants such as rhododendrons, azaleas and some other evergreens need an acid substrate. In this case, you should prepare the soil by adding peat, or use special ericaceous potting compost. Shrubs have a resting period in winter, beginning with leaf-fall in autumn and ending when the new leaves begin to grow in spring. The best times to plant, therefore, are after the leaves have fallen – so long as the ground is not frozen yet – or in spring just before the buds break. The planting hole should be twice as wide and deep as the root-ball of the shrub, which must be well watered before planting. The shrub should not be placed any deeper in the soil than it was in the nursery; the right level will be clearly visible on the collar of the root. It is usually stressful for the plant to be moved, and pruning will help to create a good balance between the part of the shrub above the ground and its roots, making it easier for it to establish itself. However, even if the shrub was planted in autumn, pruning should be left until spring, before the leaves begin to show. As a general rule, cut back the branches by one-third, but it is always a good idea to get expert advice when you are buying. Some shrubs, including magnolias and rhododendrons, should be left unpruned.

Western prickly Moses

Acacia pulchella

ⓘ

Family: Mimosaceae
Flowering season: spring
Height and spread: 5 × 5 ft
Situation: ○
Moisture requirement: ◌
❄
Pests: mealy bugs and scale insects

This acacia species is native to Southeast Asia. It forms a bushy shrub with arching branches and will grow into a small tree with time. The small, bright yellow, spherical flowers are grouped in loose spikes. The most distinctive feature of this small, evergreen shrub is that it has so-called phyllodes instead of leaves, which are flattened leafstalks which look and function as leaves. They are triangular and blue-green on both sides with a single thorn on the underside. Because the shrub is sensitive to frost, it is usually cultivated in a tub so that it can be brought indoors in winter. Acacias need a humus-rich compost and regular watering. The branches should be cut back after flowering. It is raised from previously soaked seed in spring. It is prone to attacks by mealy bugs and scale insects.

Japanese maple

Acer palmatum

ⓘ

Family: Aceraceae
Flowering season: spring
Height and spread: 13 × 13 ft
Situation: ○ – ◑
Moisture requirement: ◗
❄ ❄ ❄

The Japanese maple is native to Japan and Korea. There are hundreds of varieties with different habits and foliage which comes in a variety of shapes and colors. The species itself grows into a large shrub or small tree with a low, compact crown and thing purple-red branches. The small red flowers are borne in umbels and are rather inconspicuous. The fruits are obtuse-angled and winged and are carried in pendulous or erect clusters on the branches. The most striking feature of this species is its magnificent foliage. The leaves are palmate and divided into five to seven lobes with pointed ends. They are bright green in spring and develop brilliant autumn colors; orange, fire-red or yellow, depending on the variety. The Japanese maple grows best in moist, well-drained, humus-rich soil and requires protection from cold winds and early morning sun. Pruning is not necessary. It can be propagated in spring by cuttings.

*A*melanchier, June berry, Snowy mespilus

Amelanchier laevis

The amelanchier is native to North Africa where it grows in damp woodland and wetlands. This early-flowering shrub has a spreading, open habit and with time grows increasingly tree-like. The white, star-shaped flowers are carried in pendulous clusters and exude a honey-like fragrance which attracts many insects. Together with the beautiful, bronze-brown leaves, they are a magnificent sight in spring. The red to purple-black berries which appear in August are very juicy and taste quite delicious. In autumn, the dark green ovate leaves turn a striking orange and red. The amelanchier thrives in neutral to acid humus-rich soil and does not need pruning. In the case of grafted specimens, it is important to remove the suckers that grow at the base. Propagation is by seed or rooting suckers.

ⓘ

Family: Rosaceae
Flowering season: spring
Height and spread: 10–20 × 26 ft
Situation: ○
Moisture requirement: ◖
❄ ❄ ❄
❀

Arundinaria

ℹ️

Family: *Poaceae*
Height and spread: 13 × 13 ft
Situation: ◐
Moisture requirement: ◊
❋ ❋ ❋

Bamboo

Arundinaria

In the past, botanists included the evergreen bamboo, native to the Himalayas and China, in the *Sinarundaria* genus, so bamboo is often still sold under this name in nurseries. Two species are particularly suited for cooler climates because of their hardiness: *A. murielae* (syn. *S. murieliae*, *Thamnocalamus spathaceus*) with an attractive arching habit, and the erect-growing *A. nitida* (syn. *S. nitida*). *A. murieliae* has bright green leaves 4 in long and 1/2 in wide on orange-yellow stems, while *S. nitida* has fine, dark green leaves and dark green stems which turn red-brown towards the top. The leaves of *A. murieliae* turn a beautiful yellow in autumn. These bamboos do not require much care but they do not like waterlogged soil or windy places. However, they do need a lot of water and food so that they should be watered regularly in dry weather (also in winter when there is no frost) and given fertiliser between May and August. Rolled-up leaves are a sign that the plant needs water. Both species can be propagated in spring by division of the clumps.

ℹ️

Family: *Poaceae*
Height and spread: 16 × 16 in
Situation: ◐
Moisture requirement: ◊
❋ ❋ ❋

Thicket-forming bamboo

Arundinaria

Arundinaria is a genus which includes species with very different habits, shape and size. Many plants reach a height of 13 ft while A. *variegata* (syn. A. *fortunei* 'Variegatus'), A. *pumilus* and A. *viridistriatus* are low evergreen shrubs which make excellent ground cover. A. *variegata* has narrow, oblong-lanceolate leaves with striking white or yellow stripes on green stems. The slightly taller A. *pumilus* also has green stems but plain green leaves. The leaves of A. *viridistriatus* are usually yellow when they first come out and turn green in summer. These bamboos develop a lot of new shoots if the soil is rich. However, they dislike waterlogged soil as do the other bamboo species and, like them, they need regular watering in dry weather conditions and fertiliser during the summer. If cut down to nearly ground level, the bamboo will produce new shoots with a particularly luminous color.

Aucuba

Spotted laurel

Aucuba japonica

The spotted laurel is native to southern Japan, China and Taiwan. It forms a round, compact shrub with thick, forked branches. The plant is unisexual which means that the male and female flowers appear on separate plants. The small purple-brown male flowers are carried in erect panicles 4 in high. The female flowers are also reddish-brown and rather inconspicuous, but develop into 3/8 to 3/4 in long, elliptic stone fruits whose bright scarlet berries contrast beautifully against the glossy, dark green leaves. These are oblong ovate with a leathery texture and evergreen. There are many forms in cultivation, such as 'Crotonifolia' which has magnificent foliage, mottled with gold. Because it is only half-hardy, it must be protected against the cold. Young plants should also be protected against intense winter sun. In spring, old branches should be cut back so that the shrub keeps its shape. The plants are propagated by cuttings in summer.

Family: Cornaceae
Flowering season: spring
Height and spread: 8 × 8 ft
Situation: ◖
Moisture requirement: ◌
❄ ❄

Barberry
Berberis julianae

ℹ

Family: Berberidaceae
Flowering season: spring
Height and spread: 10 × 10 ft
Situation: ○ – ◐
Moisture requirement: ◊
❀ ❀ ❀
❀

This beautiful plant is native to China. It forms a magnificent dense evergreen shrub and is therefore ideally suited as hedging. Another advantage is that the strong branches are covered with thorns so that it forms quite an impenetrable barrier both to animals and people. The beautiful, narrow, leathery, dark green leaves are shiny on top and have a prickly, serrated edge. The small clusters of tiny yellow flowers appear in the middle of spring and are slightly scented. In autumn, they develop into long, blue-black fruits with a gray bloom. The shrub must be cut back after flowering. It is propagated by cuttings taken in summer.

Barberry
Berberis linearifolia

ℹ

Family: Berberidaceae
Flowering season: spring
Height and spread: 5 × 3 ft
Situation: ○ – ◐
Moisture requirement: ◊
❀ ❀

This evergreen barberry is native to Chile and Argentina. It is a medium-sized shrub with stiff, upright branches. The orange-yellow flowers, borne in long clusters, appear in spring between narrow, shiny, dark green leaves. The vigorous-growing 'Orange King' is the most striking form. It has darker, narrower leaves than the species and its large flowers are a brilliant orange-red. It flowers so profusely that the leaves are almost completely concealed. In autumn, the shrub is covered with long black fruits covered with bluish bloom. Like the previous barberry, it prefers fertile, humus-rich soil and should be planted in a sheltered position. It is propagated by cuttings in summer.

Berberis thunbergii

Berberis thunbergii

This variety of Berberis, native to Japan, is probably the most popular and most common of evergreen barberries. There are many forms available in nurseries, whose leaves differ in color and shape. This variety of barberry forms a strongly branched, compact shrub with long clusters of yellow flowers. One of the most outstanding features are the orange to scarlet-red autumn colors of the otherwise bright green ovate to spatula-shaped leaves. An additional benefit in autumn are the bright red, shiny, elliptic fruits which remain on the shrub for a long time. In contrast to the other barberry varieties, this one needs a sunny position to ensure good flowering and autumn colors. Because the shrub is robust and requires little care, it also grows in partial shade. It can be propagated in summer from herbaceous or semi-ripe cuttings and can be pruned if necessary.

ⓘ

Family: Berberidaceae
Flowering season: spring
Height and spread: 6–10 × 10 ft
Situation: ○ – ◑
Moisture requirement: ◊
❋ ❋ ❋

Berberis thunbergii

Butterfly bush
Buddleia davidii

ⓘ

Family: Buddlejaceae
Flowering season: Summer
Height and spread: 13 × 13 ft
Situation: ○
Moisture requirement: ◊
❆ ❆
❁

The butterfly bush, which originates from China, can now also be found in parts of Central and Western Europe as well as in California. This vigorously growing shrub has erect branches which arch slightly at the top with lanceolate leaves, arranged in opposite pairs, dark green on top and tomentose underneath. The Butterfly bush is particularly beautiful in summer when it is in full bloom: the sumptuous, plume-shaped clusters of violet flowers of the species or the white, blue, pink or purple flowers of the varieties attract large numbers of butterflies – this is a characteristic common to all the species of the Buddleia genus and why it is known as the butterfly bush. Buddleias must be pruned back vigorously every year and all dead wood must be removed in order to ensure a profusion of flowers the following year. The plant is propagated by herbaceous cuttings in summer.

Butterfly bush
Buddleia globosa

ⓘ

Family: Buddlejaceae
Flowering season: Summer
Height and spread: 16 × 16 ft
Situation: ○
Moisture requirement: ◊
❆

This species of butterfly bush is native to the Andes in Argentina, Chile and Peru and is very easy to look after. In addition, it has beautiful foliage and interesting flowers. This species has loosely arranged, erect branches which arch slightly at the top and lanceolate, dark green leaves with brown woolly hairs underneath. The numerous globular heads of orange-yellow flowers appear in May and June on the previous year's wood and contrast beautifully against the dark leaves. It prefers good loamy soil and sunny position where it is also protected from the wind. Although pruning is not required, it is recommended to remove dead wood and unsightly shoots. This species is propagated by semi-ripe cuttings, taken in summer.

Common box

Buxus sempervirens

ⓘ

Family: Buxaceae
Flowering season: spring
Height and spread: 10 × 10 ft
Situation: ○ – ◑
Moisture requirement: ◌
❄ ❄ ❄
✖

This evergreen plant is native to southwest and Central Europe, North Africa and Asia. Because of its vigorous growth and wide range of habits, it is widely popular. Depending on the variety, it forms a dense shrub or small tree which can grow up to 23 ft high. However, dwarf varieties are more often used for edging such as 'Suffruticosa' which barely grows up to 39 in. The color of the leaves is as varied as the habit. While those of the species are dark green, those of 'Golden Tip,' for instance, are golden-tipped, those of 'Elegantissima' have creamy-white edges and those of 'Aureovariegata' are mottled with creamy-white flecks. The inconspicuous greenish-yellow flowers are found in the axils of the ovate, leathery leaves. The brown fruit capsules burst open in autumn. The common box grows very slowly and is an ideal topiary plant. It also makes beautiful hedges and provides an ideal background for roses. It thrives in calcareous, humus-rich soil and is propagated by cuttings. Great care should be taken when pruning box because it is very poisonous.

Buxus in the garden 'Ton ter Linden'

Callicarpa bodinieri

Callicarpa bodinieri

This round, deciduous shrub, native to China, has ovate, pointed, pale green leaves. The young leaves of the *C. bodinieri* variety are dark brown. The violet flowers which appear in summer between the opposite leaves are barely visible among the foliage. However, the shrub's attraction lies in the profusion of violet, berry-like stone fruits which are grouped in large clusters and are a real eye-catcher in the autumn. Even after the leaves have fallen off, the berries remain on the bush for a long time because the birds are not interested in them. The twigs also look very decorative in a vase. *Callicarpa* must be planted in a sheltered position and young plants should be protected from frost at ground level. Apart from thinning and removing the frost-damaged branches, it does not need any pruning. Several plants should be planted so that cross-pollination can take place. It is propagated by cuttings in summer.

Family: Verbenaceae
Flowering season: summer
Height and spread: 6 × 6 ft
Situation: ○
Moisture requirement: ◊
❁ ❁ ❁

Ling, heather

Calluna

Heather grows throughout Europe, in the northern parts of Asia Minor and northern Morocco. The *Calluna* genus contains only one species but a very large number of varieties. They are low, vigorously growing evergreen shrubs with a compact habit whose size depends on the variety. The flowers and leaves also come in a wide range of colors. The scale-like, linear leaves range from dark to bright green and from gray to brown and gold-yellow. Many varieties have magnificent orange or red autumn colors. A sunny position is important to ensure a profusion of pitcher-shaped or bell-shaped flowers which range from white to bright pink and dark-purple or red in color. In the wild, heather grows over large areas, creating a spectacular landscape. In the garden, it is better to plant several shrubs together to increase the effect. *Calluna* needs a humus-rich, acid soil and should be cut back in spring. The species can be propagated by seed in spring and by division or runners in summer. Varieties can only be propagated vegetatively.

Family: Ericaceae
Flowering season: summer/autumn
Height and spread: 21 × 21 in
Situation: ○
Moisture requirement: ◊
❁ ❁ ❁

Camellia

Camellia

The camellia originates in China and Japan. The evergreen shrub with its glossy, pointed, dark green leaves has beautiful bowl or cup-shaped flowers. In spite of their reputation as demanding plants, they are extremely popular – as is reflected by the 10,000 varieties. These handsome, vigorously growing shrubs with their elegant flowers are a magnificent sight in early spring. The colors range from white to carmine red depending on the species and variety. *C. chrysantha* is an exception with its yellow flowers. The shape and size of the flowers vary enormously. They may be single, semi-double or double, anemone, peony or rose-like with a diameter ranging from 2 to 6 in. Unfortunately, camellias are not completely hardy and need a sheltered position. Winter morning sun and rain should be avoided because they damage the delicate blooms. That is why the plants are often cultivated in tubs so that they can be brought into a cool greenhouse or conservatory when the weather conditions are not right. Moreover, because camellias only grow in good, lime-free soil, cultivation in tubs is also recommended if the soil in the garden is unsuitable. Pruning is not necessary except in the case of young plants whose growth is sometimes straggly. Camellias can be propagated from of half-ripe lateral shoots from June to August and layering in September.

ⓘ

Family: Theaceae
Flowering season: winter/spring
Height and spread: 33 × 16 ft
Situation: ○ – ◑
Moisture requirement: ◊
❄❄ – ❄❄❄ *(to 23 °F)*

Common camellia

Camellia japonica

ⓘ

Family: Theaceae
Flowering season: spring
Height and spread: 33 × 16 ft
Situation: ◑
Moisture requirement: ◊
❋ ❋

The species itself is now rarely cultivated, but the varieties are increasingly numerous in gardens. They form a large shrub or small tree with ovate to lanceolate glossy, dark green leaves and the flowers come in a wide range of colors ranging from white to pale pink and dark red. There are also variegated flowers such as the double white or pale pink 'Lavinia Maggi,' streaked with red. *C. japonica* is hardy to 5°F and more resistant to frost than many other varieties. Apart from that, they still need the same growing conditions as the other camellia varieties.

Camellia reticulata

Camellia reticulata

ⓘ

Family: Theaceae
Flowering season: spring
Height and spread: 33 × 16 ft
Situation: ◑
Moisture requirement: ◊
❋ ❋

This species with its many varieties is an extremely popular camellia. It forms an imposing, large shrub or tree whose growth is more vigorous than that of other camellia species. The glossy, dark green leaves are mostly ovate. When in full bloom in spring, it is a spectacular sight. 'Captain Rawes' is a particularly handsome shrub with beautiful flowers: between March and April it is covered with a profusion of large, semi-double, carmine flowers. Unlike other camellias, C. *reticulata* can be grown outdoors all year round if it is in a sheltered position. However, in very cold regions, it should be brought into a cool greenhouse during winter. Apart from that, it need the same care and conditions as other camellias and can be propagated in the same way.

Camellia japonica

Williamsii hybrids

Camellia × williamsii

These popular hybrids were developed by crossing *C. japonica* and *C. saluenensis*. They are small to medium-sized shrubs with an erect habit and often a spreading growth. The leaves are similar to those of *C. japonica* while the flowers resemble those of *C. saluenensis*. The hybrids are particularly floriferous and start flowering in winter. The flowers vary in shape, size and color depending on the form. The colors are the usual camellia shades, ranging from white to red. Like *C. japonica* and *C. reticulata*, these camellias are relatively very hardy. The hybrids need the same care and conditions as the varieties and are propagated in the same way.

ⓘ

Family: Theaceae
Flowering season: winter/spring
Height and spread: 13 × 10 ft
Situation: ◗
Moisture requirement: ◌
❄ ❄

Chamaecyparis lawsoniana 'White Spot'

🛈

Family: Cupressaceae
Flowering season: spring
Height and spread: 33 × 16 ft
Situation: ○ – ◑
Moisture requirement: ◊
❅ ❅ ❅
✿
✖

Lawson cypress
Chamaecyparis lawsoniana

This species of hardy, evergreen coniferous tree is native to the northwest of the United States where it grows up to 200 ft high. It is therefore not suitable for growing in gardens, but its many forms vary in size and shape and are extremely popular among gardeners. They range from bushy dwarf shrubs such as 'Gnome' which only grows to a height of 20 in, to the columnar 'Allumii.' Most varieties form a narrow spherical or columnar tree with a pendulous crown and scale-like leaves ranging from gold-yellow to green, blue-green and silver-gray. The male and female flowers grow separately on the trees and are inconspicuous. The globular cones appear in profusion in autumn. The Lawson cypress requires very little care and is very robust. The tall varieties look very good planted on their own, while the medium-sized make excellent hedges and screens and provide excellent wind protection. They are propagated by cuttings. Be careful: all parts of the cypress are poisonous.

Cornus mas

🛈

Family: Cornaceae
Flowering season: spring
Height and spread: 20 × 16 ft
Situation: ○
Moisture requirement: ◊
❅ ❅ ❅

Cornelian cherry
Cornus mas

This deciduous plant is native to Central and southern Europe as well as Asia Minor. The compact, densely branched shrubs and small trees look very striking in late winter and early spring when the bare branches are covered with a profusion of small yellow flower clusters. The ovate, pointed, dark green leaves only appear after the shrub or tree has finished flowering. In autumn, the foliage turns a beautiful yellow. But before this happens, the oval red stone fruits will have appeared among the green foliage. Although not very nice raw, they make delicious jelly and jam which is packed with vitamin C. Cornelian cherry is one of the most robust cornus varieties and can be planted on its own or as a hedge. It does not to be pruned but can be cut back if necessary. It can be propagated from cuttings or rooted suckers.

Dwarf medlar

Cotoneaster frigidus

This deciduous dwarf medlar is native to the Himalayas. It forms a large, fast-growing shrub or small tree with large, elliptical leaves reminiscent of those of magnolia. At first they are mid-green and covered with silvery hairs, later they turn dark green and smooth. Clusters of small, yellowish white flowers appear in June, followed in autumn by orange to coral-red fruits. They are not edible but they are extremely decorative and remain on the shrub all through the winter. The dwarf medlar is robust and easy to grow. However, like all other medlars, it is sensitive to fire blight. If necessary, it can be pruned back severely. The dwarf medlar is propagated by cuttings.

Family: Rosaceae
Flowering season: summer
Height and spread: 23 × 23 ft
Situation: ○ – ◑
Moisture requirement: ○
❋ ❋ ❋

Cotoneaster horizontalis

Cotoneaster horizontalis

This variety is native to western China. It is a low semi-evergreen or deciduous shrub depending on its position. If trained against a wall, it will behave like a climber and grow up to 6 ft 6 in high. The branches are arranged in a herringbone pattern and have ovate, glossy, dark green leaves which turn orange or scarlet red in autumn. The small, reddish-white flowers appear in early summer, followed in August by a profusion of tiny, decorative, coral-red fruits. This shrub demands little attention and will also grow in partial shade. However, it will produce more flowers and fruits in a sunny position. It can be pruned if necessary and is propagated by cuttings.

Family: Rosaceae
Flowering season: summer
Height and spread: 6 1/2 × 5 ft
Situation: ○ – ◑
Moisture requirement: ○
❋ ❋ ❋

*E*vergreen dwarf medlar

Cotoneaster sternianus

ⓘ

Family: Rosaceae
Flowering season: spring/summer
Height and spread: 10 × 10 ft
Situation: ○ – ◑
Moisture requirement: ○
❊ ❊ ❊

This graceful shrub originates from Tibet. It is a semi-evergreen or evergreen depending on its position, and has elegant arching branches. Its small, elliptic leaves are gray-green on top and light green with white silvery hairs underneath. The small, white-pink flowers appear in late spring, followed in autumn by numerous large, orange-red fruits. This dwarf medlar looks particularly beautiful on its own but it is also very good for hedging. It is easy to grow and does not need any special care, although it dislikes badly drained soil. It is propagated in summer by cuttings of half-ripe shoots.

Broom

Cytisus nigricans 'Cyni'

This plant can be found in Central and southeastern Europe as well as northeastern Russia. This deciduous shrub has many branches with very small dark green leaves and an erect bushy habit. The species can grow up to 7 ft high but the variety 'Cyni' is usually shorter. In early summer, this handsome shrub stands out with its profusion of fragrant, yellow, sweetpea-shaped flowers, borne in dense terminal racemes. Brooms sometimes flower again in September. They are undemanding and thrive in ordinary, well-drained garden soil. They require pruning in spring and are propagated by half-ripe cuttings. Like all brooms, this species is poisonous.

ⓘ

Family: Fabaceae
Flowering season: summer
Height and spread: 5 × 2 ft
Situation: ○
Moisture requirement: ◊
✾ ✾ ✾
✖
✿

Cytisus nigricans 'Cyni'

Warminster Broom

Cytisus × praecox

Cytisus × praecox

ℹ

Family: Fabaceae
Flowering season: spring
Height and spread: 2 × 5 ft
Situation: ○
Moisture requirement: ◊
❄ ❄ ❄
✖
❀

This hybrid forms a densely branched, somewhat stocky shrub which can reach up to 80 in height. It is a very popular shrub because of its breathtaking appearance in spring. The slender, slightly arching branches are covered with a mass of wonderfully beautiful, cream-yellow flowers. Depending on the form, the flowers can also be white, gold-yellow or purple-red ('Hollandia'). Its very strong scent is not liked by everyone, but the beauty and profusion of the flowers makes up for it. In fact, the small leaves are barely visible amongst the flowers. Although it is such a magnificent sight when in bloom and would be breathtaking planted on its own, it is rather boring the rest of the year so it is best to combine it with other shrubs or herbaceous plants. This hybrid must be cut back strongly to encourage new growth. The plants are propagated in late summer by cuttings. Be careful when handling it because all parts of the plant are poisonous.

Heather

Daboecia

ℹ

Family: Ericaceae
Flowering season: summer/autumn
Height and spread: 20 × 24 in
Situation: ○
Moisture requirement: ◊
❄ ❄

This genus grows wild in the coastal regions of Western Europe and in the Azores. It comprises two species of evergreen shrubs with oblong, dark green leaves and a robust, low habit: *D. Azorica* and *D. cantabrica*. In addition, there a few varieties which differ in size and habit as well as in the color of the flowers. The nodding, bell-shaped flowers vary in color from white to pink and purple-red. This genus is related to the *Erica* and *Calluna* genera and like them, it should be planted in large drifts. Being lime-haters, they prefer peaty, acid soil. Although they grow in shade and partial shade, they produce more flowers in a sunny position. The shrubs should be cut regularly in spring as they have a strong tendency to spread. *Daboecia* is propagated by cuttings and layering. The species can also be raised from seed in spring.

318

Deutzia

Deutzia gracilis

This small, elegant deciduous shrub belongs to the vast *Deutzia* genus and produces very pretty flowers in May. Originally from Japan, it is now one of the most popular shrubs in our gardens. The erect growing branches bear ovate to elliptic, medium-green leaves with serrated edge. The characteristic white flowers with five petals are grouped in erect racemes or panicles and appear in late spring. Deutzias will grow in any ordinary well-drained garden soil. During the flowering season, they need to be watered regularly. Shoots which have finished flowering should be cut back at ground level to promote new growth. It is propagated by cuttings in summer.

🛈

Family: Hydrangeaceae
Flowering season: spring/summer
Height and spread: 3 × 6 ft
Situation: ○
Moisture requirement: ◌
❄ ❄ ❄

Deutzia gracilis

Heather

Erica

Erica is a genus which includes more than 550 evergreen species, most of which are native to South Africa but a few originate from south and Western Europe. In their country of origin, they grow in large drifts which gives the landscape a very distinctive appearance. The main features of these dwarf shrubs are their tiny needle-like leaves, borne in whorls, and the small, bell-shaped or tubular flowers. Besides the low-growing shrubs, the genus also includes species which grow as high as small trees, such as the tree heath *E. arborea* which can reach a height of more than 16 ft. Heather is mostly grown as groundcover and provides an interesting sight throughout the year with its interesting foliage and flowers whose colors vary according to the species and variety. The leaves range from gold to copper hues to gray and dark green, while the flowers vary from white to yellow, pink and violet red. Like *Daboecia* and *Calluna*, most *Erica* species need an acid soil. However, there are a few species which tolerate chalky soil such as *E. carnea*. Most species are not completely hardy and need a certain amount of protection in winter. Pruning in spring will encourage bushier growth. Heather is propagated by cuttings.

🛈

Family: Ericaceae
Flowering season: acc. to species and variety
Height/spread: 21 × 21 in;
tree heath: 16 × 16 ft
Situation: ○ – ◑
Moisture requirement: ○
❄ ❄ – ❄ ❄ ❄

Erica arborea 'Alpina'

Erica arborea 'Alpina'

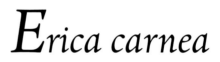

ⓘ

Family: Ericaceae
Flowering season: spring
Height and spread: 3 × 3 ft
Situation: ○ – ◐
Moisture requirement: ◌
❀ ❀
❀

This variety of tree heather is native to western Spain. The species grows up to 16 ft high but this variety never reaches that height, only growing to 3 ft. It is a dense, erect growing shrub with needle-like leaves which are fresh green, as is usual in the species. The large, fragrant snow-white flowers, grouped in long racemes, appear in spring. Unlike the other Erica species, this one tolerates chalky soil provided it is rich in humus and not too shallow. Although it is hardier than the type species, it needs some protection in severe winters. But it will not be harmed by frost damage since this only helps to generate new growth.

Erica carnea

Erica carnea

Erica carnea

ⓘ

Family: Ericaceae
Flowering season: winter/spring
Height and spread: 12 × 12 in
Situation: ○ – ◐
Moisture requirement: ◌
❀ ❀ ❀

This species originates in southern Europe. It is a popular garden plant which, in contrast to other species and varieties, not only survives relatively harsh winters but also flowers in late winter, thereby providing color at one of the gloomiest times of the year. There are many varieties of this small, strongly branched shrub which all differ in the color of the leaves and flowers. For instance, the popular 'Ann Sparkes' has golden-yellow leaves which turn bronze in winter and carmine-pink flowers. 'Loughrigg,' on the other hand, has dark green leaves and dark pink-red flowers, and 'Foxhollow' has yellow-green leaves and pale pink flowers. Unlike almost all the other species, E. carnea tolerates chalky soil, provided it is rich in humus and not too shallow. Furthermore, it need not be cut back in spring as other heathers.

Dorset heath

Erica ciliaris

This species is native to the coastal regions of southern Ireland, south-west England and north-west Morocco. It is a low growing shrub with ovate to lanceolate, dark green leaves with long, grey-white gland-bearing hairs underneath, which have inspired the Latin name of the species. The terminal racemes are 4 in long, white ('White Wings') or pink-red ('Corfe Castle'), and appear in early summer depending on the variety. The calyx is also ciliate. Like almost all its relatives, this species requires acid soil and pruning in spring. Because Dorset heath is not completely hardy, it needs to be well protected in winter.

ⓘ

Family: Ericaceae
Flowering season: summer
Height and spread: 12 × 12 in
Situation: ○ – ◑
Moisture requirement: ◊
❊ ❊

Bell heather

Erica cinerea

This species of Erica grows in the wild in the coastal regions of Western Europe and northwest Africa. The small, strongly branched shrub is low growing with gray, tomentose branches covered with dark green, lanceolate leaves. There are many garden forms of bell heather whose color is more intense than the light violet-red of the species. For instance, 'C. D. Eason' has dark pink flowers, 'P. S. Patrick' has carmine-red flowers, and the forms of the 'Eden Valley' variety have white flowers with violet-pink tips. Like all heathers, it is not entirely hardy and must therefore be protected from frost in winter. It requires pruning in spring.

ⓘ

Family: Ericaceae
Flowering season: summer
Height and spread: 24 × 24 in
Situation: ○ – ◑
Moisture requirement: ◊
❊ ❊

Spindle tree

Euonymous fortunei

Family: *Celastraceae*
Flowering season: spring
Height and spread: 7 × 5 ft
Situation: ◯ – ◖
Moisture requirement: ◌
❄ ❄

This evergreen shrub, which is native to China, is very popular in gardens because of its habit and hardiness. Its long, creeping branches make it ideal as groundcover while it can also be trained against a wall to provide a screen. The ovate to elliptic leaves are dark green. But there are a few varieties with striking variegated leaves such as 'Emerald 'n' Gold' (dark green with yellow edges), 'Silver Queen' (dark green with creamy-white edge), and 'Sunspot' (dark green a yellow fleck in the middle). The leaves usually turn red in autumn. The inconspicuous greenish-white flowers, followed in autumn by greenish-white fruits, appear in May and June. The spindle tree is easy to grow and even tolerates shade. It is propagated by cuttings in summer.

Forsythia × intermedia

Forsythia × intermedia

Family: *Oleaceae*
Flowering season: spring
Height and spread: 10 × 10 ft
Situation: ◯
Moisture requirement: ◌ – ◖
❄ ❄

This is a hybrid between *F. suspensa* and *F. viridissima* which are both native to China. This erect, vigorous growing, deciduous shrub is one of the most popular spring-flowering shrubs. In spring, its mass of luminous yellow flowers make it a real eye-catcher in the garden: because the flowers appear before the leaves, the shrub looks like a cloud of flowers. They look particularly good when planted as a hedge. A few flowering branches also look very attractive in a vase. The ovate to lanceolate dark green leaves with serrated edge are 4 in long and appear after the shrub has flowered. The hybrid is easy to grow and requires little attention. It thrives in ordinary garden soil and, although it prefers a sunny position, it will also tolerate partial shade. In order to ensure plenty of flowers and a beautiful shape, the shrub should be cut back after flowering. It is propagated by cuttings in summer.

Forsythia × intermedia

*F*orsythia suspensa

Forsythia suspensa

This species includes two varieties: one native to China, *F. fortunei*, whose branches grow upright when young but become arching when older, and the other native to Japan, *F. sieboldii*, which has arching branches from the beginning. While *F. fortunei* can grow up to 10 ft in height and bears numerous dark yellow flowers, *F. sieboldii* is smaller with a maximum height of 8 ft and flowers less abundantly with pale yellow blooms. The dark green leaves of the species are ovate, slightly smaller than those of the hybrid. *F. suspensa* is as easy to grow as the hybrid: it looks particularly good against a wall. It thrives in good ordinary garden soil and prefers a sunny location although it tolerates partial shade. It needs to be thinned after flowering in order to keep its shape and encourage flowering. It is propagated by cuttings in summer.

🛈

Family: Oleaceae
Flowering season: spring
Height and spread: 10 × 7 ft
Situation: ○
Moisture requirement: ◊
❄ ❄

325

Fuchsia

Fuchsia

This is a genus of more than 100 species, native to Central and South America, Tahiti and New Zealand. They are deciduous or evergreen shrubs, small trees or climbers, depending on the climate, which produce an abundance of flowers. They were so popular in Central Europe that since their introduction in the 18th century breeders have developed several thousand varieties, although only a few of these are still available at nurseries. The plants owe their popularity to the delicate elegance of their very beautiful, pendulous flowers which consist of long, tubular calyx ending in four spreading sepals which reveal the petals. The protruding stamens and very long style are distinctive features of the fuchsia flower. There are single, semi-double and double flowers which come in all shades of red, but also in white and orange hues. The tubular calyx and sepals are a different color from the petals. Some of the color combinations are quite extraordinary, yellow and purple-violet for instance. The pendulous flowers are usually borne in loose clusters or panicles or grow singly in the leaf axils. They can be as small as 1/8 in and as long as 4 1/2 in. The foliage seems to provide only a background for these spectacular blooms. However, there are some interesting leaf colors such as dark green, yellow-green and variegated. The oval to oblong leaves are borne in whorls or arranged in opposite pairs on the branches. Fuchsias are very versatile plants and, depending on their habit, they can be grown as a bushy shrub, pyramid or tree. The hanging forms are perfect for balconies and hanging baskets. One of their greatest disadvantages is that, with a few exceptions, they are not hardy. Fuchsias thrive in any well-drained garden soil enriched with humus and prefer a sheltered position. Regular pruning in spring will promote bushier shrubs. They can be propagated all year round by cuttings.

Family: Onagraceae
Flowering season: according to species and variety: spring/autumn
Height and spread: according to species and variety: 16 ft × 7 ft
Situation: ○ – ◑
Moisture requirement: ◐
✿ – ✿ ✿

327

Fuchsia boliviana

Fuchsia boliviana

This elegant variety is native to the South American rain forest. It forms an erect, compact, deciduous shrub or small tree whose mid to dark green leaves which can reach up to 10 in in length and are arranged in opposite pairs. The relatively short red petals and stamens project from the slender, dark red, tubular calyx. The 'Alba' variety with white tubular calyx and sepals is more contrasting than the species. The dark purple-red, 3/4 in berries are particularly attractive. Because this fuchsia is not hardy and needs to overwinter in a cold greenhouse or conservatory, it is best to grow it in a tub so that it can also be protected from the fierce sun on a hot summer's day.

Fuchsia 'Rose of Castile'

🛈

Family: Onagraceae
Flowering season: summer
Height and spread: 10 × 3 ft
Situation: ◑
Moisture requirement: ◐
❄

🛈

Family: Onagraceae
Flowering season: summer
Height and spread: 10 × 3 ft
Situation: ○ – ◑
Moisture requirement: ◌
❄

Fuchsia fulgens

Fuchsia fulgens

Native to Mexico, this species is a large deciduous shrub with an erect habit. It has large ovate to heart-shaped leaves with finely serrated edges and a bulbous rootstock which is unusual in fuchsias. The gray-green foliage provides a wonderful background to the bright orange flowers borne in clusters in early summer. The flowers are very striking, with their long, tubular calyx and pale-green tipped sepals over dark orange petals. The large berries are a deep purple-red. This species must spend the winter in a cool greenhouse because they need a minimum temperature of 41°F.

Fuchsia magellanica

Fuchsia magellanica

This species is native to southern Chile and Argentina along the Magellan straits. The deciduous, very floriferous shrub has an erect, compact habit. The ovate to lanceolate dark green leaves have dark red veins and are only 1 in long. The slender dark carmine red flowers with violet petals are followed in autumn by black-red berries. The flowering period lasts from July until October. Unlike most fuchsias, this species (and its varieties) is hardy. However, this hardiness applies more to the roots than the branches. In spring, it is cut down to 4 in from ground level to encourage new growth. It requires partial shade and thrives in humus-rich soil.

ⓘ

Family: Onagraceae
Flowering season: summer
Height and spread: 10 × 7ft
Situation: ◑
Moisture requirement: ◊ – ◊
❄ ❄ ❄

Fuchsia procumbens

Fuchsia procumbens

This deciduous species native to New Zealand has a very distinctive habit. It is a small-leaved, prostrate plant which only grows 4 in high and is ideal for growing in a hanging basket. The erect flowers which appear in profusion in spring are different from those of other fuchsias. They have no petals, but compensate by an extraordinary color combination: the tubular calyx is yellow, the sepals are purple-violet and the stamens are red and blue. The flowers are followed by large deep red berries which remain on the shrub for a long time and are very decorative. In milder climates, *F. procumbens* is hardy enough to survive winter so that it can be used as ground cover.

ⓘ

Family: Onagraceae
Flowering season: spring
Height and spread: 4 in × variable
Situation: ◑
Moisture requirement: ◊ – ◊
❄ ❄

Spanish Gorse

Genista hispanica

ℹ

Family: Fabaceae
Flowering season: spring / summer
Height and spread: 2 × 5 ft
Situation: ○
Moisture requirement: ◊
❋ ❋
✖

This species, native to Spain and southern France, forms a low, compact deciduous shrub. Its spine-covered branches have small, deep green, lanceolate leaves. The gold-yellow papilionaceous flowers, borne in terminal clusters, appear in late spring and continue to flower until early summer. Spanish gorse grows well even in poor soil as long as it is well-drained. It even tolerates chalky soil. Because it is not entirely hardy, it needs protection against frost. All dead wood must be removed after winter and after flowering, it should be be cut back to encourage bushy new growth. The plants can be propagated by cuttings in summer. Be careful: all parts of the plant are poisonous.

Chinese witch hazel

Hamamelis mollis

ℹ

Family: Hamamelidaceae
Flowering season: winter / spring
Height and spread: 16 × 20 ft
Situation: ○ – ◐
Moisture requirement: ◊
❋ ❋ ❋
✿

As the name indicates, this species is native to China. It is a deciduous shrub with a spreading, funnel-like habit and green leaves which have a metallic sheen on top and are felted underneath. The foliage turns a beautiful yellow in autumn. At the beginning of the year, fragrant, gold-yellow, spidery flowers appear on the bare branches. The flowers do not mind the frost – they merely stop appearing for a time and start again later, the petals curling up in the meantime. In autumn, they are followed by woody fruit capsules which burst open with a loud cracking noise, thus scattering their seeds. It is easy to grow and requires little care; it should not be pruned. *H. mollis* can be raised from seed.

Hamamelis mollis

Common witch hazel

Hamamelis virginiana

The western relative of the Chinese witch hazel is native to the eastern United States and Canada. This deciduous upright shrub has slightly broader leaves than *H. mollis* and unlike the latter, it flowers in autumn before or after the yellow autumn leaves have fallen off. The very fragrant, bright yellow flowers do not stand out against the yellow autumn leaves. The fruits only ripen the following year. Like the Chinese witch hazel, the common witch hazel is easy to grow and requires very little care. It tolerates chalky soil although it prefers a slightly acid soil. Like other *Hamamelis* species, it does not need pruning and can be raised from seed.

ⓘ

Family: Hamamelidaceae
Flowering season: autumn
Height and spread: 16 × 16 ft
Situation: ○ – ◑
Moisture requirement: ◌
❄ ❄ ❄
✿

331

Common hydrangea

Hydrangea macrophylla

The common hydrangea is native to Japan and China and is one of the most popular deciduous flowering shrubs in our gardens. There are many species which vary mainly in color and flower shape. However, all species have an upright habit and ovate to elliptic leaves between 3 and 8 in long in a wide range of greens which are, depending on the species. But the most remarkable feature of the common hydrangea are the extraordinarily decorative flower heads which, even when faded, remain attractive both on the shrub and as dried flowers in a vase. Besides white, pink, red and violet flowering hydrangeas, there are also blue flowering varieties. In soil with a high pH, or alkaline soil, the flowers will be red, while in soil with a low pH, or acid soil, they turn blue. The small flowers are borne in round or flat corymbs, 4 to 8 in across, and consist only of large, sterile florets, unlike the flower heads of the Lacecaps which have fertile inner florets surrounded by sterile florets. 'Bouquet Rose' has particularly large round flower heads while 'Masja' has large round flat flower heads. Hydrangeas need good loamy soil, enriched with humus and are best grown where they are protected from the wind. Hydrangeas need regular watering in summer and in winter they must be protected from the cold at ground level. They do require any pruning, but damaged or weak shoots should be removed. Removing the dead flower heads after winter will encourage the following season's flowering. Hydrangeas are propagated by cuttings in summer.

ⓘ

Family: Hydrangeaceae
Flowering season: summer
Height and spread: 10 × 10 ft
Situation: ○ – ◑
Moisture requirement: ◐
❄ ❄

Lacecap

Hydrangea macrophylla

Lacecaps are also common hydrangeas but, because of their different flower heads they are treated separately. In contrast to the round or flat corymbs of the mop-head hydrangeas, the flat flower heads consist of tiny, inconspicuous but fertile inner florets surrounded by large, striking, sterile florets which attract insects: the flower heads are delicate and look like lace, inspiring their name 'lacecap.' The outer florets are usually a different color from the inner florets: in 'Veitchii' the inner florets are violet-blue surrounded by white outer florets, in 'Mariesii Perfecta' the inner florets are blue and the outer florets are bluish or pink. Like the mop-head hydrangeas, the lacecaps are not completely hardy and the roots should be protected from frost. The dead flowers should be removed in spring to promote flowering.

Hydrangea macrophylla

ⓘ

Family: Hydrangeaceae
Flowering season: summer
Height and spread: 10 × 10 ft
Situation: ○ – ◑
Moisture requirement: ◐
❋ ❋

ⓘ

Family: Hydrangeaceae
Flowering season: summer
Height and spread: 10 × 10 ft
Situation: ○ – ◑
Moisture requirement: ◐
❋ ❋ ❋

Hydrangea arborescens

Hydrangea arborescens

This hydrangea, native to northeast America, forms an upright deciduous shrub with loose habits. Its bright green leaves are ovate to elliptic with serrated edges, 2 1/2 to 8 in long, depending on the species. It flowers throughout summer with flat corymbs of creamy white, mostly sterile florets which reach a diameter of 7 in in the 'Grandiflora' variety and an amazing 10 in in the 'Anabella.' These hydrangeas should be planted in a sunny position, but sheltered from the strong sun. Like other hydrangeas they need a lot watering in summer in dry weather conditions. Pruning is not absolutely necessary, but it will lead to more beautiful flowers.

Hydrangea aspera ssp sargentiana

Hydrangea aspera ssp sargentiana

This sub-species, native to southwest China, forms an erect deciduous shrub with vigorous, densely hairy branches. The leaves are lanceolate to ovate, dull green with velvety hairs on top and whitish-gray and downy underneath. The leaves can be up to 14 in long depending on the variety. The very large, flat flower heads with white ray florets, tinged with pink, and purple inner florets are particularly beautiful. This hydrangea should be grown in well-drained but moisture-retentive soil in a place where it is protected from the strong sun and wind. Light pruning in spring will produce more beautiful flowers.

ⓘ

Family: Hydrangeaceae
Flowering season: summer
Height and spread: 10 × 10 ft
Situation: ◯ – ◑
Moisture requirement: ◐
❆ ❆

Hydrangea paniculata

Hydrangea paniculata

This deciduous species, which can grow into a 33 ft high tree, is native to China and Japan. However, in gardens of the western world, they usually form an upright shrub with arching branches which can be kept low by frequent pruning. Its ovate to elliptic dark green leaves have a serrated edge and are covered with bristly hairs underneath. In summer, the shrub is a real eye-catcher with its 10 in long, pyramidal terminal panicles. While the small inner florets remain white, the large, white outer ray florets gradually become flushed with pink as time goes by. The panicles of the variety 'Grandiflora' consist entirely of sterile ray florets. The shrub will benefit from pruning in spring which will promote new growth and more prolific flowering.

Hydrangea

ⓘ

Family: Hydrangeaceae
Flowering season: summer
Height and spread: 10 × 10 ft
Situation: ◯ – ◑
Moisture requirement: ◐
❆ ❆ ❆

English or common holly

Ilex aquifolium

Family: *Aquifoliaceae*
Flowering season: *spring/summer*
Height and spread: *to 33 × 20 ft*
Situation: ◑
Moisture requirement: ○ – ◐

This evergreen holly species grows wild in Asia Minor, North Africa and Atlantic Europe, where it grows into a tree 40 ft high. The varieties suitable for growing in the garden do not grow as high, usually forming a large, spherical shrub which is particularly popular because of its attractive fruit. The elliptic to lanceolate, dark green leathery leaves of the species are about 3 $\frac{1}{2}$ in long and have a strongly wavy edge with sharp spines. There are many varieties which differ mainly in the shape and color of the leaves: those of 'Argentea Marginata' have a white edge, and those of 'Aurea Marginata' have a gold-yellow edge. The small, fragrant, white flowers appear in late spring. In order to ensure the production of the celebrated shiny berries – which are poisonous – male and female specimens must be planted together so that pollination can occur. Holly thrives in good moist soil, rich in humus but it must not be waterlogged. It will also tolerate shady positions. Common holly does not need pruning and is ideal for hedging. It is propagated by cuttings.

Ilex aquifolium

336

Ilex serrata (syn. I. sieboldii)

Ilex serrata (syn. I. sieboldii)

This species of Ilex, native to Japan and China, is a large shrub with erect habit. It is deciduous in contrast with many other ilex species. The elliptic to lanceolate, deciduous, dark green leaves have serrated edges and are smaller than those of *I. aquifolium*, being only 2 in long. In autumn, they a beautiful gold-yellow. The bright red flowers which appear in early summer are followed by red fruits which remain on the shrub for a long time after the leaves have fallen. They are very attractive in a vase. The 'Leucocarpa' variety has creamy-white fruits. In order to ensure the production of berries, male and female plants must be planted together to enable cross-pollination. This species prefers acid soil and a sunny position. It is propagated by cuttings.

Family: Aquifoliaceae
Flowering season: summer
Height and spread: 13 × 8 ft
Situation: ○
Moisture requirement: ◐
❁ ❁

Ilex verticillata

Ilex verticillata

This species is native to North America. Like its relative *I. Serrata*, this large shrub is also deciduous. Its elliptic to lanceolate, pale green leaves have serrated edges. They are abour 3 in long and turn yellow in autumn. The inconspicuous white flowers of the female plant are followed by a mass of shiny red fruits which remain on the shrub for a long time and are beautiful in flower arrangements. In order to ensure the production of berries, male and female plants must be planted together to enable cross-pollination to occur. This species does not tolerate chalky soil or shade, but it will thrive in moisture-retentive soil and is frost-resistant. This species is poisonous, as are all *Ilex* species.

Family: Aquifoliaceae
Flowering season: summer
Height and spread: 10 × 10 ft
Situation: ○
Moisture requirement: ◐
❁ ❁ ❁
✖

337

Jasminum humile

Jasminum humile

ℹ

Family: Oleaceae
Flowering season: summer
Height and spread: 8 × 8 ft
Situation: ○
Moisture requirement: ◌
❄ ❄

This bushy shrub grows wild from Burma to India and as far as western China. Its evergreen to semi-evergreen, brilliant green leaves are ovate to elliptic. This shrub looks very attractive in early summer when the bright yellow, star-shaped flowers appear at the end of the thin branches. The flowers may be small, but they are very abundant and pleasantly fragrant. If planted against a wall it can be trained like a climber but it will need a trellis to climb against. It requires rich soil and a warm, sheltered position. Extensive pruning is not necessary. Just cut back slightly after flowering. The shrub is propagated by cuttings in summer.

Procumbent juniper

Juniperus procumbens

Juniperus procumbens

This very low-growing juniper species originates from the mountains in southern Japan. The vigorous-growing branches of this dwarf conifer spread in a prostrate manner close to the ground. Their branches are densely covered with fragrant, short, pointed, evergreen needles which are bright green to yellow-green on top and blue-green underneath. The almost spherical black-brown berries have a diameter of 3/8 in. The particularly small 'Nana' form forms a dense mat with its compact branches and twigs and is therefore very suitable in the rockery. Juniper is easy to grow and requires little care. It also thrives in poor soil, but prefers a sunny position. It is propagated by cuttings. The shrub is poisonous, as are all Juniper species.

ℹ

Family: Cupressaceae
Height and spread: 1 × 7 ft
Situation: ○
Moisture requirement: ◌
❄ ❄ ❄
✖

Pencil cedar

Juniperus scopulorum

This tree juniper is native to the mountainous regions of western North America. It is tall tree with a distinctive, slender, columnar habit. In the garden form 'Sky-rocket', which is often regarded as a variety of *J. virginiana*, the branches and twigs are erect and very dense. Even the blue-green needles are arranged like scales on the thin branches. The spherical pine cones are also blue and covered with a bloom. They are smaller than those of *J. procumbens*, measuring only 1/4 in. Like the latter, this tree juniper is easy to grow and requires little care. It prefers poor soil and a sunny position. It can be propagated by cuttings. Be careful when touching the plant, since all parts are poisonous.

ⓘ

Family: Cupressaceae
Height and spread: 26 × 2 ft
Situation: ○
Moisture requirement: ◊
❋ ❋ ❋
✖

Privet

Ligustrum lucidum

This evergreen species which is native to China and Korea forms a large shrub or small tree which can grow up to 33 ft high. However, garden forms do not grow so high. The glossy dark green, ovate to lanceolate leathery leaves may be up to 5 in long. The panicles of white flowers, almost 8 in long, appear in autumn and are followed by small, blue-black poisonous fruits. The leaves and flowers are not unattractive, but the shrub's main attraction is the fact that it does not mind pruning. It is therefore an ideal hedging plant, but it is also ideal for topiary. It will grow well in any ordinary garden soil, in either sun or shade and requires very little care. It is propagated by hardwood cuttings.

ⓘ

Family: Oleaceae
Flowering season: summer/autumn
Height and spread: 20 × 20 ft
Situation: ○ – ◑
Moisture requirement: ◊
❋ ❋
✖

Magnolia
Magnolia

Magnolias are native to eastern Asia and also the eastern parts of North America and Central America. This large genus includes large deciduous and evergreen shrubs or small trees; the early-flowering varieties are often deciduous while the summer-flowering are mostly evergreen. Magnolias from eastern Asia are smaller than those from North America and are therefore more common in gardens. Although the shrubs have beautiful large leaves which range from pale green to dark green, the main feature of magnolias are the flowers. Most magnolias have beautiful, elegant flowers which develop from velvety buds at the end of the branches. The large, solitary flowers range from white to pink and purple-red in color. Asian magnolias have a bushy habit and flower in early spring before the leaves develop. A spectacular eye-catcher in the garden, it overshadows all other plants. Magnolias are shallow-rooted and therefore need a position with light, well-drained, loamy soil where their roots can develop undisturbed. Most species prefer a light acidic soil although there are a few species which will tolerate a chalky soil. Magnolias are hardy plants but a thick layer of mulch will help protect the shallow roots from harsh frost. Because a late frost can damage early blooms, magnolias should be planted in a sheltered position. Magnolias should not be pruned. They are propagated in summer by cuttings or grafting.

ⓘ

Family: Magnoliaceae
Flowering season: according to species and variety: winter - summer
Height and spread: according to species and variety: up to 65 × 33 ft
Situation: ○ – ◑
Moisture requirement: ◊
❄ ❄

341

Magnolia liliiflora 'Nigra'

Magnolia liliiflora 'Nigra'

ⓘ

Family: Magnoliaceae
Flowering season: spring
Height and spread: 13 × 13 ft
Situation: ○
Moisture requirement: ◌
❀ ❀ ❀

This magnolia species is native to China. However, in gardens in the western world, it is the 'Nigra' variety, a compact plant, which is most widely cultivated. This large deciduous shrub is slow-growing with an erect habit and large, glossy dark green leaves. As soon as the leaves begin to unfold in May, the 5 in long flower heads emerge from the purple-red buds. This species has the darkest red-purple flowers of all magnolia flowers, but this is only on the outside; as soon as the petals have opened, they reveal a whitish-pink interior. In the species, the petals are purple on the outside and white inside. The flowers of the purple magnolia make it a spectacular solitary plant. Magnolias thrive in well-drained, loamy, slightly acidic soil in a sunny, sheltered position. It is propagated by cuttings.

Magnolia stellata

Magnolia stellata

This slow-growing magnolia, native to Japan, is the most decorative of the genus. As a young plant, M. *stellata* has a round, compact habit but with time, it grows increasingly tree-like. Unlike those of many other magnolias, the deciduous, dark green leaves of M. *stellata* are narrow and lanceolate and only appear after the flowers have emerged from the silky buds. In early spring, the shrub develops an abundance of fragrant, white, star-shaped flowers after which the species is named. There are varieties with double flowers such as 'Royal Star' and purple-pink flowering varieties such as 'Rubra.' 'Waterlily' has larger flowers than the species. Because M. *stellata* flowers so early, it could easily be damaged by late frost. It is therefore advisable to plant it in a sheltered location where it is protected from cold winds. It thrives in slightly acidic, humus-rich soil and will tolerate shade. It is propagated by cuttings in late summer.

ℹ

Family: Magnoliaceae
Flowering season: spring
Height and spread: 10 × 10 ft
Situation: ○
Moisture requirement: ◊
❄ ❄ ❄
❀

Mahonia aquifolium

Mahonia aquifolium

Mahonia aquifolium

This species of mahonia is found in the wild in western North America where it grows in coniferous forests as low, bushy evergreen shrubs. The unevenly pinnate leaves are ovate and have wavy, spiny, serrated edges. The shiny dark green leaves turn an intense bronze-red in autumn. The numerous, dense terminal clusters of pale yellow to gold-yellow flowers, often flushed with red, appear in spring and are followed by blue-black berries, covered with hoary bloom. *M. aquifolium* is ideal as undergrowth because it grows well in shade. It can be pruned to keep it into a particular shape. It is a vigorously growing shrub which will grow in any soil as long as it is moist, well-drained and rich in nutrients. It spreads by underground suckers and is propagated by cuttings.

ⓘ

Family: Berberidaceae
Flowering season: spring
Height and spread: 3 × 5 ft
Situation: ◑
Moisture requirement: ◌ – ◗
❊ ❊ ❊

Common myrtle

Myrtus communis

This well-known plant is native to the whole of the Mediterranean region, southwest Europe and western Asia. It used to be part of the traditional bridal attire and its essential oil is used in the cosmetic industry. Myrtle is a bushy, evergreen shrub with small glossy, dark green leaves which are pleasantly fragrant. The small white, equally fragrant flowers appear in mid-summer, followed by almost black berries. Because myrtle is not completely hardy, it is often cultivated in pots or tubs so that it can be brought into a cool greenhouse in winter. When growing it in a pot or tub, it is important to make sure that the soil never dries out completely. In summer, myrtle loves a sunny, sheltered position, preferably against a wall, and does well in a slightly acidic soil. The young shoots should be supported in spring. Myrtle is propagated by cuttings.

ⓘ

Family: Myrtaceae
Flowering season: summer
Height and spread: 10 × 10 ft
Situation: ○
Moisture requirement: ◌
❊ ❊

Pernettya mucronata

Pernettya mucronata

Pernettya is native to southern Chile and is an evergreen shrub with a low, bushy habit. The glossy, leathery dark green leaves are ovate to lanceolate and only 3/4 in long with a thorn-like, pointed end. The small, nodding, white flowers, tinged with pink, appear in late spring. The poisonous red fruits which follow in autumn, remain for a long time on the shrub, often throughout the winter. The garden forms also include varieties with white, pink-red and purple-violet berries. Because *P. mucronata* is dioecious, male and female specimens must be planted together to enable cross-pollination to occur and thus ensure fruiting. It requires acid, humus-rich soil and partial shade. Because the plant is not completely hardy, the roots need protection from severe frost. The plant spreads by underground suckers but can also be propagated by cuttings.

ⓘ

Family: Ericaceae
Flowering season: spring
Height and spread: 4 × 4 ft
Situation: ◐
Moisture requirement: ○– ◐
❄ ❄
✖

Pernettya mucronata

345

Mountain pine

Pinus mugo

This pine species is native to the mountainous regions of Central and southern Europe and distinguishes itself by its wide range of habits, ranging from small to medium-sized shrubs to small trees. The branches grow level or upward and are densely covered with needles, arranged in pairs. The shade of green varies according to the species. The cones grow on their own or in groups of up to three, arranged symmetrically. There are several garden forms of which 'Gnome' is one of the most popular: it has dark green needles and forms a very compact, round shrubs. Mountain pine is very easy to grow and will do well in any soil, even a poor one. Being robust, very hardy plants, they make an ideal screen against the wind, but they do need plenty of light. Light pruning helps prevents unsightly bareness. It can be raised from seed or propagated by grafting.

ⓘ

Family: Pinaceae
Flowering season: spring
Height and spread: 10 × 10 ft
Situation: ○
Moisture requirement: ◌
❈ ❈ ❈

Cinquefoil

Potentilla fruticosa

The large potentilla genus includes mainly herbaceous perennials and a few shrubby species such as the evergreen *P. fruticosa* native in northern Asia and America. It forms a small, erect bushy shrub with gray-green, pinnately-lobed, lanceolate leaves with curled up edges. The numerous, yellow, saucer-shaped flowers appear between late spring and late summer. There are several varieties which vary mainly in the color of the flowers: in 'Abbotswood,' they are white, in 'Red Ace,' they are orange-red, and in 'Tangerine,' they are orange-yellow. *P. fruticosa* will tolerate shade, but grows much better when in full sun, although the red flowers will fade in the strong sun. Pruning in spring will promote abundant flowering. The plants are propagated by cuttings.

ⓘ

Family: Rosaceae
Flowering season: spring - summer
Height and spread: 5 × 5 ft
Situation: ○
Moisture requirement: ◌
❈ ❈ ❈

Potentilla fruticosa

*J*apanese apricot

Prunus mume

The name is misleading because the Japanese apricot is native to China. But it is so popular in Japan because of its intensively fragrant white flowers, particularly lovely in the evening, that it has been cultivated there for a very long time. It is now also very popular in European gardens where it can grow into a tree up to 33 ft high with a round crown. The small, pale pink flowers appear in late winter on the still bare branches and make a truly breathtaking sight. There are other varieties available with flowers in a wide range pinks and different shapes of flowers such as 'Omoi-no-mama' with white-pink, semi-double flowers, and 'Beni-chidori' with single carmine-red flowers. The shiny green shoots with fresh green, ovate leaves with finely serrated edges are also very attractive. The yellow to greenish round stone fruits have a bitter or sour taste and are processed in various ways in Japan. Pruning after flowering will encourage next season's flowering. It is propagated by cuttings in summer.

Prunus mume

ⓘ

Family: Rosaceae
Flowering season: winter/spring
Height and spread: to 33 × 8 ft
Situation: ○
Moisture requirement: ◌
❅ ❅ ❅
❀

347

Rhododendron

Rhododendron

In the past, this vast genus was divided into two genera: the evergreen rhododendron and the deciduous azaleas which also include the so-called Japanese azaleas, evergreen dwarf shrubs. Although botanists have merged the two genera, there is still a lot of confusion because the 1,300 or so species have countless varieties and hybrids. However, apart from these taxonomic problems, rhododendrons are wonderful flowering shrubs or small trees, native to eastern Asia and North America as well as southern and Central Europe, growing in mountainous regions as high as the snow line and also in coastal regions. In gardens in the western world they are grown mainly for their magnificent flowers, although many deciduous species develop very beautiful autumn colors, ranging from red and orange to golden-yellow. The flowers come in various shapes and sizes: they can be bell or funnel-shaped, tubular or saucer-shaped, and they can be borne singly or in large terminal clusters or umbels. They come in a wide range of colors, ranging from white to yellow, red and blue in which the reddish tones predominate. The leaves can also vary enormously, from linear to round in a wide range of shapes and sizes. But they are all alternate, undivided with smooth edges. Rhododendrons need partial shade, sheltered from the wind and acidic, moist soil. Many species will tolerate sun, but the soil must never be allowed to dry out. Because they are shallow-rooted, rhododendrons should only be planted under deep-rooting trees so that they do not compete for water and nutrients. Pruning is not necessary. Propagation is by cuttings, layering and grafting.

ⓘ

Family: Ericaceae
Flowering season: spring/summer
Height and spread: according to species and variety: 16 × 16 ft
Situation: ◐
Moisture requirement: ◌– ◗
❄ ❄ ❄

Rhododendron auriculatum

Rhododendron auriculatum

Family: Ericaceae
Flowering season: summer
Height and spread: 10 × 10 ft
Situation: ◐
Moisture requirement: ◌– ◖
❋ ❋ ❋
✿

This species, native to China, grows to 20 ft in its country of origin. However, in gardens in the western world this species usually only forms a low shrub with an erect, bushy habit with large, oblong leaves. The delightful, fragrant, white tubular to funnel-shaped flowers are borne in large clusters from late July or August onward. It grows well in partial shade in moist, acid soil. Although this species is hardy, extreme frost can damage the leaves and branches. This is why it should be planted in a sheltered position.

Forrest rhododendron

Rhododendron forrestii var. repens

Rhododendron repens

Family: Ericaceae
Flowering season: spring
Height: 6 in;
Hybrids: 3 × 5 ft
Situation: ◐
Moisture requirement: ◌, acid soil
❋ ❋ ❋

This shrub, originally known as *R. repens*, is native to China, southeast Tibet and Burma. It is a low shrub with a creeping habit and with its height of 6 in, and is one of the smallest rhododendrons. Its small, round, evergreen, glossy, dark green leaves are often purple-red or blue-green underneath. The crimson, bell-shaped flowers, which are borne singly, are not always reliable in the species. This is why breeders are constantly searching to improve the flowering potential of the shrubs – with great success because the *R. repens* hybrids flower abundantly in a wide range of reds. In addition, these hybrid shrubs grow higher, reaching almost 3 ft. Because the flowers appear early in the year, they are often at risk from late frost and should therefore be planted in a sheltered position. These rhododendrons grow well in partial shade in moist, acid soil where they form a thick carpet.

Rhododendron occidentale

Rhododendron occidentale

This azalea is native to the western United States where it grows as undergrowth in coniferous forests. It is an deciduous shrub with a round, erect habit which can reach a height of 23 ft in its country of origin. The ovate to elliptic, shiny green leaves turn yellow, orange or crimson in autumn. However, this shrub is particularly beautiful in late spring when the large clusters of fragrant white or pink flowers appear. One of the distinctive features of this species is the yellow blotch at the base of the wide, funnel-shaped flowers – a characteristic which together with intense fragrance is common to all *R. occidentale* hybrids. These azaleas grow best in moist, acid soil and partial shade.

ⓘ

Family: Ericaceae
Flowering season: spring/summer
Height and spread: 8 × 8 ft
Situation: ◐
Moisture requirement: ◌*, acid soil*
❀ ❀ ❀
❁

Indian azaleas

Rhododendron simsii

In spite of their name, these azaleas are native to China and Taiwan. *R. simsii* hybrids are usually sold in pots because, unlike all other rhododendrons, they are not hardy. This bushy, evergreen species has narrow, oblong, dark green leaves, covered with bristly hairs. The large, funnel-shaped flowers are pink or dark red appear in late spring. At the same time, the hybrids produce large, funnel-shaped flowers which may be single, semi-double or double and come in a wide range of colors, from white to pink and violet-blue; and there are also forms whose flowers are mottled or flecked with another color. These azaleas in pots need moist soil and a light position, but not in direct sunlight. It is important that they should be watered with soft water and placed in a cool room during winter.

Rhododendron simsii

ⓘ

Family: Ericaceae
Flowering season: spring,
hybrids: autum - spring
Height and spread: 20 × 20 in
Situation: ◐
Moisture requirement: ◌ – ◑
❀

351

Weeping willow

Salix babylonica

ℹ

Family: Salicaceae
Flowering season: spring
Height and spread: 33 × 20 ft
Situation: ○
Moisture requirement: ◊ – ◖
❁ ❁ ❁

This deciduous tree, which is native to China, is smaller than most species in the genus, only growing to a height of 33 ft. It is, therefore, suitable for small gardens. However, with its larger arching branches and slender drooping branches it forms quite a spreading tree. The narrow, lanceolate, dark green leaves are gray-green underneath and have a finely serrated edge. The catkins appear in spring at the same time as the leaves. In male plants, the catkins are an attractive yellow while in female plants they are green. The weeping willow is easy to grow, but it needs a sunny position and moist soil but not waterlogged. Pruning after flowering will encourage the growth of long twigs with many catkins. Weeping willows are propagated by hardwood cuttings.

Salix hastata

Salix hastata

ℹ

Family: Salicaceae
Flowering season: spring
Height and spread: 5 × 5 ft
Situation: ○
Moisture requirement: ◊ – ◖
❁ ❁ ❁

This low, deciduous shrubs can be found in northern Europe, the mountainous regions of southern and Central Europe and also in northeast Europe. Usually, nurseries offer the male variety 'Wehrhahnii.' This shrub has an erect habit with densely hairy shoots and oblong, dark green leaves with gray-green undersides. It looks most attractive in spring when, just before or at the same time as the leaves come out, the catkins appear, at first silvery and later yellow. Like its relative, the weeping willow, this shrub needs moist soil and a sunny position. Young plants do not require pruning, but it does produce larger catkins. Older plants benefit from a rejuvenating pruning. Propagation is by hardwood cuttings.

S*kimmia japonica*

Skimmia japonica

This plant grows wild in the mountain forests of Japan and Taiwan. The evergreen, compact shrub is densely branched with ovate to elliptic leaves which are pale to yellow-green in the species but are dark green and similar to laurel leaves in the more common 'Rubella' variety. Skimmias look very decorative all year round, whether in spring when the small, very fragrant, yellowish-white flowers are borne in long, terminal panicles, or in autumn when the female plants are covered with bright red, fleshy, berry-like stone fruits which remain on the shrub all through the winter. The Japanese skimmia is dioecious so that you must plant male and female plants together to in order to ensure cross-pollination and the production of fruit. It grows best in partial shade in slightly acidic soil, rich in humus. In regions where the winters are very cold, the shrub must be protected against frost and winter sun. Pruning is not usually necessary but damaged wood can be removed. The plants are propagated by cuttings.

ℹ

Family: Rutaceae
Flowering season: spring
Height and spread: 5 × 5 ft
Situation: ◑
Moisture requirement: ◌ – ◗
❄ ❄ ❄
✿

Spiraea canecens

Spiraea canecens

Family: Rosaceae
Flowering season: spring/summer
Height and spread: 8 × 7 ft
Situation: ○
Moisture requirement: ◊
❀ ❀ ❀

This species which is native to the Himalayas is a popular flowering shrub in gardens in the western world. Its branches become increasingly arching with age while young plants have a rather erect habit. Its slender branches are covered with deciduous oval, matte-green leaves which are gray underneath. The shrub is a real eye-catcher in spring with its profusion of creamy-white flowers, borne in umbels on old wood. The dead flower heads must be removed just above the old wood. If the shrub needs to be thinned out, this should be done after flowering. This robust shrub grows best in a sunny position in fertile soil. The plants are propagated in summer by cuttings.

354

Spiraea japonica 'Little Princess'

*S*piraea japonica

Spiraea japonica

This species is native to Japan, but also grows wild in China. In contrast to *S. canecens*, the branches of this deciduous shrub do not become arching with age but grow upright and are covered with bright green leaves. However, there are also varieties with leaves whose color ranges from dark green to yellow. This species is a summer-flowering shrub with pink flowers borne in large, flat umbels. The low compact variety, 'Little Princess,' flowers prolifically and has beautiful red foliage in autumn. Late-flowering shrubs need pruning in early spring. They grow best in well-drained, not too dry soil. They are propagated by cuttings in summer.

ⓘ

Family: Rosaceae
Flowering season: summer
Height and spread: 3 × 3 ft
Situation: ○
Moisture requirement: ◌
❄ ❄ ❄

355

*L*ilac

Syringa meyeri

ⓘ

Family: Oleaceae
Flowering season: spring
Height and spread: 5 × 5 ft
Situation: ○
Moisture requirement: ◊
❀ ❀ ❀
❀

This species which is native to northern China forms a small, compact, round shrub. Its numerous branches are covered with ovate to elliptic, deciduous mid-green leaves with hairy undersides. The small violet flowers which appear in late spring are borne in hairy panicles 4 in long, which exude a delicate fragrance. *S. palibiniana* is a very popular species because of its compact growth and purple-red flower buds which open into pale violet flowers, borne in round panicles. This species needs a rich, moisture retentive soil. Young plants must be pruned, but older plants need not be. Wild suckers growing at the base of a grafted varieties must be removed. Species can be raised from seed and offshoots or runners while varieties are propagated by heel cuttings of half-ripe shoots and grafting.

Syringa vulgaris

ⓘ

Family: Oleaceae
Flowering season: spring
Height and spread: to 20 × 20 ft
Situation: ○
Moisture requirement: ◊
❀ ❀ ❀
❀

*C*ommon lilac

Syringa vulgaris

The common lilac is native to southeastern Europe but has also has become naturalised in Central Europe. This erect, deciduous shrub or small tree can reach up to 23 ft in height, but most known lilac varieties do not reach this height. The erect pyramidal panicles 8 in long appear in May and June, surrounded by almost heart-shaped, bright green flowers. The species has lilac-colored flowers, but there are many varieties on the market with double and single flowers in a wide range of colors, ranging from white to creamy-yellow and mauve-pink to purple-red. Many of them are two-tone, such as 'Michel Buchner' with white and violet-pink flowers. All varieties have a wonderful fragrance. Lilacs need fertile soil and a sunny position. The species will also tolerate partial shade but will flower less abundantly. Lilacs spread spontaneously through vigorous-growing suckers but in grafted specimens wild suckers must be removed. The species is raised from seed and varieties are propagated by cuttings and grafting.

Common yew

Taxus baccata

ⓘ

Family: Taxaceae
Flowering season: spring
Height/spread: 3–33 × 10–26 ft
Situation: ◑
Moisture requirement: ◌
❋ ❋ ❋
✖

The yew genus is native to Europe, Asia and North Africa and forms a tall, evergreen tree with several trunks growing from the base. Young plants are conical in shape, but become oval with age. The branches are covered with glossy, dark green, linear needles. Several varieties are available on the market which differ from the species both in habit and in the color of the needles: for example, 'Fastigiata' (Irish yew), a columnar-shaped yew which grows 10–16 ft high, and 'Dovastonii' (Westfelton yew) with a short central trunk, long, upward growing branches and hanging branchlets. Both varieties also have a golden form. In contrast, the dwarf variety 'Repandens' is only 20 in high, but its branches can create a spread of 13 ft. The plant is dioecious. The small female flowers are green and inconspicuous while the male flowers are yellow. The female flowers are followed by bright red fruits. One of the yew's advantages is that it does not mind pruning which makes it an ideal hedging plant as well being ideally suited for topiary. It grows well in rich soil in a sunny position, partial shade and deep shade. Propagation is by cuttings. But be careful: all parts are poisonous.

Taxus baccata

White cedar

Thuja occidentalis

Like *T. plicata*, this species is native to North America which differentiates them from the other thuja species which are all native to Asia. The white cedar is an evergreen tree which can grow up to 66 ft high. It produces several trunks from the base, forming a narrow, conical tree with erect branches. Its flattened branchlets or sprays are densely covered with aromatic, needle-like, scale leaves are dark green on top and bright green underneath. In autumn, the plant develops long greenish cones which later become brown. There are several garden forms of this species which are divided into tall-growing and dwarf varieties: the columnar-shaped 'Columna' with glossy, dark green scale leaves, and the compact conical 'Smaragd' which has bright green foliage all year round. 'Globosa,' 'Danica' and 'Golden Globe' are spherical dwarf forms which only reach 3 ft in height. This vigorous plant grows well in sunny position in moist, but not swampy, soil. Because it does not mind pruning, it is an ideal hedging plant. Thuja is propagated by cuttings. Be careful: all parts of the plant are poisonous.

ⓘ

Family: Cupressaceae
Height/spread: 3–66 × 3–16 ft
Situation: ○
Moisture requirement: ◐ – ◉
❄ ❄ ❄
✖

Thuja orientalis

Thuja orientalis

The eastern relative of *T. orientalis* which originates from China and Korea can reach 50 ft in height – a little shorter than *T. orientalis* – with several trunks. It too is cone-shaped with erect branches and flattened branchlets or sprays covered with needle-like, scale leaves. The foliage is not as aromatic and the cones are blue-green with a hoary bloom before turning brown. The varieties available on the market differ mainly in their habit: 'Aurea Nana' forms a round shrub, about 24 in high and wide, while 'Elegantissima' grows into a broad 16 ft high columnar tree. The yellow-green varieties are slightly hardier than the species. They too can be pruned strongly if required. They grow best in moist, well-drained, deep soil in a sheltered position in full sun. Like all thujas, every part of the plant is very poisonous. It is propagated by cuttings.

ⓘ

Family: Cupressaceae
Height/spread: 3–50 × 3–50 ft
Situation: ○
Moisture requirement: ◐ – ◉
❄ ❄
✖

Vibernum × carlcephalum

Vibernum × carlcephalum

opposite: Viburnum × carlcephalum

The evergreen hybrid is a cross between the Korean *V. carlesii* and *V. macrocephalum*. The round, bushy shrub with ovate leaves, dark green on top and gray-green underneath is very slow growing. In autumn, the leaves turn red before falling. The shrub looks particularly beautiful in full bloom: the pink flower buds develop into large, globular white flower heads which exude a delicious vanilla-like fragrance. This shrub, which is easy to grow in full sun, will also grow in partial shade. Regular thinning of old and damaged wood is advisable. It is propagated by cuttings. This hybrid is poisonous as are many of the viburnum species.

ⓘ

Family: Caprifoliaceae
Flowering season: spring
Height and spread: 12 × 12 ft
Situation: ○
Moisture requirement: ◌– ◑
✻ ✻ ✻
❀
✖

Wayfaring Tree

Viburnum lantana

This species which is native to Europe, Asia Minor and North Africa forms a medium-sized, deciduous shrub of erect habit when young which becomes spreading with age. The oval, matt-green leaves are densely covered with gray-brown hairs underneath as are the branches – a feature which has given the species its name. The equally hairy, dense umbels of white flowers appear in late spring which are not particularly fragrant. They are followed by red, shiny, poisonous fruits which later turn black. Unlike other viburnums, this species needs a warm, sheltered position and it will also grow in dry soil. This shrub should also be thinned regularly to promote abundant flowering. It is propagated by cuttings.

Viburnum lantana

ⓘ

Family: Caprifoliaceae
Flowering season: spring / summer
Height / spread: 8–13 × 8–13 ft
Situation: ○
Moisture requirement: ◌
✻ ✻ ✻
❀
✖

Climbers

The cultivation of climbers, or plants which grow up trees, walls and other supports by means of twining leaf stalks, leaf tendrils or aerial roots, has a long tradition. In antiquity, vines were trained in such a way as to provide protection from the sun as well as to produce delicious fruit. In some countries, climbers almost disappeared from the townscape in the 1920s and 1930s because they did not fit in with the functional approach to architecture and were considered old-fashioned and unattractive. Today, they are more popular, both for their creative and aesthetic effect and for their architectural and ecological applications. Particularly in urban environments where green spaces are rare, climbers succeed in providing this green effect without requiring much horizontal space. They can be used as screen and sound insulation, to cover facades with greenery, to provide shade and as protection from the weather. The group of climbing plants is very large. It includes hardy or tender species of annuals, herbaceous perennials and woody plants, which may be evergreen or deciduous. They are usually divided according to the way they attach themselves: self-climbers such as ivy and Virginia creeper attach themselves by adhesive pads and do not require a trellis or similar support. Other climbers like clematis and sweet peas use their twining leaf stalks and leaf tendrils to attach themselves to the support provided. Winding climbers such as hop and honeysuckle wind themselves upwards around the support. Climbing roses and brambles attach themselves by hooking their thorns to trees, shrubs or other supports.

Actinidia kolomikta

Actinidia kolomikta

ⓘ

Family: Actinidiaceae
Flowering season: summer
Height/Spread: 16 ft × 15 ft
Situation: ○
Moisture requirement: ◗
❋ ❋ ❋

This hardy climber comes from the forests of eastern Asia and was introduced to Europe at the end of the 19th century. It thrives in a sunny or partially shaded, sheltered position against walls and on trellises. In the garden, it is grown particularly for its decorative leaf coloring. The oblong-ovate alternate dark green leaves are up to 6 in long. They are flushed with pink in young plants, and in older specimens the upper part is patterned with pink and white. The flowers develop in June, consisting of bunches each of three fragrant white flowers 3/4 in wide. Male and female flowers appear on separate plants, so both are needed for pollination. The oblong-ovate fruits are about 1 in long, yellow-green, tender and edible, maturing on female plants in September until October. Propagation is by cuttings in late summer, thriving best in full sun in fertile, well-drained soil.

Actinidia kolomikta

Bougainvillea

Bougainvillea

The genus of 14 evergreen bush or tree species and climbers is a native of the tropical and subtropical latitudes of South America. Bougainvillea is a spiny spreading climber that can completely cover a whole house with its floral splendor in regions with a Mediterranean climate. In cooler climates, the temperature-sensitive plant requires a protected, frost-proof area on a bright, sunny wall and pots or tubs should be over-wintered indoors. Bougainvilleas have insignificant small tubular flowers encircled by three petal-like bracts and increase in axillary or terminal clusters. They bloom throughout the summer with violet, red, pink or yellow bracts according to species. The alternate leaves are mostly smooth-edged and ovate. Among the most popular varieties are the pink 'Apple Blossom,' the orange-yellow 'Orange King' and the purple-violet 'Alexandra.' The plant is propagated by soft cuttings in the spring or half-ripe cuttings in the summer. For strong growth, it should be fed and watered weekly in summer, but do not allow it to become waterlogged.

ℹ

Family: Nyctaginaceae
Flowering season: summer/autumn
Height: 3 1/2–40 ft
Situation: ○
Moisture requirement: ◗
❄

Bougainvillea

Clematis

Clematis

Clematis is a genus of over 200 evergreen and deciduous species, mostly climbing shrubs. They are among the most popular climbers because of their magnificent blooms and long flowering period. The wild forms can be found in both northern and southern hemispheres, including Europe, the Himalayas, China, Australia and North and South America. The individual species and the 400 or more varieties are all very different in habit and foliage. For instance, low-growing shrubs and climbers which can reach a height of 30-50 ft, making them perfect for growing over porches, trellises, pergolas and unsightly walls. The climbing species cling to trees and other supports by twining leaf stalks. The leaves are pale to dark green, hairy or smooth, whole or compound, or digitate or biternate with smooth or serrated edges. The shape, size and color of the flowers also varies enormously. They may stand singly or be grouped in cymes or panicles; they can have from four to ten petals (or correctly, sepals) and they may be single or double, saucer, star, tulip, bell or funnel-shaped. Just three contrasting examples of the range are the species *Clematis montana*, a vigorous climber with numerous small white flowers in late spring, the early flowering hybrid 'Jackmanii,' one of the early large-flowered climbers covered with single, velvety, deep-purple blooms which later turn violet; and the *C. viticella* varieties which offer many medium-sized flowers in a range of colors from late summer to early autumn.

Clematis alpina

Clematis alpina

ⓘ

Family: Ranunculaceae
Flowering season: spring/early summer
Height/Spread: 7–10 ft × 5 ft
Situation: ○ – ◐
Moisture requirement: ◌
❄ ❄ ❄
Diseases: clematis wilt

The *Clematis* genus has more than 200 evergreen and deciduous species with many varieties and hybrids in both northern and southern hemispheres. *C. alpina* is native to the Alps and Siberia. It is completely frost-hardy and can even be planted in an exposed north-facing position. It reaches a height of 6 1/2–10 ft and is particularly happy scrambling over or through other low woody plants and shrubs. The flowers appear separately in the leaf axils of the previous year's growth. They are bell-shaped when closed and open into nodding, lantern-like blooms. Apart from the blue color and white centers characteristic of the species, varieties include 'Constance' with semi-double, deeply purple-pink flowers, 'Frances Rivis', medium-blue, and 'Pink Flamingo' with semi-double pale-pink flowers. It is propagated by cuttings or sowing in the open ground. Like all clematis, *C. Alpina* requires a shaded root run while the upper part of the plant is in the sun. Feed the plant in late winter with garden compost or well composted manure, keeping it out of contact with the stem.

Clematis 'Jackmanii'

Clematis montana

Clematis montana

ⓘ

Family: Ranunculaceae
Flowering season: spring, early summer
Height/Spread: 46 ft × 10 ft
Situation: ○, ◐, ●
Moisture requirement: ◌
❄ ❄ ❄
❀
Diseases: clematis wilt

C. montana is native to the Himalayas as well as western and central China and was introduced to Europe in 1831. With a height of up to 46 ft, it is a very strong, extremely vigorous climber which can clamber over whole buildings and trees. The numerous white flowers are small, 2 in across, filled with yellow stamens. They appear separately or as short cymes in the leaf axils of the previous year's growth. There are many varieties, some with flowers tending towards pink, such as 'Tetrarose,' 'Pink Perfection' and *C. m. rubens*. In summer, fleecy seed heads develop from the flowers, which are usually scented. The leaves are usually slightly pinnate and slightly serrated. Propagation is by seeds or cuttings. Pruning the plant is not necessary since it blooms on the previous year's growth. But pruning may have to be undertaken to keep the plant within bounds, in which case it should be done immediately after flowering. *C. montana* should be planted with the top of the root ball about 3 in below the surface of the soil in order to reduce the danger of clematis wilt and to encourage the formation of new basal growth.

Clematis 'Fuji Musume'

Clematis viticella

Clematis viticella

C. viticella is a floriferous, rather elegant species from southern Central Europe and is an old garden plant which was already being cultivated in the 16th century. Alongside as the large-flowering hybrids of C. viticella, there is a great number of varieties with a wild character (among others, 'Albiflora', 'Purpurea Plena Elegans' and Rubra). The wild species has pinnate leaves with 5-7 leaflets. The open bell-shaped flowers 1 1/2 in wide appear separately in the leaf axils from mid-summer until early autumn. According to variety, the flower colors range from purple-pink to violet. Seed heads develop from the flower. Propagation is by seeds and cuttings. C. viticella requires very heavy pruning in early spring, cutting back the previous year's growth to a pair of shoots about 8 in above the soil.

ⓘ

Family: Ranunculaceae
Flowering season: summer/early autumn
Height: 7–13 ft
Spread: 5 ft
Situation: ○, ◑, ●
Moisture requirement: ◐
❄ ❄ ❄
Diseases: clematis wilt

369

Russian vine, Mile-a-minute

Fallopia baldschuanica

ⓘ

Family: Polygonaceae
Flowering season: late summer/autumn
Height: 40 ft
Situation: ○ – ◑
Moisture requirement: ◐
✿ ✿ ✿

Russian vine or *Fallopia baldschuanica* (syn. *Polygonum baldschuanicum*) is native to southeast Russia and spread all over Europe in the 19th century. Today, it is one of the most popular climbers because of its ability to conceal ugly buildings, but it is so rampant that it should only be planted after serious consideration. The unpretentious, perennial plant thrives in all aspects and covers walls, walls, pergolas and tall trees by twining all over them. Because of its strong growth, Russian vine is hard to control. It needs a strong support since its weight increases very quickly. It can be a problem on houses where it can lift bricks and grow into lofts. Between July and October, the plant develops wide, almost hairless panicles with small tubular flowers which are white at first, then slightly pink. In the autumn small, triangular, pale pink fruits appear. The dark green leaves are heart-shaped and up to 4 in long. Propagation is by seed in spring, by cuttings in summer and hardwood cuttings in the winter. The plant likes moist, alkaline soil and should be trimmed annually in the early spring to prevent the growth at the foot becoming too thick.

Fallopia baldschuanica

370

Glory lily

Gloriosa superba

The glory lily is one of many varieties of tuber-forming climber originating in forests in tropical Africa and India. In the garden, it is grown particularly for its striking flowers and its ability to climb up other plants upwards. After flowering, the tubers should be dried at a temperature of 59–68°F and overwintered. They are planted in the early spring about 3–4 in deep in pots or in a warm, protected situation in the garden with a suitable climbing support. About eight weeks later, the flowers, measuring 2–4 in across with six or so petals (according to variety), appear in the leaf axes. The, unevenly marginated petals are red or purple, frequently yellow bordered. The lanceolate leaves are glossy and bright green. They end in a tendril which winds firmly round the climbing support. The fruit appears as a tripartite capsule with red seeds. The glory lily is highly toxic and handling the tubers can cause skin irritations. Propagation is in spring by sowing the seeds at a temperature of 66–75°F, or by division of the finger-shaped tubers.

ⓘ

Family: Colchicaceae
Flowering season: summer/autumn
Height: up to 7 ft
Spread: 12 in
Situation: ○
Moisture requirement: ◑
❄
✖

371

Common ivy
Hedera helix

Family: *Araliaceae*
Flowering season: *autumn*
Height: *33 ft*
Situation: ○, ◑, ●
Moisture requirement: ◊
❋ ❋ ❋
✖

This species of ivy native to Europe has a very wide area of circulation and is frequently grown. The evergreen climber adheres to masonry and other climbing supports. The creeping perennial develops adhesive roots. The common ivy occurs in various sub-species and many cultivars. It has three to five-lobed, broadly oval to triangular leaves which are 3/4–3 1/2 in long according to variety. Some varieties such as 'Atropurpurea' become reddish colored in winter. The variegated light and dark gray-green leaves of the variety 'Adam' are flushed with yellow when fully grown. 'Goldheart,' with a yellow central marking contrasting with the dark green edges of the leaf has the most striking coloring. Older plants have the unlobed form of the leaves and in light conditions, small, green flowers appear on a massive scale in the autumn, attracting insects. These produce numerous globed black fruits which are eaten with pleasure by birds. All ivy varieties can cause serious illness if eaten. Contact with the sap of the plant can cause strong irritation. Propagation is very easy by cuttings or rooted runners.

Hedera helix

Irish ivy

Hedera hibernica

Irish ivy *H. hibernica* is a native of the Atlantic coast climate of Western Europe and is therefore less hardy than common ivy. Nevertheless, it is outstanding for covering walls and as a quick-spreading ground cover. The climber has dark green, oval to triangular five-lobed leaves, 2–3 in long. Like the common ivy, Irish ivy only flowers when mature, bearing green and rather inconspicuous umbels in the autumn which develop into small, black globular fruits. The plant flourishes in well-drained fertile soil. It is propagated by planting a runner in soil in a pot, where it will form new roots at the nodes. As a shade-tolerant ground cover plant, Irish ivy is especially suitable as a lawn replacement.

Family: Araliaceae
Flowering season: autumn
Height: 33 ft
Situation: ○, ◑, ●
Moisture requirement: ◍
✾ ✾ ✾
✖

Japanese hop

Humulus japonicus

The annual Japanese hop comes from Japan and China, and is related to the common hop used in brewing beer (*H. lupulus*). The flowers, borne in midsummer, are unspectacular compared to the fragrant female flowers of the Common hop. The most striking decorative features are the hand-shaped leaves, up to 8 in large and covered with rough hairs. This climber's vigorous growth and its dense mass of leaves make it extremely suitable for covering pergolas, arbours, or ironwork balconies, where it will soon form a natural sight-screen. The hop is dioecious: that is to say, male and female flowers are borne separately on different plants. Sow in spring under cover, and do not plant out until all danger of frost is gone. As the plants will spread rapidly, they should not be placed too close together. The Japanese hop likes moist but not water-logged soils. Besides the green species which will also grow in shade, there is a variegated variety, 'Variegatus,' which is particularly suitable for sunny positions.

Family: Cannabaceae
Flowering season: summer
Height: up to 20 ft
Situation: ○ – ●
Moisture requirement: ◍
✾

Climbers

Climbers

Climbing plants will quickly and easily provide privacy from prying eyes, or create a shady, secluded spot in the garden. They grow rapidly, sometimes reaching a considerable height, and with the aid of simple trellises, strings or canes, they will soon cover walls, fences, balconies or pergolas. If they are grown, in tubs and containers, they can also be moved. Climbing plants are natives of the tropics, where they usually grow as perennials. In moderate climates, however, they are generally cultivated as annuals because of their sensitivity to frost. Their extremely beautiful flowers attract the eye and, depending on the species, may be large and funnel-shaped, as in *Ipomoea tricolor* and *I. indica*, or tubular, with an exotic appearance, as in *I. lobata*. The flowers form an effective contrast with the robust green leaves, which may be heart-shaped or finely divided and are always quick to create a dense curtain of foliage. Given a warm situation well protected from the wind, climbers are very undemanding plants. In very windy places, however, even young plants should be loosely tied in to their supports. During the growing season they will need plenty of water and nutrients. Either feed them with liquid manure once a week, or add slow-release fertiliser to the substrate when you are planting them. If the lower leaves turn yellow, feed with fertiliser at once. You can give the plant a good start by adding well matured garden compost to the soil. Sow in spring at a temperature of 64–68°F, but do not plant the seedlings out until all danger of frost is gone. Shrubs or semi-shrubs overwintered in a warm greenhouse can also have softwood cuttings taken from them in spring.

Ipomoea hederacea

Ipomoea hederacea

ⓘ

Family: Convolvulaceae
Flowering season: summer
Height: 6 1/2–10 ft
Situation: ○
Moisture requirement: ◐
✳
✖

This climber is a native of tropical Central America and it is only grown in temperate areas as an annual summer plant because it cannot survive frost. In the garden it is used to cover fences, trellises and pergolas; it can also be grown in pots or tubs. It is a gorgeous climbing plant with slim, densely hairy stems bearing heart-shaped, mostly three-lobed medium to dark green leaves tapering off to a point at the ends, 2–5 in long. In the summer, cymes develop with two to five blue or sometimes purple trumpet-shaped flowers 3/4–1 1/2 in wide, with a white throat and long green sepals. The seeds are extremely toxic if eaten. Propagation is by seed under glass or by sowing in the open in a sunny, protected location in spring. Before, the seeds should be notched, or soaked for 24 hours. Like most morning glory plants, it requires a well-manured, humus-rich well-drained soil and full sun.

Ipomoea hederacea

Morning glory

Ipomoea tricolor

This convolvulus from tropical Central and South America was brought from Mexico to Great Britain by the British officer Samuel Richardson in 1834 and has been widely used to cover fences, trellises and walls in gardens all over Europe ever since. Usually grown as an annual, it is rapidly growing but very wind-sensitive climbing plant. It is extremely prolific. Its light to medium green leaves are smooth-edged with a heart-shaped base and thin tip. I. tricolor is one of the commonest summer climbers in cultivation. There are many varieties distinguished particularly by the color of the trumpet-shaped flowers, up to 3 in wide, which appear in summer singly or in group of three to five. The variety 'Heavenly Blue' has azure flowers with a white throat, while 'Flying Saucers' is marbled white and purple-blue and 'Crimson Rambler' is red with white throat. The plant flowers early in the morning and wilts in the late afternoon, but on gray days the flowers will not open until evening. The seeds are toxic. Propagation is by sowing in the spring, and also by cuttings.

Family: Convolvulaceae
Flowering season: summer
Height: 10–13 ft
Situation: ○
Moisture requirement: ◗

Ipomoea indica

Ipomoea indica

I. indica is a spectacular tropical species grown domestically in warmer climates as a perennial climber. In the garden, it requires fertile, well drained soil, full sun and protection from cold, drying winds. The growth should be supported by a climbing support. The evergreen leaves 2 1/2–7 in long are heart-shaped or triangular with thinly pointed extremities. The plant blooms from late spring until autumn in purple-blue to blue colors. The trumpet-shaped flowers are 2 1/2–3 in wide and appear in bunches of three to five. The color later changes to purple. The seeds are poisonous if eaten. The plant is propagated by seeds in the spring or cuttings in the summer. It is vulnerable to viruses and mildew. When grown under glass, it may be subject to the pests white fly and red spider mite.

Family: Convolvulaceae
Flowering season: summer/autumn
Height: 20 ft
Situation: ○
Moisture requirement: ◗

Diseases: various viruses, mildew
Pests: white fly, red spider mite

Primrose jasmine

Jasminum mesnyi

ℹ

Family: Oleaceae
Flowering season: Spring/summer
Height: 10 ft
Spread: 3–7 ft
Situation: ○, ◑
Moisture requirement: ◐
❄
❀
Pests: aphids, mealy bugs

The evergreen primrose jasmine, native to the southwest regions of China, reaches a height of up to 10 ft as a light, slender-stemmed bush. It is a scrambling climber which can be supported on pergolas, fences, trellises or large bushes. Its pinnate, dark green, glossy leaves are divided into three oval leaflets. The primrose jasmine is a scented plant with a delightful fragrance during the spring and summer flowering season. Then semi-double, pale yellow flowers appear in several flower heads. The fruit are black clusters. Propagation is in the summer by cuttings of semi-ripe growth. The primrose jasmine requires a fertile, well-drained soil and full sun or light shade in the open. The plant should be pruned annually after flowering in order to encourage the young growth. Aphids and mealy bugs are the main pests which can damage the plant.

Pea family

Lathyrus

The pea family *Lathyrus* has about 150 different annual and perennial species including evergreen shrubs, also evergreen herbs. They originate from the northern temperate regions as well as from northern and eastern Africa and South America. They are cultivated as a garden plant for their attractive white, blue, red and pink flowers, frequently strongly scented. Some of the climbing sweet peas are suitable for covering fences, trellises and walls, and they can scramble over slopes and through bushes. They also provide a constant source of flowers for cutting. *L. odoratus* is one of the climbing species and is itself divided into numerous varieties. The fruit and seeds are inedible. According to species, propagation is by sowing, cuttings or division. The seeds should be soaked or cracked before. Plants of the pea family require fertile, well-drained humus-rich soil and thrive best in sunny or lightly shaded locations. Regular cutting and application of manure will prolong flowering. Aphids, slugs, snails and thrips are the main pests.

Family: Fabaceae
Flowering season: summer/autumn
Height: up to 10 ft
Situation: ○, ◑
Moisture requirement: ◊
❁ ❁ ❁
Pests: aphids, slugs and snails, thrips

379

Everlasting pea

Lathyrus grandiflorus

ℹ️

Family: Fabaceae
Flowering season: summer
Height: 5 ft
Situation: ○, ◑
Moisture requirement: 💧
❋ ❋ ❋

This herbaceous perennial climbing species family is native to Italy, Bulgaria and parts of Slovenia and Albania. The plant expands with shoots and reaches a height of about 5 ft. Its growth needs a climbing support. It has unwinged shoots and medium-green elliptical leaves, usually in pairs, with leaflets up to 2 in long. In the summer, clusters of 1–2, or sometimes up to 4 flowers develop in the leaf axils; they are pink-purple or tending to red and about 1 in wide. For strong, growth *L. grandiflorus* needs a fertile, not too dry soil in as sunny a situation as possible. Flowers should be regularly removed when over.

Perennial pea

Lathyrus latifolius

Lathyrus odoratus

ℹ️

Family: Fabaceae
Flowering season: summer, autumn
Height: 7 ft
Situation: ○, ◑
Moisture requirement: 💧
❋ ❋ ❋

This perennial climber native to southern Europe is a popular garden plant. It growth each year, up to 7 ft high, which needs supported. It has winged stems and pairs of blue-green, oblong-elliptical leaves, with leaflets 3–4 1/2 in long and two broad stipules. The plant has panicles of small flowers from summer until early autumn. The variety 'Blushing Bride' is very abundant with pinkish white flowers, 'White Pearl' has pure white flowers, and 'Rose Queen' has deep pink flowers. To minimise seed production and to encourage further flowering, the wilted flowers should be regularly removed. The perennial should be pruned after flowering. Propagation is by sown seed in autumn in a mild position in the open, or in colder climates in a cool greenhouse in pots. The species breeds true from seed. The perennial pea thrives best in fertile, well-drained soil in full sun or partial light shade.

Lonicera × heckrottii

Lonicera × heckrottii

The honeysuckle *L. x heckrottii* is a climbing, bushy shrub which is probably a hybrid of *L. americana* and *L. sempervirens* honeysuckle. It is particularly suitable for growing in the garden through netting or thin trellis. The plant has pairs of dark green oval or elliptical leaves, 1–2 1/2 in long, with blue-green undersides. In the summer, it has tubular two-lipped flowers, about 1 1/2 in long, pink to violet-red with a yellow-white interior. They are strongly scented and particularly attractive to bees. In the autumn, strongly toxic red berries are sometimes produced. *L. x heckrottii* has a variety 'Gold Flame' with deeper-colored, more orange flowers. Propagation is by cutting. This plant is one of the longest-lived and least demanding climbers. It thrives in fertile, moist but well-drained soil and is best in full sun. In partial shade, the plant is somewhat vulnerable to aphids.

ℹ

Family: Caprifoliaceae
Flowering season: summer
Height: 16 1/2 ft
Spread: 23 ft
Situation: ○, ◐
Moisture requirement: ◊
❄ ❄ ❄
✿
✖
Pests: aphids

381

Parthenocissus tricuspidata

ⓘ

Family: Vitaceae
Flowering season: summer
Height: 66 ft
Situation: ○, ◑, ●
Moisture requirement: ◔
❅ ❅ ❅

Boston ivy, Japanese ivy

Parthenocissus tricuspidata

This climber was introduced to Europe from its native eastern Asia to Europe in 1862. It supports itself with sucker-like pads. In the garden, it is presents a particularly striking picture with its long-stemmed, broad leaves, which turn to spectacular shades of orange and scarlet in the autumn. The plant is grown up large trees or against walls and fences. The mature Boston ivy has three-lobed leaves up to 10 in long; in young plants they are undivided. The upper side of the leaf is a striking glossy green and the underside is bronze in color. The variety 'Beverley Brook' has smaller leaves flushed purple in summer, the foliage turning bright red in autumn; 'Veitchii' has a dark crimson-purple autumn color; and 'Lowii' has small deeply cut leaves with 3–7 lobes. In the summer inconspicuous, greenish-yellow flowers appear which mature to round black fruits of up to 1/3 in. The fruit causes illness if eaten. Propagate in the autumn with seed sown in pots or by soft cuttings in early summer and by hard cuttings in winter. In very cold winters, the plant is sometimes cut back, but it always grows up again from the base in spring. Boston ivy is robust and makes few demands, thriving in any fertile garden soil that is not too dry.

Parthenocissus tricuspida

Passion flower

Passiflora

Passiflora is a genus of more than 400 species mainly native to the warmer regions of North, Central and South America, but also to the Asia, Australia, New Zealand and the Pacific Islands. Mostly they are woody climbers which cling with axillary tendrils. Half-hardy species as *P. caerulea* are excellent for growing on trellises and walls, while tender species should be kept in the greenhouse. The usually palmate leaves of the passion flower are round to oval and elliptical, and are normally pinnate. The exotic flowers appear individually or in clusters in the upper leaf axils in summer. Each has a wide base and ten, or sometimes five, petals. A stalk in the centre carries the ovary and stamens and is surrounded by a corona of fleshy threads. In hot summers, the flowers are succeeded by oval or round, usually yellow fruits. These are edible and the source of passion fruit juice. Propagation is by cuttings or by seeds sown in the spring. Passion flowers require open ground and a fertile, moist, but well-drained soil. It tolerates full sun or partial shade.

Passiflora

ℹ

Family: Passifloraceae
Flowering season: summer/autumn
Height: 16 ft
Situation: ○ – ◑
Moisture requirement: ◗
❄ – ❄ ❄

Potato vine

Solanum jasminoides

This evergreen or semi-evergreen climber, with tendrils that encircle any support, is native to Brazil. It is fast growing and can reach up to 20 ft in one season. In spite of its name, *S. jasminoides* is not a fragrant plant. It has oval to lanceolate, three to five-lobed dark green leaves that are about 2 in long. In the summer and autumn, bunches of blue-white flowers 2–3 in across develop in leaf axils at the ends of the main and lateral growth. The variety 'Album' has pure-white flowers. It has small oval fruits 1/4 in across, but these seldom mature in mild climates. They are poisonous if eaten. Propagation is by sowing in the spring or by semi-ripe cuttings summer or early autumn. It is overwintered by taking rooted cuttings or by keeping pruned plants in pots in frost-free conditions. The jasmine-like potato vine should be grown in full sun in open ground in fertile, moist, but well-drained, neutral to weakly alkaline soil.

Solanum jasminoides

ℹ

Family: Solanaceae
Flowering season: summer/autumn
Height: 20 ft
Situation: ○
Moisture requirement: ◗
❄
✖

Vitis vinifera

Grape vine

Vitis vinifera

ⓘ

Family: Vitaceae
Flowering season: summer/autumn
Height: 23 1/2 ft
Situation: ◯, ◑
Moisture requirement: ◐
❀ ❀ ❀

The grape vine, whose many different varieties provide bunches of delicious grapes, was already being cultivated in Egypt 5,500 years ago. Today, it occurs in forests, at the edges of woods and in thickets in temperate climates. The herbaceous, thickly foliaged scrambling climber thrives best in a wind-protected, sunny position on pergolas, fences and walls, or as large bushes and trees. The leaves, up to 6 in long with 3–5 lobes, turn a wine-red-purple color in the autumn. According to variety, light green, yellow, red or purple fruits develop from the inconspicuous greenish flowers. To ensure high-yielding strong plants, a variety proven in the region should be selected from a local nursery or garden center. Recommended old varieties include 'Blue Muscat,' 'Medina' and 'Bianca.' Choice varieties should be planted in well-drained humus-rich neutral to slightly alkaline soil. Lateral growth should be cut back to two flower buds, or just one bud if the grape yield is valued more than the growth of the vine. The later shoots can be cut back in the winter and also in the summer where appropriate.

384

Japanese wisteria

Wisteria floribunda

This clockwise-twining, leafy climber of the wisteria family is native to Japan and was introduced to Belgium in 1830. Today, it is one of the species most widely grown in gardens. It enhances houses, arbours, pergolas and othen supports with its floral splendor. It has pinnate leaves, each consisting of 11–19 oval to lanceolate leaflets. The fragrant flowers hang in pendulous racemes about 12 in long and are violet, pink or white according to variety. The flowers mature successively from the stem to the tip. They mature into velvety, hairy, bean-like, green seed pods about 6 in long. The variety 'Alba' forms longer racemes, up to 24 in long with white flowers; 'Macrobotrys' has even longer racemes of lilac flowers, up to 4 ft long. All parts of the plant are poisonous and can cause serious illness. Propagation is usually by cuttings in autumn. The long-racemed varieties do best in moist, neutral to slightly acid soil.

ⓘ

Family: Fabaceae
Flowering season: spring/summer
Height: 30 ft and more
Situation: ○, ◑
Moisture requirement: ◍
❄ ❄ ❄
✖
❀

385

Chinese blue rain

Wisteria sinensis

ⓘ

Family: Fabaceae
Flowering season: spring
Height: 30 ft and more
Situation: ○, ◑
Moisture requirement: ◌

❀ ❀ ❀

✖

❀

As the name suggests, this wisteria species is native to China. It was introduced to Europe in 1816. Today, it is probably the species most widely cultivated in gardens. It has alternate, pinnate leaves with 7–13 oval to lanceolate leaflets. Depending on the variety, the flowers are lilac-blue to white, about 1 in long, in hanging racemes 8–12 in long, all flowering at about the same time. The flowering season is April–May, before the leaves on the new growth are mature. The variety 'Alba' has white flowers, 'Sierra Madre' has lavender-violet flowers with standards tinged with white. Prolific flowering does not occur until the fourth or fifth year after planting. In early summer, the flowers mature into green, hairy, bean-like pods, 6 in long. All parts of the plant are poisonous. The plant is propagated by cuttings in autumn. The size and weight of this strongly growing climber should be considered in choosing its site and climbing support. For instance, it can cause damage to rainwater gutters and down pipes.

Blue rain hybrids

Wisteria × formosa

ⓘ

Family: Fabaceae
Flowering season: spring/summer
Height: 30 ft and more
Situation: ○, ◑
Moisture requirement: ◌

❀ ❀ ❀

✖

❀

This wisteria species is the result of crossing *W. floribunda* and *W. sinensis*. Its pinnate leaves consist of 9–15 oval to elliptical leaflets. Young growth is covered with silver-white hairs. Scented violet-blue flowers with white and yellow markings appear in late spring and early summer, opening almost simultaneously in pendulous racemes up to 10 in long. The flowers mature to green bean-like pods, 6 in long. All parts of the plant are poisonous. Propagation is by cuttings in the autumn or by grafting in winter. The plant requires fertile, moist but well-drained soil which must be completely lime-free. This hybrid is pruned at the same as the other species, strongly in late winter and again less severely after flowering.

Wisteria × *formosa*

Pests and Diseases

Prevention is often the best medicine, and plant protection should begin well before it becomes necessary to combat pests and diseases. The selection of strong, healthy plants, a careful choice of situation and good cultivation are crucial for plant development. For instance, setting plants out too close together, or in excessively dark, damp situations, can encourage pests and diseases just as much as watering and fertilising the plants either too much or too little. Working compost into garden soil will give it a crumbly structure and promote the development in it of living organisms which make nutrients available to the plants. A natural garden will attract beneficial creatures to take up residence. You can encourage birds to visit your garden by installing nesting boxes and drinking troughs, and piles of twigs and leaves can be left around as shelter for animals such as hedgehogs and shrews which eat slugs.

Plants will usually tolerate a certain number of pests without suffering too much themselves. If there are enough natural predators present, and a good biological equilibrium is preserved, then it is not usually necessary to resort to chemical pesticides. However, if their use becomes unavoidable, then make sure that you buy substances which are **not harmful to beneficial creatures**, so as to avoid killing such insects as ladybirds, lacewings and hoverflies which tirelessly devour aphids. In treating flowering plants, it is essential to use methods which are not harmful to bees.

It is advisable to use **plant preparations** in the form of teas, brews or liquid manures to strengthen the plants and deter pests. They can now be bought ready prepared, or can easily be made at home: as a rule of thumb, add 2 1/4 lb fresh plants or 5 oz dried plants to 2 gal water. Teas are usually boiled and must then stand for 24 hours; brews are boiled up a second time after this first 24 hours. Liquid manures must ferment for about two weeks, and should be sprayed on the plants only in diluted form. For instance:

- Use stinging nettles, male fern or bracken to make liquid manure or a brew for use as a fertiliser, or in diluted form to control aphids
- Use horsetail grass to make a brew or tea to control mildew, rust and scab
- Garlic and onion liquid manure builds up resistance to fungal diseases in general.

Pests:

Aphids: Aphids are very common garden pests, with over 220 species. Typical symptoms of aphid infestation are deformed, shrivelled or rolled leaves, shortened shoots, and withering. Aphid colonies settle on the undersides of leaves and are particularly fond of feeding on the young, soft parts of plants. The honeydew they secrete encourages the formation of sooty molds. In addition, aphids are carriers of many dangerous viral infections. Using a well-balanced fertiliser not too high in nitrogen is a good preventive measure. In a mild attack, remove the affected parts of the plant or dip them in a solution of soft soap. An extract of stinging nettles made with cold water and used undiluted as a spray is said to be very effective against aphids; steep 2 1/4 lb of nettles in 2 gal water for 12 to 24 hours. *In the case of a severe attack, use a pesticide which will not affect such beneficial creatures as lacewings and ladybirds, the natural enemies of aphids.* Many creatures such as lacewings, ladybirds and gall midges can be bought for biological control in the greenhouse.

Scale insects: These flat or domed insects, yellowish to brown in color, sit motionless on branches and leaves. They attack coniferous and deciduous shrubs, fruit trees and bushes, and houseplants and container-grown plants. The honeydew they secrete often causes infestation with sooty molds. If the attack is mild, it is best just to brush the insects off. *In the case of a severe attack, a preparation containing mineral oil can be sprayed several times on plants with strong foliage, smothering the insects under the film of oil. This process should not be repeated too often, or the pores of the leaves may become clogged.* In the greenhouse, ichneumon flies are useful, and can be ordered from specialist commercial sources.

Woolly aphids: These small creatures, which are covered by white, waxy secretions, colonize the undersides of leaves, leaf stems, shoots, and in particular leaf axils. Unlike scale insects, they move, but they are just as much of a nuisance. The honeydew they secrete is frequently followed by an attack of sooty moulds, and the leaves become sticky and shiny. In conifers, the needles turn yellow and fall; pine, larch and Douglas fir are particularly susceptible. Use the same measures as for controlling scale insects. A useful tip is not to keep sensitive houseplants and container-grown plants in too warm an atmosphere during the winter, to prevent the woolly aphids from reproducing.

Spruce aphids: These dreaded pests, particularly on Colorado and Sitka spruces (*Picea pungens, P. sitchensis*), cause yellow spots to develop on the needles, which then turn brown and fall. Inner, older shoots are the first to suffer, while the new shoots put out in May will not be affected until later in the summer. As a result, whole sections of branches can be left bare. The secretion of honeydew often leads to attacks of sooty molds, and in addition, spruce aphids carry viral diseases. The symptoms of infestation are similar to those of the spruce spider mite, and the two pests quite often occur together. Eggs overwinter on the tree, and if the weather from December to March has been mild, the aphids may reproduce in large quantities in spring. Early checking for any attack is therefore important, sometimes starting as early as February, depending on the weather. Knock any aphids off the branches over a sheet of white paper, so that you can assess the gravity of the infestation. *In the case of severe infestation, it is advisable to treat the plants with a pesticide containing mineral oil, preferably before the new shoots grow.*

Spider mites: These tiny pests cause pale dots to appear on the upper surfaces of leaves. The leaves wither and finally die. The insects themselves colonize the undersides of leaves, and their host plants range from houseplants to fruit trees. Typical symptoms are white webs in the leaf axils and on the undersides of leaves. Spider mites are especially prolific in dry, warm weather, which encourages them to reproduce. Dry air, therefore, is a danger. In the garden, predatory mites and bugs which are the natural enemies of spider mites should be encouraged. *Resort to pesticides which will not harm beneficial insects (e.g. potash soap preparations) only in the case of a bad attack.* Predatory mites can be bought for biological control in the greenhouse.

Whiteflies (snowflies): These winged, powdery white insects and their immobile larvae colonize the undersides of leaves, where they lay large quantities of eggs. The adult insects fly away as soon as they are touched. Their sucking causes yellow mottling of the upper surfaces of leaves, which will then wither and finally drop off. The secretion of honeydew often leads to an attack of sooty molds. As a preventive measure, avoid fertilisers with a high nitrogen content, so that the plant tissues do not become too soft and vulnerable to attack. Whiteflies are common pests in winter quarters in the garden, and it is a good idea to hang up yellow flypapers so that you can assess the severity of any attack, as

well as keeping the greenhouse thoroughly aired, or if necessary introducing ichneumon flies. *In the case of a severe attack, apply commercial preparations which will not harm beneficial insects in good time.*

Thrips (thunderflies): Typical symptoms of thrips infestation are silvery mottling on leaves and flower petals, which later develop cork-like patches. The leaves become deformed, dry up and die off, and the growth of the whole plant is poor. The insects often suck at the undersides of leaves and are particularly common in wet weather with high humidity. When they attack plants grown in the open ground, it is advisable to choose a different situation or grow something else, since thrips can overwinter in the soil and on remains of plants – even on the compost heap. Blue flypapers in the greenhouse will help you to check the severity of any attack. Here, as in other enclosed areas, beneficial insects such as lacewings and predatory mites and bugs can be used very successfully. *Only in the case of a severe attack is it advisable to use an insecticide which will not harm beneficial creatures; it is best to remove severely affected plants entirely.*

Gladiolus thrip causes white spots to appear on leaves and flower petals. The buds dry up and do not open, and affected flowers are deformed or rot. The gladiolus thrip prefers large-flowered gladioli, but will also feed on amaryllis, daffodils and callas.

Capsid bugs: Bugs can be recognised by their flat bodies and relatively small heads. The forewings lie flat beside the body, and the elytron wings overlap, unlike those of beetles. They cause yellow mottling on leaves, which later turn brown and disintegrate so that the leaf is perforated to a greater or lesser extent. The buds and young shoots of roses are also affected, and become deformed. *If the bugs are troublesome, treat plants frequently with potash soap preparations which are not harmful to beneficial insects, preferably in the morning when the temperature is still too low for the bugs to fly.*

Leafhoppers: The sucking of the grown insects and their larvae causes white mottling on the upper surfaces of leaves resembling a spider mite attack. Both creatures are often found on the same plant, but can easily be told apart. The yellowish-green leafhoppers jump away when touched and when they cast their white skins, they usually leave them on the plant. Prevention consists in choosing an airy situation and a well-balanced fertiliser not too high in nitrogen. *In the case of a severe attack, spray the undersides of leaves repeatedly with a suitable commercial insecticide.* Leafhoppers often infest rhododendrons, roses, deciduous shrubs and perennials.

Stem and bulb eelworms: Typical symptoms of eelworm infestation are weak, inhibited growth and a swollen, crooked stem. In *Phlox*, the nematodes cause the tissues of the leaves to die away, leaving only the central rib. Affected parts of the plant should be removed at once. As a preventive measure, plant well apart. It is advisable not to grow plants prone to infection continuously, and to practise mixed cultivation. Weeds are often host plants, and are best removed to avoid new infestation. Stem and bulb eelworms attack perennials and also plants growing from bulbs and corms (tulips, daffodils, crocus), and annuals of the pink family.

Winter moth caterpillars: The green caterpillars of the Lesser and Greater Winter Moth cause a great deal of damage in spring when they feed on the leaves and new shoots of deciduous shrubs. The young leaves become stuck together. The 'looper' caterpillars are recognisable by their five pairs of legs and the typical arching of their backs, and the caterpillars of the Greater Winter Moth also have striking white stripes down their sides. Encourage such natural enemies as ichneumon flies and birds: a pair of tits raising a brood of young can consume up to 66 lb of caterpillars in a season. Grease bands placed around trees in autumn will catch the flightless females on their way to lay eggs at the top of the tree. Hornbeams, oaks and fruit trees are most at risk.

Vine weevil: This beetle takes semi-circular bites out of the edges of leaves, and also attacks buds. The small white larvae feed on roots, causing withering and poor growth. Both larvae and beetles overwinter in the soil. The flightless, nocturnal beetles stay in the soil during the day, but can be collected in the evening. Parasitic nematodes (*Heterorhabditis*) can be applied during watering in spring and autumn to control the larvae; these nematodes can be ordered from garden suppliers, and are also useful as biological control in roof gardens, containers and window boxes. Weevils often attack rhododendrons and yew, perennials, strawberries, vines and houseplants such as cyclamen.

Slugs: Slugs eat leaves and fruits, and are particularly destructive to tender young plant tissues. Sometimes, they can eat a plant bare in a single night. They come out during the day only in wet weather. The ingenious ideas devised by gardeners to keep them away from plants are as varied as the damage caused by the slugs themselves, ranging from collecting them, laying down protective strips of sawdust or sand, setting slug traps (drowning them in beer, for instance), to building little fences to keep them off plants. It is also useful to clear out nooks and crannies where they may hide, to avoid excessive moisture and to encourage their natural enemies such as birds, hedgehogs, frogs and toads. *If all else fails, sprinkle slug pellets round the plants, but remember that they are poisonous to domestic pets.*

Voles: These creatures can be a great nuisance, and occur chiefly where the garden adjoins open meadows or woodland. They nibble busily at roots and bark, and can destroy entire vegetable beds. They are particularly fond of young fruit trees and roses. The animals, which are up to 8 in long, leave their burrows only at night. Unlike the mole, the vole casts up shallow heaps of earth rather than mounds, and its underground passages are straight. An effective measure of prevention is to line the hole with wire netting or rabbit wire when planting, and wrap it round the root ball of the plant. The main enemy of the vole is the domestic cat, but birds of prey and polecats are also its natural predators. Strong-smelling plants such as crown imperial and garlic are said to keep voles away. Traps set in their burrows are useful, but in order not to endanger moles it is best to use humane traps which will catch them alive.

Plant diseases

Grey mold (botrytis): Symptoms of this fungal disease are brown, rotting patches on leaves and flowers, sometimes reaching the stem. In fruits, soft, rotten places coated with mould develop, and they smell musty. Attacks occur mainly in damp, warm weather. The best prevention is an airy position with the plants spaced well apart, so that they can dry off quickly. Trees and shrubs should be thinned out if necessary and it is advisable to place a mulch round such plants as strawberries which grow close to the ground. Avoid using fertiliser with a high nitrogen content, to keep the plant tissues from becoming soft and vulnerable. Remove dead parts of the plant on which the fungus can overwinter as soon as possible. *If chemical treatment during the flowering season is necessary, make sure you choose a fungicide which will not harm bees.*

Rust: In spring, pustular patches of spores form, particularly on the undersides of leaves, yellowish to rusty brown in color depending on the type of parasitic fungus causing them. Leaves wither and rot, and plant growth is weak. To reduce the risk of attack, avoid high humidity and getting the leaves wet, and do not use a fertiliser high in nitrogen. The parts of the plant carrying spores must be removed and destroyed to keep the fungus from surviving on them. Rust fungi are often transferred from one host plant to another, so such plants should be removed; do not hesitate to seek expert advice. Pear tree rust, for instance, overwinters on junipers. Extracts of horsetail grass and tansy will help to strengthen plants, and are also a good method of controlling mildews. *Vulnerable plants can be given preventive treatment with a commercial fungicide. It is important to apply it to the undersides of leaves.*

Root and root collar rot: The collar of the root and the base of the stem turn brown, the roots rot and the plant withers. The fungus prefers young, vulnerable tissue, and chiefly attacks seedlings. The appearance of *Pythium and Phytophthora* rot is frequently the result of a water-logged situation caused by compacted soil and over-watering. Special attention should be paid to maintaining a well-drained soil, and humidity in the greenhouse should not be too high. Affected plants must be removed and destroyed. *As a preventive measure, vulnerable plants grown in a frame can be watered with a fungicide suitable for controlling disease on seedlings.* Heather die-back is particularly feared; it is caused by *Phytophthora cinnamomi*, which can destroy a whole bed of plants.

Wilt: In the various wilt diseases, leaves wither on one side of the shoot first, and hang there in a dry state. In other cases, single shoots die off. Growth will be stunted, and later the plant will collapse. If you cut the stem, the vascular bundle inside shows brown discoloration. Roots are not affected. The only remedy is to remove affected plants, and replant the area with others which are not attacked by *Fusarium* and *Verticillium* wilts or are resistant to them, for instance asters. Special attention should be paid to hygiene when you are working with plants, and it is particularly important to use clean pots and a sterile substrate. *Fusarium oxysporum* causes rot at the base of the bulb of flowering bulbous plants.

Powdery mildew: The typical symptom is a mealy white coating found mainly on the upper surfaces of leaves, and on flower calyxes and young, soft shoots, but in fruit trees, the fruits and blossom are also affected. Leaves turn brown, shrivel and dry up. The fungus reproduces particularly fast in warm, damp weather, especially on hot, sunny days after dew has fallen overnight. It is advisable to choose an airy situation, space plants well apart, and feed with a well-balanced fertiliser not too high in nitrogen. Liquid manure or extracts of horsetail grass or tansy are effective. It is also a good idea to choose less vulnerable or mildew-resistant varieties (for instance when growing grapes). In perennials, affected parts of the plant must be carefully cut back to healthy wood.

In the case of a severe attack, you can use a commercial fungicide containing sulphur. The fungi causing powdery mildew often specialize in one particular plant genus.

Downy mildew: Obvious symptoms are patches between the veining of the leaves, pale to dark purple in color (the latter in roses) depending on the fungus which causes them. White to pale brown spores cluster on the undersides of leaves. This fungus also affects fruits and tubers; grapes attacked by downy mildew turn bluish brown and dry out to a leathery consistency. Cool, damp weather encourages the fungus to spread, so do not set plants too close together, but leave them plenty of room to dry off. Thinning out shrubs in good time is advisable. Since the fungus usually overwinters on fallen remnants of leaves, they should be swept up and preferably destroyed. Remove badly infected plants entirely. Make sure the greenhouse is well aired, and buy resistant varieties (for instance of lettuce).

Leaf spot diseases: Dark, round spots on leaves occur chiefly in long periods of damp weather when the leaves are wet. Depending on the fungus causing them, the spots are surrounded with a reddish to purple border, and black fungal receptacles may form on them. In high humidity and when the plant tissue is injured, for instance by sucking insects, the fungus will spread rapidly. To control it, affected parts of the plants should be removed in good time. Leaves must be able to dry off fast, so do not set plants too close together, and thin out trees and bushes where necessary. Feeding with a well-balanced fertiliser is important, since tissue which is too soft will encourage leaf spot.

Black spot: A typical rose disease. Its symptoms are dark purple leaf spots, usually with fringed edges. The leaves turn yellow and die off prematurely. The danger of attack is particularly high in wet weather, so it is advisable to plant roses in a sunny, airy situation where the leaves can dry off quickly. Regular thinning during pruning and the selection of resistant varieties are also helpful. Infected leaves should be quickly removed and destroyed, since the fungus will overwinter in them and re-infect the plants next year. *In the case of a severe attack, there is usually little to be done but use a fungicide at regular intervals; choose one which will control both black spot and powdery mildew.*

Coral spot: The fungus makes its way into the plant tissue through injured areas and causes tissue to die off. Later on, pinhead-sized pink to red pimples (fungal receptacles) will form on shoots, branches and trunks. Cutting the tree back will help; it is advisable to paint the cut surfaces with a special sealant. Prunings must be removed to prevent re-infection. *In the case of a severe attack, apply a copper-based fungicide in autumn after leaf-fall, to prevent infection through the leaf scars.* Such trees as maple are vulnerable.

Viral diseases: Depending on the particular virus, symptoms vary a good deal, from growth disorders combined with mosaic-like, sharply defined patches on leaves and flowers (flowers will develop mottling), to deformed leaves, flowers, fruits, shoots and roots, and even complete dying of the affected tissue. The viruses frequently specialise in one plant genus. Important measures in countering infection are the control of virus carriers such as aphids, bugs and leafhoppers; the removal of host plants (in other words weeds); the use of healthy plant stock; selection of virus-resistant or robust varieties; and scrupulous observation of hygiene during plant propagation (disinfect your tools and plant pots).

Bacterial diseases: Depending on the particular kind of bacteria, they can produce many different symptoms, ranging from mottled leaves to the formation of cankers and bacterial blight, the development of rotting slimy patches, stem and root rot, and diseases causing withering (for instance *Erwinia, Pseudomonas, Xanthomonas*).

Fireblight is a notifiable disease: flowers discolor first, and then the leaves turn dark brown and hang from the shoots looking burnt. In high humidity, drops of slime containing the dangerous bacteria can form on the affected places. Infection is carried by insects visiting the blossom. The main host plants are of the rose family (Rosaceae): the service-berry, japonica, cotoneaster, hawthorn, quince, apple, pyracantha, pear and rowan. There are no chemical fungicides to control bacterial diseases, fireblight in particular. Infected plants, and even those suspected of infection, should be removed immediately and destroyed.

Glossary

The glossary explains botanical terms used in this book or in other gardening books. The words in italics refer to the corresponding entry.

Achene: Fruit which does not open to release its seeds. See also *fruit types*.

Acid: Soil with a pH of under 7. See also *alkaline* and *neutral*.

Adventitious: Grows in places where normally there is no growth; for instance, adventitious roots can develop from a shoot. In a geobotanical context, adventitious plants are introduced into distant countries; for instance. the seed is transported by birds, ships etc.) and displace indigenous plants, for instance, agaves, Indian figs on the Canaries and *Solidago* from Canada.

Adventitious bud: See *bud*.

Aerial roots: Roots which develop far above ground to secure the plant, as in the case of epiphytes, to absorb the moisture in the air. They develop, for instance, on the shoots of *Ficus* species. When they reach the ground, they root and form secondary trunks.

Air layering: See *layering*.

Airing: Breaking up the soil by mechanical means to allow air (oxygen and carbon dioxide) to penetrate.

Alkaline: Soil with a *pH* of more than 7; the soil is rich in lime. See also *acid* and *neutral*.

Alpine house: Well-ventilated, unheated greenhouse for alpine plants and bulbs.

Alpine plants: Plants which grow above the tree line. The term is also used for rockery plants.

Alternate: Leaves which grow spirally along stems, shoots or branches at alternate levels

Annual: A plant whose life cycle (germination, flowering, seed formation, dying) is completed in one year.

Anther: The part of a flower which produces pollen; situated at the top of the filament.

Approved: Plants which have been declared free of certain pests and diseases by the agricultural authorities.

Asexual reproduction: A form of propagation without fertilisation which often requires mechanical intervention. See also *vegetative reproduction*.

Awn: Bristly hairs on the flowering *glume* of grasses, particularly long in oats.

Axillary bud: See *bud*.

Axillary bulbil: Small bulb- or tuber-like organ, often developing in a *leaf axil*, occasionally along a stem or flower head (as in the case of *Dentaria bulbifera* for instance), which detach themselves, root and form new plants.

Axillary shoot: A shoot developing from an axillary bud (see *bud*).

Bare-rooted: Plants which are sold with roots bare, without soil. Compare *container plant*.

Bark: The outer layer on the outside of a tree or shrub which protects the *cambium*.

Basal: Emerging at the base of a plant.

Basal fleck: The fleck at the base of a petal or a flower.

Beard: Sulcate growth, often on the perigonium, in orchids and some species of iris.

Bedding dahlias: Low-growing varieties which are grown as annuals, being raised from seed every year.

Bedding plants: Annual or biennial plants, or plants grown as such, which are cultivated in a bed until mature and then planted out, often in large groups.

Biennial: A plant which completes its life cycle in two seasons, after which it dies.

Blade: The two-dimensional main part of the leaf.

Blanching: The practice of preventing light from reaching developing leaves or stems so as to keep the plant tissues white and enhance the taste.

Bleeding: Loss of cell juice through a cut or wound in the plant; it is created by root pressure which pushes the water up until the level of solutions in the water in the soil and in the cells is equal.

Blind: A plant which fails to produce flowers, or a flower which does not open properly and rots as a flower bud. Also a stem in which the vegetation point has been damaged.

Bloom: A bluish-white wax-like coating on fruits, leaves etc.

Bolting: The premature production of flowers and seeds.

Bract: A modified, often protective leaf, situated under the flower. Bracts can look like normal flowers but they may also be small and scale-like or large and colorful.

Branch structure: The permanent branch structure of a tree or shrub, its main branches determining its final shape.

Brassica: Belonging to the cabbage family.

Broadcasting: To sprinkle seed or fertiliser evenly over the soil, without furrows and not in rows.

Bromeliad: Belonging to the *Bromeliaceae* family.

Bud: Rudimentary or shortened shoot which contain the structures of leaves and flowers: AXILLARY BUD: a bud emerging from a leaf axil; ADVENTITIOUS BUD: a bud appearing in an unusual position, for instance on a stem instead of from a leaf axil; LEAF BUD: bud from which a leaf develops; WOOD BUD: bud from which a shoot develops; FLOWER BUD: bud from which the flower develops, followed by a fruit; TERMINAL BUD: a bud at the tip of a stem.

Bud eye: A bud-like growth consisting of tiny, tightly curled petals in the center of many roses.

Bud rot: This occurs especially in spells of wet weather. The flowers do not open properly and rot while still at the bud stage.

Bulb: Modified stem which acts as a storage organ, consisting mainly of fleshy scale leaves (modified flower bud), more or less separated or closely packed on a much shortened stem (*bulb stem*).

Bulb stem: Compressed stem at the top of a bulb.

Bulbil: See *offset*.

Callus: Protective tissue formed by plants at the site of an injury, especially in woody plants.

Cambium: New actively growing tissue below the bark which increases the thickness of trunks and branches.

Capitulum: Inflorescence consisting of a disc-shaped center with tubular florets, surrounded by *ray florets*.

Capsule: Dry seed pod that bursts open when ripe, thus releasing the seeds it contains. See *fruit types*.

Carina: Lower part of the flower of *Papilionaceae*, consisting of two modified petals.

Carpel: Part of the *ovary* which contains the *ovule*.

Catkin: Pendulous, ear-like inflorescence, with striking *bracts* enveloping the tiny, often unisexual, flowers with no petals.

Cell sap: Watery content of the central vacuole of a cell. Also the juice of a plant contained in the cells and tissues.

Cilium: Part of a plant with a hairy, frayed edge.

Claw: Stem-like lower part of a petal.

Climbers: Plants which use other plants or structures as support in various ways. 1. The woody stem winds upward around the support. 2. The woody branches climb and attach themselves loosely by means of thorns or prickles. 3. The plant attaches itself by means of aerial roots (e.g. ivy). 4. The plant attaches itself with discoid adhesive pads (e.g. Virginia creeper). 5. The plant winds itself round its support by strong stems (e.g. nasturtium). 6. The plant attaches itself by means of terminal leaflets (e.g. crown vetch).

Cloche: Glass or plastic cover placed over the plants to protect them from frost or rain. It is also used to warm up the soil a little before sowing or planting.

Clone: Group of plants which are genetically identical, produced by vegetative propagation from a single specimen.

Cold frame: Box-like construction made of brick, wood or glass with a hinged, glazed (glass or transparent plastic) cover that can be raised to provide ventilation. It is used to protect plants from harsh frost and to bring on seedlings before planting out in open ground.

Compacted soil: Crust which forms on the surface of soil after damage by condensation, strong rain or excessive irrigation.

Companion planting: Growing two kinds of plants together, one of which is known to have a beneficial effect on its neighbour, by discouraging pets or diseases and by encouraging growth.

Compositae: Family of plants with daisy-like flowers (a central disk surrounded by petals) such as asters.

Compost: Organic material rich in *humus*, containing broken down vegetable matter, used to improve the soil and as a *mulch*.

Compound: Leaf made up of two or more similar units, such as *digitate* and *palmate* leaves. See also *pinnate*.

Cone: The flowers and fruits of conifers and some flowering plants (for instance *Liriodendron*), grouped in dense ears, with bracts at the base of each flower; often appearing as woody seed bearing structures as is the case in conifers.

Conifers: Usually evergreen trees and shrubs with needle-like leaves, cones and gymnosperms, such as larches, deciduous cypress and metasequoia. They differ from angiosperms (flowering plants) by the exposed ovules which are not enclosed in an ovary; the cone is the enlarged, woody female flower.

Container plant: Plant grown in a container in which it can be conveyed from the point of purchase to the garden. As well as being convenient, it saves the roots being damaged by transplanting.

Cool greenhouse: Unheated but frost-free greenhouse in which tender plants can overwinter.

Coppice shoots: A number of more or less even shoots arising rise from the base of some trees and shrubs which are cut back regularly to regenerate.

Cormlet: Small corms which develop on the mother corm such as in gladioli.

Corolla: Inner whorl-shaped floral envelope, consisting of separate or partially fused petals.

Corona: The central, usually trumpet or cup-shaped, part of the flower of genera such as *Narcissus*. Usually known as the trumpet.

Corymb: Raceme reminiscent of an umbel in shape. See *inflorescence*.

Cotyledon: Seed leaf; the first leaf or leaves which emerge from the seed after germination has taken place and which are often different from the mature leaves. Flowering plants (angiosperms) are divided into mono-cotyledons and dicotyledons, depending on the number of seed leaves contained in the ripe seed. In gymnosperms (conifers) they are often arranged in whorls. Seed leaves contain nutrients for the seedling.

Crocks: Crocks are pieces of old, broken earthenware flowerpots used to cover the holes in planting containers. In this way, the soil is not rinsed out through the holes, nor can it clog them. The water drains through well and the roots are aerated sufficiently.

Cross-fertilisation: The fertilisation of the flower of one plant by another.

Cross-pollination: The transfer of pollen from the anthers of a flower to the stigmas of another.

Crown grafting: A kind of grafting in which a narrow scion is inserted into cuts in the bark of the stock. See *grafting*.

Crumb structure: Ideal soil structure where it crumbles into small particles. This result can be achieved by cultivating the soil to loosen it.

Cultivar: A variety of a plant produced from a natural species and preserved by cultivation.

The word is a contraction of 'cultivated variety'.

Cup-shaped: Spherical to cylindrical with a slightly narrower opening.

Cutting: Part taken from the plant (leaf, shoot, root or bud) from which a new plant will be grown. HEEL CUTTING: with a piece of bark or the previous year's wood at the base; EYE CUTTING: cutting containing an eye or bud; LEAF-PETIOLE CUTTING: consists of a small piece of stem with one or two pairs of buds or leaves; LEAF CUTTING: consists of a leaf or pieces of a leaf; SOFTWOOD CUTTINGS OF DECIDUOUS WOODY PLANTS: taken from the soft tip of a stem during the growth period; SOFTWOOD CUTTINGS OF EVERGREEN WOODY FOLIAGE PLANTS: taken from the soft tips of young twigs after the spring growth has ended (a little harder and woodier than the greenwood cuttings of deciduous woody plants); TIP CUTTING: taken from the end of a shoot (often used in the case of softwood cuttings); STEM CUTTING: taken from any part of the stem; HARDWOOD CUTTING: taken from ripe wood from both deciduous and evergreen plants at the end of the growth period.

Cutting back: The radical pruning of a tree by cutting the branches back to the main stem or major branches. Cutting a shrub to about half its height.

Cutting back to ground level: The radical rejuvenation of a woody shrub whereby it is cut back to the ground every year in order to stimulate the growth of vigorous shoots.

Cyme: Also called false umbel. A flower head in which the first bud to flower is situated at the top of the main stem, the remaining buds flowering at the end of lateral stems.

Daisy-like: Flowers consisting of central and ray florets.

Deciduous: Plants which shed their leaves every year at the end of the growing season.

Dentate: Small, often sharp indentations along the margin of a leaf, calyx or corolla.

Dicotyledon: Flowering plants whose seed contains two seed leaves.

Digitate: With 3 or more leaflets spreading from a common point.

Dioecious: Plants having its male and female reproductive organs on different plants.

Disc floret: Disc formed of small, inconspicuous, usually tubular-shaped flowers, situated in the center of a composite flower.

Distal end: The end of a cutting which was furthest from the root of the parent plant.

Distichous: Leaves alternately on opposite sides of the stem and encircling it.

Division: Propagation method which consists in dividing a plant into several parts, each one with a root system and a few shoots (or eyes).

Dormant season: Period during which growth stops and other processes are slowed down in the plant. This normally occurs in the winter.

Double: Flower with several rows of petals.

Double digging: Digging the soil to the depth of two spade blades, usually 2 ft.

Dwarf shrub: Low-growing woody plant, less than about 20 in; for instance, heather.

Earthing up: Heaping up soil round a plant in order to protect it from the wind, blanch the stems and encourage the stem to develop roots.

Elliptic: A leaf which is wide in the middle and narrower at the ends.

Epiphyte: A plant which exists on another plant but is not a parasite and does not root in the earth, such as some orchids.

Erect: With vertical or semi-upright main branches.

Ericaceous compost: Compost with the correct acidity for ericas and other lime-hating plants.

Ericas: Plants which belong to the *Ericaceae* family, usually lime-hating (apart from *Erica carnea*), requiring a soil with a pH of 6.5 or lower.

Espalier: Method of training apples and pairs flat with opposite horizontal branches (tiers), supported by a structure of stakes and wires, sometimes in the open and sometimes against a wall.

Evergreen plants: Plants which keep their leaves throughout the year; semi-evergreen plants keep only some of their leaves.

Explant: To transfer a small piece of a plant to a culture medium for propagation purposes.

Eye: 1. A dormant, latent bud, for instance stem buds or 'eyes' in potatoes or tuber buds in dahlias. 2. The center of a flower when the colour is different from that of the petals.

Eye cutting: See *cutting*.

F1 Hybrids: The first generation resulting from the crossing of two selected, homozygous parents planted in order to obtain homogeneous, vigorous but also fertile offspring. Seeds of F1 hybrids do not develop true to type.

F2 Hybrids: Plants resulting from the self- or cross-fertilisation of F1 hybrids. They are less homogenous than the parent plants.

Falls: The drooping or horizontal petals of irises and other related plants.

Family: A category in the systematic classification of plants which includes several related genera. For instance, the *Rosaceae* family includes the *Sorbus*, *Rosa*, *Rubus*, *Prunus* and *Pyracantha* genera, while the *Iridaceae* family includes the *Iris*, *Crocus*, *Dierama*, *Crocosmia*, *Freesia* and *Gladiolus* genera.

Farinose: Wax-like, white or blue deposit occurring on the stems, leaves or fruit, particularly of primulas.

Feature plant: Striking individual plant, usually a tree or a shrub, grown as an eye-catcher in a prominent place.

Feeding: Applying fertiliser to the surface of the soil around a plant. See also *manuring*.

Fertile: Plant which produces viable seeds; floriferous shoots are also described as fertile in contrast to non-flowering (sterile) ones.

Fertilisation: The fusion of the nucleus of a pollen grain (male) with an ovule (female), producing a fertile seed.

Fibrous compost: Loam containing fibres of decayed vegetable matter.

Fibrous roots: Fine, dense roots, often branched.

Filament: The stem of a stamen bearing the anther.

Fire blight: A bacterial infection which first affects the flowers, then the branches and leaves and finally causes the plant to die.

Flower head: A mass of tiny flowers that together appear as one flower with a disc-shaped center, surrounded by ray florets.

Flower spike: Inflorescence which consists not of an individual flower but a spike of vertically arranged smaller flowers which open from the bottom (e.g. delphinium).

Forcing: To encourage the early growth (usually of flowers but also of fruit) of a plant by manipulating the conditions in which it grows, usually by raising the temperature.

Forcing: Artificial stimulation to encourage the plant to produce flowers during the plant's rest period.

Form: A variation within a species which only differs in minor details: for instance, *Clematis montana grandiflora* is a larger-flowered, stronger form of *C. montana*.

Frond: 1. Leaf-like organ of a fern. Some ferns produce both sterile and fertile fronds, the latter carrying the spores. 2. Also used to designate the large, fan-shaped leaves of a group of palms.

Fruit: The fertilized, ripe ovary of a plant, containing from only one to a large number of seeds, e.g. grapes, hips, capsules and nuts. See also fruit types.

Fruit types: 1. Dry single fruits which usually open spontaneously: follicle, from a carpel, bursts open at the tip (snapdragon); pulse, from a carpel, opens lengthways (peas, laburnum); pod consisting of two carpels separated by a septum and opening lengthways (wallflower); capsule with several carpels, opening in several ways (*Impatiens*). 2. Closed single fruits which do not open spontaneously (achenes): fruit with a hard (walnut) or pergameneous (beech nut) shell. 3. Aggregate or pseudocarp fruit: strawberry with flesh consisting of thickened receptacles. The 'stones' or 'kernels' are the nuts; rose-hips, flesh contained in urceolate pods; raspberry, blackberry, each carpel develops into a stone fruit; apple, aggregate fruit consisting of five leathery single fruits (pyrenes).

Furrows: Narrow, straight grooves in the soil in which seeds are sown and seedlings planted.

Garden soil: Ordinary soil occurring naturally in gardens and fields and used for growing plants and produce.

Genus: A category in the systematic classification of plants which is part of a family and includes several species which share common features. For instance, all the horse chestnut species are part of the *Aesculus* genus. Plural 'genera'. See also *family, sub-family, variety, form* and *hybrid*.

Germ: An embryo without chlorophyll, produced by a seed and fed by the nutrients contained in this seed.

Germination: The physical and chemical process which occurs when the seed begins to grow and develops into a plant.

Germination rest: The non-germination of seeds in spite of favourable conditions is caused by physical, chemical or other factors within the seed itself; double germ rest refers to the non-germination of seeds caused by two factors within the seed itself. See also *dormant season*.

Glume: Chaffy, scarious bracts present on the flower spikes of grasses and sedges.

Graft binding: A wrapping to hold the graft together and protect it during the healing process.

Grafting: A method of propagation whereby a scion, taken from one plant is artificially joined to the stock of another so that they finally form and grow as a single plant. There are several methods such as budding, splice grafting, whip and tongue grafting, crown grafting and saddle grafting.

Grafting site: The place where the scion and stock are joined to each other.

Green manure: Fast-growing, leafy plants such as mustard which are dug into the soil in order to enrich it.

Greenhouse: Building with glass roof and walls which let in the light so as to provide plants with the best possible growing conditions. There are several types of greenhouses: the cool greenhouse, unheated but insulated to be frost-free; the temperate greenhouse, heated to a minimum temperature 45°F; and the warm greenhouse or hothouse, heated to a minimum temperature 65°F. Running costs mean that the latter is very uncommon.

Ground cover: Mostly low-growing plants which spread quickly and cover large areas, often used to suppress weeds.

Growing medium: Medium in which plants can be grown or propagated, such as compost, soil or other material.

Habit: The characteristic shape of a plant.

Half-hardy: Plants which are susceptible to frost although they can stand lower temperatures than tender plants.

Half-standard: Tree or bush with a trunk or stem 3–5 ft high before it begins to branch out.

Halm: The hollow stem of grasses with transverse walls at the nodes from where the stem-hugging leaves grow, enveloping the stem like a sheath.

Hardening off: The gradual acclimatisation of plants to outdoor conditions after being cultivated in a cold frame or greenhouse.

Hardwood cutting: A woody cutting which is taken from the plant at the end of the growing season for propagation purposes.

Heated greenhouse: Artificially heated greenhouse, suitable for overwintering tender plants, depending on the temperature.

Heavy soil: With a high proportion of clay.

Heel: Cutting with a piece of bark or wood from the previous year's growth attached at one end.

Heeling in: Burying the roots loosely in the earth to preserve a plant temporarily before planting it in its final situation.

Herb: 1. Plants cultivated for their medicinal and culinary properties. 2. Botanically: a *herbaceous* plant.

Herbaceous: Non-woody plants which die down to root level at the end of the growing season. Generally used to describe perennial plants but from a botanical point of view it can also refer to *annual* and *biennial* plants.

Herbaceous perennial: Herbaceous or mostly herbaceous plants which last at least three years, dying down partially in the autumn and reappearing from the basal woody stem in spring.

Hermaphroditic: With both male and female sex organs.

Honeydew: Sticky substance on leaves, secreted by pests such as aphids, whiteflies etc.

Humus: The chemically diverse, organic residue from dead vegetable matter in the soil. The term often describes partially decomposed substances such *leaf mould* or *compost*.

Hybrid: Plant resulting from the crossing of genetically different parents. Hybrids resulting from the crossing of species of the same genus are called interspecific hybrids; hybrids resulting from the crossing of different but related genera are called intergeneric hybrids. See also *F1 hybrids* and *F2 hybrids*.

Hybridisation: The process which leads to the creation of hybrids.

Hydroponics: The cultivation of plants in a nutrient-rich water solution, often with sterile growing medium.

Hypocotyl: The part of an embryo plant between the *cotyledon* and the *radicle*.

Incurved: The petals of flowers and individual florets which curve inward to form a compact, round shape. Incurved flower heads are less compact and form a less dense shape.

Inflorescence: A mass of individual flowers which together appear to form a single flower. The main types of flower heads are: RACEME, erect with flowers all round the spike (lupin), with flowers only on one side of the spike (lily-of-the-valley), or pendulous (laburnum); UMBEL, domed umbels with equally long stems borne on long axillary stems (chervil), flat umbels (carrot) with longer outer flower stems; CAPITULUM, with small, equally long terminal flowers (red clover), raised or flat center with tubular florets surrounded by bracts and no outer florets, centre with tubular florets surrounded ray florets (Rudbeckia) or with only long tubular florets (dandelion).

Initial pruning: Pruning of young trees and shrubs in order to develop the basic branch structure of the shape desired.

Intermediate: Hybrids whose characteristics are half way between the two parents.

Internode: The part of the stem between two nodes; it is clearly visible in grasses, for instance.

Involucre: Ring of bracts found beneath the flower of some plants, such as the daisy.

Laced: Term used of *Dianthus* species in which each petal has a narrow edging whose colour contrasts with the rest of the petal.

Lamina: The flat blade of a leaf or petal (not including the *petiole*).

Lanceolate: Narrow and tapering to a point at both ends.

Layering: A method of propagation whereby a branch is bent down to soil level where it will develop roots while still being attached to the mother plant. This method is based on the principle of self-layering which occurs naturally in some plants. There are several methods of layering such as serpentine layering, tip layering, drop layering and air layering.

Leading shoot: 1. The central, erect main trunk of a tree. 2. The terminal shoot of a plant.

Leaf: A plant organ which varies in color and shape, usually flat and green with a stalk; it enables photosynthesis, respiration and transpiration to take place.

Leaf axil: The angle between a leaf and a shoot, between a stem and a bract. See also *bud*.

Leaf bud: See *bud*.

Leaf cutting: See *cutting*.

Leaf mould: Fibrous material consisting of broken down, decayed leaves, used in compost and to improve the quality of the soil.

Leaf shapes: Leaf shapes: the numerous leaves shapes are grouped roughly into divided and undivided. For instance, UNDIVIDED LEAVES can be needle-like (*Erica*); linear (pink, carnation); elliptic (forget-me-not); lanceolate (cornflower); ovate (greater plantain); obovate (*Azara microphylla*); round (nasturtium); kidney-shaped (marh marigold); heart-shaped (violet). DIVIDED LEAVES can be palmate, digitate (horse chestnut); tripartite (strawberry); pinnatifid (thistle); paripinnate (honeysuckle); imparipinnate (raspberry).

Leaflet: Individual part of a compound leaf.

Light: Soil with a high proportion of sand and little clay.

Lime: Calcium carbonate. It is the amount of lime in the soil which determines whether it is alkaline, acid or neutral.

Lime hating: Plant which will not tolerate alkaline soil, such as azaleas, rhododendron, and ericas with the exception of *Erica carnea*.

Lime tolerant: Plant which tolerates alkaline soil.

Linear: Description used for a very narrow leaf with largely parallel sides.

Lipped flowers: Flowers with a protruding, lip-like lower part.

Lithophyte: A plant that grows on rocks or very stony ground, usually obtaining most of the water and nutrients it needs from the atmosphere.

Loam: Soil of average texture, easy to work, consisting of roughly equal parts of sand, silt, clay and humus. If the proportion of one constituent is particularly high, the description is modified accordingly, for instance, sandy loam.

Lobe: The division of part of an otherwise undivided leaf into separate areas.

Low bush: Fruit tree with a stem or less of 36 in or less, such as currant or gooseberry bushes.

Maintenance pruning: The normal cutting back of woody plants by thinning out the stems while preserving the shape of the bush; cutting the top is usually to be avoided.

Manuring: Digging fertiliser, compost or humus into the soil before sowing or planting, or sprinkling it on the surface around a plant or on the lawn to replace nutrients.

Marginal plant: Plant whose natural location is permanently moist or wet, or one which thrives under such conditions.

Medium soil: Soil which is between heavy and light. See also *loam*.

Medulla: Pith, the soft vegetable material in the interior of a stem.

Meristem: The continually dividing tissue of a plant, responsible for its growth. It enlarges the cambium round the trunk, the leaf axils and the leaves themselves, as well as the tips of shoots and roots. Without the meristem, no grafting of any kind would be possible. If the bark of a plant is cut or damaged, the meristem forms a callus to repair it.

Microclimate: The particular climate of a limited space within a larger once, for instance in a greenhouse or in a protected part of a garden.

Midrib: The main vein of a leaf, running down its centre.

Mixed: Collections of summer flowers which differ in only one feature, usually the color. They are available in individual colors or more commonly as a mixture.

Monocarpic: Plants which flower and bear fruit only once before they die. They take several years to reach flowering size.

Monocotyledon: Flowering plant with only a single seed leaf. The leaf has parallel veins.

Monoecious: Describes a plant which has both male and female flowers on the same plant.

Monopodium: Predominantly vertical axis of growth, with an upright main stem from which side shoots grow. See also sympodial.

Mulch: Layer of organic material; to if it is deposited onto the surface of the soil in order to decrease the spread of weeds, to conserve moisture and to maintain a cool, uniform root temperature. In addition to organic materials such as stable manure, leaf mold, forest bark, garden compost and straw, plastic sheeting and pebbles can also be used.

Mutation: Genetic change of properties occurring spontaneously in a plant, for instance flowers colored differently from those of the parent. A mutant is also known as a *sport*.

Mycelium: The vegetative body of fungi, consisting of microscopically small filaments known as hyphae.

Mycorrhiza: The symbiotic association of fungi and plant roots which live together for mutual advantage, for instance with forest trees.

Native: Species originating in the wild in a particular area.

Naturalisation: Growing plants in conditions similar to their native ones, so they thrive as they would in the wild.

Nectar: Secreted by the nectaries; it has a strongly attractive effect on pollinating insects.

Nectary: Glandular tissue that mostly occurs in flowers, for instance in the spur (as in the case of violets, for instance), but sometimes also on leaves or stems. It secretes nectar.

Neutral: Soil with a pH value of 7, i.e. neither acid nor alkaline.

Nicking: 1. Nicking or scratching the coating of hard-coated seeds before sowing in order to accelerate its uptake of water and hence the process of germination. 2. Removal of a small piece of bark from the trunk or the boughs of specific fruit trees, in order to encourage strong growth and to increase the yield of fruit.

Node: Section of the stalk (often slightly swollen) from which leaves, shoots, twigs or blossoms arise.

Non-recurrent: Used of roses which flower and bear fruit only once during the season. See also *recurrent*.

Nutrients: Minerals, proteins and other compounds which are necessary for plant growth.

Offset: Young plants in the form of small bulbs developing on the edge of a parent bulb (such as tulips and daffodils), which are used for vegetative propagation. If only one or two larger specimens are formed, these are known as daughter bulbs, while if they are more numerous but smaller in size, they are often known as bulbils. These terms overlap and are not strictly defined.

Opposite: Two leaves or other plant organs facing each other on the same level on opposite edges of a stem or other axis; the opposite of alternate.

Organic: 1. Chemical compounds which contain carbon, which comes from decomposed plant or animal organisms; therefore used to describe compost etc. formed from such decayed organisms. 2. Used to describe plants, fruit and other organisms fertilised and treated only with materials made from organic materials, without the application of any synthetic (inorganic) preparations.

Ovary: The lower part of the carpel which contains one or more ovules, developing into a fruit after fertilisation. See also *carpel*.

Ovule: The part of the ovary which develops into the seed after pollination and fertilisation.

Own-rooted: Roses grown on their own roots, not budded onto a rootstock of a different (wild) variety. The advantage of growing on its own roots is that it does not produce suckers.

Palmate: Hand-shaped leaf rounded with three or more finger-like or pointed lobes.

Panicle: A large, open, branched flower cluster, often composed of many flowers with individual stalks.

Papilionaceous flowers: Flowers of members of the pea family whose irregular form is reminiscent of a butterfly with its wings folded.

Parent plants: Plants from which propagating material, whether seed or vegetative material, is collected.

Parterre: A formal terrace with ornamental beds, usually filled with low-growing plants enclosed by low hedges, often box.

Parthenocarpy: Producing fruit without fertilisation having occurred.

Pathogen: Any micro-organisms or other agents which can cause disease.

Peat: Partially decomposed vegetable matter making a humus-rich open soil which is very water-absorbent. MOSS PEAT comes from partially decomposed sphagnum moss, formed in bogs, and is used for peat compost. SEDGE PEAT comes from the roots of sedges and similar plants, formed in fens; it is coarser than moss peat and less suitable as peat compost.

Peat bed: Bed made from blocks of peat and filled with very peaty soil; designed for acid-loving plants, for instance where the natural soil is neutral or alkaline with a high pH value.

Peat pot: Pot made of compressed peat which decomposes when planted in the soil; it avoids the need for transplanting.

Peat substitute: Any of a large number of different organic materials, such as coconut fibre, which can used in place of peat in compost and as a soil conditioner, supplying humus and improving the drainage.

Peduncle: The stalk of a flower.

Perennial: Strictly speaking, any plant, which lives for at least three growing seasons. In gardening it is general used to mean herbaceous plants, although it can include woody perennials such as trees and shrubs.

Perianth: Term describing combined sepals and petals when they cannot be distinguished from each other, for instance tulips.

Pericarp: The external covering of a fruit or seed.

Perlite: Small granules of volcanic mineral consisting of many tiny granules, added to soil to improve drainage and aeration.

Pesticide: Chemical, frequently synthetically produced, used for killing pests including insects, mites and nematodes.

Petal: A modified leaf, often brightly coloured, forming part of the flower. They may be separated or fused, when they are known as the *corolla*. See also *tepal*.

Petiole: The stalk of a leaf.

pH level: Measure of the acid or alkaline content of a substance, which in gardening is invariably the soil. The scale runs from 1 to 14. A pH level of 7 is neutral; numbers above 7 indicate increasingly alkaline soil, while numbers below 7 indicate increasingly acid soil.(see also acid, alkaline and neutral.

Photosynthesis: The production of the organic compounds needed for plant growth by a complex process involving the interaction of chlorophyll, light energy, carbon dioxide and water.

Phyllode: A flattened stalk of leaf-like appearance, which also undertakes the functions of a leaf. Also known as a cladode.

Pinching out buds: The removal of superfluous flower buds in order to encourage the optimal development of the remaining flowers.

Pinching out growing tips: Pinching out the growing tip of shoots, using thumb and forefinger, to stimulate the growth of side shoots or flower buds.

Pinna: The individual leaflet of a pinnate leaf.

Pinnate: Description of a compound leaf divided into a number of leaflets arranged opposite each other in pairs on a central stem. The number varies from a single pair (e.g. *Trifolium*), to many (e.g. *Rhus*). See also *leaf shapes*.

Pinnule: The individual leaflet of a bipinnate leaf.

Pistil: The female reproductive organ of flowering plants, consisting of *ovaries*, *style* and *stigma*.

Pod: See *fruit types*.

Pollarding: The regular cutting back of the main branches to the main stem, usually to a height of 6 ft 6 in. Willows are commonly treated in this way to harvest the stems for basket weaving etc.

Pollen: The male cells of a plant, which are contained in the *anther* or in pollen sacs.

Pollination: The transfer of pollen from the *anthers* to the *stigmas*. See *cross-pollination* and *self-pollination*.

Polyembryony: Containing more than one embryo in an ovule or a seed.

Pompon: Small, mostly spherical flower formed of numerous individual florets.

Potting compost: A mixture of loam, peat or peat substitute, sand and nutrients in various proportions. Soilless compost contains no loam but for instance peat with added nutrients.

Potting up: Planting individual seedlings in pots.

Pricking out: Planting out seedlings once they have germinated, in pots, pans, boxes or trays, or in a nursery bed, so that they have enough room to grow and develop.

Propagating case: Closed case, in which young seedlings, cuttings and other plant propagating material can be kept in conditions of increased air humidity.

Propagation: The increase of plants either by seed (sexual) or through the use of vegetative methods.

Prostrate: Spreading low over the soil.

Proximal end: The end of a cutting which was initially nearest the root of the parent, the opposite of the *distal end*.

Pruning: The annual cutting back of trees and shrubs in order to obtain stronger branches and shoots. This must be carried out with great care in order to maintain the shape of the plant.

Pseudobulb: False bulb, the thickened, bulb-like part of stem of some orchids, arising at the end of a sometimes short rhizome.

Pulse (Legume): See fruit types.

Raceme: Unbranched flower head bearing many flowers attached to the main stem by *peduncles*.

Radicle: The part of the embryo of a seed which develops into the main root. In the case of bare seeds and *dicotyledons* this is the tap root; in the case of *monocotyledons* it forms a root which dies and is replaced by secondary roots.

Rain shadow: Area near a wall or a fence that is protected against the prevailing winds and therefore receives less rain than the open ground.

Ray florets: The outer ring of petals of a flower of the daisy family (*Compositae*).

Recurrent or remontant: Plant which flowers more than once during the season, as is often the case with some roses or strawberries for instance. See also *non-recurrent*.

Reflexed: Petals which are curved back on themselves more than 90°. Less accurately used to describe all flowers in which the petals are bent back to a lesser degree.

Rejuvenation pruning: Pruning method in which the side shoots are cut back constantly in order to induce the growth of new shoots in their place. It is not always appropriate since it can spoil the appearance of the plant.

Respiration: The process of releasing carbon dioxide while creating energy through the breakdown of organic molecules.

Revert: Returning to the primary state, for instance when a variegated leaf becomes a plain green leaf.

Rhizome: A specialist, normally horizontal creeping, thickened or slim, subterranean stem. It acts as a storage organ. Vertical stems break out at the tip and along it.

Root: The normally underground part of plants; it anchors the plant, as well as taking up water and nutrients from the soil. See also aerial root.

Root attachment: The point in a herbaceous plant which is level with the soil, where the roots and the stems join and from which new shoots are formed.

Root ball: The clump formed by the roots and the soil or compost surrounding them, visible when a plant is being planted or transplanted.

Root-balled plants: When transplanting trees and large shrubs, the root ball with its soil is wrapped in cloth or other material to preserve it until it is replanted.

Root nodules: Growths on roots containing bacteria which fix the nitrogen in the air. This characteristic, a notable feature of leguminous plants, means that the fertility of the soil is improved by planting them.

Root run: The area of soil equivalent to the extent of the plant's roots.

Root runner: A usually slim shoot growing from a plant's root system. It can be cut off with its own roots to form a new plant.

Rosette: Bunch of leaves radiating from the same point, often at ground level from a very short stem.

Runners: Side shoots which roots and form new plants, either on the surface, as in the case of strawberries, or underground as in the case of ground elder.

Saddle graft: See *grafting*.

Sapling: A young tree about 3–7 ft tall; a tree seedling or every young tree, before the wood hardens.

Scale leaf: A small, rudimentary non-foliage leaf.

Scion: A piece cut from a selected variety to be increased which is grafted onto a stock.

Scorching: Wilting, burning or discoloration of aplant through exposure to excessive heat or light.

Scree: Slope formed of pieces of weathered rock. Similar scree beds are sometimes created in gardens as stony beds for alpine plants, having excellent drainage.

Scutate: Shield-shaped leaf where the stalk is attached at the centre of the leaf, or sometimes away the centre, e.g. nasturtium.

Seed: Ripe, fertilized *ovule* containing the dormant embryo which will develop to a plant.

Seed bed: Bed of soil or compost in which seeds are sown to germinate or in which young plants are cultivated before being planted out in the flowering position.

Seed leaf: See *cotyledon* and *dicotyledon*.

Seedling: A young plant raised from seed.

Selection: Plant selected for its special features. It is usually propagated to preserve these features

Self-fertile: Plant that produces seeds which are viable after fertilisation by its own pollen. See also *fertilisation*, *pollination*, and *self-sterile*.

Self-layering: see shoot

Self-pollination: The transmission of pollen from the anthers to the stigma of the same flower or of another flower of the same plant.

Self-seeding: Seeds from a plant which freely produce seedlings around its parent.

Self-sterile: Plant which can form no viable seeds by self-pollination. The pollen of another plant is necessary for fertilisation to occur.

Semi-evergreen: See evergreen.

Semi-hardwood cuttings: Cuttings towards the end of the current year's growing season, woody at the base but soft and tender at the tip.

Sepals: Modified leaves forming the outer *whorl* of the flower. Usually small and green, they are sometimes colored and similar to *petals*.

Sets: Small offset bulbs (such as onions or shallots) or potato tubers selected for growing.

Sexual reproduction: Reproduction by fertilisation; seeds are the result.

Shoot: A branch, stem or twig.

Show plant: A striking plant, normally a tree or shrub of merit in outstanding state, in a situation is where it can be seen to advantage.

Shrub: Woody plant only a few metres (feet) high, branching from the bottom equally in all directions.

Side shoot: Lateral shoot growing sideways from the main stem.

Single: Flower with a single row of petals.

Single digging: Digging the soil to the depth of the spade blade, usually 10–12 in.

Single floret: Small floret in a multiple cluster or flower head.

Smooth-edged: Description of leaf with non-serrated edges.

Softwood cuttings: Cuttings from the tips of non-flowering shoots.

Sowing in rows: Sowing seeds individually or in small groups, in furrows at specific distances apart.

Spadix: A fleshy flower spike in which numerous single flowers are embedded.

Spathulate: Spoon shaped, such as the individual flowers of chrysanthemums. The term can also describe a leaf or a bract.

Species: A category in the systematic division of plants; applied to a group of closely related plants within a genus.

Sphagnum: Water storing moss, a constituent of growing mediums, and when partially decomposed, peat.

Spike: See flower head

Spikelet: A small spike; part of a small compound flower head; often seen in grasses and sedges, in which the flower head consists of several small flowers with basal bracts.

Sporangium: Organ in fungi in which the spores are produced.

Spore: The tiny single-celled reproductive body of non-flowering plants such as ferns, fungi and mosses. With ferns, they originate on the undersides of the fronds in sporangia; ripe spores fall onto the soil. There they form prothalli, which have male and female sex organs. Fertilisation produced a new fern (vegetative generation).

Sport: Gardening term for a mutation caused by a induced or spontaneous genetic change, resulting in different features and/or the differently coloured flowers from those of the parents.

Spur: 1. Short lateral shoot with flower buds, as in fruit trees; or with leaves, as in deciduous trees and conifers. 2. The hollow projection of a petal, seen for instance in violets, columbines, and toadflax; it often makes nectar.

Stalk: Common term for the petiole of a leaf or the peduncle of a blossom.

Stamen: The male reproductive organ of a plant, consisting of the pollen-making anther and the filament on which it is carried.

Standard: 1. Rose or shrub grown so that it has a stem about 3–4 ft high or more before the first side shoots. 2. The larger, upstanding back petal of a flower belonging to the *Leguminosae* genus such as sweet peas. 3. In irises, the three inner petals which are usually erect.

Stem: The main support of a herbaceous plant, largely above the soil; it carries leaves, flowers and fruits.

Sterile: 1. Producing no flowers or viable seeds. 2. Flowers without operative *anthers* and *pistils*.

Sterilisation: The removal of the *anthers* before the pollen is dispersed in order to prevent *self-pollination*.

Stigma: The flower's female reproductive organ, the tip of the *pistil*; supported by the *style*. It becomes sticky when ready for pollination.

Stock: A plant to which a scion is grafted.

Stolon: A low-growing horizontal-creeping stem which roots and forma new plants at the nodes.

Stone fruits or drupes: Fruits with one or more seeds ('stones'), surrounded by fleshy tissue or drupe such as fruit from the *Prunus* genus (apricots, plums, cherries) and a few other plants such as mangoes which produce woody achenes. See also fruit types.

Stratifying: Storing seed under warm or cold conditions, in order to overcome its dormancy and to encourage germination.

Style: Stalk linking the ovary and stigma of a flower; not always present (e.g. poppy flowers do not have styles).

Sub-family: A category in the systematic classification of the plants; a group within the *family*.

Sub-lateral: Side shoot from a lateral shoot.

Sub-shrub: Plant that is woody at ground level and herbaceous above; this part dies at the end of the season.

Sub-soil: The soil below the topsoil; it is usually less fertile and with a poorer structure and texture than topsoil.

Sub-species: The sub-division of a species, at higher level than variety or form.

Succulent: Plant with thick, fleshy stems and/or leaves, used for storing water.

Sucker: With plants grown on a rootstock, any shoot arising from below the grafting point.

Sucker: Stem growing on the side from a shoot or a root.

Suckers: *Adventitious* shoots which arise from underground roots.

Surface roots: Large roots above the surface which help to support a tree or shrub.

Sympodium: A mainly horizontal growth habit, characteristic of the grape vine for instance. The main stem ends in a flower or ceases to grow, while further growth is by lateral branches. Compare *monopodium*.

Systemic: Term describing fertilizers and weed-killers which are applied when watering the plant and taken up with the water, thus working from the inside out.

Tap root: The largest and most important root of a plant growing vertically downwards, particularly trees. The term is generally used too for any strongly downward-growing root.

Taxon: Any taxonomic group, classifying plants with specific features together. Plural taxa.

Tendril: Modified twig, stalk or leaf, normally thread-shaped (long and slim) which is able to attach itself to a solid support. See also *climber*.

Tepal: Individual section of a *perianth* which cannot be identified as either a *petal* or a *sepal*.

Terminal: Inflorescence borne at the end of a stem so that the latter cannot grow taller any more. See also *cyme*.

Terminal bud: The tip of a stem, usually referring to a flower bud or flower.

Thicket: Group of shrubs or small trees growing close together.

Thinning: The removal of seedlings, shoots, flowers or fruit buds to encourage the growth and improve the quality of the remaining ones.

Tilth: A fine, crumbly surface layer of the soil resulting from cultivation, the ideal condition for sowing seeds.

Tissue culture: Propagation of plants under sterile conditions in synthetic mediums.

401

Topiary: The art of pruning trees and shrubs to form various, usually complicated, geometric shapes, or imaginative creatures.

Transpiration: Water loss by evaporation from the leaves and stalks of plants.

Triploid: A plant with three sets of chromosomes; such plants are usually sterile.

True to type: The characteristic properties of the parent plants which are not always preserved when reproducing from seed.

Trunk base: The part of a plant where roots and stalks meet.

Tuber: A thickened, usually underground organ for storage of nutrients, growing from a stem (in the case of a potato) or a root (in the case of a dahlia).

Tubular flower: The tubular-shaped individual disc florets forming the centre of a flower of the *Compositae.*

Tufa: Porous limestone with water-retentive properties; it is used to make garden soil suitable for growing alpines.

Tunic: The paper-like or fibrous outer skin of bulbs and corms.

Turning the soil: Digging method in which the soil is dug one spit deep with a spade and turned over.

Umbel: See *inflorescence.*

Underplanting: Planting low-growing plants with taller ones.

Variable: Plant which will not reliably reproduce the features of the type; it happens for instance with plants grown from seed, when the characteristics will vary from those of the seed source.

Variety: Group of plants within a species, or a plants within a group, differentiated by one or more distinguishing features which are maintained through sexual or non-sexual propagation; particularly common in growing flowers for cutting.

Variety: In botanical classification, a variant of a wild *species*, between the statuses of *subspecies* and *form.*

Vegetative growth: Non-flowering, mostly leafy growth.

Vegetative reproduction: Propagation of plants by non-sexual methods by which genetically identical individuals almost invariably result.

Vermiculite: A mica-like material providing good water storage and aeration. It is often added to potting compost to improve its performance in these respects.

Watering: To irrigate a plant there are many methods, ranging from a watering can or hosepipe to sophisticated built-in irrigation systems. To ensure the intended plant fully benefits from it, a useful technique is to form the earth round the plant into a surrounding bank, making a basin into which the water is poured. This prevents it running all over the place.

Whip and tongue graft: Grafting method where the scion and stock are cut with tongues so that they interlock.

Whorl: Arrangement of three or more leaves or flowers arising from the same point.

Whorl-like (leaf arrangement): Leaf arrangement with at least 3 leaves growing at every node.

Wild shoot: Shoot arising directly from the stem or underground from a root.

Wind protection: Structure protecting plants from strong wind; usually a hedge, a line of trees, a fence or a wall.

Wind rock: The loosening of a plant's roots by the effect of a strong wind.

Winged seed: A flying seed, such as that formed by the sycamore, *Acer pseudo-platanus.*

Winter wet: Excessive water stored in the soil during the winter months.

Winter hardy: Describes a plant which survives all climatic conditions throughout the year, including frost, without needing special protection.

Wood bud: See *bud.*

Woody: Stems of hard, woody fibres which, unlike tender herbaceous stems, survive over the winter. A half-hardy plant contains more tender material and may not survive the winter.

Index

Acacia pulchella 300

Acanthus spinosus 120

Acer palmatum 300, 301

Achillea filipendulina 120

Achillea millefolium 121

Achillea ptarmica 122

Aconitum carmichaelii
    'Arendsii' 122

Actinidia Kolomikta 364

Adiantum pedatum 123

African daisy 94

African lily 80

African marigold 113

Agapanthus africanus 80

Ajuga reptans 232

Albarose 273, 283

Alcea rosea 80

Alchemilla mollis 124

Alisma plantago-
    aquatica 125

Allium giganteum 10

Allium sativum 232

Allium schoenoprasum 233

Alpine aster 132

Amaranthus caudatus 81

Amaryllis 41

Amelanchier laevis 301

Amelanchier, 301

Anemone 126

Anemone coronaria
    'De Caen' 10

Anemone hupehensis 125

Anemone sylvestris 126

Anemone x hybrida 'Honorine
    Jobert' 126

Anemonopsis macro-
    phylla 127

Anethum graveolens 234

Annuals 78, 79

Anthemis tinctoria 127

Anthriscus cerefolium 234

Antirrhinum majus 81

Antler dahlia 29

Apple mint 249

Aquilegia canadensis 128

Aquilegia vulgaris 128

Argyranthemum frutes-
    cens 82

Armeria maritima 129

Arnica 235

Arnica montana 235

Artemisia 235

Artemisia alba
    'Canescens' 130

Artemisia ludoviciana 235

Artichoke 238

Arugula salad or garden
    arugula 240

Arum 11

Arum lily 77

Aruncus dioicus 131

Arundinaria 302

Asplenium trichomanes 131

Aster alpinus 132

Aster novi-belgii 133

Aster pringlei 'Monte
    Cassino' 133

Astilbe 134

Astilbe x arendsii 134

Astrantia major 135

Aubrieta x cultorum 135

Aubrietia 135

Aucuba jaonica 303

Auricula cultivars 212

Aurinia saxatilis 136

Authemis tinctoria 127

Autumn crocus 12

Avens 169

Ayssum saxatile 136

Ball-flowered dahlias 25

Bamboo 302

Barberry 304

Basil 250

Bay 243

Bay laurel 243

Bear's breeches 120

Beard tongue 204

Bearded iris 46

Begonia 83

Begonia Semperflorens 83

Begonia Tuberhybrida 83

Bell heather 323

Bellis perennis 84

Bells of Ireland 103

Shell-flower 103

Berberis julianae 304

Berberis linearifolia 304

Berberis thunbergii 305

Bergenia 136

Bergenia cordifolia 136

Bistorta officinalis
    'Superba' 137

Black mustard 237

Black-eyed susan 110,
    114, 220

Blanket flower 162

Bleeding heart 155

Bloody-crane's bill 168

Blue rain hybrids 386

Blue-eyed Mary 197

Blue poppy 192

Bluebell 41

Borage 236

Borago officinalis 236

Boston ivy 382

Bougainvillea 365

Bourbon rose 296, 297

Brassica nigra 237

Broom 317

Buddleja davidii 306, 307

Buddleja globosa 306

Bugbane 141

Bugle 232

Busy lizzie 98

Buttercup 68

Butterfly bush 306

Buxus sempervirens 308

Cactus-flowered dahlia 27

Calceolaria intetgrifolia 85

Calendula officinalis 237

Californian poppy 95

Callicarpa bodinieri 309

Callistephus chinensis 85

Calluna 309

Caltha palustris 138

Camellia 310, 311

Camellia japonica 310, 312

Camellia reticulata 312

Camellia x williamsii 313

Campanula carpatica 138

Campanula persicifolia 139

Candytuft 182

Canna 11

Cape marigold 94

Carex hachijoensis
    'Evergold' 139

Carnations and pinks 91

Carthamus tinctorius 86

Castor oil plant 110,
    255

Catnip 250

Celosia-plumosa 87

Centaurea 140

Centaurea 87

Centaurea americana 87

Centaurea cyanus 88

Centaurea montana 140

Centranthus ruber 141

Chamaecyparis
    lawsoniana 314

Chelone barbata 204
Chervil 234
China aster 85
China rose 270, 271
Chincherinchee 66
Chinese blue rain 386
Chinese witch hazel 330
Chives 233
Christmas rose 174
Chrysanthemum frutescens 82
Chrysanthemum
    leucanthemum 184
Cimicifuga simplex 141
Cinquefoil 211, 346
Clematis 366, 367
Clematis alpina 368
Clematis montana 368
Clematis viticella 369
Climbers 362, 363
Climbers 374, 375
Climbing rose 265, 275, 279,
    284, 286
Colchicum autumnale 12
Coleus blumei 113
Collerette dahlias 25
Columbine 128
Common arrowhead 221
Common box 308
Common buttercup 219
Common camellia 312
Common daisy 84
Common elder 258
Common hydrangea 332, 333
Common ivy 372
Common lilac 356
Common myrtle 344
Common or wild
    marjoram, 252
Common white water lily 196
Common witch hazel 331
Common yew 357
Consolida ajacis 88
Continental wild thyme 261

Convallaria majalis 142
Coral flower 177
Coreapsis lanceolata 142
Coreopsis 142
Coriander 238
Coriandrum sativum 238
Cornelian cherry 314
Cornflower 88
Cornus mas 314
Cortaderia selloana 143
Corydalis lutea 215
Cosmos 89
Cosmos bipinnatus 89
Costmary 258
Cotoneaster frigidus 315
Cotoneaster horizontalis 315
Cotoneaster sternianus 316
Cotton lavender 222
Cowslip 214
Crane's bill 166, 167, 168
Crocosmia masoniorum
    'Lucifer' 13
Crocosmia masoniorum 12
Crocus 14, 15
Crocus chrysanthus 16
Crocus speciosus 16
Crocus tommasinianus 17
Crocus vernus 17
Crowfoot 68
Crown anemone 10
Crown Imperial 32
Cyclamen 18
Cyclamen mirabile 18
Cyclamen persicum 19
Cynara scolymus 238
Cytisus nigricans 'Cyni' 317
Cytisus x praecox 318
Daboecia 318
Daffodil 60, 61
Dahlia 20, 21
Dahlia 'Akita' 22
Dahlia 'Bantling' 22
Dahlia 'Brandaris' 24

Dahlia 'Charles Dickens' 25
Dahlia 'Don Lorenzo' 25
Dahlia 'Gay Princess' 26
Dahlia 'Horido' 27
Dahlia 'Jescot Julie' 27
Dahlia 'Loki Schmidt' 28
Dahlia 'Tsuki yori no
    shisha' 29
Dahlia 20, 21
Damask rose 273, 282, 285
Darwin hybrid tulips 74
Day lily 176, 177
Dead nettle 184, 185
Decorative-flowered
    dahlias 22
Delphinium 'Berg-
    himmel' 146
Delphinium 'Black
    Knight' 146
Delphinium 'Fanfare' 147
Delphinium 'Völker-
    frieden' 147
Delphinium-hybrids 144, 145
Dendranthema x grandiflorum
    'Ritter Tom Pears' 151
Dendranthema x
    grandiflorum 150
Dendranthema-hybrids 149
Deutzia 319
Deutzia gracilis 319
Dianthus 91
Dianthus barbatus 90, 92
Dianthus caryphyllus 153
Dianthus deltoides 154
Dianthus plumarius 154
Dicentra spectabilis 155
Digitalis grandiflora 93
Digitalis purpurea 93
Dill 234
Dimorphotheca pluvialis 94
Dog rose 292
Dorinicum parda-
    lianches 156

Dorset heath 323
Dotted loosestrife 189
Double early tulips 76
Dryopteris filix-mas 156
Dutch irises 47
Dwarf medlar 315
Dwarf rose 295
Eagle-likebrake 216, 217
Easter lily 55
Echinacea 39
Echinacea purpurea 239
Echinops ritro 157
English or common
    holly 336
English rose 269, 270, 272,
    277, 282,
Eremurus robustus 158
Erica 320, 321
Erica arborea 'Alpina' 322
Erica carnea 322
Erica ciliaris 323
Erica cinerea 323
Erigeron 'Dunkelste
    Aller' 158
Eruca sativa 240
Eryngium 159
Eryngium x oliverianum 159
Erysimum cheiri 94
Euonymus fortunei 324
Eupatorium purpureum 160
Euphorbia 160, 161
Euphorbia characias ssp.
    wulfenii 160
Euphorbia cyparissias 161
Euphorbia polychroma 161
Evening Primrose 251
Evergreen dwarf medlar 316
Everlasting or straw
    flower 97
Everlasting pea 380
Fallopia baldschuanica 370
False anemone 127
Fennel 240

Filipendula palmata 162
Five-fingered maidenfair
    fern 123
Fleabanet 15
Floribunda rose (patio rose)
    269, 276
Floribunda rose 290, 293
Florist's cyclamen 19
Foeniculum vulgare 240
Forget-me-not 103
Forrest Rhododendron 350
Forsythia suspensa 325
Forsythia x intermedia 324,
    325
Fountain grass 204
Foxglove 93
Foxtail lily 158
Freesia 30
Freesia species 30
Freesiea varieties 30
French Marigold 114
Fritillaria 32
Fritillaria imperialis 32
Fritillaria meleagris 33
Fritillary species 32
Fuchsia 326, 327
Fuchsia boliviana 328
Fuchsia fulgens 328
Fuchsia magellanica 326, 329
Fuchsia procumbens 329
Gaillardia x grandiflora
    'Kobold' 162, 163
Galanthus 35
Galium odoratum 241
Gallica rose 271, 274, 276
Garden chrysanthemums 148,
    149, 150, 151
Garden lupin 187
Garden pansy 117
Garden peony 200
Garden thyme 259
Garlic 232
Gaultheria procumbens 241

Gazania 95
Genista hispanica 330
Gentian 163
Gentiana sino-ornata 163
Geranium 164, 165, 253
Geranium grandiflorum 166
Geranium himalayense 166
Geranium renardii 167
Geranium sanguineum 168
Geranium sylvaticum 168
Geranium x magnificum 166
Geum coccineum 169
Gladiolus 36, 37
Gladiolus callianthus 39
Gladiolus cardinalis 39
Gladiolus papilio 40
Gladiolus 'Peter Pears' 38
Gladiolus 'Rose Supreme' 38
Gladiolus tristis 40
Glechoma hederacea 169
Globe flower 228
Globe thistle 157
Gloriosa Superba 371
Glory lily 371
Glyceria 170
Glyceria maxima 170
Glycyrrhiza glabra 242
Goat's beard 131
Golden marguerite 127
Golden rayed lily 54
Golden rod 226
Gooseneck loosetrife 188
Granny's bonnet 128
Grape hyacinth 58, 59
Grape vine 384
Great leopard's bane 156
Ground cover rose 280, 290,
    295, 296
Ground ivy 169
Guernsey lily 65
Gypsophila 170
Gypsophila elegans 96
Gypsophila paniculata 170

Hamamelis mollis 330, 331
Hamamelis virginiana 331
Hare's tail grass 99
Heather 309, 318, 321
Hedera helix 372
Hedera hibernica 373
Helenium 'Moerheim
    Beauty' 172
Helianthus annuus 96, 97
Helianthus x multiflorus 173
Helichrysum bracteatum 97
Heliopsis 173
Heliopsis helianthoides 173
Heliotrope 98
Heliotropium arborescens 98
Helleborus niger 174
Helleborus orientalis 175
Hemerocallis 'Marion
    Vaughn' 177
Hemerocallis fulva 176
Hemerocallis lilioas-
    phodelus 176
Hemp agrimony 160
Herbs 230, 231
Heuchera micrantha diversi-
    folia 'Palace
    Purple' 177
Hippeastrum 41
Hollyhock 80
Horsemint 249
Hosta 'Hadspen Blue' 180
Hosta sieboldiana 181
Houseleek 225
Humulus japonicus 373
Hyachinthoides hispania 41
Hyacinth 42
Hyacinthus orientalis 42, 43
Hybrid teas 268, 274, 279
Hydrangea arborescens 334
Hydrangea aspera ssp
    sargentiana 335
Hydrangea macrophylla
    332, 333, 334

Hydrangea paniculata 335
Hymenocallis calathina 42
Hymenocallis
    narcissiflora 42
Hypericum 242
Hyssop 243
Hyssopus officinalis 243
Iberis sempervirens 182
Ice plant 224
Iceland poppy 202
Ilex aquifolium 336
Ilex serrata (syn. I.
    sieboldii) 337
Ilex serrata 337
Ilex sieboldii 337
Ilex verticillata 337
Impatiens 98
Incense rose 289
Indian azaleas 351
Inula 182
Inula hookeri 182
Ipomoea 375
Ipomoea hederacea 376
Ipomoea indica 377
Ipomoea tricolor 377
Iris barbeta 44, 46
Iris chrysographes 47
Iris histrioides 48
Iris magnifica 48
Iris reticulata 49
Iris x Hollandia 47
Irises 44, 45
Irish ivy 373
Ismene calathina 42
Ivy-leaved geranium 107
Japanese apricot 347
Japanese hop 373
Japanese ivy 382
Japanese maple 300
Japanese wisteria 385
Jasminum humile 338
Jasminum mesnyi 378
June berry, 301

405

Juniperus procumbens 338
Juniperus scopulorum 339
Kansas gay feather 185
Kniphofia caulescens 183
Knotweed 137
Lacecap 334
Lady's mantle 124
Lagurus ovatus 99
Lamb's tongue 227
Lamium maculatum 184, 185
Lamrum maculatum 184
Large flowered bush rose 280,
    281, 284, 288, 289,
Large-cupped daffodils 63
Large-flowered gladiolus
    hybrid 38
Larkspur 88, 144, 145, 146,
    147
Lathyrus 379
Lathyrus grandiflorus 380
Lathyrus latiflorus 380
Laurus nobilis 243
Lavandula angustifolia 244
Lavatera cachemiriana 99
Lavatera trimestris 100
Lavender 244
Lawson cypress 314
Lemon balm 245
Lemon thyme 261
Lily (Lilium) 52, 53
Lent lily 64
Lenten rose 175
Lesser celandine 254
Leucanthemum vulgare 184
Leucojum aestivum 50
Leucojum Vernum 50
Levisticum officinale 244
Liatris spicata 185
Licorice 242
Lilac 356
Lily (Lilium) 52, 53
Lilium 'Black Beauty' 57
Lilium 'Bright Star' 57

Lilium auratum 54
Lilium candidum 54
Lilium longiflorum 55
Lilium regale 56
Lily of the valley 142
Lily-flowering tulips 72, 73
Limonium latifolium 186
Limonium platyphyllum 186
Limonium sinuatum 100
Ling 309
Lobelia 186
Lobelia erinus 101
Lobelia x speciosa 186
Lobularia maritima 102
Lonicera x heckrottii 381
Loosestrife 190
Lovage 244
Love-in-the-mist 105
Love-lies-bleeding 81
Lungwort 217
Lupinus hybrids 187
Lychnis coronaria 188
Lysimachia clethroides 188
Lysimachia punctata 189
Lythrum virgatum 190
Macleaya cordata 190
Madonna lily 54
Magnolia 340, 341
Magnolia liliiflora
    'Nigra' 342
Magnolia stellata 343
Mahonia aquifolium 344
Maiden pink 154
Maidenhair spleenwort 131
Male fern 156
Mallow 99
Malva moschata 191
Marguerite 82, 184
Marjoram 252
Marsh Africaner 41
Marsh marigold 138
Masterwort 135
Matricaria recutita 245

Matteuccia struthiopteris 192
Matthiola incana 102
Meadow phlox 208
Meadow saffron 12
Meadowsweet 162
Meconopsis grandis 192
Melissa officinalis 245
Mentha 247
Mentha suaveolens 249
Mentha x piperita 248
Mentha x smithiana 248
Mertensia 193
Mertensia simplicissima 193
Michaelmas daisy 133
Mile-a-minute 370
Mints 246, 247
Miscanthus 194
Miscanthus sinensis
    'Silberfeder' 194
Miscellaneous daffodils 64
Molucella laevis 103
Monarda 249
Monkshood 122
Montbretie 12, 13
Morning glory 377
Moss Phlox 209
Moss rose 281, 287
Mountain pine 346
Mullein 229
Muscari latiflorum 58
Musk mallow 191
Myosotis palustris 195
Myosotis sylvatica 103
Myrtus communis 344
Narcissus 60, 61, 62, 63
Narcissus 'Tête-a-Tête' 64, 65
Narcissus pseudonar-
    cissus 64
Nasturtium 262
Nepeta cataria 250
Nerine sarniensis 65
Nicotiana alata 104
Nicotiana x sanderae 104

Nigella damascena 105
Noisette-Rose 279
Nuphar lutea 195
Nymphaea alba 196
Obedient plant 210
Ocimum basilicum 250
Oenothera biennis 251
Omphalodes verna 197
Orchid-flowered dahlia 27
Oregano 252
Oriental hybrids 57
Oriental poppy 203
Origanum majorana 252
Origanum vulgare 252
Ornithogalum thyrsoides 66,
    67
Osmunda regalis 197
Ostrich fern 192
Ox-eye daisy 184
Paeonia 'Kamada-nishiki' 201
Paeonia lutea 201
Paeonia officinalis 198, 202
Paeonia species and
    hybrids 199
Paeonia 'Globe of Light' 200
Palma Christi 110
Pampas grass 143
Papaver 106
Papaver nudicaule 202, 203
Papaver orientale 203
Parrot tulip 72
Parsley 254
Parthenocissus tricuspi-
    data 382
Partridge berry 241
Passiflora 383
Passion flower 383
Patio rose 294
Pea family 379
Peach-leaved cam-
    panula 139
Pelargonium 253
Pelargonium peltatum 107

Pelargonium zonale 107
Pencil cedar 339
Pennisetum alopecu-
    roides 204
Pennisetum compressum 204
Penstemon barbatus 204
Peony 198, 199, 202
Peppermint 248
Perennials 118, 119
Perennial pea 380
Pernettya mucronata 345
Petroselinum crispum 254
Petunia 108, 109
Phlomis 205
Phlomis russeliana 205
Phlomis samia 205
Phlox 206, 207, 208
Phlox maculata 208
Phlox paniculata 206, 208
Phlox species and
    hybrids 207
Phlox subulata 209
Physostegia virginiana 210
Pink 154
Pinks and carnations 90, 91,
    152, 153
Pinus mugo 346
Plantain lily 178, 179
Plume poppy 190
Polygonatum x hybridum 210
Polystichum luctuosum 211
Polystichum tsus-
    simense 211
Pompon dahlia 22
Poppy 106
Pot marigold 237
Potato vine 383
Potentilla aurea 211
Potentilla fruticosa 346
Primrose 109
Primrose jasmine 378
Primula 213
Primula auricola 212

Primula officinalis 214
Primula pulverulenta 213
Primula veris 214
Primula vulgaris 109
Primula-Polyantha group 212
Privet 339
Procumbent juniper 338
Prunus mume 347
Pseudofumaria 215
Pseudofumaria luea 215
Pseudolysimachion (spiked
    speedwell) 216
Pseudolysimachion 215, 216
Pseudolysimachion longi-
    folium 215
Pseudolysimachion
    spicatum 216
Pteridium aquilinum 216, 217
Pulmonaria saccharata 217
Pulsatilla 218
Pulsatilla vulgaris 218
Purple cone flower 39
Puschkinia scilloides 66
Rambler rose 268, 293
Ranunculus acris 219
Ranunculus asiaticus 68
Ranunculus ficaria 254
Red mint 248
Red moss 281
Red valerian 141
Red-hot poker 183
Regal lily 56
Rhododendron 348, 349
Rhododendron auri-
    culatum 350
Rhododendron forrestii var.
    Repens 350
Rhododendron occi-
    dentale 351
Rhododendron simsii 351
Ricinus communis 110, 255
Rodgersia 219
Rodgersia aesculifolia 219

Rosa 'Albertine' 268
Rosa 'Alexander' 268
Rosa 'Anna Ford' 269
Rosa 'Charles Austin' 269
Rosa 'Charles de Mills' 270
Rosa chinensis 'Cécile
    Brunner' 270
Rosa chinensis 'Old
    Blush' 271
Rosa 'Complicata' 271
Rosa 'Constance Spry' 272
Rosa 'Cuisse de
    Nymphe' 273
Rosa 'Duc de
    Cambridge' 273
Rosa 'Duchesse de
    Montebello' 274
Rosa 'Duftzauber 84' 274, 275
Rosa eglanteria 292
Rosa 'Félicité et
    Perpétue' 275
Rosa 'Gentle Touch 276
Rosa 'Gertrude Jekyll' 277
Rosa Glauca 277
Rosa 'Gloire de Dijon' 278, 279
Rosa 'Gloria Dei' 279
Rosa 'Graham Thomas' 280
Rosa 'Heidetraum' 280
Rosa Henri Martin 281
Rosa 'Heritage' 281
Rosa Iceberg 293
Rosa 'Ispahan' 282
Rosa 'Jayne Austin' 282, 283
Rosa 'Magenta' 284, 285
Rosa 'Maigold' 284
Rosa 'Mme Hardy' 285
Rosa 'New Dawn' 286
Rosa 'Nuits de Young' 287
Rosa 'Peace' 279
Rosa 'Penelope' 288
Rosa 'Pink Grootendorst' 289
Rosa primula 289
Rosa 'Queen Elizabeth' 290

Rosa 'Queen of Denmark' 283
Rosa 'Rosy Cushion' 290
Rosa 'Royal Wiliam' 274
Rosa rubiginosa (R. eglanteria)
    292
Rosa 'Schneewittchen' 293
Rosa 'Seagull' 293
Rosa 'Sheri Anne' 294
Rosa 'Snow Carpet' 295
Rosa 'Sommerwind' 295
Rosa 'Sonnenschirm' 296
Rosa gallica 'Versicolor' 276
Rosa Gentle Touch' 276
Rosa pimpinellifolia hybrids
    284
Rosa rubiginosa 292
Rosa rubrifolia 277
Rosa x borboniana 'Mme Isaac
    Pereire' 296
Rosa x borboniana 'Variegata
    di Bologna' 297
Rosa x centifolia
    'Muscosa' 281, 287
Rose campion 188
Rosemary 255
Roses 264-267
Rosmarinus officinalis 255
Royal fern 197
Rudbeckia fulgida 220
Rudbeckia hirta 110
Rudbeckia purpurea 239
Rue 256
Russian vine 370
Ruta graveolens 256
Safflower 86
Sage 221, 257
Sagittaria sagittifolia 221
Salix babylonica 352
Salix hastata 352
Salomon's seal 210
Salvia officinalis 257
Salvia x sylvestris 221
Sambucus nigra 258

Santolina chamaecy-
    parissus 222
Scabiosa atropurpurea 111
Scabiosa caucasica 222
Scabiosa stellata 112
Scabious 222
Scilla siberica 69
Sea lavender 100, 186
Sedge 139
Sedum 223
Sedum reflexum 224
Sedum rupestre 224
Sewdum species 223
Sedum spectabile 224
Semi-cactus-flowered
    dahlias 24
Sempervivum species and
    hybrids 225
Senecio cineraria 112
Shell-flower 103
Shield fern 211
Shuttlecock fern 192
Shrubs 298, 299
Siberian squill 69
Single early tulips 75
Single late tulips 76
Single-flowered dahlia 28
Skimmia japonica 353
Snake's head fritillary 33
Snapdragon 81
Sneezeweed 172
Sneezewort 122
Snowdrop 35
Snowdrop windflower 126
Snowy mespilus 301

Solarum jasminoides 383
Solenostemon scutalle-
    roides 113
Solidago virgaurea 226
Spanish Gorse 330
Species crocus 16
Species tulips 77
Spider lily 42
Spiked speedwell 216
Spindle tree 324
Spiraea canecens 354
Spiraea japonica 355
Spotted laurel 303
Spring snowflake 50
St John's Wort 242
Stachys byzantina 227
Stachys lantana 227
Stock 102
Stone orpine 224
Striped squill 66
Summer snowflake 50
Sunflower 96, 173
Sweet scabious 111
Sweet William 92
Syringa meyeri 356
Syringa vulgaris 356
Tagetes erecta 113
Tagetes patula 114
Tanacetum 258
Tawny day lily 176
Taxus baccata 357
Tazetta daffodils 63
Thicket-forming bamboo 302
Thrift 129
Thuja occidentalis 359

Thuja orientalis 359
Thunbergia alata 114
Thymus serpyllum 261
Thymus vulgaris 259
Thymus x citriodorus 261
Tobacco plant 104
Trailing petunia 108
Trailing Verbena 115
Tree mallow 100
Tree peony 201
Triumph tulips 73
Trollius chinensis 228
Tropaeolum majus 262
Trumpet daffodils 62
Tuberous begonia 83
Tulip 70, 71
Tulipa 72, 73
Tulipa 'Apeldoorn' 74
Tulipa 'Apricot Beauty' 75
Tulipa 'Prof. Röntgen' 72
Tulipa Queen of the Night 76
Tulipa praestans 'Unicum' 77
Tulipa 'Willemsoord 76
Valerian 263
Valeriana officinalis 263
Verascum olympicum 229
Verbascum olympicum 229
Verbena 115
Veronica longifolia 215
Veronica spicata 216
Viburnum lantana 361
Viburnum x carlce-
    phalum 361
Viola cornuta 116
Viola wittrockiana 117

Vitus vinifera 384
Vivernun x carlce-
    phalum 361
Wallflower 94
Warminster Broom 318
Water forget-me-not 195
Water lily-flowered
    dahlias 26
Water plantain 125
Wayfaring Tree 361
Weeping willow 352
Western prickly Moses 300
White Cedar 259
Wichuraina-Rambler 286
Wild camomile 245
Williamsii hybrids 313
Wisteria 363
Wisteria floribunda 385
Wisteria sinensis 386
Wisteria x formosa 386, 387
Woodruff 241
Wormwood 130
Yarrow 120, 121
Yellow alyssum 136
Yellow foxglove 93
Yellow water lily 195
Zantedeschia aethiopica 77
Zinnia 117
Zinnia elegans 117
Zonal peragonium 107